Praise for **MUSTANG**

"A stunner and a heartbreaker." — NPR's *On Point*

"Brisk, smart, thorough, and surprising." — *Atlantic Monthly*

"Extraordinary . . . a true American tragedy. [Stillman] tells the infuriating but inspiring story of the destruction and survival of a noble icon perfectly — you'll never forget it." — *Penthouse*

"In *Mustang,* her new history of the wild horse in North America, Deanne Stillman explores why America is destroying the horse it rode in on." — *Newsweek*

"A colorful story of America's 400-year-old love affair with the horse."
— *Denver Post*

"The author's impassioned investigation results in an epic history of the horse . . . absorbing." — *Dallas Morning News*

"Well-researched and written, and might well be essential reading for Westerners." — *Missoulian*

"A hard, albeit sympathetic look at mustangs that remain on the range today and the situations arrayed for and against them, and their defenders and their detractors, round-ups, adoptions and other ends." — *Reno Gazette-Journal*

"Fervent and exhaustive . . . less of a manes-a-flying romance than a long consideration of the wild horse and its treatment."
— *Cleveland Plain Dealer*

"Stillman's work is a must-read, a must-know, and a call to action for all those who hope to save the American mustang."

— *Equestrian News*

"This urgent, compelling, and unforgettable book builds a convincing case that wild horses are an essential part of both our national history and character." — *King Features Syndicate*

"An eloquently written wake-up call." — *Pasadena Weekly*

"Particular books both define a topic and become the defining book on that topic. I am thinking of John McPhee's *Oranges*, Jessica Mitford's *The American Way of Death*, and Mike Davis's *City of Quartz*, and today add to that list Deanne Stillman's *Mustang*."

— KPFK's *Bibliocracy*

"A stampeding, crusading history of horses in America during the last half-millennium . . . a spirited defense of the wild horse, as well as a rousing, sweeping account of the horse from the arrival of the conquistadors, who would not have been able to subdue North America without it . . . a well-written, welcome work of history and advocacy."

— *Kirkus Reviews*

"Mustangs, an iconic element of the American West, receive their due in this history of the horses of the New World . . . the controversy over these tough little horses has not abated, and Stillman brings their story to the present and the continued political maneuvering around the mustang question." — *Booklist*

"Deanne Stillman has given horse lovers a remarkable book which includes everything one needs to know about our mustangs. Don't miss it — and if you loan it to a friend, make him sign for it. He will be passing it along to his friends, and you will have to get yourself another one." — Tony Hillerman, author of *Dance Hall of the Dead*

"Told with passion and skill, filled with drama and dust and fascinating facts, *Mustang* is a worthy addition to the literature of the horse in the American West." — Ian Frazier, author of *Great Plains*

"In *Mustang*, Deanne Stillman has written a classic in equine literature, an exhaustively reported and beautifully told tale of the American mustang viewed in the full sweep of his cultural and evolutionary development. The mustang is a national symbol and treasure. And, from beginning to end, now so is Stillman's book — in the end, a riveting, compelling testimonial on why this free-roaming animal must be saved." — William Nack, author of *Secretariat: The Making of a Champion*

"Deanne Stillman's writing, research, and inspiration in the creation of *Mustang* is stunning. When finished, readers will fret over how the U.S. government can continue to allow the destruction of those who have been our brothers and sisters for centuries: America's wild horses." — Michael Blake, author of *Dances with Wolves* and *The Holy Road*

"It's been said that the history of this nation was written from the back of a horse. But not until now — with Deanne Stillman's *Mustang* — has that history come to epic life. At once an important, comprehensive study and a spellbinding read, *Mustang* is ultimately a hymn to our homeland. Deanne Stillman makes a compelling case for the preservation of wild horses." — John Fusco, screenwriter of *Hidalgo*, *Thunderheart*, and *Spirit: Stallion of the Cimarron*

"Stillman's masterfully crafted work demands that we examine our American identity and humanity." — Samantha Dunn, author of *Not by Accident*

MUSTANG

THE SAGA OF THE WILD HORSE IN THE AMERICAN WEST

Deanne Stillman

MARINER BOOKS

HOUGHTON MIFFLIN HARCOURT

BOSTON • NEW YORK

First Mariner Books edition 2009

Library of Congress Cataloging-in-Publication Data
Stillman, Deanne.
  Mustang : the saga of the wild horse in the American West / Deanne Stillman.
    p. cm.
  Includes bibliographical references and index.
  ISBN 978-0-618-45445-7
  ISBN 978-0-547-23791-6 (pbk.)
  1. Mustang — History. 2. West (U.S.) — History. I. Title.
  SF293.M9S75 2008
  599.665'50978—dc22   2008004732

Book design by Melissa Lotfy

Printed in the United States of America

DOC 10 9 8 7 6 5 4 3 2

Passages from this book first appeared in the *Los Angeles Times, LA Weekly, 111 Magazine,* the *Boston Globe,* and the *Chronicle of the Horse;* on slate.com, world-hum.com, newwest.net, and huffingtonpost.com; and in the anthologies *Naked: Writers Uncover the Way We Live on Earth* and *Unbridled: The Western Horse in Fiction and Nonfiction.*

The author is grateful for permission to quote from "The Misfits" by Arthur Miller. Copyright © 1957 by Arthur Miller, reprinted with permission of The Wylie Agency, Inc.

PHOTO CREDITS   p. ii–iii: Challisherd, central Idaho, Elissa Kline (2005 All Rights Reserved); p. 13: Bancroft Library, University of California, Berkeley; p. 20: The Mariners' Museum, Newport News, Virginia; pp. 52: Library of Congress; p. 59: Laurent Martres; pp. 62, 65, 81, 106: Library of Congress; p. 109: National Anthropological Archives, Smithsonian Institution; p. 141: Library of Congress; p. 155: Denver Public Library, Western History Collection; p. 173: Library of Congress; p. 192: Dickinson Research Center, National Cowboy and Western Heritage Museum; p. 203: Courtesy of Special Collections, University of California, Santa Cruz; p. 224: Cornell Capa, Magnum Photos; p. 251: International Society for the Protection of Mustangs and Burros; p. 277: Betty L. Kelly; p. 278 (both photos): Flora Steffan; p. 279: Cindy Lawrence; p. 291: Marilyn Newton/Reno Gazette-Journal; p. 301: Mark Lamonica; p. 308: Library of Congress; p. 337: LRTC Wild Horse Mentors

*This book is dedicated to my mother, Eleanor Stillman,
a free spirit, and to my sister, Nancy Stillman,
who understood the magic of horses before I did*

Contents

Introduction

FOR A LONG TIME, the American desert has been my beat and my passion. The reasons are many, but really, there is only one. In the desert, the chatter of city life fades away and my own thoughts vanish; I get quiet and I hear things. The beating of wings. The scratching of lizard. The crack of tortoise egg. The whisper of stories that want to be told.

In 1991, I walked into a bar on Highway 62, the desert two-lane that stretches from Interstate 10 in California eastward into the far Mojave. I had just finished a hike in Joshua Tree National Park. It was twilight. Thunderclouds were rolling in, and the perfume of creosote was in the air. Inside the Josh Lounge, people sat at the bar, guarding their pitchers of beer, talking of sports, the weather, local news. After a while, I heard the first few notes of a dark desert tale. Two girls had been "sliced up" by a Marine, someone said; probably they deserved it. "Who were they?" I asked. "Just some trash" came the reply. I sought more information but people shrugged and then someone punched the jukebox and "Dirty White Boy" came on and the conversation was over. A frequent visitor to the area, I knew something about the girls who took care of local members of the military, and I vowed to bear witness to their story. A decade later, it became my book *Twentynine Palms: A True Story of Murder, Marines, and the Mojave.*

But before I was finished, another terrible tale was unfolding and I couldn't shake off its call. A few days after Christmas in 1998, I was waiting to meet with a source in another desert bar. I picked up the local paper and read that six wild horses had been gunned down in the mountains outside Reno. The next day, the body count had grown to twenty. By the end of December, thirty-four dead mustangs had been found in the Virginia Range, and the hideous news was announced to the world on the ticker tape at Times Square. A few days later, three men were arrested. Two of them were Marines and one of them was stationed at Twentynine Palms.

I was surprised — and then I wasn't. I knew that a number of grisly crimes had emanated from the military base hidden away in that remote desert town. Now, the victims were wild horses, and their story also spoke of our history, our heritage, and our land. But what exactly was their story? I wondered as the Reno incident began to take over my life. Why would someone go out and kill the animals that had blazed our trails, fought our wars, served as our most loyal partners? As I began looking into the story, I realized that what had happened to the wild horses in Reno was about much more than that particular event. It went right to the heart of who we are as Americans.

With all due respect to our official icon, the eagle, he of the broad wingspan and the ability to see across great distances, of patience born of the ages and of majestic flight, it is really the wild horse, the four-legged with the flying mane and tail, the beautiful, bighearted steed who loves freedom so much that when captured he dies of a broken heart, the ever-defiant mustang that is our true representative, coursing through our blood as he carries the eternal message of America. Many have read *Moby Dick,* but few — including me, until I began my wild horse research — remember that in his tribute to that which man should not possess, Melville devoted a passage to the other great white, the one that ranged the Great Plains:

> Most famous in our Western annals and Indian traditions, is that of the White Steed of the Prairies; a magnificent milk-white charger, large-eyed, small-headed, bluff-chested, and with the dignity of a thousand monarchs in his lofty, over-scorning carriage. He was the elected Xerxes of vast herds of wild horses, whose pastures in those

days were only fenced by the Rocky Mountains and the Alleghenies ... The flashing cascade of his mane, the curving comet of his tail, invested him with housings more resplendent than gold- and silver-beaters could have furnished him.

As I read this passage in light of the horse killings, I started to wonder about the men who would do such a thing. Were they modern Ahabs? Or were they more prosaic — just a bunch of drunks with guns? Or perhaps they were a strange new iteration of the American psycho, or maybe even some sort of full-on combination platter of all of the above?

To see this killing for what it was, I realized, I needed to learn the story of the wild horse before the Reno massacre — the facts of its life along the trail, at war, at play, in our literature and lore, how it got here and where it came from. This was a large and at times daunting endeavor but one that I felt compelled to undertake. Quite simply, the horse deserved its own account, and no such thing existed — at least not in the way I wanted to tell it, by traveling with the horse across space and time, right through the entire American saga.

Then, also, there was a personal connection. Years ago, when my parents got divorced, my mother, sister, and I moved from an upper-middle-class suburb of Cleveland, Ohio, to a blue-collar community. Suddenly, most of our friends in the old neighborhood — and even some relatives — stopped talking to us, and it didn't take long to figure out that our new address had made us social pariahs. In addition, my mother had become the breadwinner in an era when there were few jobs for women outside of the secretarial pool. Typing wasn't an option because she didn't know how, but she did have another skill that, due to her persistence and desire, was something she could transform into a living. It was riding a horse.

Soon after our move, she got a job as what was then called "exercise boy" at the racetrack. There were few women working in that capacity at the time (we later found out that she may have been the first in the country to do so); among those women who tried out for the job, most didn't qualify for various reasons or were not given the chance to prove themselves. After all, the job wasn't called "exercise boy" for nothing. But my mother was an expert equestrienne; she'd ridden with the local hunt club and shown her own horses on the competitive circuit, impressing the local gentry and winning many prizes. And so her skills did not go unnoticed at the track and she quickly became the talk of northeastern Ohio.

In fact, early on during her career at Thistledown Racetrack, a reporter from the *Cleveland Plain Dealer* arrived to profile my mother, the novelty act. As she breezed around a bend on Lord Fleet at six in the morning, a photographer snapped a picture of me and my sister looking on across the guardrail. I'll never forget the caption that appeared the next day under the photo. "Nice going, Mama," it quoted me as saying. Now, I should mention that I had been reading newspapers since I was a toddler. As the family story goes, when my sister was born and came home from the hospital, the first thing I did was place a newspaper in her crib. By the time I was nine or ten, when the reporter from the *Plain Dealer* knocked on the door, I had a pretty good sense of what newspapers were up to, and somehow, I knew that they dressed things up. Yet as proud as I was of the article about my mother, bringing it to school to show my friends, I was also slightly annoyed. I never used the phrase "nice going" and I never called my mother "Mama."

Actually, the reporter was right. Things were going rather nicely. For the next five years, my mother got up every day at dawn and headed for the track to ride. It wasn't a high-income gig but it helped her return to college so she could get a master's degree. It also took us into an enchanting world of misfits and outcasts who, like us, did not have traditional families. They had one another, and their sanctuary was the racetrack, and their best friends and saviors were horses. The horses all seemed to offer a kind of protection; to me, as lots of little girls come to find out, it was by dint of their size and power, even — perhaps especially — when they were in their stalls and being still, whinnying occasionally or nickering when I scratched their flanks. One of my fondest memories is walking through the barns in the morning after it had snowed and being enveloped by great puffs of steam coming from the horses as they breathed the cold air.

There was safety in the vapors, in the sound of the exhales up and down the row, as if they were blowing out the cares of the world, like Melville's mythical great white creature, I see now, echoing the earth's very rhythm, perhaps huffing its infinitesimal though mighty turns. Sometimes, I would sit on a bale of hay inside the entrance to the barn and listen to the horses, and after a while, my breathing would sync up with theirs and I would forget about my shattered life from which my father had suddenly vanished.

Often, on such mornings, my mother would take me and my sister to the track kitchen for breakfast, where everything was slathered with gravy or cream sauce, and you could get as many helpings as you liked. But more important, the kitchen was where I first met the oddballs of the world. Sitting at our table were poor young jockeys who had trained on nags and fled the hollows of Appalachia hoping for a break, grooms as old as the stars who seemed happy to live in their small quarters next to the horses, toothless track wags who eked out food money at the low-ball betting windows and made their home at motels across the street, lifelong circuit trainers who had finally come into possession of a winner. The community was driven by heart, uplifted by belief in the racetrack version of sunrise (every day is a new chance), and held together by firsthand knowledge that outside the track there was one damn cruel world.

And always, the horse, waiting to carry us all across the finish line, and beyond. For during those years, the horse had become my means of escape in every way. Prior to my parents' divorce, my father and I would sit in his library, where he would read aloud from his favorite authors — Hemingway, Steinbeck, O'Hara. One of the works my father most liked to recite was Edgar Allan Poe's "Eldorado," the sad poem about a wandering knight's search for the land of gold. Together, my father and I traveled the path of the perpetually questing knight, and I remember the sense that Eldorado was a land far beyond the borders known to either of us, an enchanted place to be found somewhere in the books from which my father loved to read aloud, perhaps in the reading itself.

After my parents parted, Poe's poem about the questing knight and the pilgrim who urged him to "ride, boldly ride" was my salvation, my ticket away from the wintry shores of Lake Erie. It soon took me to the frontier of Zane Grey and Cochise and Geronimo, and later to many others who became my guides. While everyone else was ice-fishing or partaking in league night at the Kingpin Lanes, I would vanish into the red rock and mesquite of Western literature, finding refuge on the path to Eldorado. When not in school, I wore fringe and cowboy boots. I sent away for seeds from Kaktus Jack's. I read encyclopedia entries about the James gang and Doc Holliday, pioneer diaries of survival and hardship. I wrote my own stories of flight, always disappearing in a swirl of magic dust.

Years later, when I moved to New Mexico to attend college, I began exploring the dusty byways of our history, on foot and on horseback, and I began to realize exactly how lucky I was. Atop a horse, I could ride to those red-rock mesas I had read about and survey the land that had fueled the American dream, and I could gallop across a *bajada* and, as I did so, enter a warp that was filled with the great characters of our history, from cowboys to Indians to outlaws to hardscrabble pioneers. Their partner was the horse and so was mine, and as I rode with the enduring spirits of the West on the animal that had carried them all, I truly felt free.

Yet it was not until I learned of the Reno massacre that I began to take a really close look at the wild horse. The mustangs that had perished, I learned, were among the last in the country. Once they had roamed our land by the millions. Now the mustang population was dwindling to a number from which it might not rebound. What had happened to our beautiful, steadfast partner? I wondered. To understand the end and perhaps try to stop it, I had to go back to the beginning. My journey took me into deep time and across vast swaths of the western terrain, to far-flung libraries and archives by way of airplanes, cars, and the Internet, to the open range where wild horses still roam, crowded government corrals where they are fenced in and sent down the pipeline, and sanctuaries that have become their final home.

I began my investigation in a place I have been exploring for years, the Mojave Desert. In this case, the destination was Death Valley, where wild horses had flourished millions of years ago, leaving their hoof tracks on a vast stone panel in a remote canyon that you can hike to at certain times of the year. Where did they go from here? I wondered one February afternoon as I traced the outlines of the ancient glyphs. The magic site began to unlock the rest of the story; "Follow the tracks," I kept hearing along the way, and as I proceeded, they became both moor and marker.

The tracks led to the Ice Age, at which point the horses of this continent vanished, but not before they had headed north across the Bering land bridge and populated the rest of the world. I picked up the tracks thousands of years later, when sixteen horses were loaded onto ships in Cuba, a staging ground for conquistadors, and reintroduced to the mainland of the New World, helping Hernando Cortés bring down the Aztec empire and launching the American *entrada*. I continued to follow the horses' return as they carried priests and warriors toward El Norte, heading across the Rio Grande and into the deserts of Texas, Arizona, New Mexico, and California. They kept moving and so did I, traveling with them as they made their way onto the Great Plains and into the world of Native Americans, forming a partnership that seemed as old as forever, and then joining up with the U.S. cavalry (or perhaps it was the other way around), and I visited the battlefield of the Little Bighorn, where they served white and red men alike in the bloody moment that changed history.

Of course their work was not done, and I retraced their service on cattle drives, in rodeos, and in the early Westerns, and I traversed the washes and mountains of Nevada, where, of all the states, they still roam in the greatest numbers. Now, I continue to follow the mustangs as they wage their own last stand, battling to save themselves in the remote high desert where they went — like a lot of misfits — to be left alone and flourish and finally to hide from those who want to destroy them, including not just those who killed them in 1998 but a parade of such men who have carried out acts even more horrific, as well as all the others who want the land for livestock, fuels, and themselves.

As I take you through this epic, sad, grand, and still unfolding saga of the wild horse, I'll introduce you to some of the great equine characters in American history (along with some of their human friends and enemies) — and tell you what they did and how they did it. You'll meet Comanche, the cavalry horse that survived the Little Bighorn and lived out his years in a strange retirement at an army fort. You'll meet Fritz, America's first movie star; Buffalo Bill's cast of four-legged celebrities; the painted pony that carried Crazy Horse across the Badlands; and, finally, you'll meet Bugz, silent witness to the massacre of the Virginia Range horses, rescued during a snowstorm by two women who have devoted their lives to taking care of the wild ones at their sanctuary in Carson City.

I've spent a lot of time with Bugz, who lost her family but has a new one. In fact, her best friend is a little brown mustang named Mona, who was taken in after she came down from the mountains and was found wandering a well-traveled road near tract homes in Reno. If you didn't know these horses were once wild, you might not be able to tell just from being around them. While they have the scruffy look of mustangs, they seem tame; they are happy at the approach of those who saved them and sometimes nicker when people they don't know proffer apples or carrots. But, as scientists have noted, if they were returned to the mountains tomorrow (depending on which range, not permissible, according to Nevada statutes), the veneer of domestication would fade away quickly, and once again they would go wild.

This is the great paradox of the horse. It possesses a wild spirit but serves as the greatest helpmate this country — and all of civilization — has known. Other wild animals have been pressed into service or entertainment, but it is only the horse — the beautiful, mysterious, powerful great white — that consistently moves back and forth between there and here, horizon and corral, range and rodeo, inspiring centuries of song, art, literature, and worship, and stirring passions that have wreaked havoc in everyone from King Solomon to the ancient Greeks to cowboy poets. We see your fire, all have said. We want it. And the horse has responded, let us restrain it with ropes and things that pull on its mouth and all manner of gear — giving up its freedom so that we can have ours, slipping easily, quickly, back into the wild when it can, serving as avatar, martyr, and friend.

How and when did the moment of partnership first occur? No one knows for sure, and there is much speculation on this subject. But however it happened, it's clear that the horse's ability to provide flight was universally desired, and nowhere is this desire more pronounced, more extreme, than in America, where escape and the chance to start over is not a pipe dream but a birthright. We may not think of ourselves as part of a horse culture, like the nomads of Mongolia, for instance, but in our own way, we are; we worship cowboys and we're jacked on freedom and we love moving fast through wide-open space, preferably on a cactus-lined highway in our most iconic car, the Mustang, whose grille features a galloping pony. Yet as we ply the road, many of us do not realize that the real thing is fighting for its life on the rocky playas just over yonder, staking out the dream, being wild and free for the rest of us.

In the nineteenth century, some thought that the great dream of unfettered territory had died with the birth of barbed wire and the fencing-off of the range. Yet it endured. As the twentieth century approached, when Native Americans and hundreds of thousands of wild animals had been purged from the land, historian Frederick Jackson Turner made it official. At the Chicago World's Fair, while exhibits representing the Wild West played on stages around him, Turner announced that the frontier was closed. Across the way, Buffalo Bill and his cast galloped on mustangs, tame but with spirit unbroken, evoking the American promise even as its end was declared. Yet again, the dream endured.

Today the West is constrained by more than barbed wire; it's dammed up, walled up, paved over, chopped down, dumped on, stripped, mined, and cleared. But still the dream lives on. You can buy a piece of it through the government's controversial adopt-a-horse program, which markets mustangs culled from the range — "living legends" — at auctions around the country. Yet with too many horses for too few adopters, they often meet a sad fate, shipped to the slaughterhouse or fenced in at federal corrals, where they can gaze out at their dwindling families and what's left of the range.

As you follow the tracks of the wild horse, perhaps you'll agree that it deserves a safe haven in the country it helped to build, deserves the protections it once had and were only recently unraveled; perhaps you may have a greater understanding of the forces that are contriving to wipe out our loyal partner, the one in whose hoof sparks this country was born. We may be fighting wars around the world, but in the West, to paraphrase the great environmental writer Bernard DeVoto, we are at war with ourselves. To me, there is no greater snapshot of that war than what we have done and continue to do to the wild horse. As it goes, so goes a piece of America, and one of these days, bereft of heritage, we may all find ourselves moving on down the road.

PART I

NEW WORLD

1

The Horses Return

THEY MUST HAVE KNOWN they were coming home for nothing else can explain their survival, and perhaps only that knowledge deep in their cells sustained them. Horses are animals of prey and they like the wide open and to be constrained on the decks in the hot sun or between decks without light or means of escape for two or three months would have overloaded their circuits. Threats hung in the air and everything was new and strange. Where once they had smelled land and grass and legumes, they now smelled salt air mixed with the galleon stench; where once they had heard the sounds of their own hooves on the fields of Europe, they now heard the uneasy creak of wood as the giant brigantines hove through walls of water; where once they had been calmed by the nuzzling and grooming of their band and family members in one another's manes and necks, they now were held in place with slings and hoists, touched and reassured not by their own kind but by the men who were in charge of making sure they had safe passage.

These were the horses that carried Spain to victory in the New World. During the years of the conquest, thousands of them were shipped across the Atlantic. More than half died on the way. Sometimes when rations ran low, they were killed for food. Sometimes the ships sank in hurricanes, taking the horses to a howling and watery grave, along with slaves who had been kidnapped from Africa and chained to one another in the ships' galleys. Often the ships were becalmed midway; between 30 to 35 degrees north and south of the equator, the barometric pressure often increased, and the hot dry breezes called the westerlies stopped blowing. The procession of proud, defiant galleons would come to a halt, mired in the tropics for endless days, their massive sails limp in the blistering sun, and the cargo — man and animal alike — slowly going mad.

At that point, it was time to lighten the load. The horses were removed from their slings and taken above deck. At long last they saw light and could move freely, although they were still hobbled by their weak legs, and they probably faltered as the conquistadors urged them to the gangplank. Perhaps as they faltered they took in the sweep of the peripheries with their big satellite eyes and then gazed across the seas where an albatross was passing, following it all the way to the equator and beyond, and as their eyes swept the horizon, they may have experienced a vestigial sense memory of the wide-open space in the New World where they had once roamed before it had a name. Perhaps they felt that strange tingling of hot, dry no-wind that raises the hack on all living creatures and makes the neurons crackle and the ganglia dance, while sea monsters and dolphin pods and vast armies of seaweed growing from canyons whose rims were the ocean floor encircled the brigantines and waited. Perhaps, as they drank in the air — for the last time — they never felt more alive. And then they were spooked down the plank by thirsty, desperate men who cursed loudly and waved things to scare them, and they skidded down the gangway shrieking in fear, thrown to the seas so the armada could catch the wind.

And as the sea was swallowing them, the ships rose in the water, lighter now, and the sails again furled with the crackling air, and the procession left the region that sailors came to call the horse latitudes. Of course, not all the horses were jettisoned on those terrible crossings. Perhaps the ones that were passed over when the men went below decks to make their grisly selection sensed — in the way that all animals have a homing instinct, and generation after generation make their way back to their ancestral turf — that they would soon be home, back on the continent that had spawned them, thirteen thousand years after they had dispersed and mysteriously disappeared from their birthplace. In fact, it must have been more than a sensation or a feeling; it must have been a kind of certainty that ran through their bones, down through their legs and into the ground they would soon churn up as they headed for the range. Yes, they had to know, for how else to explain the ease and speed with which they adapted to the American desert? The thing is, they just needed a little help . . .

Horses have a way of entering dreams and visions, even those of people who do not know exactly what they are dreaming about. Long before the Spanish conquistador Hernando Cortés and his crew began crossing the sea, Montezuma, the ruler of the Aztec empire in the lush inland valley of Mexico, had dreamed of Quetzalcoatl. This was the fair-haired god who was said to have deserted his people; someday he would return, the dream said, riding a fierce animal and breathing fire. And that day would mark the beginning of the end.

As the desire of the Old World was acted out on the stage of the New, Aztec artists drew pictures of the invasion, and two Spaniards wrote the whole thing down. One was the official scribe of the Cortés expedition, Bernal Díaz del Castillo, who penned a detailed and evocative account of the landing and ensuing battles in his book *The Conquest of New Spain*. The other scribe was Cortés himself, who wrote a series of detailed letters to the man who had dispatched the conquerors, Charles V, the holy Roman emperor who was also known as the Prince of Light Cavalrymen. The letters of Cortés described the terrain, the Indians, their religion, the fighting, the gold. He was not as good a writer as Díaz del Castillo, but no matter; together, the two books are an astonishing chronicle of *la conquista*. But the bigger surprise is that they paint a portrait of the sixteen horses that began the chain of events that brought the Aztec empire to its knees.

It is rare in historical chronicles — especially those that recount battles and wars — that we learn of the horses who served. Considering the millions of equine warriors who have figured in human history, there are precious few whose stories we know. Of course, there is Pegasus, the mythological winged horse who helped Bellerophon fight the Chimera and who gave Zeus thunderbolts, then returned to the sky as a constellation to live forever in the Western psyche as the ultimate symbol of freedom. There is Bucephalus, the mighty wild horse who carried Alexander the Great into ferocious battles from Macedonia to the Indian subcontinent. He was buried in a splendid tomb of gold leaf and alabaster tiles on the banks of the Hydaspes River, and in his honor Alexander built the city called Bucephala around it. And there is Incitatus, the famous white steed belonging to Caligula, the psychotic Roman emperor who raised appreciation of the horse to its most exquisite level. If there is anything good to be said for Caligula, it's that he loved horses — except when they belonged to his enemies, in which case he poisoned them. At home, Incitatus was his partner. Often the horse issued invitations for banquets — at least, that's whose name was at the bottom of requests. If guests declined, they were tortured. The many who came were greeted by Incitatus and a troop of slaves in a marble stall. Draped in a purple blanket of silk and a collar of gems, the equine host would dip into his ivory manger for a dinner of finely milled grain mixed with flakes of gold and drink wine from a golden goblet. Incitatus was also a priest, accompanying Caligula to public assemblies, then later promoted to senator. Just before he was assassinated, Caligula appointed Incitatus as his second in command. It would be a very long time before another figure of power acknowledged the role of *Equus*. Long after the fall of Rome and the fall of Constantinople and the rise and fall of old and new capitals and towns and kingdoms across all the lands, it was Hernando Cortés, one of the most audacious and bloodthirsty knights in human history, who finally spoke the truth: "We owe it all to God, and the horse."

While 1492 is the year from which the New World is tracked, we must look to 1519 as the date that horses put hoof to soil on the mainland of their origin, pulling the chariot of Western empire behind them. After some months in Cuba, where he survived infighting and intrigue among other conquistadors who vied for prestigious expeditions, Hernando Cortés defied his nemesis, the Cuban governor Diego Velázquez, and headed across the Atlantic to take Mexico, departing quickly before he could be stopped. Like many of the sixteenth-century adventurers, he had come from Extremadura, Spain, a rural region about 120 miles north of Seville that became known as the cradle of the conquistadors. For the ambitious young men in the expanding empire, the call to travel was irresistible. The strange land across the sea was said to hold vast repositories of gold and human treasure. Sometimes, all the men in a particular extended family shipped out, and a few returned with tales of astonishing discoveries that would alter the faces of maps. In fact, Cortés's second cousin was Francisco Pizarro, who was with Balboa at the first sight of the Pacific Ocean; later, after Cortés had laid waste to the Aztecs in Mexico, Pizarro wiped out the Incan empire in Peru.

In the year 1501, Cortés had made his decision: he would not go off to war in Italy and he would not become a lawyer like his grandfather. He would join the fleet and see the world. He was twenty-two, and he left for Cuba. Thirteen years later, after marrying, raising a family, and acquiring vast holdings of land and many slaves, he wanted more. So he rolled the dice again and prepared to leave for a new adventure. He assembled a fleet of eleven ships, including one that weighed a hundred tons, trailed by smaller brigantines. Among his crew of six hundred, there were thirty crossbowmen and twelve men with harquebuses; he also had over a dozen pieces of small artillery and several portable breech-loading cannons, weaponry unknown to the Aztecs. Many soldiers in his army had come from families of minor nobility in Extremadura; like Cortés, they were hidalgos. A number of men in the expedition were Jews fleeing the Inquisition.

Jews had been an important minority in Spain since the time of Christ. Yet in 613, after centuries of persecution, they were ordered to convert or leave. Those who remained were enslaved. In 711, shortly after the founding of Islam, Muslims invaded and conquered the Iberian Peninsula. They immediately freed all slaves and allied with the Jewish minority, with whom they had much in common; both cultures placed importance on the arts and education and both had originated in the same region. With their desert roots, they shared common stories about hardship and wandering, and some of their most important religious myths were bound up with animals — horses in particular.

It wasn't just on foot that Jews had fled into the sands from Egypt; it was on the backs of horses and burros. The Old Testament makes much of the beauty and might of horses. "Hast thou given the horse strength?'" it is written in the Book of Job. "Hast thou clothed his neck with thunder? . . . He paweth in the valley, and rejoiceth in his strength: he goeth on to meet the armed men. He mocketh at fear, and is not affrighted; neither turneth he back from the sword . . . He saith among the trumpets, Ha, ha; and he smelleth the battle afar off, the thunder of the captains, and the shouting." In Song of Songs, King Solomon's erotic ode to an Egyptian princess, Solomon compares his beloved to a company of horses in Pharaoh's chariots. In Kings I, we learn that Solomon himself had a formidable cavalry, consisting of 1,400 chariots and 12,000 horses. "Of all that I have inherited from David," he once said, "nothing is dearer to my heart than these horses."

In Muslim culture, we see a kinship with the horse that perhaps ran even deeper than that of its Hebrew forebears. In many ways, the culture itself revolved around the enduring and fleet desert steed. According to an old Bedouin saying, when God created the first mare, he spoke to the South Wind, saying, "I will create from you a being which will be a happiness to the good and a misfortune to the bad. Happiness shall be on its forehead, bounty on its back and joy in the possessor." Muhammad himself compared the horse to an arrow, and decreed that every Muslim should have one. To that end, the tribes of the Sahara bred the famous Arabian horse, which came from the five mares of Muhammad. As the story goes, the Prophet selected one hundred of his finest mares and locked them in a corral under the blazing sun not far from a pond. Every morning he would blow his horn, and the mares learned to answer his call. Yet they yearned for the water just beyond the fence, and, denied food and shade, they began to falter. Finally, he opened the gate and the thirsty animals ran to the water. But as they were about to drink, Muhammad blew his horn. Five mares of skin and bone turned from the pond and staggered to Muhammad. With tears of gratitude, he gave them water and named them, and they went on to foal the legendary Arabian horse. It was on this "son of the desert" and this "daughter of the wind" that Muslims conquered Spain, following the horse's arrow to the heart of their desire.

The next four hundred years were a period known as the golden age of Spain, during which an alliance between Jews and Arabs is said to have flourished. Many Jews served as middlemen between the

Islamic and Christian worlds, even guarding Muslim forts. Others functioned in key cultural roles, including the noted Hebrew scholar and physician Maimonides, who was court physician to the Kurdish warrior Saladin. But recent reappraisals of the golden age have cast it in a different light, with the good news of cooperation now considered along with the fact that, all too often, Jews and Christians were not allowed to ride horses, the most sacred animal in the kingdom. In other words, they were deprived of flight. Even the beloved Maimonides was deemed not worthy of the noble four-legged creature; in the twelfth century, as the Islamic caliphate began to crack down on infidels, Maimonides was ordered to bear the humiliation — and emasculation — of riding a donkey.

By the early fifteenth century, Spain began to cast off Muslim rule, and Jews came under widespread attack from Christian zealots. Most Jews submitted to baptism and came to be known as Conversos. But hundreds were massacred, and in 1480, the Church appointed two Inquisitors to root out the Hebrew population. Guided by medieval texts, they held secret tribunals, unmasking hidden Jews and denouncing them in public at autos-da-fé, where they were burned at the stake. Those who escaped were burned in effigy, and others were marched barefoot through the streets, dressed in *sambenitos*. Although the *sambenito* looked like a priest's garment, with its chasuble and long pointed hat, its purpose was to mock the wearer; its name means "to brand or disgrace," and it was yellow — a color that is most significant in terms of our story because its use as a slander dates from a medieval superstition about dun, or yellow, horses: they were considered inferior. As Spain was about to lay claim to foreign lands, the fate of Sephardic Jews became linked forever with horses — going way beyond the *sambenito,* taking them back to their Old Testament roots as they found refuge across the sea.

Within a century, some of these Jews became the first cowboys in the New World — yes, the original high plains drifter of American legend was not Clint Eastwood but a son of Moses who had been kicked out of Spain. In 1492, King Ferdinand and Queen Isabella issued the Alhambra decree, a cataclysmic document concocted by the deranged Inquisitor Torquemada. Read by town criers across the land, it asserted that Jews were wreaking evil and that it was time for them to leave. So the tribe fled, descendants of ancient shepherds whose communion with oxen and mules and horses was recorded in the Psalms and the more esoteric texts of another age, wandering again after the original desert exile, many heading for the New World, where over time, traveling on the backs of horses, they would find their way to another desert and make the wide-open space their home.

There were others who sailed with Cortés seeking a new life, a strange assortment not unlike those who had colonized Cuba under Columbus. "They ran the scale from governing officials and men of noble birth," writes Arthur Strawn in *Sails and Swords,* referring to the first wave of the conquest, "down to jail-birds who had been granted immunity to settle in the colony, and whose missing ears gave eloquent testimony of their former mode of living." With Cortés there were at least eight women, including a *conquistadora;* there were carpenters; there was a doctor. And there were also those who were not there by choice — a Mayan-speaking Indian fisherman who had been captured in the Yucatán in a previous expedition, slaves from Cuba, livestock, and war dogs — also unsung participants in the settlement of the New World.

In 1513, when Balboa seized Panama, he credited his dog Leoncico — Little Lion, the first named animal in the conquest histories — who killed so many Indians that he was given his own slaves and piles of gold, making him the Spanish empire's canine Incitatus. The wolfhounds and mastiffs of the Spanish cavalry may have been formidable warriors, but their primary task was to form a flank around the advancing line and protect the horses.

After Cortés had made all of the preparations for his journey to Mexico — the men recruited and assembled, provisions for a trip of indefinite term gathered — he "then gave orders to all his soldiers to furbish up their arms, and to the blacksmiths in the town to make helmets, and to the crossbowmen to overhaul their stores and make arrows," recounted Díaz del Castillo. "A town crier moved through the streets and alleys, calling for blacksmiths. Some of the men then boarded ships off the south coast of Cuba in Trinidad; others traveled overland to Havana, picking up additional recruits from farms along the road, and bringing the horses overland for the three-week voyage to Mexico." On February 18, 1519, the fleet was blessed and the cavalry set sail, flying the flags of the Holy Roman Empire and the kingdom of Spain, and ferrying horses back to their land of origin. Thanks to Bernal Díaz, we know not only the names of some of these horses, but also each one's rider, color, and, in some cases, personality traits — a picture of the very steeds that made the New World possible.

"I wish to put down from memory," Díaz wrote in his war diary, "all the horses and mares that we embarked." Cortés had a "vicious dark chestnut" who died in the first port, so he purchased another one from a member of his crew. Pedro de Alvarado and Hernando Lopez de Avila shared a bright bay mare. "She turned out very good," he noted, "both for tilting and to race." Alonzo Hernandez took a fast gray mare whom he had won from Cortés in a bet. Juan Velazquez de Leon had a strong gray mare called Bobtail. "She too was fast, and had a splendid mouth," Díaz wrote, describing her quick responses to the painful chain bit. Cristóbal de Olid brought a dark bay, a very able horse. Francisco de Montejo and Alonso de Avila shared a dark chestnut horse who lacked the temperament for war. "Francisco de Morla had a dark bay," reported Díaz, "who was very fast and well-bitted." Juan de Escalante had a skittish light bay with three white feet. Diego de Ordas had a barren gray mare who paced, but not quickly. The first-rate rider Gonzalo Dominguez brought a fast dark brown horse. Pedro Gonzalez de Trujillo had a bay horse that was also very fast. Baena from La Trinidad had a piebald horse, inclining to black in the markings, with white forefeet. "He turned out worthless," said Díaz. Moron of Bayamo had a piebald with white feet and a very responsive mouth. Another fine horseman, Lares, had a good bay horse who was light and a fine galloper. Ortiz the musician and Bartolome Garcia, who owned gold mines, shared a good black horse called both El Arriero, "the Drover," probably because he was or looked like a pack mule, and El Morzillo, "the Black One." Juan Sedeno from the Habana "had a brown mare," Díaz recorded. He was the richest conquistador in the fleet, a soldier of fortune who had brought his own vessel, a black slave, and plenty of cassava bread and bacon. On the way to the New World, Juan Sedeno's mare gave birth to a foal.

After sailing west for about fourteen days, the eleven galleons reached the eastern coast of Mexico and headed north along the palm-studded shoreline of Yucatán, stopping for a few days at the is-

land of Cozumel. On this tropical outpost, Cortés ordered an inspection — yes, the men were fit, the crossbows and harquebuses worked
properly, and the horses were weary but in good health. Perhaps most
important, the Spaniards learned that one of their compadres, Jeron-
imo de Aguilar, had been captured in an earlier, failed expedition and
taken as a slave. Cortés made a deal with local Indians, and Aguilar
was returned. It was obvious to the conquistadors that he had gone
native — dressing and talking and in every way appearing to be indigenous. A huge asset for the invaders, Aguilar now re-joined the cavalry as an interpreter.

The fleet left to continue its storied quest, and it was not long before Montezuma's vision was fulfilled. On April 21, 1519, the year 1
Reed on the Aztec calendar, Cortés spotted an inlet about forty miles
north of their earlier forays, and he headed up the passage to begin
the assault. As the galleons closed in, the horses must have sensed
that change was in the air. They had already picked up the strange
scent from a distant jungle blowing through their nostrils, and their
large ears had heard the call of tropical birds from a far-off grove
of palms. Now, as they were brought into the sunlight, their wide-
ranging eyes perceived a figure, or many, with vibrant feathers, duck-
ing between rocks or hiding in trees. The ship slowed just offshore
and the men scurried along the decks, preparing for exactly what, no
one knew, and as horse and man alike tasted the perfume of the New
World, the conquistadors donned their chain mail and some helpers
hauled into a bark the heavy wooden cross that would accompany
them through the empire of the Aztecs, and the bark was dropped
and the men rowed ashore. It was Good Friday, and the priest said
a prayer.

Hernando Alonso, the Hebrew blacksmith who was fleeing the
Inquisition as a secret Jew, one of the many Conversos on board, also
said a prayer as he checked the shoes of the horses and perhaps fitted
some with new ones for the tough days ahead. The Spaniards had a
special incantation that was designed for such occasions; the length
of time it took to say it permitted the iron to get as hot as necessary
before it was shaped and nailed to the horses' hooves. "For *Christo y
Santiago*," Alonso said, and then repeated it several times, perhaps
adding in a furtive whisper as he hammered, "*Shema Yisrael, Adonai
Eloheinu, Adonai echad*" — and then the horses were saddled, their

breastplates bedecked with bells, and they were lowered into shallow water, for there were no piers or points of debarkation awaiting the visitors, and they swam ashore. It was difficult for them, as their legs were stiff from the containment during the passage, but instinct prevailed and the little band that would change the world forever scrambled onto the land their masters would call Eldorado.

Drawing by a Spanish count from an eighteenth-century horsemanship guide titled *Manejo Real*, or *True Handling*.

Here is how the scribe Díaz described that day's landing:

The river, its banks, and the mangrove swamps were crowded with Indian warriors drawn up for battle. Cortés told Aguilar the interpreter to ask why they were so alarmed, since we had not come to do them any harm, but would give them some of the things we had brought with us, and treat them like brothers ... The more Aguilar talked, the more defiant they became. As soon as Cortés knew that the Indians intended to attack, thirteen gentlemen were chosen to go on horseback ... The Indians wore great feather crests, they carried drums and trumpets, their faces were painted black and white, they were armed with large bows and arrows, spears and shields, slings and stones and fire-toughened darts ... They rushed on us like mad dogs, discharging a rain of arrows, darts, and stones ... They shouted and whistled and cried, "Alala! Alala!" and were so crazed by their attack that they did not at once see the horsemen approaching behind their backs ... The horses were very nimble, coming quickly upon them and spearing them as they chose ... The Indians had never seen a horse before.

Within an hour, the Indians fled and the conquistadors planted the cross, thanked God, and founded a new town in honor of their first battle: Santa Maria de la Victoria. More than eight hundred Indians had been killed by sword, cannon, musket, or crossbow. Many lay groaning on the ground. Two Spaniards were dead and several horses wounded. "We sealed the wounds of our horses with fat from the corpse of an Indian we had cut up for the purpose," Díaz wrote, and then the invaders returned to camp with prisoners and took their supper. Later, an advance party headed by the cavalryman Francisco de Morla on a dapple-gray horse joined the men, leading the triumphant Cortés. Someone had a vision of the apostles James and Peter. Some of the captured Indians were dispatched with trinkets and told to return to their villages and let their chiefs know the Spaniards had arrived — and had come in peace.

The next day, forty chiefs returned with objects of gold and fowls, fruit, and baked fish. Not to be outdone, Cortés arranged for a most ingratiating gift to be sent to Montezuma, offering the Indians an exquisitely carved armchair inlaid with precious gems and packed in musk-scented cotton. "Take this to your prince," he said, "and this too" — adding a crimson cap with a gold medal engraved with a figure of Saint George on horseback, slaying a dragon with his lance. "When I come to talk with Montezuma, perhaps he'll sit in this chair and wear this hat."

Among Montezuma's emissaries were artists, and after the ceremony of the gifts had concluded, they unraveled broad scrolls of fabric and with colorful pigments made full-length portraits of Cortés, his captains and soldiers, the ships, sails, and horses, the Indian mistress Cortés had taken after the first battle and baptized, his interpreter, a pair of greyhounds, and even the cannon and cannonballs.

Lest Montezuma understand the pictures and prepare for the invaders' next move, Cortés had earlier decided to play a trick. "You know, gentlemen," Cortés had said to his men before the chiefs came, "I believe it is the horses that the Indians are most frightened of ... I have a way of confirming their belief. Let us bring Juan Sedeno's mare, which foaled the other day, and tie her up here, where I am standing. Ortiz the musician's stallion is very randy, and we can let him get a sniff of her. Then we will have both of them led off in different directions, and make sure that the chiefs who are coming do not hear them neighing, or see them, until they are standing and talking to me." And so the mare and stallion were brought, and the male caught the female's scent.

"You should not have attacked my men," Cortés said after the celebration, as the chiefs prepared to depart. "That was a crime. You should be executed," he continued, "like this" — and he gave a sign. A loaded cannon was fired, and it thundered, and the ball whistled over the hills. "It was midday," Díaz reported, "and very still." The Indians were terrified. Then the stallion was brought to Cortés, who was standing near the chiefs, where the mare had been tethered. Having caught her scent, the excited horse pawed the ground and neighed fiercely. "The *caciques* thought he was roaring at them," Díaz continued, "and were terrified once more." Then Cortés said something to the horse and told two orderlies to take him away. "He then informed the Indians that he had told the beast not to be angry," Díaz noted, "since they were friendly and had wanted to make peace."

And so Montezuma's vision had been satisfied, and the Indians sent word of the fire-breathing animals that danced up and down the shoreline and the strange-looking men who were covered in sheets of silver and attached to the animals so that each pairing of man and animal appeared to move as one, all in a unison that they did not understand. The startling news preceded the painted proof—"live coverage" of the cataclysmic meeting of two civilizations—the information finding its way up the streams and rivers and canals, and through the dense thickets of palm trees and ancient rain forest, and soon all the tribes in the land knew that the time had come for alliances. Some tribes chose to fight with Cortés, and others remained loyal to Montezuma, and by the time the dispatch reached the man who expected it, the mighty ruler knew the game was up.

Cortés had learned that Montezuma lived about two hundred miles from the port where he had landed, in a fabulous, golden city called Tenochtitlán. The city was beyond a mountain range, in the middle of a lake, surrounded by vast garrisons, approachable only by a heavily guarded causeway. In his second letter to Charles V, Cortés laid out his plan: march through the interior and bring back the Aztec leader "either dead or in chains" if he refused to submit to the Spanish Crown. Leaving a small party behind in the base camp that was now called Veracruz ("true cross"), the conquistadors began their advance. It took seven months to get to the fabled city; along the way the Spaniards traversed plains and jungle swamps, crossed mighty rivers, climbed through snow-packed mountains, passed under the shadow of smoking volcanoes, and finally came face to face with Montezuma.

When the conquistadors began their advance, they were down to fifteen horses, including the foal that was born along the way. As there is no further mention of the foal in the chronicles of the conquest, we may assume that the foal accompanied the mare, for it needed milk, and the gold seekers would not have left the newborn on a ship because they would not have wanted to lose a precious steed. Perhaps Alonso the Hebrew farrier said a prayer over the foal as the cavalry trekked on, or perhaps as his fellows marched with him he asked the Virgin Mary for protection—after all, Christo, her son, was born in a manger, and was that not a sacred place? Then again, perhaps he furtively (lest he be accused of Judaizing and then executed in a land where no one would remember his story) invoked the God of Abraham, Isaac, and Jacob, nomads all, shepherds whose very name, Hebrew, derived from *apiru*—"donkey caravaneer." And perhaps he even tended the foal as danger lurked, fashioning a coat of chain mail from scrap iron and hoping that the war dogs would scent and nail a jaguar before it sank its teeth into the neck of the young horse.

And what of Montezuma when he received word, the word-pictures, that his vision had been fulfilled? Yes, he was prepared for the end, and yes, he knew it would come in the form of man-animals that breathed fire, but he would meet the enemy on his terms, for he was also a student of fear. Quite possibly he did what he and his priests had done for centuries—carved open the chest of a drugged virgin with a shaft of obsidian, tossed her throbbing heart down his bloody temple steps, and then tore her limb from limb, throwing her head on a massive pile of rotting skulls where eagles and snakes feasted. Eventually Montezuma would administer the "sweet obsidian death" to some of the marauding knights who climbed the temple steps, and he would do the same to the horses, on the same steps; a few years later, when it was all over, a band of Indians formed a cult that worshipped a massive stone effigy of *Equus* seated on its haunches.

But what of the horses who were not forced to climb the altar? After trekking for three months, the cavalry came out of the mountains and into the sprawling valley of Mexico, an emerald gateway that led to Tenochtitlán. For another two months, the men and their horses moved ahead; they endured sieges along the way, but with the help of their allies, they steadily approached the capital city. Then, on September 1, outside the Aztec stronghold of Tlaxcala, there was intense skirmishing with Montezuma's army. Juan Sedeno's mare, the mother of the foal, was carrying the respected horseman Pedro de Moron; why he was not riding his own horse, the piebald with the white feet, we do not know, but Sedeno had been wounded in a previous battle and did not fight that day. Charging through rows of mud houses and plantations of maize, Cortés and his crew battled for hours as hundreds of Indians responded with a relentless fusillade of arrows and darts. That night, the conquistadors slept near a stream and, as was their habit, dressed their wounds "with the fat from a stout Indian whom we had killed and cut open, for we had no oil," recounted

Díaz. "We supped very well on some small dogs, which the Indians breed for food. For all the houses were deserted and the provisions had been carried away. They had even taken their dogs with them, but these had returned home at night, and we captured them ... We kept on alert all night, with sentries, patrols, and scouts on the watch and our horses bitted and saddled, for fear the enemy might attack."

The next day, the Spaniards said a prayer and marched on. They were met by six thousand warriors, again hurling arrows and darts as a jungle orchestra of drums and trumpets sounded the pagan defense. "Halt!" Cortés ordered his company, and he sent forth three Indian prisoners who had been captured the previous day, commanding them to tell their brothers the invaders meant no harm. But "the Indians became much more savage," Díaz wrote, "and attacked us so violently that we could not endure it." "Saint James and at them!" Cortés shouted, and the men from the Old World rushed the men from the New, killing three captains and sending the warriors back into the woods. The Spaniards pursued them — into an ambush of another forty thousand Indians, who cut them off on all sides. "The ground was somewhat broken," Díaz recalled, "so we could make no use of the horses, though by careful maneuvering we got them over it ... but the Indians' shooting was extremely good, and they did us great damage with their spears and broadswords, also with the hail of stones from their slings."

The cavalry faltered, and a chief decided to capture a horse. The Indians escalated their attack, launching another barrage of stones and darts. Pedro de Moron formed a line with three other horsemen and charged into enemy ranks. The men held their lances short, close to the hilt, and when they broke through the ranks, they aimed at the Indians' faces and made repeated thrusts to prevent them from grabbing hold of the lances. If an Indian managed to seize a lance, the horseman knew what to do next — dig in with his spurs, so that the leverage of the lance under his arm and the headlong rush of the horse enabled the rider to rip the lance free or drag the Indian with him. But before de Moron could make his defensive move, the Indians grabbed his lance and hacked him with their machetes, then sliced through the mare's neck until it hung by the skin. She dropped in her tracks, and the Spaniards quickly cut the girth around her belly and took the saddle, while others dragged the half-dead rider from the battlefield. Later, the Indians went to work on the fallen horse.

Centuries earlier, the Celts and the Etruscans and the Scythians had found magic in the horseshoe, invoking its power in secret rites. Centuries later, when Custer's horse fell at the Little Bighorn, his men would seek the same thing, taking not just the shoes but the hooves, chopping them off and turning them into inkwells. Now the Aztecs succumbed to the spell of the mare's shoes, cutting them away and offering them to their gods, for what purpose we can only guess. Good luck, perhaps? Protection? A magic shield of some sort? When the battered men and wounded horses returned to their camp at the banks of the stream, perhaps the mare's foal—now six months old—listened for the march of the approaching hooves, her mother's distinctive neigh, looked for her mother in the bedraggled and tired band; perhaps the stallion who had scented the mare when Cortés played the trick on the Indians also looked expectantly to the returning horses. This is not the stuff of cheap sentiment, for that is what horses do—they have families and companions and they recognize one another by way of their heightened senses. In any case, the horses were now fourteen, and they marched on, their cuts and scrapes dressed with human oil, closing in on their ancestral turf.

The chronicles mention that three more horses were killed in the next battle, which brings the roll to eleven. Still, with the remaining horses and superior arms, the Spaniards subdued town after town. But six months into the siege, the men had grown weary, and finally, by late fall, some of them had lost faith in the mission and threatened to return to Cuba. Ever the gambler, Cortés repelled the mutiny with another astonishing move. He hurried back to Veracruz and ordered his men to scuttle the fleet; the galleons were stripped of rigging, gear, sails, metal, and other things of value, piled ashore, and set on fire. "On this all abandoned any hope of leaving the land," he wrote in his second letter to Charles V, "and I set out relieved from the suspicion that once my back was turned I should be deserted by the men whom I had left behind in the town." There would be no more help or assistance except from God, he told his men, and they resumed the next phase of their siege, penetrating deeper into the forests of Mexico and seizing another settlement, although the closer the men got to Montezuma, the more it seemed as if they were traversing the labyrinth in Dante's *Inferno* — everywhere they went there was a new horror. As Díaz wrote:

> I remember that in the square [there] were many piles of human skulls, so neatly arranged that we could count them, and I reck-oned them at more than a hundred thousand. I repeat that there were more than a hundred thousand. And in another part of the square there were more piles made up of innumerable thigh-bones. There was also a large number of skulls and bones strung between wooden posts, and three papas, whom we understood to have charge of them, were guarding these skulls and bones.

Sights such as these combined with the fact that there was no es-cape must have given the march new urgency, and as the men be-came more agitated and frightened, so too did the horses, for horses

In a daring move, Cortés scuttles his ships and resumes his march through the jungle.

respond to the moods of their riders. Even if the men had withheld their true feelings, the remaining horses would have smelled the fear on their sweat, and perhaps they stepped with nervousness, more anticipation, and perhaps the farrier Alonso again uttered incantations from Testaments Old and New, asking for protection from the Trinity whose auspices the expedition invoked, and from *Adonai Eloheinu,* the one God, whose name he would whisper, perhaps to the foal. And the Spaniards began to close in on the heart of Mexico, the very chamber where Montezuma waited, ready to see the fire-breathing animals his emissaries had sketched on their scrolls.

Of what lineage were these animals? How were they able to survive the rigors of cavalry life in a strange land, taking their riders through charge after charge even while bleeding from wounds and suffering countless hardships? The original horses of the conquest had come with Columbus in 1493, on his second voyage, pressed into service for gold and God. They were traveling under a royal edict that said:

> The Twenty-third of May, 1493. Archive of the Indies. The King and the Queen: Fernando Zarpa, our Secretary. We command that certain vessels be prepared to send to the Islands and to the mainland which has been newly discovered in the ocean sea in that part of the Indies, and to prepare these vessels for the Admiral Don Christopher Columbus ... and among the other people we are commanding to go in these vessels there will be sent twenty lancers with horses ... and five of them shall take two horses each, and these two horses which they take shall be mares.

These horses (fifteen stallions and ten mares; in the parlance of the time *horses* meant "stallions") became the foundation stock for hundreds of horses that would serve in dozens of waves of a conquest that would effectively attain victory in about twenty years. Spain itself had once been conquered by a horse cavalry, Berbers from North Africa, who rode hot-blooded desert steeds that became known as barbs. Unlike the large Spanish horses that had been bred to carry knights and armor, the horses brought to Spain during the Muslim invasion were smaller and lighter—looking much like many of the mustangs in the American West today. Over the seven-hundred-year period that the Arabs ruled Spain, from 711 to 1400, the barbs

crossed with the larger European horses. As Robert Moorman Denhardt writes in *The Horse of the Americas:*

> These animals no longer showed the large, thick body and coarse,
> hairy legs which indicate north European and Germanic origin;
> they were light, clean-legged saddle horses, not the plate-armor
> type. So many Barb horses had been brought in and crossed on
> them that they were more like the Barb than any other horse. Al-
> though they were light animals, they were broad between the shoul-
> ders and across the hips and deep through the heart — characteris-
> tics that the Barb often lacked. In other points they were like the
> Barb, being of small to average height, having on occasion a long,
> round body, a strong head sometimes Roman-nosed, thick-necked,
> with full loin, sloping rump, the color often some shade of line-
> backed buckskin, and a smooth gait ideal for a saddle horse.

As Spain absorbed the smaller, faster, and more agile barb, it also
appropriated the Berber riding style, known as *a la jinete* (spelled
differently over time), which most likely originated with the Zenetes,
a notorious tribe of North African horse warriors. It was the opposite
of the traditional chivalric style favored by knights, *la brida,* in which
the rider — loaded down like his horse with heavy armor — sat erect
and rode with long stirrup leathers. He had little maneuverability
other than to charge. Horsemen who rode *jinete* had shorter stirrups,
and their legs were bent so that they appeared to be almost kneel-
ing. This gave them a greater level of control; in addition to using the
reins and bits, they could now use their legs. With saddles that were
smaller and less confining, they could more effectively throw lances
or fire guns. "My country was won *a la gineta,*" wrote Garcilaso de la
Vega, the half Incan, half Spanish scribe of the Pizarro expedition, in
what was one of the first published accounts of Western history.

When it comes to style, all roads lead to Italy, and the conquest of
the New World is no exception. The *jineta* style of riding may have
come from North Africa but it was perfected at post-Renaissance
cavalry schools in Naples, which was at the time ruled by Spain. During the Dark and Middle Ages, horses were considered vicious animals and were often beaten into submission. As the Renaissance began, an ancient manuscript that would change attitudes toward the

horse was resurrected by Italian monks, who had begun to assemble
libraries of Greek literature. This was *The Art of Horsemanship* by
the great Greek horseman and warrior Xenophon, who wrote his famous manual (still used today) in 360 B.C. He was the first person
on record to advocate kind treatment and training of horses. At the
same time that knights were replacing *la brida* with *la jineta,* Italian
schools of cavalry began to adopt some of Xenophon's rules. "Whenever you induce [the horse] to carry himself in the attitude he naturally assumes," wrote the equestrian, "when he is most anxious to
display his beauty, he will do the very things in which he himself de-
lights and takes the greatest pleasure."

As Italians were learning about Xenophon's equestrian codes,
they were also advancing a revolution in how to live, shedding the
coarse behavior of the plague years in favor of the mannered. The
finer aspects of life were initially spelled out by Baldassare Casti-
glione in his famous book *Il Cortegiano* (*The Courtier*), in which he
suggested that social interaction be carried out with *sprezzatura* — a
kind of carelessness that concealed art, a breezy performance of the
complex, that in modern times would be embodied by, say, Marcello
Mastroianni, or by the Ferrari. In a way, the dressage that came out
of the post-Renaissance schools — the formalized equestrian warfare that defeated millions of aboriginals in the New World — was a
highly refined embodiment of *sprezzatura,* with guns and war dogs
added by the Spanish to create a deadly army that not only pirouetted, kicked, and stomped on command but also had fangs and appeared to breathe fire.

It was in the kingdom of Naples, ruled by Spain from 1502 to 1714,
that this seminal style of riding was developed. The first cavalry re-
forms of that period were instituted by a viceroy of Naples, Gonzalo
Fernández de Córdoba, also known as "el Gran Capitán." Under his
reign, Spanish barb mares from Iberia were brought to the studs in
Naples — descendants of horses left over from invasions by Saracens
and Normans (Arabians, barbs, and bigger horses from the Christian West) — and bred to produce the Neapolitan, a trim and strong
horse. A preferred steed for cavalry training, the Neapolitan was used
to enhance the performance of many European breeds.

At the same time, in nearby Mantua, Francesco Gonzaga was

breeding his fabled Gonzaga horse—a combination of horses from Spain, Ireland, Africa, Thrace, and Cilicia—considered the fleetest, most beautiful, and fittest breed of its time. These new types were constantly tested at racetracks all over Italy, then reconfigured and refined to meet the demands of expanding European monarchies. Again and again, the Gonzaga horses outran the others, and they were quickly purchased or requisitioned for military service. In 1532, the famous Neapolitan Riding School was founded, and it was here that the monarchs of Europe, including Henry VIII, sent their representatives to learn from Italian masters.

In 1550, Federico Grisone's seminal book on warhorse training, *Gli Ordini di Cavalcare* (*Orders of Riding*), was published. Xenophon may have been saved from oblivion by monks who revered the classics, but Grisone ignored his teachings and put forth his own very brutal techniques, which were a throwback to the Middle Ages and followed for decades all over Europe. To break a horse's spirit, he advocated such things as beating him between the ears and other sensitive areas, and as a punishment, he suggested tying a cat to a long pole and placing it under the horse's belly and hind legs, or putting a live hedgehog under his tail. The martially constructed spurs that he favored drew blood. His student Giambattista Pignatelli designed a widely used bit that was very heavy and hurt the horse's mouth simply by its presence; the Pignatelli bit was used in many variations until the eighteenth century. Yet Grisone also promoted the idea of good health and proper care of horses; his book *L'arte Veterale* is one of the first known accounts of veterinary science, and in it he discussed, among other things, the "marvellous secrets" of blacksmithing.

Another influential horseman of the time was the Bolognese Count Fiaschi, whose book *Trattato del Imbrigliare, Maneggiare, et Ferrare Cavalli* was published in 1556. His methods were similar to Grisone's, but he was the first to advocate the use of voice as well as music in horse training. But it was the Frenchman Antoine de Pluvinel, a student of Pignatelli, who fully returned to the spirit of Xenophon. "Anything forced or misunderstood can never be beautiful," Xenophon had written, and Pluvinel brought a modicum of kindness back into the training of warhorses. Contending that the use of spurs and whips was a confession of failure, Pluvinel relied on praise and reward, writing in his seventeenth-century manual that men must be

"lavish with caresses" and "sparing with punishment." He also pioneered the carousel — the forerunner of Buffalo Bill's equine spectacles as well as of today's mounted drill — in which a group of horses
performed a ballet to music; his most famous carousel involved more
than a thousand horses and riders.

When you watch dressage today, or even the U.S. Marines'
Mounted Color Guard (which uses palomino wild horses from Nevada), remember that the beautiful and ritualized moves you see
were once performed on the battlefield — and in fact are essentially
the same ones that the sixteen horses of Cortés carried out as they
marched into the heart of Mexico, laden with chain mail and the
weight of heavily protected riders. "The horse is a generous animal,"
wrote the sixteenth-century priest Luis de Granada, "well-bred and
high-spirited. When he leaves the stable, he prances in a way but little fitted to the narrowness of the streets, dancing to one side and the
other, arching his neck to show how well he knows the bit. He seems
to understand the beauty of his trappings, and that he is obliged to
show his spirit and his strength."

In the decades that followed the first Atlantic horse crossing,
countless other horses were shipped on frequent voyages from Spain
to join the original ones. Some were listed in a kind of equine census or in records of provisions and livestock. On April 9, 1495, for instance, "there were four caravels with a quantity of livestock aboard,
including six mares," writes Denhardt. Mares were needed for the
obvious reason — to breed more horses. Shortly after his second voyage, Columbus wrote to Queen Isabella with the following request:
"Each time there is sent any type of boat there should be included
some brood mares." "On April 23, 1497, fourteen mares were sent,"
Denhardt continues, adding that there was another billet for 106
mares who were sent around that time from Seville, Sanlucar, and
Huelva. "In 1498, when the Admiral was organizing his third voyage,
he was authorized to carry to the island of Hispaniola forty horsemen
and their horses." These horses were switched with nags at the point
of debarkation, with the horsemen pocketing a hefty profit. In Cuba,
when Columbus found that inferior horses had been shipped, rather
than punish his men, he punished the horses, withholding feed until
he felt all parties had learned a lesson.

Animals have always borne the ill behavior of their partners and masters, particularly those animals that are beasts of burden, and the horses that helped to found America were both pawns and treasure. "In 1501," Denhardt notes, "Don Nicolas de Ovando took only eighteen horses, but they were the best available ('*de distinguida casta*') ... by 1500 the Crown had one ranch on Hispaniola that boasted sixty brood mares." By then Columbus had laid waste to the Indian population of Cuba and fully taken the island; soon it became the primary breeding ground for horses in the New World. Before they headed for the jungles of Mexico, Panama, Venezuela, Bolivia, Nicaragua, Florida, and Peru, Spanish explorers stopped in Santo Domingo to pick up mounts and to get the other animals — mules, cattle, sheep, pigs, and dogs bred expressly for fighting — that carried and fed the conquistadors and the padres who accompanied them. By 1510, so many horses had been shipped from Spain that the Crown outlawed further export, and New World prices for horses jumped from one peso to the equivalent of hundreds of dollars.

Except for the foal born at sea on the way to the temple steps of Montezuma, no one knows if the sixteen horses on the Cortés expedition originated in the Caribbean or if they were shipped from Spain or even Naples to Cuba and then shipped out again, but one thing is certain: it was the stamina, endurance, and courage flowing from their ancient desert bloodlines that carried them through the horse latitudes and finally to the shores that would take them home. And on those shores, around 1519, the remaining band of eleven faced their most difficult task — surviving Tenochtitlán, the Aztecs' capital city, home of Montezuma.

After a long trek, the conquistadors had climbed to the top of snowcapped mountains. The volcano Popocatépetl puffed smoke in the distance, and splayed out before them was the valley of Mexico, the source of the siren call that had traveled the sea all the way to their haciendas in Spain, penetrated their dreams and their every waking moment, made them sick with gold fever, commanding them to give up everything and risk all to come. Now, the caravan made its way down the pass, thick forests of pine with a floor of ash, and as the invaders neared their quarry, they were met by a few of Montezuma's ambassadors, who welcomed them with gold and feathers. According to Aztec eyewitnesses whose accounts were recorded in the *Florentine Codex* in 1540 by the missionary Bernardo de Sahagún:

> The Spaniards ... seized upon the gold like monkeys, their faces flushed. For clearly their thirst for gold was insatiable; they starved for it; they lusted for it; they wanted to stuff themselves with it as if they were pigs. They went about fingering the streamers of gold, passing them back and forth, grabbing them one to the other, babbling, talking gibberish among themselves.

And then the men resumed their march, Cortés on El Morzillo leading the way, the other horsemen following, the cavalry surrounded by a phalanx of dogs, the infantry next in the column, trailed by thousands of Indian allies who were opposed to Montezuma, and many slaves captured during the six-month siege. And then, it was as if the whole ordeal had been worth it — as they proceeded deeper into the valley, they saw a vision, rising out of the lake on the horizon; in a way, the original Emerald City. Díaz could barely contain his ecstasy:

> And when we saw all of the cities and villages built in the water, and other great towns on dry land, and that straight and level causeway leading to Mexico, we were astounded. These great towns and temples had buildings rising from the water, all made of stone ... Indeed some of our soldiers asked whether this was not all a dream ... It was all so wonderful that I do not know how to describe this first glimpse of things never heard of ... [The causeway] was so crowded with people that there was hardly room for them all, so we could barely get through ... The towers and temples were full, and they came in canoes from all parts of the lake. And no wonder, since they had never seen horses, or men like us, before.

Montezuma, the dreamer of horses and men on their backs, was now about to welcome them to his enchanted and bizarre domain. Quite aware of his power, he was forty but looked much younger; he was tall with long dark hair, said to be spare and thin, quick to laugh when entertained by the dwarves and deformed creatures he kept in cages, serious and even morose in public matters such as the one at hand. Just as serious was Cortés, now thirty-five, a man who had scuttled ships and rendered his men castaways just to prove a point. Call it what you will — Christian versus pagan, guns versus poison darts, linear versus cyclical interpretations of time — their meeting was possibly the most monumental encounter in the course of human history. Imagine the two entourages from distant worlds — one covered in armor and carrying the flag of Christ, the other brandishing colorful shields and dressed in a profusion of jungle finery — entering from opposite sides of the stage, sizing each other up, sniffing, eyeing, and in fact there are records of the words that representatives of the two kingdoms said to each other as their men fell away so the two could engage. But the words that were not spoken are the truth of this scene, and after the introductions, after "Hernando Cortés, meet Montezuma; Montezuma, meet Hernando Cortés," what the Spaniard did not say was this: "I am here, sir, to cause your death and wipe out your people."

"Oh, yes, my lord," the Aztec did not respond, "and it will happen. But along the way, I will rip your animals limb from limb and I will tear the hearts of your men from their chests and feed them to my snakes. This is the year 1 Reed and this is the day 1 Wind. It is Quetzalcoatl's moment and I have been expecting you and your foam-flecked monsters. Come."

And so Cortés and his column followed Montezuma into his capital's glittering and golden heart. Temples of white stone inlaid with turquoise rose from the canals; gaily festooned warriors with pet jaguars and ocelots watched from rooftops bedecked with bright flags. It hurt to look at the many wonders, and finally, Montezuma took the men to the top of a pyramid and into a shrine dedicated to the war god Huitzilopochtli. Human organs were burning on a grill. Cortés told Montezuma that he was doing the Devil's work and asked for permission to erect a Christian altar. No, Montezuma replied, these are good things, they bring fertility and rain, and that was the end of the conversation.

Eight days later, Cortés placed Montezuma under house arrest, instructing him to act as if all were well. For the next six months, that is exactly what he did. Life in the kingdom was as always; in fact, so convincing was the play that a newcomer might have thought that the conquistadors were guests. But one spring day in 1520, Cortés got word that his enemy Panfilo de Narváez had landed at Veracruz, sent from Cuba to punish him for leaving without permission. He chained Montezuma and handed off control to Alvarado, his second in command, then left with most of his men to confront Narváez.

While Cortés was gone, Alvarado took the shadow play to its next act. First, he locked up two Indians, shot a king with arrows, then burned him alive. Two days later, as gaily bedecked singers and dancers assembled in a temple for the spring festival, he launched a killing spree. The musicians were attacked first—old men who played the drums; the invaders "slashed open their backs," witnesses later reported, "and their entrails gushed out. Of some they cut their heads to pieces ... They split bodies open..." The slaughter continued for three hours, until all the singers and spectators were dead. The conquistadors then moved through the temple and killed everyone else—"those who were carrying water, or bringing fodder for the horses, or grinding meal, or sweeping the floor." As word of the massacre spread across the city, a mob of women carrying torches swarmed the temple, throwing themselves on the corpses, wailing and crying. Aguilar the interpreter said he had never been so afraid.

By this time, Cortés had reached Veracruz; in a rainstorm on Easter night, he surprised and defeated Narváez. We do not know what part, if any, horses played in this battle, for there is no mention of their role in the records, no mention of the foal, who would have been about a year old. But we do know that with Narváez came plenty of reinforcements—including eighty fresh horses, already saddled. It was a lucky break for Cortés, because when he returned to Tenochtitlán on June 25, the lamentation of the Aztecs had turned into a revolt, and Montezuma was unchained.

At midnight on July 1, under a light rain, Cortés organized his caravan—his men, his Indian allies, all the women—and tried to sneak out of town. A greedy bunch, they were not traveling light: the gold yielded by the City of Dreams had been melted down for easy carrying back to Spain, and the horses designated for that purpose—"seven wounded and lame and one mare"—were heavy with it. So too the men, whose pockets were stuffed with bars of gold. The hooves of all of the horses had been muffled to silence the escape, but just as the caravan started to cross a bridge from the city to the other side of the lake, they were besieged by thousands of warriors on foot and in the water; "the whole lake was so thick with canoes," Díaz reported, "that we could not defend ourselves." Some of the brigade, including Cortés and the horses with the gold, crossed the bridge and reached safety, but others could not. Two horses slipped and fell into the water because of the rain, and soon "the channel filled up with dead horses, Indians of both sexes, servants, bundles, and boxes."

Cortés got word that some of his men were still under attack, and he took several horsemen back toward the lake but was stopped by Alvarado, who was badly wounded, on foot, holding his spear. The Indians had killed his sorrel mare. "Don't go back," he warned the men. "Save yourselves."

The night was filled with charges and retreats, charges and retreats, and in the thick of it, the Aztecs hurled five heads at the soldiers, streaming with blood, cut from men they had just captured.

Later, Cortés was dragged from his steed, wounded. Many soldiers rushed to the aid of their captain, hauling him out of the mud even as he killed four Indians with his lance. Eight more horses were killed, and then someone brought Cortés another mount. The army retreated, and there came the haunting sound of drums, conches, whistles, and horns. Finally, the men reached safety, but the sound of the drums continued, and when they looked across the lake to the shrine from which it came, they saw their captured comrades being hauled up the temple steps. Plumes were placed on their heads and they were made to dance before the war god Huichilobos. Then the priests laid them down on their backs, cut open their chests, took out their beating hearts, and offered them to their idols. The Indians kicked the carcasses down the steps, and later, the hands and feet of the Spanish soldiers, the skin of their faces, and the heads of the horses that had been killed were sent to the towns of those who had allied with Cortés. History books — that is, history books of the West — refer to that night as La Noche Triste — "the night of tears."

But Montezuma did not survive that night either — according to legend, he was killed by his own people for collaborating with the Spanish. "Cortés said to us that although we were so few," Díaz wrote, "only 440 of us surviving, with twenty horses, twelve crossbowmen, and seven musketeers — almost the same number as had followed him into Mexico in the first place — and though we had no powder and were all wounded, lamed, and maimed, we could clearly see that it had been Jesus Christ's pleasure to spare our lives, and that we must always give Him great thanks and honour." Yet the thing that had lured them in the first place — the gold — had been lost. It was now lying at the bottom of the lake, in the pockets of the men who were so laden with it that they could neither run nor swim when they were attacked. So after the surviving conquistadors thanked the Lord, they came back one more time, six months later, with fresh horses. Cortés was riding El Morzillo. His army was swarmed by thousands; Cortés was hit by an arrow and wounded by rocks. As he slipped from his saddle, a feathered shaft penetrated Morzillo's mouth. Angered, the big black steed quickly rallied, biting and striking at the Aztecs with his hooves until Cortés managed to remount and launch the final, victorious charge. It was August 13, 1521 — day 1 Serpent in the year 3 House. Two years after the Spanish had landed, the Aztec empire was vanquished.

In 1524, Cortés again rode the black, when he returned and led a march to Honduras. The column entered a valley where a Mayan tribe tended sacred deer. The Spaniards fired at the deer. These Indians had not yet seen horses or weapons such as the conquistadors', and like the others before them, they surrendered in awe. But a splinter had entered one of Morzillo's hooves, and Cortés was forced to leave him with the Mayans. "Take good care of him," he said. "I'll be back."

The Indians installed El Morzillo in the largest temple on their island in a lake, and they worshipped him as the god of thunder and lightning, just as some aboriginals in America later did, and as they recounted in their legends that they had always done. Like Incitatus, El Morzillo had his own attendants, young maidens who placed wreaths of flowers around his neck and offered him chickens and other delicacies on which to dine. But the war-torn horse could not eat such food and wasted away.

A hundred years later, a pair of Franciscan monks came upon the Mayans bowing down before an equine idol. "This is no god but only the image of an unthinking beast!" one said, and the other picked up a club and shattered the horse's head. But not his spirit; according to legend, should you happen to find yourself in a canoe on a clear, moonless night on the lake whose waters the ancient Mayans once plied, you might just see the likeness of the Black One in the depths below.

"We have a disease of the heart," Cortés had told Montezuma, "which is only cured by gold." For the next two decades, the Spanish continued to lay siege to the New World, sending wave after wave of warriors and horses and war dogs and armaments, and priests and settlers and livestock and Bibles. Among these ambitious invaders was Hernando de Soto, a young knight who made bold claims of adding more gold to the country's overflowing coffers. In 1539, he led a doomed, three-year expedition through the treacherous mangrove swamps of La Florida and into the marshy lowlands of what later became Alabama, Georgia, Mississippi, Louisiana, Tennessee, and North and South Carolina. It was one of the most brutal marches in the annals of Western history, with horses — as always — witnesses to the beheadings, the eviscerations, the gougings, one more hideous extirpation carried out in the name of Christ. Yet there were survivors, and, unlike certain Indians of Mesoamerica, they were not at all in awe of the strange, four-legged creatures that carried the army.

For much of the expedition, de Soto's army was lost in the swamps. When lunar charting failed, the men relied on their mounts. "The [horses] thrust their noses to the ground like hounds or bird dogs," Garcilaso de la Vega wrote in his colorful account of the expedition, *The Inca's Florida,* one of the first works of Western history. "As if possessed by human intelligence, [they] set about tracing and following the path left by the Spaniards in coming there. Not comprehending the intention of the animals, the riders at first drew in the reins, but the horses would not lift their heads from the trail and, to find it when it was lost, gave great puffs and snorts."

As the cavaliers moved through the woods, the Indians were studying their animals. By the time the intruders got to Georgia, the Chickasaw had figured out the most effective way to kill the horses — multiple arrows or long poles with fire-hardened shafts that they plunged through the hearts. As the gruesome *entrada* stretched into its third year, not even half of the 340 original horses remained. The men themselves succumbed to attack, starvation, and the wages of their own putrefying flesh, but they tried mightily to protect their steeds. "Horses are the nerve and sinew of our army," a captain proclaimed, and sometimes the soldiers killed an aboriginal just for his fat and used it to treat the wounds of their animals. Like the Chickasaw, the Apalachee Indians near present-day Tallahassee figured out how to fend off the four-leggeds; they planned their battles around them, having learned during an earlier Spanish invasion how the conquistadors waged war. Often, they engaged the enemy in the woods and swamps where the horses could not charge, and they also constructed rope-and-cane fences across paths to stop or slow down the animals.

In the winter of 1541, they routed de Soto and harried the expedition out of their lands. After months on the trail, the voracious knight and his weary men reached the area of what is today Mobile, Alabama. The faltering horses grazed on grasses, fattened up, and regained their high spirits. Lest they escape, the Spaniards fashioned special halters and shackles of large iron chains. One night while the soldiers were sleeping, the Indians attacked once more, torching the encampment and stables. The horses went up in flames — in all, eighty were raked by arrows while staked to the ground.

De Soto and his crew retreated. Racked by fever, de Soto degenerated quickly, falling into a coma on May 21, 1542, and dying later that day. He was buried in secret on a deserted plain. Pursued by Indians, the soldiers wandered for months, back through the swamps as winter set in, coming almost full circle to the point of their original landing at Tampa, navigating by the stars. Near the Gulf of Mexico, a search party found them — the final weary two hundred and their last sixty horses. Twenty of the animals were not fit for further travel. The men tied them to stakes and opened their veins. After the horses bled to death, the men ate them, and took the hides.

To get the other horses to the ships, they procured canoes and tied them together in twos; in each pair of canoes they loaded one horse, its forefeet in one and its hind feet in the other, and then they pushed the canoes through the water to the ships. With hundreds of Indians on their trail, they paddled quickly toward the anchored ships, taking cover under the skins of their freshly killed horses even as they stood by the living ones. But they had no defense against the massive storm of arrows and set off for the ships themselves, leaving their animals alone in the small boats.

One man, the clown of the expedition, remained with his horse in a canoe. This was Estevan Anez, and his horse, too, was something of a joke, "of comic shape, but nevertheless strong and robust; and because of being so, or more likely because no arrow had struck it in the proper place, the animal had served until the end of the expedition." Anez stood in his tiny vessel, taunting the Indians to come and get him. Together the pair foretold Don Quixote and his skinny horse Rocinante (which means "nag"), and perhaps Cervantes had heard this tale by the time he wrote his famous knight's tale, *Don Quixote.* In any case, the more Anez taunted the Indians, the more the cavaliers urged him on, and some even joined his rebellion, until finally the commander ordered a squadron to capture him and string him up.

With all men now safely on board the ships, the horses stood alone, stranded on the canoes, taking arrows until they all went down. But there were eight that the Spaniards had left ashore as they were fleeing. The Indians took off their halters and saddles and set them loose, and as the animals were running, they launched another fusillade of arrows until the last horses of the grand *entrada* had fallen.

No one knows how many Indians were killed by the time it was all over. In the final siege of Tenochtitlán alone, as many as a hundred thousand perished. Some say that the populations of Mexico, Peru, Bolivia, Nicaragua, Honduras, the islands of the Caribbean, and all the adjoining lands in that part of the world had been reduced by tens of millions. Disease had done its part, along with murder and slavery. Such things take their toll on their progenitors, and although Cortés received much fame and fortune upon his return to Spain, his life was said to be empty.

Many of his old compadres turned against him, accusing him of war crimes and of misappropriating Montezuma's gold. Others had remained in Mexico, particularly the Jews who had been hiding as Catholics. The farrier Alonso, who had uttered the special prayer while fitting the horses of the conquest with shoes, established the first ranch in the New World, outside Mexico City. But by 1529, the Inquisition had ranged across the ocean. What prayer did he utter when the soldiers came for him in the jungles of Mexico? Of course we do not know, for there is no record of his last words as a free man, but we do know that the Church rendered him another sort of pioneer — the first Jew to be burned at the stake in the New World; he was carried to the outdoor furnace in a procession on a horse while draped in the dun-colored *sambenito* of shame that might have matched the coat of his four-legged companion.

After the auto-da-fé in Mexico City, other secret Hebrews who had fled Spain as conquistadors volunteered for assignments in the most rugged parts of Mexico, where they thought they could be safe. And so was established another first — the biggest ranch in the New World, in the sere province of Nuevo León, near what became the modern city of Monterrey. It was started by the Carvajal family, a famous Converso dynasty that bred the first horses and cattle in the conquered lands. Father and nephew, wife and nieces were burned at the stake as the *conquista* pressed on.

From the time of de Soto and for the next fifty years, there came more explorers with more horses and cattle and sheep and burros, wanting so much more than the glittering innards that they had already hauled out of the mountains in the New World, not satisfied but taunted by the large gold horse in a church in Seville built by Columbus after one of his expeditions. There was Coronado, who traveled with five hundred horses up the Devil's Highway into Arizona, the treacherous, desolate, delicious, vast, and lonely route through the Sonoran Desert plied today by migrants who might stumble over shards of conquistador armor and bones and die of thirst along the way. There was Oñate and his fifteen hundred horses and mules trekking into New Mexico, and in the next century, there was Father Kino, a sort of anti-conquistador, a padre known for his kind treatment of Indians and animals, a dedicated missionary who for twenty years traveled thousands of miles on horseback, establishing missions up and down the Rio Grande. "He died as he lived," said a priest at his funeral, "in the greatest humility and poverty, not even undressing during his last illness and having for his bed two sheepskins for a mattress and two small blankets of the sort that the Indians use for cover, and for his pillow a packsaddle."

The record tells us that the original sixteen horses that came with Cortés — the two bays, the light bay with the three white feet, the piebald with the black markings, El Morzillo, and the others — perished during the early years of the conquest. And so too did the 350 that came with de Soto, according to history. But there's a legend that says otherwise. It says that the foal born to the brown mare en route from Cuba survived, escaped at some unknown time, and ran toward its ancestors, over mountains and across valleys and canyons and rivers, through cloudbursts and dust storms and days of no water, left to carry on by jaguars and wolves and snakes, perhaps aided by animal spirits, particularly chattering birds that urged the foal onward as it grew older, and eventually finding its own kind — six horses that are said to have escaped the de Soto campaign and moved westward. This small band too had traveled great distances, across wetlands and then into the parched flats just beyond the Rio Grande, like the foal, getting a reprieve from predators, or perhaps not appealing to them for reasons that we do not know, drawing ever closer to the American West, possibly sensing in their bones and marrow that one of their own was waiting for them, needed their kinship, and it was in the Sonoran Desert possibly, or the Mojave, that one day the six happened upon the one, drinking at a depression in a canyon rock, or grazing on some rabbit brush, and then they exchanged some information and headed for freedom, El Norte, their home.

2

Dawn of the Mustang

Eohippus to Equus

SIXTY-FIVE MILLION YEARS AGO, the North American continent was molting. The vast inland seas that had covered it began to recede, and large swaths of land appeared. Tectonic plates shifted and volcanoes blasted, throwing forth the Rocky Mountains and the Tetons and the Sierras. Stretching away from the ranges were rolling hills and savannas, nourished by river systems and freshwater lakes and marshes. In the new subtropical climate, grasses flourished and there were fruit trees and big flowers and forests of hickory and oak. The Age of Mammals unfolded; free of the vanished and predatory dinosaur, the animals evolved accordingly. They fed on the proliferating forage and increased in number and species. Within ten million years, there were mammals everywhere — in the air, the sea, and on land. Among the animals that now appeared on the plain was the very first horse. This was eohippus, also known as "dawn horse."

For millions of years the horse continued to evolve, adapting to the shifting geography and climate by way of teeth and leg bones and size. Some branches became extinct, and others sent forth bigger and faster new lines. As the horse changed, it traveled north, crossing the

Bering land bridge from America to Asia and then points beyond, re-
peating the pattern of survival and extinction wherever it went. Four
million years ago, right where it had started, the horse and nature
conspired one more time — *Equus* emerged, the fleet, bighearted ath-
lete of the plains.

Eohippus barely resembles *Equus*, and it's hard to believe that the
animals are related. Dawn horse was just ten to twenty inches tall, no
bigger than a fox terrier. It had an arched back, short neck, short face,
short, flexible legs, and a long tail. Scientists believe that it scam-
pered through forest thickets like a deer, aided by pads on its feet.
It had four toes on each front foot and three on each hind foot, with
vestiges of earlier toes on the front and back. Its teeth were typical of
omnivorous browsers, with three grinding molars on each side of its
jaw. This progenitor horse lasted for twenty million years, spinning
off three species, including *Orohippus*, which continued the horse
line. It looked very much like the dawn horse, but its vestigial toes
were gone and two teeth had evolved into new grinding molars, to accommodate plants with tougher leaves.

About forty million years ago, there was another cataclysmic shift
in geography and climate. North America and Greenland had separated from Europe, and the continents began to drift toward their
current positions. With the land on the move, the patterns of ocean
and air currents changed. The earth cooled and seasons emerged,
and the weather became much dryer. Some of the giant forests with-
ered, and new grasses flourished on the developing stretches of open
land. Many mammals did not make the transition, but within five
million years *Mesohippus* arrived — a significant advance in horse
evolution.

While still small at twenty-four inches, *Mesohippus* was less dog-
like, with legs, face, and neck that were longer than its predecessors'.
Moreover, it had fewer toes; with three each on both its front and
hind feet, and the fourth front toe becoming another vestige, *Mesohippus* was that much closer to the single-toed — or hoofed — horse
of today. In addition, its brain had grown larger, and the horse now
had a total of six grinding teeth, with sharp crests on each tooth to
help it survive on new forms of vegetation. Shortly after *Mesohippus* appeared, another horse variation split off. This was *Miohippus*,

which was larger and had a longer skull. For a short period, the two species lived side by side on the fields of Wyoming, until a new epoch arrived and *Mesohippus* vanished. This was the Miocene, and it began about twenty-three million years ago. During its course of nearly twenty million years, the continents assumed their present configuration. The climate changed again, warming up, and the woodland regions became meadows of grass. The number of species of mammal exploded in response; in the American West, nearly twenty different species of horse crisscrossed the land.

The early part of the Miocene saw a quick division of the *Miohippus* line, with the equine taking several detours and spinning off two trajectories, one of which produced a horse called *Mercyhippus* about seventeen million years ago. While not as glamorous in name as "dawn horse," *Mercyhippus* was nearly as pivotal; in the words of anthropologist Kathleen Hunt, this was "the first, bona fide, speedy plains grazer." As such, *Mercyhippus* blazed the path for *Equus*, the horse of today. For the first time in equine evolution, the classic horse look emerged. At forty inches, or about ten hands, *Mercyhippus* was taller than the earlier horses. It had a longer muzzle, deeper jaw, and eyes that were far apart, which provided room for larger and stronger teeth, an adjustment for grazing. In addition, it had a larger brain and was much smarter than its ancestors.

But *Mercyhippus* also embodied other refinements, and these were in its legs and feet. Its legs had become longer, and it now was able to bound away when threatened. "It stood permanently on tip-toe," observes Hunt, "supported and propelled by strong, springy ligaments that ran under the fetlock." It still had three toes on each foot, but "the side toes began to be of varying sizes." Some variations of this species retained full-size side toes, while "others developed side toes that only touched the ground while running. The central toe developed a large, convex, 'horsey' hoof. All these changes made the legs of *Mercyhippus* specialized for just one function — rapid running over hard ground." With increased speed, the horse could locate remote sources of food and also outrun predators such as saber-toothed tigers and wolves.

By the late Miocene epoch, fifteen million years ago, *Mercyhippus* was not just running but also throwing off new evolutionary lines.

Within a period of several million years, nineteen new horse species in three major groups appeared on the plains. A final succession of mercihippines produced a wave of larger horses, some of which had one toe. Scientists refer to these one-toed horses as "true equines"; with this one toe, or hoof, horses have left their iconic tracks across time, for all to follow.

As the curtain descended on the rich Miocene epoch with a drying and cooling trend, horse populations went into decline. But *Dinohippus,* a genus of one-toed horse that appeared twelve million years ago, endured on the plains of the West, grazing on prairie grasses and casting off two new lines before it died out. One line disappeared, and the other was *Equus.*

This genus appeared about four million years ago, during the Pliocene epoch, when grasslands continued to spread and stretches of desert and tundra began to appear. At 13.2 hands, *Equus* was five times bigger than the dawn horse and would soon increase in size. It had powerful, straight teeth and a brain that was larger than its forebears'. It had a long neck, long legs, and long muzzle; its mane was short and stood upright, its ears were medium-size, and it had stripes on its legs and back. It looked very much like a donkey. Like *Mercyhippus,* it quickly split off into a number of variations; within three million years there were twelve species in four groups. Some of them headed north across the land bridge and made their way to Africa, where they evolved into zebras, and others remained in the American West while at the same time finding their way to the mountains of China, the deserts of Asia, and the hills of Europe.

Among these migrating species was *Equus caballus,* which emerged about 1.7 million years ago. Often referred to by scientists as "the true horse," it is linked by mitochondrial DNA with the horses of Cortés, and it is a direct descendant of the mustangs that roam the West today. This true horse was a finely calibrated collaboration of the environment and animal, a specimen of locomotion that had been in the works through four geologic epochs. As a prey animal, it was fast, able to cover thirty miles in an hour and sometimes more. Its famous satellite eyes — bigger than a whale's or an elephant's, and just as haunting — gave it a wide range of lateral vision, with a nearly full-circle sweep of about 340 degrees. It also had a special light refractor — the *tapetum lucidum* — that enhanced its night vision. The ability to constantly scan for threats, even in the dark, helped the horse to survive. Any visual disturbance on the horizon would trigger flight — birds that were suddenly on the wing, or a waterfall. Another aspect of horse radar was its hearing. Like its eyes, its large ears were always scanning its surroundings, and often, it was through sound that a horse first picked up news of danger. The early rumbles of an earthquake, thunder in the distance, the rustle of leaves — all these sounds and many more would set it off, sometimes causing it to run for miles.

Yet even as the horse had reached its evolutionary peak, sheets of ice were sweeping across the continents and ushering in a new age. During this cataclysmic epoch — the Pleistocene — vast populations of mammals in North America were wiped out, including the dire wolf, the mammoth, and the saber-toothed cat. Among the vanished species was *Equus caballus* (hereafter referred to simply as *Equus*), which disappeared about twelve thousand years ago. But exactly why the true horse became extinct is a mystery. Some scientists believe that it was not a victim of climate, but of man, who was traveling south across the Bering land bridge and hunting the horse, who was going north. A controversial theory called Pleistocene overkill suggests that too much hunting — combined with a deadly new arrowhead called the Clovis point — drove many mammals, including the horse, to the brink of extinction and beyond.

Other scientists believe that something else happened. During the Ice Age, the horse represented as much as one-third of this continent's megafaunal population. It would have been impossible, they say, to destroy all of them with the hunting methods of the time. In fact, large horse-kill sites have not been discovered on this continent. This suggests to some analysts that pockets of Pleistocene horses survived, linking up thousands of years later with the horses of the conquest to form new herds. The theory is backed up by oral histories of certain Native American tribes. For some students of equine history — scientists and the self-taught alike — the possibility is so compelling that they have devoted their lives to proving it, traveling to far-flung fossil sites to gather remains, meeting in secret chat rooms, unearthing obscure frontier chronicles, and calling reporters at odd

hours with urgent news of post-Pleistocene, pre-Columbus wild
horses on the frontier. A continuous line of horses on this continent
would prove that they are indigenous rather than non-native, which
is a widely held opinion and a factor — as we shall see — that has contributed to the modern wars against them, playing out to this day
across the West, where they are sometimes gunned down for sport.

But by most accounts, *Equus* seems to have disappeared from its
homeland during the Ice Age. Its bones and hides and manes have
been preserved on the Yukon tundra, where it faltered or was killed
during migrations. It was also in decline in faraway lands. Paradoxically, there was only one thing that saved it from vanishing forever — a
partnership with man, who would become its greatest predator.

In the nineteenth century, the horse came to serve man even in death,
helping him understand the past. When its bones were first discovered on the Great Plains, the story they told was so graphic, so startling, so apparent, that they were used to prove the strange new theory of evolution. In his book *The Gilded Dinosaur,* journalist Mark
Jaffe recounts the story: At a train stop in Nebraska in 1868, on his
first trip to the West, famed paleontologist O. C. Marsh made a significant discovery. He had heard that the skeleton of a "pre-Adamite
man" had been found while members of an expedition were digging
a well. He didn't believe it; hoping to debunk the rumor, he asked the
conductor to stop at the Antelope railroad station so he could look
around. He found lots of bones in the dirt near the railhead. As he
was sifting through the gravel, the train whistled and started to leave.
Marsh ran to catch it, unable to complete his survey. As he hopped
aboard the caboose, he asked the station agent to pick up all the
bones, promising to pay him when the train returned.

A few days later, the agent handed off a hatful of bones, possibly as the train rattled by. As the locomotive headed east, Marsh
sorted through the ancient quarry as his fellow passengers excitedly
watched. The scientist spotted evidence of eleven extinct animals,
but one group of bones especially caught his attention — the remains
of a tiny horse. The horse "was then and there christened *Equus parvulus,*" Marsh later wrote. "During his life he was scarcely a yard in
height, and each of his slender legs was terminated by three toes."

Marsh's discovery of *Equus parvulus* was one more link in a chain that would lead from the earlier dawn horse to the modern four-legged horse, which was hauling its own ancestors out of the fossil-studded layers of rock in the giant library of the West.

But the astonishing find was not the first discovery of the prehistoric horse on this continent. In 1847, the Civil War surgeon Joseph R. Leidy, known as the country's first paleontologist, examined classified bones sent to him from expeditions in Florida and South Dakota. His paper "On the Fossil Horse" would influence scientists for decades to come, bolstering Darwin's scientific narrative on the chain of life, which was based on the idea that evolution was a series of continuous links.

Long before the white man unearthed the four-leggeds, Native Americans had come upon the ancient remains of horses. They chronicled their knowledge in their own way and sometimes spoke of such remains to the white men who were moving them onto reservations. Sometime around 1873, when U.S. Army scout James H. Cook visited the Red Cloud Agency on the White River in northwestern Nebraska, an Indian showed him a petrified tooth. As it happened, the Indian who explained its provenance was, like many Indians, named for a horse. "American Horse explained that the tooth had belonged to a 'Thunder Horse' that had lived 'away back,'" Cook wrote, "and that this creature would sometimes come down to earth in thunderstorms and chase and kill buffalo. His old people told stories of how on one occasion many, many years back, this big Thunder Horse had driven a herd of buffalo right into a camp of Lakota people during a bad thunderstorm, when these people were about to starve, and that they had killed many of these buffalo with their lances and arrows. The 'Great Spirit' had sent the Thunder Horse to help them get 'food' when it was needed most badly."

As we shall see, such accounts were generally cast aside, leading the white man to underestimate the Indian's connection with the horse. Lakota tales of the animal world were superseded by the discoveries and interpretations of a parade of scientists that had begun with Yale graduate Marsh and was now joined by his rival Harvard graduate E. D. Cope. This resulted in a strange fossil war that played out across the Great Plains—a kind of shadow dance behind the more visible and much deadlier war that was annihilating the Native American.

Under the protection of Buffalo Bill and army scouts, squads of paleontologists fanned out across the West, sometimes as battles unfolded in the nearby canyons or buttes, no doubt amplifying the Native American view that the white man was crazy. In fact, one of the first paleontologists into the Great Plains was Ferdinand Vandeveer Hayden, who collected fossils in the 1850s and 1860s, apparently so feverishly that the Indians dubbed him "He Who Picks Up Stones Running." Later, while rooting around in Utah, one of Marsh's students said, "We have literally had to crawl over the country on our hands and knees. To see these minute bones the eye must be brought within three or four inches of the white clay on which they lie." It's an image of the West about which we rarely hear — arrows and bullets flying in the distance while academics sift through time to figure out how we got here. The Yale-Harvard bone battles were so intense that Cope went into Montana just after the Battle of the Little Bighorn, paying reluctant men hefty fees to hunt for skeletons even as those remains were being covered by fresh kills of horse and man alike.

Yet from the chaos of war and the strange rummaging around in the dirt emerged important information. The horse, Marsh learned, had been here for sixty million years. Others would disagree with him, but he was the first to suggest that its genealogy had been worked out on this continent. Over time, Marsh's presence in the wilderness was not seen as especially strange, and the Pawnee, for instance, began to bring him horse bones, even referring to him as the "Bone Medicine Man." By the end of the nineteenth century, the West had yielded up so many fossils that the secrets of evolution were being found almost too fast for words — and many of the secrets were coming via the horse.

Marsh himself became obsessed with the animal, and he ultimately documented thirty different species, from a version of the fox-sized *Hyracotherium* (which was the same as eohippus) to a spinoff of the donkey-sized *Mercyhippus* to the modern *Equus complicatus*. Meanwhile, not to be outdone, Cope had been discovering and hauling bigger and more glamorous prey out of the vast and sere field station — dinosaurs. Some of these discoveries began to go on display

back east, in circuses and expos. For the American centennial celebration in Philadelphia, Cope unveiled a restoration of a dinosaur
called *Hadrosaurus,* to the endless delight of huge crowds. But it was
the horse in its many incarnations that caused the most discussion, as
if daring academics, and through them the world, to understand its
meaning and its gift.

On September 18, 1876, a little over two months after the Battle of
the Little Bighorn, a Marsh protégé named Thomas Huxley began a
series of three talks on evolution at New York's fashionable Chick-
ering Hall on Fifth Avenue. Across the West, mounted posses were
pursuing Crazy Horse, Sitting Bull, and thousands of Native Americans and their large pony herds as newspapers clamored for revenge against the killers of George Armstrong Custer. In New York,
the house was packed every night, and Huxley regaled the chic and
powerful with tales of paleo drama. But it was his final talk on September 22, Mark Jaffe recounted, that brought round after round of
applause. The lecture was all about the horse, an object of great fascination at the time — one of them, a cavalry horse named Comanche, had survived the Little Bighorn and become a national celebrity. "The horse," Thomas Huxley told the crowd, "is in many ways
a most remarkable animal inasmuch as it presents us with an example of one of the most perfect pieces of machinery in the animal kingdom. And as a necessary consequence of any sort of perfection ...
you find that he is a beautiful creature."

As he spoke, he unveiled sketches made by Marsh that portrayed
the evolution of the horse, pointing out how the hooves and legs were
built for speed, and its mouth and teeth were an outstanding "appa-
ratus for providing the mechanism with the fuel which it requires."
He compared the evolution of the horse with the evolution of man,
suggesting that the straight-line mechanics of development were so
similar that no one could argue with the new theory about how mammals evolved. The next morning, it was official: Huxley's talk was the
lead story in the *New York Times,* with a lengthy headline proclaim-
ing similarities in the development of man and horse.

Seven weeks after the talk on Fifth Avenue, Marsh discovered
the dawn horse, the very first link in the long, stunning line. The old
bones were covered with so much Eocene mud, Marsh wrote to Hux-

ley, that he almost didn't know him from *Orohippus*. "I promise you his grandfather," he said, "in time for your next Horse Lecture if you will give me proper notice."

As of this date, no one has found the grandfather of eohippus. And the prevailing views of the nineteenth century — that horses and men evolved in a straight line with adjustments and adaptations that were constantly improving — have been revised. Evolution is thought to be more of a branching bush, with many false starts and a few that work. Yet of all the animal kingdom's fossil discoveries, it is those of the horse that are still among the most prolific and diverse, and it is the American West that remains their tomb and their cradle. Despite the scientific predations of Yale and Harvard, prehistoric horse bones are still strewn across the dry lands of the West, buried in crevasses, mired in ooze, encased in layers of stone. To see them, it is not necessary to mount your own expeditions; there are horse fossil sites in many regions: the Hagerman in Idaho, the La Brea tar pits in Los Angeles, the Ashfall beds in Nebraska — a mammal version of the last days of Pompeii with equine families apparently buried alive.

There's also a place known in paleontology circles as "the Barnyard." The Barnyard has tracks, not bones — tracks of camels and elephants and birds, but mostly horse tracks, thousands of them, coming from the past and going toward the future, preserved forever in a mountain range that wasn't there when they were, magic ciphers embedded in a permanent and ever-open ancient scroll.

These horse tracks are on a wall in a secret location inside Death Valley National Park. They are accessible only by way of ranger-led hikes. I visited them two years ago, after reading about them in an obscure park service newsletter and then making a reservation months in advance. To get there, I took an interstate to a highway to a desert two-lane deep inside the park, where I joined a small group of pilgrims. We followed the ranger up an alluvial fan, through giant washes where tender once-a-century flowers were blooming after the recent rains. After two or three miles, the desert street began to shrink and we were on a narrow path that wound through slot canyons lined with sandstone, and, except for the crunching of hiking boots, all was silent.

As time passed, the path got thinner still, winding along a ribbon

of sand that was lined by sheer granite walls. We traversed upward
across rough desert gravel at an incline of about 15 degrees. As the
sun neared the high-noon mark, we stopped for a rest, then trekked
on as a stir of air came down off the higher elevations. The path emp-
tied into a sprawling white *bajada* crisscrossed by fault lines and
ringed by mineral-veined mountains. After a while, we reached the
far side where the path resumed. We walked another hundred yards
or so until we reached the seven-mile mark, the outside bend of a
steep and craggy gypsum slope.

"Okay, everybody," the ranger said, pointing to a wash. "This is it.
The Barnyard. Put down your backpacks and go in single file. Take
your time." I was talking with a companion, and my voice fell to a
whisper, lest I somehow derange the invisible horses and make the
tracks vanish. I gingerly clambered over giant boulders and chunks
of gravel as the sun—rising higher—illumined the ancient hoof
prints. They were scattered across the wall of rock, equine signals
that appeared to be heading in every direction, thisaway, thataway,
away away home. Some of the prints faced upward to the sky, some
down, some east, others west and northwest. It was a Miocene movie,
an antediluvian Western, with hundreds of hoof prints left in the dust
but no vestiges of the animals they came from—just tracks, running
across a wall.

Like all deserts, Death Valley was once composed of many lakes.
In the lakes were vast islands of grass where mammals gathered to
feed during seasonal monsoons—horses on the lush flora, saber-
toothed tigers on the flesh of horses. As they fed, the ranger explained, they made tracks in the mud, and when the waters receded
and they moved on, the tracks were preserved. This process repeated
itself over thousands of years, with animals leaving tracks in different
layers of mud. As the terrain evolved and sheets of rock were thrust
upward through the earth's crust, the tracks emerged—on slabs, cre-
ating an equine Rosetta stone. I placed my hand inside a hoof print,
the timeless cipher that had become a talisman for warriors and
barbarians of nations old and new. It was as big as my outstretched
palm, and many others appeared to be the same size.

The Shoshone Indians of this region may have known about this
site for a long time, our guide explained, but it was officially discov-

ered in 1932 by Donald R. Currey, the first ranger of what was then called Death Valley National Monument. So many anthropologists and paleo devotees began to visit the site that officials scheduled visits for certain days at certain times of the year, like the one I was on. Now, with the winter light fading, it was time to go.

We headed out of the Barnyard, stopping for a late lunch at — appropriately — Carnivore Ridge, another sprawling animal-track site. Then we packed up our gear and retraced our steps, our tracks, down the rocky paths and through the slot canyons and across the alluvial fan that led to our cars. As I later found out, because of budget constraints we were the last group outside of academia and the strange and flourishing world of anthro crooks to take the hike — an obscure event on a Park Service calendar that just happened to link today to always, an expedition to an accidental stone mural upon which horse tracks, the very beginnings of the American story, are forever preserved.

As Thomas Huxley lectured over a hundred years ago, the evolution of horses and humans had much in common. But the most striking thing is not how horse and man evolved — it's that they were destined to be a pair. How else to explain the diastema, the gap between the horse's front incisors and rear grinding teeth? As nature writer Stephen Budiansky has observed, it's the perfect place for a bit. Moreover, the horse lacks horns or antlers, which made it ideal for driving other animals, hauling wagons, and warfare. Another trait that made the horse desirable was its own form of communication, a rich body language consisting of various signals for aggression and submission. A man who could understand that language could train the horse and even mirror its own patterns of "talking" in order to bond — what horse whisperers do today. Finally, the horse positioned itself near human settlements, where it was much safer from predators and also fed on the crops.

And thus, millennia ago, *Equus* and man became acquainted. Certainly man, the predator who had been hunting him for eons, already knew some things about the horse. He had learned long ago that the horse was fast. He may have wanted to run with the four-leggeds, to possess their speed. Man also knew that the horse traveled in large herds. Perhaps he noticed the similarity between these populations and his own — large groups of living things that were nomads, following food. And perhaps he understood that the horse had families and that within these arrangements, there was an order — again, not unlike his own. In the case of the horse, there was a lead mare, and the herd followed her while the stallion stayed behind, watching for danger and keeping other stallions away. In the stallion, perhaps man found a kindred spirit.

From the archaeological record, we can say for certain that man studied the horse and considered him a powerful creature: in 6000 BC, in a village called Dereivka on the steppes of the Ukraine, he sacrificed the animal and used the remains to guard sacred sites, fashioning replicas of the horse by mounting his skulls and forelegs on poles and covering them with hides. The Copper Age people who engaged in such rituals were known as the Sredni Stog, and they were the first to domesticate the horse. Among the remains at these sites, anthropologists have found horse teeth that bear the mark of wear and tear from the bit. These teeth predate the invention of the wheel by at least five hundred years, a stunning discovery that reverses decades of thinking about why the horse was first domesticated. Scientists now believe that the horse may have been ridden before he was used to pull carts or chariots — an act that required a stunning leap of imagination.

How did it happen? In 1944, Danish author Johannes V. Jensen won the Nobel Prize in Literature for his series of novels about evolution. In one of them, *The Glacier,* he told a story that is famous in equestrian circles for its captivating and quite plausible rendition of how man and horse may have become a pair. In a large corral outside a settlement, a family kept a band of horses for meat. One day, while taking a horse back to the village, their son tried to climb aboard. The horse threw him off, and the boy tried again; in a series of tries, the boy was repeatedly ejected as the horse pitched sideways and bucked. Finally, the boy gave up. But soon, he discovered how to tap "the secret sympathy" between horse and man, an "obscure memory" that dated back to a time when the ancestors of both lived side by side in the wild.

He befriended a stallion born in captivity, always feeding him by hand and talking in sweet tones when he groomed him. Whenever the boy approached the horse, he made sure to do so quietly. The stallion's "innate shyness lay so deep in its blood that it was ready to start off all the time as though possessed by a thousand promptings of light," Jensen wrote. "Its ear, twitching nervously, lay back flat while its teeth showed in an ugly grin . . . It wanted to be patted and yet did not want it, swung its flank forward and drew back ticklishly, as though it was fire it felt and not a human hand; its mood shifted like a breeze on the water; only after a long, long time of tireless overtures would it accept the relationship, but really tame it never was."

Soon, the boy could lean against its side and drape his arms across its back, getting the horse used to his weight. Then one day, the moment arrived — the boy hoisted himself onto the back of the horse. The stallion did not throw him off, and in fact accepted him; the horse began to walk and then gallop around the corral and, finally, across the steppe. "The first horseman," Jensen wrote, "with a scrap of wolf's skin tied about his middle and his fiery hair flying about his ears . . . moulded in one with the wild horse, still half-striped like a zebra, its shoulders marked with lightning, and with the thunderbolt under each of its heart-shaped hoofs!"

It's also possible that the moment of domestication may have been much more brutal, with hunters running horses into a trap and then breaking them down over a period of time until they could be mounted.

However it happened, within a short period of time, the world underwent a dramatic change as humans began to subjugate the horses that had congregated near their villages. With the invention of the wheel in 4000 B.C., there came carts and wagons and plows. By 3000 B.C., horses joined oxen at the harness in the Near East. Five hundred years later, they were pulling war wagons in southern Mesopotamia. By 1800 B.C., teams of horses were deployed in the hauling of Hittite chariots on the battlefield, and around 1300 B.C., the Hittite king's horse master Kikkuli wrote the first training manual for equines. Incised in cuneiform on clay tablets, the ancient trainer's text outlined a seven-month training program that went through three stages and included designated workouts and rest days, as well as a special diet. "Pace two leagues," went the instruction for day five.

"Run twenty furlongs out and thirty home. Put rugs on. After sweating, give one pail of salted water and one of malt water. Take to river and wash down. Swim horses. Take to stable . . ."

In 700 B.C., from the steppes of central Asia came the first mounted marauders. These were the Scythians. Although people had already been on horseback for thousands of years, to hunt and travel and fight, the Scythian was a different breed. "He was not a mere rider and keeper of horses," writes Frank Trippett in *The First Horsemen,* "nor did he simply exploit the horse: he merged with his mount in a remarkably thorough way. He reshaped his entire mode of life around the capabilities of the horse. He stripped himself of all identification with a permanent home and became a full-fledged nomad who, with his herds, followed the seasonal grasses with scant regard for distance. His dwelling had become a collapsible tent, his hearth could be anywhere." With the horse, he had formed a new creature — what Lakota Indians later called the six-legged warrior.

The Scythians controlled the region north of the Black Sea, while other horse tribes dominated the Near East, Siberia, Mongolia, and China. The Greek historian Herodotus traveled through Scythian lands and marveled at their explosive and flamboyant nature. They loved to hunt, sing, and dance, and at their celebrations, they inhaled vapors of hemp. They were festooned with pendants and rings, and their horses were bridled with silver and gold. At war they were ferocious, beheading their enemies, drinking their blood from skulls, and hanging their scalps from their bridles. In death their kings were honored with an elaborate procession; the horses were then sacrificed to join them in their graves. They clearly had animals to spare — in one grave, archaeologists found four hundred horses.

The Scythians were not the only prehistoric people to invoke horse magic. The ancient Greeks spoke of the centaurs, the mythological tribe of creatures that were half man and half horse. And the Greeks gave us Pegasus, the winged horse who flew away to join the gods in the heavens, becoming a constellation. About 3,500 years ago, a large, stylized white horse was carved into a British hillside. No one knows who dug the trenches and filled them with chalk blocks in order to make the animal, but many believe that it was an homage to Epona ("Divine Mare"), the horse goddess who was worshipped across the Roman empire, said to protect horses and riders and stables.

In his far-flung travels, there were few places *Equus* did not reach. He even got as far as Spain, as if preparing for his homeward journey. There, as everywhere, he was viewed with reverence and awe — Ice Age hunters captured him in ocher and zinc, painting his image on the cave walls of Altamira. In one of the images, his neck is arched and he seems to be bucking. Some say he is even wearing a bridle — suggesting that, perhaps even twelve thousand years ago, man dreamed of riding the horse.

Ice Age art on cave walls in Altamira, Spain.

3

Hoofbeats on the Prairie

ONCE UPON A TIME, according to an old Mandan legend, the camp crier told all the people in the village to gather at its edge. "Our little friend is leaving us," he said. And the little friend said, "Don't cry. I'll be back someday. And when I return, I'll be much changed and you may not recognize me. But those who keep the stories will know who I am. Remember, I am the one who eats the grass. When I come back, I will be tall as man and swift as the wind. I will be strong so I can carry much on my back—maybe two or three men or maybe heavy packs. I'll be gone for a while. Don't forget me."

Shortly after their return to the New World, horses swept through the deserts and plains like a fast-moving secret. They partnered up quickly with Native Americans, players taking to the script with astonishing ease. From the Apache and Comanche to the Zuni to the Hopi to the Navajo to the Ute; from the Shoshone to the Flathead, Crow, and Nez Perce; from the Arapaho to the Ponca, the Cheyenne, the Sioux, the Mandan, the Ojibwa and beyond, horses allied with tribe after tribe—perhaps not in that exact order, but the deed was done, and by the early 1700s, it was as if their kind had never disappeared from their native turf.

Certainly, it is hard to picture the Native American on foot, or even remember that this was once his situation, and remained so for many tribes whose home was the eastern woodlands, where it was difficult to ride. Westerns and dime novels rarely featured an Indian who was walking, and as we imagine him today, he is generally on a horse and he and his animal are decorated for war. Yet in the beginning, the horse was far from a partner-in-arms. The first known contact between horses and the Indians of North America happened soon after the arrival of Francisco Vásquez de Coronado in 1539. Leading a caravan of 300 men and 558 horses from Mexico into what was later known as the American Southwest, Coronado trekked for three years, across thousands of miles, through Arizona, New Mexico, Texas, Oklahoma, and finally Kansas, on what proved to be a fruitless quest for gold. Along the way, many Indians met the animals that would transform their world. Like the Aztecs, some natives were afraid at first. Others, like the Hopi in Arizona, laid down ceremonial rugs in their path. The Acoma Indians in New Mexico desired their power. When they saw the caravan passing, they descended from their sky city on a giant butte, took the horses' sweat, and anointed themselves. Soon, tribes began to simply take the horses.

By the time Coronado died in 1554 (having suffered for years after being kicked in the head by a horse), the Apache were stealing mustangs from ranches in Santa Fe and undergoing a radical change, from poverty to wealth. For the next two hundred years, many tribes across the land followed a similar path, taking horses from other tribes, the cavalry, and from missions, as well as capturing them from herds that were beginning to flourish in the wilderness. In the swift four-legged, the Indians found a kindred spirit who — like other animals — was a friend and teacher with great powers. "Horses are gods," the elders told a Hidatsa boy who guarded the herds. "Treat them well. They have minds and understand."

Like the ancient Greeks, Hebrews, and Muslims before them, Indians sang praise to the horse, but their praise was even more eloquent, with more tones and layers; in the horse they saw not only the stars, the rivers, the elements, but also the land — the very wild that was their home. His mane and tail moved like the grasses in the wind, sang the Chickasaw. His foot was like striped agate, sang the Navajo, his legs like lightning, tail like a trailing black cloud; his mane was of short rainbows, his eyes were of stars, and his teeth of white shell. No other animal took the Indian to such stunning flights of fancy, no other took him to the glory of his greatest days. As the noted cowboy scribe J. Frank Dobie wrote in his classic work *The Mustangs*:

> The horse dilated the imagination of the Indian as it has dilated the imaginations of millions viewing him horsed. It elevated him in pride and put motion into his spirits commensurate with that of his mount galloping over grass through which he had once crawled up to his game. It put him on a par with the Tartars, the Parthians, the gauchos, the cowboys on the open range and all the other free riders of remembrance whose very names stir the gasolined and the seated towards a life of movement, freedom and spaces.

While the first conquistadors had facilitated this transformation, it was the man known as the last conquistador, Don Juan de Oñate, who brought Indians the herd of horses that drastically changed life on the plains. On January 26, 1598, his expedition crossed the Rio Grande on its way from Mexico to Santa Fe. The caravan was enormous, with 600 men, dozens of families, 83 ox carts, 26 wagons and carriages, and over 7,000 animals, including horses, mules, and cows. "The horses had suffered most," a lieutenant said of the dry-lands trek. "They were almost frantic with thirst and their eyes nearly bulged from their sockets." Stopping at the river, a few horses drank until they nearly burst and then they collapsed and died. The caravan resumed its journey; along the way, hundreds of horses and mules fled, adding to the growing populations in the American desert.

By late summer of that year, the expedition arrived in New Mexico, and Oñate set himself up as the first governor-general of the state, with the capital just north of Santa Fe. He quickly became notorious for his cruel treatment of Indians (among other things, when the Acoma refused to submit to slavery, he ordered his men to cut off the left foot of the twenty-four captive warriors). After failing to find gold, he was sent back to Spain and replaced by a series of governors. In later years, he became celebrated for opening up El Camino Real, the first road through the southwest, but his greatest legacy was the horse; many had survived his original trek and flourished in Santa Fe, replenished by new arrivals. By 1680, three thousand were grazing the grounds of the new capital, emblazoned with Spanish brands and trained for warfare.

That year, the Pueblo Indians—led by their charismatic chief Pope—mounted this continent's first major insurrection against the Spanish, attacking the mission of Santa Fe after decades of subjugation, killing the soldiers and priests. Word of the siege spread quickly, but it was too late; the Indians had made off with all of the horses—many of which passed into the hands of other tribes and became the foundation stock for future generations. In 1687, their ranks were expanded when the underground Hebrew Alonzo de León, from the province of Nuevo León, began making trips into Texas. He brought hundreds of horses and mules bred on his ranch and helped the Church establish missions along the Neches River. These missions were eventually plundered, scattering the horses far and wide.

Depending on the weather, available grasses and water, and the number of natural predators such as mountain lions and bears, wild horses proliferated at varying rates. While there is ongoing debate about their rate of reproduction, mustangs foal at anywhere from 10 to 20 percent, according to modern range studies. We do not know what the rates were in the eighteenth century, but by the early 1700s, maps of Texas marked the territory between the Rio Grande and Nueces River not as a place but as "Vast Herds of Wild Horses" or "simply Wild Horses." By 1741, Indians along the upper Missouri had so many horses, donkeys, and mules that a French Canadian trader named them *gens des chevaux* (people of the horse). In 1770, the fur trader Peter Pond was trekking up the Mississippi and reported that the Sioux "have a Grate Number of Horses and Dogs which carres there Bageag when they Move from Plase to Plase ... Thay Run down the Buffelow with thare Horses and Kill as Much Meat as thay Please. In Order to have thare Horses Long Winded they slit thair Noses up to the grissel of thare head which Make them Breath Verey freely. I have seen them Run with those of Natrall Nostrals and Cum in Apearantley Not the Least Out of Breath."

On December 20, 1777, the Franciscan missionary Fray Morfi was traveling north of the Rio Grande and noted in his diary that bands of wild horses "are so abundant that their trails make the country, utterly uninhabited by people, look as if it were the most populated in the world." A week later, just north of the Nueces, he and his party saw about three thousand mustangs. In 1805, while traveling through the Rockies, Lewis and Clark traded trinkets and an American flag to the Shoshone Indians in exchange for some horses from the Indians' herd of seven hundred, thus keeping their expedition from coming to a halt. While heading west toward New Mexico territory in 1806, Zebulon Pike and his men were surrounded by three hundred Pawnee warriors riding naked. "They were yelling in a most diabolical manner," Pike said, then they rushed the explorers and surrounded them. As it turned out, the Indians were friendly. Pike soon learned that they owned "vast quantities of excellent horses, which they are daily increasing by attention to their breeding mares, which they never ride; and in addition they frequently purchase from the Spaniards."

By the 1840s, parts of Texas were actually overrun with horses; while chasing Indians into the Wild Horse Desert, Texas ranger John C. Duval reported that he saw "a drove of mustangs so large that it took us fully an hour to pass it, although they were traveling at a rapid rate in a direction nearly opposite to ours. As far as the eye could extend on a dead level prairie, nothing was visible except a dense mass of horses, and the trampling of their hoofs sounded like the roar of the surf on a rocky coast." The sight of the flowing manes and tails moving in waves across the land enchanted many travelers and gave rise to fables about mythical steeds that defied capture. White men and red men alike had stories about the Big Black Stallion and the Pacing Mustang, and these horses were desired by all. Some were retrieved from the land of myth and ended up in the circus, where they refused food until they died. Others would succumb to no one.

In 1835, Washington Irving's book *A Tour on the Prairies* was published. One of the first chronicles of Native American life, it included an account of a wild horse capture. One night, as Irving was lying by the fire and listening to stories about notorious mustangs, his expedition's half-breed scout came into camp with a wild horse. "In an instant every fire was deserted," Irving wrote, "the whole camp crowded to see the Indian and his prize. It was a colt about two years old, well grown, finely limbed, with bright prominent eyes, and a spirited yet gentle demeanor. He gazed about him with an air of mingled stupefaction and surprise, at the men, the horses, and the camp-fires; while the Indian stood before him with folded arms, having hold of the other end of the cord which noosed his captive, and gazing on him with a most imperturbable aspect."

The Indian went on to recount the story of the animal's capture. While returning to camp on his horse, he had spotted a band of six mustangs. He chased them across a stream and tried to lasso one of them. But the horse shook off the lariat and ran up a hill with his band. The Indian was close behind and closing fast but suddenly the horses jumped off a cliff. It was too late to stop his horse, so they jumped too, landing safely on a sandy floor about thirty feet below, along with the band of mustangs. He threw his lasso again, now roping the colt. Leading the colt to open country, he played the young horse until he was checked and subdued, and led him back to the river. Both horses became mired in the muck and swirling waters, and the captive mustang struggled to escape. But after a while, the scout was able to cross the stream, bringing the colt with him. "For the remainder of the evening," Irving wrote, "the camp remained in a high state of excitement; nothing was talked of but the capture of wild horses; every youngster of the troop promised himself to return from the campaign in triumph, bestriding one of these wild coursers of the prairies."

Running mustangs down in this manner was a commonly used method of capture among many tribes, and for some of them, the pictograph representing wild horses soon became a lasso. Certain tribes became more adept at capturing horses in the wild than others, but it was really through raids that Native Americans made a statement of bravado and skill. Generations later, writer Sherman Alexie recalled his tribe's heritage in a heartbreaking poem: "I would steal horses for you," he said, "if there were any left." On the frontier, some tribes were so good at horse theft that it defined them — in tribute to Pawnee stealth, other Native Americans called them the Wolf Indians. For other tribes, it was as if horses were issuing a call. The Comanche could not even wait for horses to appear in their orbit; as Dobie reported, they traveled far south of their range between the Platte and the Yellowstone, swooping down the trails "from the Rocky Mountains in Colorado to Natchitoches in Louisiana and from the Platte to Durango." In their own poetry, the Comanche were as numerous as the stars, refining their horsemanship in countless raids. Later,

American soldiers came to regard them as the finest light cavalry in the world, and the artist George Catlin watched in astonishment as a young Comanche boy

> [would] drop his body upon the side of his horse at the instant he is passing, effectually screened from his enemies' weapons as he lays in horizontal position behind the body of his horse, with his heel hanging over the horse's back; by which he has the power of throwing himself up again, and changing to the other side of the horse if necessary. In this wonderful condition, he will hang whilst his horse is at fullest speed, carrying with him his bow and his shield, and also his long lance of fourteen feet in length, all or either of which he will wield upon his enemy as he passes; rising and throwing his arrows over the horse's back, or with equal ease and equal success under the horse's neck.

Native American pictographs at Canyon de Chelly, Arizona.

But among the many tribes that acquired the mustang, it was the Plains Indians who became the centaurs of the American frontier. They called the horse *sunka wakan* — sacred or mysterious dog. "Dog" because it became the new pack animal, replacing the smaller coyote-wolf crossbreed that had served the Indian for thousands of years, and "sacred" because it was much more than a carrier of goods: it was a hunter, a warrior, wealth, and prestige; it was medicine, it was magic, and above all, it was allied with the Thunder Beings who lived in the west, where rain begins.

This horse of many talents was "about fourteen hands high," wrote Colonel Richard Dodge in his frontier memoir, "with a rather light build, good legs, a strong back, full barrel, sharp nervous ears, bright intelligent eyes; it was never stabled, curried, shod, doctored or fed." He was not always treated kindly, in spite of his revered role; in the annals of the Old West, there are tales of Indian ponies with sore and bleeding backs upon which magpies feasted, of horses being run day after day in pursuit of buffalo, without food or water. But such, alas, is the age-old lot of the horse, and it must be said that during his time on the Great Plains, he was not confined; the horse roamed free with whatever tribe he was allied, along with his family inside his herd, and in general those who were cruel to *sunka wakan* had to seek forgiveness in special ceremonies, and if at some point they themselves met with a cruel fate, it was considered retribution for their unkindness.

The horse culture of the Plains Indians lasted from about 1630 to the end of the nineteenth century, a short period of astonishing importance, reverberating across time and forever. For our purposes, "Plains Indians" refers to the Cheyenne, Crow, Arapaho, Gros Ventre, Mandan, Assiniboin, Blackfoot, Arikara, and Lakota tribes, with the last including the Lakota, Dakota, and Teton Sioux. These Indians once ranged across the Great Plains, the vast midsection of the country where the western short grasses thrived in great abundance, growing as tall as a horse's belly. The plains run west of the one hundredth meridian (where rainfall drops to fewer than twenty inches per year) to the Rocky Mountains, and north from deep Texas to the Canadian provinces of Saskatchewan, Manitoba, and Alberta, covering a length of 2,500 miles and a width of 600 miles at their broadest point.

Some of the Plains Indian tribes had lived in this sprawling region longer than the others, but by the time Lewis and Clark came through in 1804, they all called it home. The Lakota — the tribe most associated with the region and its iconic Badlands terrain — came into the heart of the plains in the 1700s, when the displacement of tribes to the east forced them out of their villages on the peripheries. As the Lakota swept onto the prairies, horses were moving their way, and thus did the famous partnership begin. Those Indians lacking horses quickly understood that they were at a distinct disadvantage. In the early 1800s, a Chippewa chief spoke to a white explorer of the threat posed by the Sioux: "While they keep to the Plains with their Horses," he said, "we are not a match for them; for we being foot men, they could get to windward of us, and set fire to the grass; when we marched for the Woods, they would be there before us, dismount and under cover fire on us. Until we have Horses like them, we must keep to the Woods, and leave the Plains to them."

Across the frontier, *sunka wakan* changed every aspect of Indian life. Whereas the Indian lodge was once small, about ten feet across, it now doubled in size, because the horse was bigger and stronger than the dog. Moreover, instead of traveling just ten miles per day on foot, an entire camp could cover twice the distance in the same time with the aid of the horse. Additionally, the horse enabled members of the tribe to trade up for more wives, guns, and other goods, launching a new class system. As one story goes, a Lakota man traded forty horses for a prized medicine pipe, and it's very likely that the same horses — or some of them — continued across the plains as currency.

And then there was the buffalo hunt. In an earlier era, Indians hunted the animals on foot and ran them off cliffs — a style that took a long time, was dangerous, and resulted in few kills. On horseback, Indians ranged across a bigger area and could kill more buffalo in a shorter period of time, riding into a herd and shooting them with guns or bows and arrows, able to flee quickly when necessary. Although such pursuits were not as perilous as hunting on foot, both horse and rider were often injured. Among some tribes, doctors were frequently among the hunting party and would treat wounded ponies and people immediately, with the same remedies, rubbing mud on broken bones and perhaps using a paste of certain dried plants and flowers for gashes and cuts.

An Old-Time Buffalo Hunt by Charles Russell.

A horse that was well suited to the hunt—a buffalo runner—was priceless. "A horse had to be fast to overtake stampeding buffaloes," Dobie observed. "He had to be alert and quick in turning. With reins dropped on his neck, he came up on the right side to within fifteen or twenty feet of the buffalo selected by his rider. If the rider missed a shot and had to reload, an operation requiring both hands, the trained horse kept on after the same buffalo."

But above all, the scruffy mustang of the Great Plains was the great Indian warhorse. In this role, he transformed the Plains Indian from a mere two-legged who skirmished with an ax and a shield to a mounted warrior who waged lethal hit-and-run missions while brandishing the latest weapons. Among the Lakota, every man between twenty-five and forty had at least two warhorses and two buffalo runners, although sometimes these horses were the same. "My horse fights with me and fasts with me," said Crow chief Plenty-Coups, "because if he is to carry me in battle he must know my heart and I must know his or we shall never become brothers." This partner-in-arms was an astonishing creature. He could receive his rider on the run, as well as keep running while the rider hunkered down on one side, continuing to shoot from under the horse's neck. He knew to leap over the body of a fallen enemy and follow his rider's call if he had to dismount quickly and run for cover. The famous red and white Sioux pony Never-Whipped could carry a wounded man to safety by letting him hold on to his tail.

To show off his skills and prepare him for battle, Indians sometimes raced the warhorse against cavalry steeds, pitting the small horse that scrounged for cottonwood bark in the winter against the bigger, corn-fed animals. The races generally happened in the spring and summer, after it warmed and the grasses came up and the Indian ponies had filled out and were ready for anything. One story tells of the famous four-hundred-yard race waged by the army against the Comanche at Fort Chadbourne on the Texas frontier. The soldiers were disappointed when a Comanche chief appeared on what one observer described as a "miserable sheep of a pony." They decided to give the chief a break, and instead of running their prized thoroughbred mare, they brought out their third-best horse. Everyone laid down bets: the Americans offered flour, sugar, and coffee, and the Comanche buffalo robes and other assorted items.

With the 170-pound chief aboard and wielding a heavy club, the "sheep" easily won the race. The soldiers were embarrassed and asked for another, now bringing out their second-best horse. The "sheep" won again. Finally, the Americans brought out their best horse, and bets were doubled. The Comanche chucked his club and gave out a yell. The "sheep" took the lead and held it. About fifty yards from the finish line, with horses at full gallop, the Indian turned his horse around and finished riding the race backward, taunting his cavalry rival as his pony handily won for the third time.

Soldiers often puzzled over what gave the Indian pony its edge. It would be inaccurate to point to any one thing, but across the plains, ritual was an integral part of the horse's preparation. Warhorses and buffalo runners were raised on holy medicine — blessings and prayers and incantations that made use of many natural things. Before battle, a special medicine bag was placed around the horse's neck, his feet were rubbed with a magic herb to enhance his swiftness, and streaks of lightning were painted on his legs and flanks, just as they were on his rider. As stunned as travelers were by the vast and infinite streams of wild horses flowing across the plain, they were more astonished by the sight of the painted Indian and pony. On a June day in 1874, buffalo hunters in the Texas Panhandle were approached by a thousand Cheyenne, Comanche, and Kiowa warriors, "mounted upon their finest horses," one of the hunters wrote, "armed with guns and lances, and carrying heavy shields of thick buffalo hides, coming like the wind, splashed the rich colors of red, vermilion and ochre, on the bodies of the men, on the bodies of the running horses. Scalps dangled from bridles, gorgeous war-bonnets fluttered their plumes, bright feathers dangled from the tails and manes of the horses, and the bronzed, half-naked bodies of the riders glittered with ornaments of silver and brass. Behind the wild-riding horsemen the plain shone dazzlingly clear to the horizon of the rising sun. They seemed to emerge from the glow."

Together, a painted Plains Indian horse and its rider were an action-adventure story, living cinema meant to mesmerize and strike fear. A rectangle on the horse's flank said that the owner had led a war party. A palm print meant that an enemy had been killed in hand-to-hand battle. A circle said that the warrior had fought the enemy from behind a breastwork, rocks, or logs. Short horizontal lines on top of one another and horizontal stripes on the horse's front legs were coup marks. A rounded or squared hoof print represented a successful horse raid. Blotchy or abstract marks meant that the horse was mourning the death of its owner. Lightning bolts invoked speed and power. Long stripes and large areas of paint specks on the horse's chest and flanks indicated to which society the rider belonged. Red or white circles around the horse's eyes enhanced the animal's vision. Sometimes golden eagle tail feathers were tied to the mane and tail. The more such markings, the deeper the narrative; emblazoned with accomplishments and medicine symbols, a mounted war party galloping through the prairie grass carried the song of the West.

When it was all over for the Indian, and *sunka wakan* was taken away, there was a new cast of human characters on the Great Plains: A Fine Horse, Lost Horse, Black Horse, Blue Horse, Red Horse, Sorrell Horse, Yellow Horse, Spotted Horse, Dorothy White Horse, Fast Horse, Many Horses, American Horse, Young Man Afraid of His

Horse, Little Horse, Long Horse, Medicine Horse, Own the White Horse, Plenty Horse, Kill Spotted Horse, Handsome Horse, Big Spotted Horse, and the most fabled of them all, Crazy Horse, who was waging raids on other tribes by the time he was twelve, and giving the freshly caught ponies to other men as the clouds of war were gathering.

Oglala war party, photographed by Edward S. Curtis in 1907 for his famous series in which Native Americans posed to recreate history.

In all of the fables about how the horse made its way to the Great Plains, little attention is devoted to what happened at the missions of California — scene of the greatest horse raids of them all. The white man has tended to ignore the Indians of the Great Basin, who mounted these raids. Their cultures were not dazzling to the gringo eye — their jewelry was not elaborate enough to charm anthropologists and neither were their rituals, at least on the face of it, and as a result a large portion of American history has been neglected, passed on only in odd and minor works and oral histories through the descendants of those who first lived in the high deserts of the West. I speak in particular of the man who led perhaps the biggest horse theft in the history of this country — a Ute highwayman named Wakara who ranged westward across the Mojave Desert and staged a lightning strike at the missions of Los Angeles in the year 1840.

He lived and flourished before the Indian wars of the frontier and after the quashing of Native Americans in the North and Southeast — a strange, in-between time when classic archetypes of the defiant, mounted warrior had not yet become immortalized in literature. One account of a white man's experience with the southern Ute, recorded by a fur trader, put it like this:

> I was much surprised at the appearance of these people. I expected to find them a poor lifeless set of beings destitute of the means or disposition to defend themselves, alarmed at the sight of a white man but to the contrary they met me with great familiarity and ease of manner ... [They] have a great number of good horses & about one half [were] well armed ... and ornamented with perl and sea shells ...

The record tells us that Wakara was handsome ("a fine-looking Indian," said an early Death Valley explorer), a dandy perhaps, in white man's terms. He always wore a tall beaver hat, stood more than six feet in his moccasins, was very clever, vain, quick-tempered, and kind. He liked to drink. He had a working knowledge of English, Spanish, and Indian languages other than his own, knew how to wheel and deal, had many wives, was a fine politician, a crack shot, an outstanding rider, and a great judge of horseflesh; and, like all operators, he was ever attuned to opportunities.

From 1769 to 1823, the conquistadors and priests established twenty-one missions in California, ranging along nearly the entire coast, from San Diego to Sonoma. As the Spaniards moved northward, horses escaped their expeditions and flourished in the wilderness. Until very recently, descendants of these mustangs lived in the Anza-Borrego Desert State Park south of Palm Springs. During the height of the mission era, the Spanish prefigured the English in various aspects of things equine on this continent; they were the first to breed horses, mules, and burros in large numbers in the West, and they started the first pony express, moving mail from mission to mission by horseback on the fabled El Camino Real. By 1772, nearly half of the state's missions had been constructed in southern and central California, and there were horses living not just inside these establishments but outside them as well — escapees and other wild horses that had wandered toward the premises, perhaps having traveled from as far away as Arizona. Outside the mission at San Juan Capistrano, there were so many unwanted mustangs that drovers herded them off the cliffs at nearby Dana Point. In Los Angeles, great numbers of wild horses came to the edge of town, ate the forage, and spirited the gentled horses away, so the local government decided to kill them. Cowboys drove the herds toward specially built pens, and as the horses ran through the gates, lancers claimed some for themselves, then speared the rest. Within a three-year period, thousands of mustangs were slaughtered in these corrals.

The Comanche were drawn to the burgeoning horse population in Texas, and so too did Wakara arrange his travels, in his case lured by the beautiful animals bred at and living in or near the missions in southern California. Wakara was probably born sometime between 1808 and 1815, most likely on the Spanish Fork River in Utah. According to the very spare record, his mother was probably from one of the California tribes and for a time was indentured at one of the missions in the Sierra Nevada. His father was probably a Ute.

No one knows exactly when the Ute got the horse but in *World of Wakara,* Conway B. Sonne recounts the following legend:

> One day some Spaniards came through [the land] ... They were mounted on what appeared to be oversized dogs ... A trade was made, and the Utes possessed their first horse. Having never seen such a beast, the chief tied the horse to a side of the wickiup. In time, the animal died from starvation, since no one apparently suspected that it required anything to eat, or an amount of food different from what would sustain a dog.

This was probably in the early 1600s, when conquistadors first passed through Ute territory. But the ways of the horse were quickly learned, and the southern branch of the tribe began trading meat and hides to the Spanish in exchange for the animals, and then, unable to continue meeting the high prices, they traded their children. One female slave would buy eight horses, and early accounts tell of the youngsters moving down the trail with their captors, their feet tethered together under the bellies of the animals, soon to become shepherds and cowherds for the conquistadors.

The caravans they joined followed a path that the Ute and other tribes had blazed across this region, and it was soon followed and widened and lengthened by an endless train of explorers and priests, and then traders, trappers, and settlers. It became known as the Old Spanish Trail, and it wended its way out of Santa Fe through the Sangre de Cristo Mountains, across the Colorado River, into the Great Basin, over the enchanting and deadly wastes of Death Valley, through the eastern Mojave, up the Cajon Pass between the San Gabriel and San Bernardino Mountains, down through the foothills, across the lush flats on the way to the Pacific Coast, and finally deposited its cargo at the pueblo of Los Angeles. The very name of this path — the Old Spanish Trail — suggests a certain romance, a hint of castanets perhaps, chivalry and doomed love affairs. But behind the lace curtain was a cast of down-and-dirty desert thieves who ran horses that were stolen or traded for on the cheap; considered a scourge on the land, these thieves even had their own name, *los chaguanosos,* the raiders, a multinational gang of American and French Canadian trappers, Native Americans, and traders from New Mexico.

The first caravan to complete the route from New Mexico to the San Gabriel Mission outside Los Angeles left Abiquiu in the fall of 1829 and arrived on January 31, 1830, trading serapes for horses at roughly two for one, acquiring animals for barely a fifth of what they would sell for in Santa Fe. A month later they returned to New Mexico with the first herd of California horses. The Old Spanish Trail soon became a horse freeway, in spite of the fact that many of the animals did not survive the trek through the south end of Death Valley, which became known as the *Jornada del Muerto.* With its long stretches of parched *bajadas* on which animals were driven for up to eighty miles without water, the path was marked by "numerous skeletons of horses," observed George Douglas Brewerton in his contemporaneous account of riding the Spanish Trail, *Overland with Kit*

Carson. "The frequent recurrence of these bleaching bones in a road so lonely," he wrote, "induced me to ask some explanation in regard to them of an old trapper belonging to our party." The trapper told him that many years before, the legendary mountain man Bill Williams had taken a crew into lower California, stolen fifteen hundred horses and mules, and fled into Death Valley. Pursued by nearly two hundred men, the *chaguanosos* desperately pressed on, losing a thousand animals along the way.

To keep the loss of horses to a minimum, raiders tried to travel the extensive stretches between watering holes without stopping. Generally they would start at around three in the afternoon, travel through the night when it had cooled down, and reach the other side on the following morning. "Sometimes the trail led us over large basins of deep sand," Brewerton wrote of the nocturnal journey, "where the trampling of the mules' feet gave forth no sound; this added to the almost terrible silence, which ever reigns in the solitudes of the desert, rendered our transit more like the passage of some airy spectacle where the actors were shadows instead of men."

For the animals, the trail was treacherous in a multitude of ways. Sometimes their hooves would be worn to the quick on the rocks and desert gravel. Sometimes they became a blood feast for mosquitoes at the water holes. "Our poor mules," wrote Brewerton, "got together in a body, standing in pairs, side by side, so that the tail of one was kept in motion near the head of the other, thus establishing an association for mutual protection." Sometimes the animals became a banquet for men. After three days of travel through the desert, Brewerton wrote, it was resolved "that the fattest of our way-worn steeds should be killed, dressed, and eaten. This idea furnished ample material for contemplation. Eat horse-meat! The very thought was revolting." At camp that night, a horse was killed, cut up, and consumed. "I alone stood aloof," Brewerton wrote, "and went supperless to bed. But Hunger gained the day at last." After forty-eight hours, he gave in, and ate horse meat for more than a week.

Horses that survived the desert trek were often stolen, again, by Paiute and other Indians who plied the trade route. From that first trade in 1830 and for the next two decades, there were dozens of hit-and-run strikes along the Old Spanish Trail and on the California missions, in which scores of animals were driven to Santa Fe, and from there to the burgeoning markets in the Southeast. In one raid in 1832, Juan Jesus Villapando and his New Mexico gang converged on southern California, posing as traders while visiting missions and making off with horses and mules as they left. In 1837, Jean-Baptiste Chalifoux and his men struck the missions at Santa Inez and San Luis Obispo and fled with fifteen hundred horses.

But Wakara and his crew mounted the most daring theft of all. It was a multipronged assault involving four missions over a period of several weeks, a heist and escape born of deep knowledge of desert washes, seeps, cracks, and wrinkles, of winds and hideouts in slot canyons, of greedy men and mustangs that longed to run free. That any horses at all would survive such a relentless drive through deadly terrain is a tribute to the stamina and will of the mustang.

The great raid and the ensuing manhunt happened during April and May of 1840. The seeds for the raid had been sown five years earlier, when Wakara had a falling-out with two members of his party, the mountain men Jim Beckwourth and Pegleg Smith. The group had just visited Los Angeles and traded slaves and animal pelts for horses and gold. Wakara felt that the number of horses received in the trade, fifty, was not enough to justify his trek across the desert. So one night he took his Indian band and raided some local rancheros, driving six hundred horses through the mountains and back toward Utah, with a posse of Spaniards in pursuit. Beckwourth and Smith just barely made their own escape. Wakara and the mountain men did not speak for several years, until the night that Smith and Beckwourth rode into Wakara's camp up in the Cajon Pass. Although Wakara didn't like "the shriveled, dark-skinned Beckwourth," according to a report, "he had genuine affection for the big-hearted, roisterous, impulsive Pegleg," so he welcomed them into his desert camp. As they passed the firewater, the mountain men had a proposal. It had been a bad year for trapping, but there were all those horses in California. Why didn't they just go there and make a big haul? Beckwourth would be the advance man, finding the horse herds before the raid and laying down all of the groundwork. Smith would round up a few trusted men for his crew and arrange to sell the horses.

Wakara liked the plan, and a month later, Smith returned to Wakara's camp with a gang of mountain men and his retinue of squaws. Leaving the women at Wakara's camp, the men trekked down the mountains and met up with Beckwourth, who had made a careful study of every Spanish herd in the region. The strategy was this: Wakara would divide his band into small groups, with each one attacking a particular ranch or mission. From each point, the horses would be run into the Cajon Pass and then down across Death Valley and east toward New Mexico. The pass would be guarded by Smith and his gnarly crew.

Meanwhile, several other bands of mountain men had set out from the Rockies and the Sierra Nevada in January to join the raiders — a dirty dozen or more of *chaguanosos*. Now they all met on the flatlands and prepared to strike. Wakara and Smith led the first raid, at San Luis Obispo, midway between Los Angeles and San Francisco, stealing into the corral at night, opening the fence, and driving the mission's twelve hundred horses north through the Tehachapis and then east to the rendezvous point. Over the next few weeks, the others swept out herds from San Bernardino to San Gabriel and Mission San Juan Capistrano. According to the records at the San Gabriel mission, there were 2,600 horses there — the largest group — and most of these were taken by the thieves.

The flight took man and horse across a fertile plain where fig and peach trees flourished. As the horses were driven, they no doubt caught these scents, and as they headed eastward into a drier zone, with the river-fed loam fading to white Mojave sand, the scents would have faded as they galloped past stretches of wildflowers if the rains had come that year and perhaps past chaparral that was black and singed, burned during the previous year's fall fires. They began to climb into the higher elevations, through ancient washes and gullies, past cathedrals of stone, and up the San Andreas fault line that is the tightly wired Cajon Pass; from the pueblo in Los Angeles, witnesses observed a mighty cloud of dust rising from the mountains in the east, and it was said that the dust was stirred by the horses' hooves, pounding hard along the packed Mojave gravel. The swirls would have been swept up and carried by the high winds that customarily blow down along this path and knock tractor-trailers on their sides; we can try to imagine the effect such a condition would have had on the horses, all now at different points in the pass, the entire swiftly moving caravan pursued by three posses of heavily armed vaqueros, including men who were freed from a Los Angeles jail, to join the desperate hunt for the rapidly disappearing animals. On the far side of the pass, Wakara drove the horses eastward, stopping to water them in a place now called Horsethief Canyon, under a stand of willows.

Soon the posse found them, and when they dismounted, Wakara's band opened fire, killing two men and sending the others scrambling on foot. Then they stampeded the vaqueros' horses into their own stolen herd. Hearing the news, the second posse stopped at the pass and waited for the third. Now the *chaguanosos* were several days ahead of the vaqueros and the jailbirds from downtown Los Angeles. They stopped at Bitter Spring to refresh their horses, but there was not enough time to adequately water the large herd, so man and animal pressed on, into Death Valley across the *Jornada del Muerto,* where the horses faltered and died every few hundred feet. The next watering hole was spent, and by the time the group reached Resting Spring on May 24, the posse was upon them. But the rear guard of twenty-five thieves made a quick getaway, leaving saddles, clothes, cookware, and their hobbled horses behind. Inside one of the abandoned coats there was a list of some of the names of the *chaguanosos* — all Americans. Their own horses too tired to continue, the vigilantes called it quits.

According to one account, fifteen hundred of the stolen horses had died on the trail. According to another account, that of the thieves, most survived. As yet another had it, a year later, one of the mountain men sold the last of the herd on the Missouri River and earned $100,000 — a fortune. Although the record differs, we know for certain that many horses perished on the trek. Others passed into the hands of various tribes and trappers. And still others escaped and established new herds in remote canyons and on mountaintops. Today, in Sulphur Springs, Utah, just east of the Nevada-Utah border, near the segment of the Old Spanish Trail that crossed the Escalante Desert, there endures one small herd in particular that is said to have descended from the horses of Wakara's raids.

As for Wakara, he considered the great raid of 1840 a profitable venture. He continued to mount raids into California until 1855,

when he died during the winter at the age of forty-seven. His two favorite wives were killed so that they could join him, and the bodies
were hauled up a mountainside near Meadow Creek, Utah, for burial.
Wakara's men slaughtered a number of his finest horses to carry him
on the eternal journey.

He was hardly the first to take such powerful companions with
him. When an ancient Scythian king died, his tribe would strangle
great numbers of the finest horses to join him in the grave. In China
during the Shang dynasty, when a rich man died he was buried with
his chariot, his charioteer, and his horses. In West Africa, some tribes
buried a man in a shroud of skin from his favorite horse, and in Pata-
gonia, when a chief died, four horses were sacrificed and propped up
on sticks around the grave. Wakara was laid to rest in a stone sepul-
cher, along with his wives, blankets, rifles, robes, buckskin clothing,
cookware, and bows and arrows. The horses were placed in an adjoining pit. The graves were covered with rocks, and then a circular
cairn was erected atop Wakara's, with a roof of fresh-cut pine. Inside
were placed two Paiute children, a girl who was sacrificed for the occasion and a boy who would watch the dead make the transition until
he could wail and watch no longer.

It is said that when Crazy Horse was born on the Great Plains, a wild
horse galloped past his mother's lodge. But the name that invoked
his magic was not yet his — in the beginning, he was called Curly.
He rode his horse every day, like other boys, and often he would
ride into the mountains, through stands of virgin pine that were so
thick the region was known as the Dark Forest. Then he would head
down through draws in canyons lined by cottonwoods and box elders, ash trees and elm and hackberry, and there were bushes of wild
plums and chokecherries that provided nourishment. After a time,
he would enter Capa Wakpala, or Beaver Valley, and pass the days
with his friends at the headwaters of Beaver Creek in northwestern
Nebraska. He later said that this was where he wanted to be buried.
From the valley, he and the other boys would raid neighboring tribes
for horses, often announcing their success by setting fires. The bigger the fire, the greater the number of horses taken, and some say that
in certain areas of the plains, the trees have yet to return.

In 1854, around the time he was twelve or thirteen, he witnessed what came to be known as the Grattan incident, the first of many increasingly violent episodes between red men and white men on the Great Plains. Not surprisingly, it involved a cow — the beleaguered animal whose cultivation changed the face of the frontier, leading to the end of the buffalo, the Indian, and, later, the wild horse itself. Although there are various accounts of the incident that propelled Crazy Horse to his famous name and legendary role, it probably happened something like this: Some Mormon settlers were passing a Sioux camp in Montana territory with their wagon and oxen and cows. A crippled or injured cow wandered near the encampment. A Minneconjou named High Forehead thought it was a stray that was offering itself for dinner, so he shot it.

A gung-ho West Point graduate named John Grattan arrived with his army unit to arrest the assailant. This was a violation of the Fort Laramie treaty of 1851, which said that Indians and Americans should determine punishments for their own citizens. Grattan ordered his men into position and they leveled their guns while the unit's drunk interpreter tried to negotiate a deal. There was a misunderstanding. When the dust settled, Grattan and every trooper except one had been killed in a volley of arrows. The Brule chief Whirling Bear had been shot in the back and lay bleeding to death. The Sioux retaliated by killing nearly everyone at a nearby trading post and then ransacking a fur depot.

Eastern newspapers clamored for revenge, and an army inspector announced that "the time has now fully arrived for teaching these barbarians ... how to appreciate and respect the power, the justice, the generosity, and magnanimity of the United States." Sensing trouble, some Arapaho and Cheyenne warriors put on defiant displays, galloping around the corral at Fort Laramie and firing off their guns. Crazy Horse had fled into the wilderness, seeking a vision. He was not yet sixteen.

For three days, he stayed on a hilltop, without food or sleep, wedging pebbles between his toes and putting rocks under his back to stay awake. Weak and dizzy, he saw a horse approach. The horse carried a warrior on its back; the warrior had long unbound hair that reached below his waist, and behind one ear there was a smooth brown pebble. His body was decorated with hail spots, and a lightning streak raced across his face, from forehead to chin. He was beset by bullets and arrows but remained untouched, and he passed unharmed through a prairie storm and swarms of people trying to hold him back. On he rode, as a red-backed hawk soared above his head. When the vision was complete, Crazy Horse knew he had received power from the Thunder Beings.

Soon, he became the warrior of his vision quest. He prepared himself for battle by painting white hail spots on his body and a red lightning bolt down a cheek; behind one ear he tied a brown pebble, and on his head he placed a red-backed hawk. To his horse, he applied streaks of dirt thrown up by the burrowing blind mole, and he touched some of it to his own hair along with several straws of grass, thus making horse and rider invisible to the enemy and impermeable to bullets and arrows. Except for moccasins and breechcloth, he rode naked. Sometimes he wore a medicine bag around his neck, and it was filled with a powder made from wild asters and the heart and brain of an eagle. He chewed this mixture on some occasions; on others he rubbed it over his body.

In a solitary charge at the age of eighteen, he killed and scalped two Arapaho. It was agreed that he was brave and courageous like his father, who relinquished the name that would reverberate across the ages and passed it to the son. From then on, he was called Crazy Horse — and soon, the warrior whose name invoked raw force and immutable strength and all manner of horse magic would help lead his people to victory over the U.S. cavalry on the Great Plains.

But the mysteries of *Equus* were not imparted to Crazy Horse alone. About ten years after the Grattan incident, a horse had appeared to a young Lakota boy named Black Elk, in a vision as far-reaching as Moses' Burning Bush. It would carry his tribe to victory in the coming trials and tribulations, and later, when defeat followed, it would take him on a great adventure to a faraway land. It would also link his people to the four-legged forever, even today as they struggle to hold on to the few remaining shards of their story.

As he lay in bed with a fever, two men with flaming spears commanded Black Elk to follow them into a cloud. The cloud took them away to a white plain with snow-covered mountains in the distance. Black Elk could hear whispers in the stillness and then the men said, "Behold him, the being with four legs!" Black Elk looked and there was a bay horse. It said, "Behold me! My life history you shall know!"

The bay horse wheeled to where the sun went down and twelve black horses appeared, with necklaces of buffalo hooves, manes of lightning, and nostrils that breathed thunder. Then the bay wheeled to the north and twelve white horses stood before him. Their manes flowed like a winter wind and their nostrils roared, and white geese circled all around and above them. Then he wheeled to the east and there were twelve sorrel horses, with necklaces of elk's teeth and eyes that glimmered like the daybreak star. And then the bay wheeled to the south and twelve buckskins stood abreast, with horns on their heads and manes that lived and grew like trees and grasses.

The horses lined up by color behind the bay, who whinnied in each of the four directions, and as he did so, the horses of the corresponding colors neighed back in response. Then Black Elk joined the bay and they walked side by side, followed by the other horses, who marched in teams of four and by color. As they danced, they were transformed into the animals and birds of the world and vanished back into the four directions, and then Black Elk was inside a tepee, where he met the Powers of the World, six men who were older than the hills and the stars.

The horses reappeared from each direction and looked in as Black Elk listened to the elders. When the sixth Grandfather—the Spirit of the Earth—had spoken, the council concluded and Black Elk followed the old man out of the tepee, and then he was on the bay horse. The bay paused before the horses of the west, east, south, and north, neighing to each as before, and the horses neighed back in response, falling in line behind Black Elk by color, now with riders.

As the procession marched, it was followed by Black Elk's people at different points in time, until dark clouds gathered and the animals grew restless and women wept and in the west there was a horse that was all skin and bones. The young boy passed an herb over the horse and it arose, a big, shiny black stallion, the chief of all horses.

When he snorted it was a flash of lightning and his eyes were like the sunset star. He dashed to the four directions and the whites and sorrels and buckskins answered his call, rejoicing in their fleetness

and strength. Then silence prevailed and the great black stallion sang
a song:

> *My horses, prancing they are coming.*
> *My horses, neighing they are coming;*
> *Prancing they are coming.*
> *All over the universe they come.*
> *They will dance; may you behold them.*
> *A horse nation, they will dance.*
> *May you behold them.*

The stallion's voice was not loud, but it filled the universe. It was
so beautiful that nothing anywhere could keep from dancing. The
leaves on the trees, the grasses on the hills and in the valleys, the water in the creeks and in the rivers and the lakes, the four-legged and
the two-legged and the wings of the air—all danced together to the
music of the stallion's song.

When Black Elk awoke, the fever was gone. Later, he danced
the vision for his tribe in a grand reenactment of the knowledge he
was given, calling on horses and riders to assemble in the formation he had witnessed during his fever dream. As the Horse Nation
had danced in the spirit world, so too did it dance on earth, in har-
mony and connection and might, and about ten years later, it would
dance again, as hooves thundered across the greasy grass, where all
visions—white and red—were converging.

4

Comanche

*The Battle of the Little Bighorn and
the Horse That Survived It*

I F THIS PAGE COULD SING as you read it, or if I could
embed an audio file, I would ask it to play the tune
called "Garryowen" as your eyes passed this way. Many
of you would recognize the tune; although you might
not know the name, the first few notes are so memorable, so force-
ful, that you would recall it as the happy fife-and-drum jig played in
countless movies as the U.S. cavalry marches off into the scenery,
leaving a trail of dust and hoofprints.

Originally, "Garryowen" was used by various Irish regiments as
their quick-march in battles such as Waterloo; in the eighteenth century, it became the drinking song for the Royal Irish Lancers, who
crooned it in pubs when they came into Limerick on payday. Here
are a few verses:

> *Let Bacchus' sons be not dismayed,*
> *But join with me each jovial blade,*
> *Come booze and sing and lend me aid,*
> *To help me with the chorus.*

Instead of spa, we'll drink down ale,
And pay the reckoning on the nail,
For debt no man shall go to jail,
From Garryowen and glory!

We are the boys who take delight in
Smashing the Limerick lamps when lighting,
Through the streets like sporters fighting,
And tearing all before us . . .

As Irish immigrants arrived on American shores and enlisted in the army, the catchy quickstep was soon taken up by soldiers in the Revolutionary War and the Civil War. By 1867, it was adopted as the regimental air of the Seventh Cavalry, the unit commanded by the Civil War hero George Armstrong Custer, who would soon march into the pages of history at the Battle of the Little Bighorn — with the notes of the melody fading across the prairie grasses. "It was an appropriate choice," wrote the editors of a book about Myles Keogh, who was a pivotal member of the Seventh, especially in terms of its equine history, and who some credit with introducing "Garryowen" to Custer. Its lilting rhythm mimicked the gallop of horses, and aside from the whistle of a soldier who may have sensed he was marching to his doom, the lesser airs that were played on various legs of the march to that fatal battle, and the series of bugle calls heard on the field on June 25, 1867, "Garryowen" was the last music heard by man and horse alike. Some say that on certain evenings on the prairie, you can see the Seventh Cavalry ghosts riding their ghost horses past silhouettes of cottonwood and sage, into a hole in the sky at the end of a hard trail lit by a full moon, and if you get very quiet and still, you can hear the music that drove men into the arms of death and complemented the steady gallop of their partners, their steeds.

Who were these horses that appear in nearly every painting of the western conquest, every barroom poster of Custer gallantly fending off his mounted opponents? Many of them were once wild, living on the open range, rounded up and pressed into service by the U.S. Army. Often they were not named but merely numbered, and they were enlisted by the thousands. These beleaguered four-legged troops were the great unsung heroes of that horrible firestorm in the greasy grass. While Custer may have gone down in history as the man who was killed as he made his last stand, so too do the horses of the Seventh Cavalry deserve their place for serving with him, protecting him, as he went down.

There was one horse who—unlike many of the others—had a name. His story has been passed down through military histories, newspaper accounts of the time, and chroniclers of matters equine. His very name embodies the fateful clash of civilizations that concluded in about twenty minutes ("the time it took the sun to pass the width of one teepee pole," according to a Native American witness); it was Comanche, assigned to replace his number because of the silent courage he once displayed while farriers removed an arrowhead embedded deep in his flesh following a battle with Comanche Indians. Comanche went on to become an American hero—"the lone survivor of the Little Bighorn"—a label that was glorious but not true because there were many survivors, including scores of Native Americans who had wiped out Custer and his gray horse unit on June 25, 1876.

Comanche was most likely born around 1862 on what was once called the Great Horse Desert of Texas, a vast region that was home to hundreds of thousands of mustangs. Comanche bore the markings of the early Spanish horses—the bay or claybank horse (inexplicably referred to as dun or buckskin in many accounts) had the telltale black dorsal stripe down his back that today can still be seen on some wild horses in the high deserts of Nevada, Oregon, Wyoming, Utah, and Montana. Like many mustangs, he was small, about 925 pounds and fifteen hands. And he had a white star on his forehead.

No one knows how old he was when he was taken off the range; it was the era of the great plundering, when immense populations of birds and mammals were ours for the taking, and detailed records of the voracious mustang roundups that continued for decades were not kept. These horses were rounded up by cowboys and mustangers for cattle drives, personal use, sport, profit, or combinations thereof, and many of them were sold to the army. The roundups were often cruel (as they still are, although today's are carried out more "humanely"), frequently employing the method called creasing, in which a bullet was fired at the upper part of a horse's neck, causing temporary paralysis by striking a nerve. Sometimes the shooter aimed badly and fatally wounded the mustang; other times he injured the horse permanently and left him to wander the desert until he bled to death or was attacked by a predator.

Comanche was a survivor, one of thousands of horses who lived through a creasing (at least without visible damage), and he was then sold to the army. It was probably in 1868 that he and an unknown number of horses were driven north across mustang and cattle trails, most likely following the Kickapoo Trace, a rutted and dusty byway that went through the unfamiliar and rough terrain of Indian territory and into Missouri, where Jesse James and other outlaws were still fighting the Civil War after it ended, ranging the state where brother had literally fought brother, carrying out raids on herds of mustangs that happened to cross their paths. The trail ended in St. Louis,

A portrait of Comanche – the so-called "lone survivor of the Little Bighorn" – and an unnamed soldier, taken in 1887 at Fort Meade, South Dakota, by the noted frontier photographer John C. H. Grabill. The plaque bears a military pledge to care for Comanche "as long as he shall live."

where just days after running free on the open range, the horses were funneled into crowded corrals, awaiting buyers from the army. According to army purchasing standards of the time, horses acquired for cavalry use were required to be "sound in all particulars, well broken, in full flesh and good condition, from fifteen to sixteen hands high, from five to nine years old, and well adapted in every way to cavalry purposes." While the mustangs were not always broken when the army bought them, they were certainly sound; wild horses have unparalleled strength, endurance, and stamina, at that time drawing on three hundred years of experience in the American desert and a pre-Columbian heritage in the same region that stretched back to the Eocene.

On April 3 of that year, 1868, Comanche makes his first official appearance in the record; according to documents, a mustang fitting his description was sold to the army for the going rate of ninety dollars. A week after his purchase, he and various other horses were loaded onto railroad cars and shipped west to Fort Leavenworth, Kansas, where they arrived around the middle of May and were each branded with the letters *US* on the left shoulder, and the regiment number and the letter *C,* for *cavalry,* on the left thigh. Sometimes the letter of the company to which the horse was assigned was added to the brand. Custer's Seventh Cavalry unit had been stationed in Kansas and had lost a number of horses that spring. Custer sent his brother, First Lieutenant Tom W. Custer, to buy remounts. After looking them over in the corrals, he purchased forty-one, including the horse that would soon be named Comanche.

Once again the horses were loaded onto a train, where they stood head to tail in crowded cars and were shipped the short distance to Hays City, near Ellis, Kansas, where Custer and his troops were encamped at a fort. Eight years later, in 1876, the year of our centennial, more horses than cavalry soldiers would perish at the Battle of the Little Bighorn.

The cavalry that fought the Plains Indians was a product of two armies — the Union and Confederate soldiers of the Civil War. In that conflagration, each side had refined its equestrian tactics. While mounted soldiers had been critical in the first wars of this country, it was not until after the Civil War that the cavalry came into full flower, as waves of settlers swarmed across the frontier and violent encounters with Indians escalated accordingly. It was among the horse tribes of the Great Plains that the cavalry found its greatest foe. With a different style of fighting, and horses that had greater stamina, the Indians fended off the white man for nearly three decades, until finally their populations were decimated and their ponies were seized or killed and they were vanquished.

In a way, the country was born by warhorse. Immortalized in the Longfellow poem about Paul Revere's midnight ride, this was the fearless steed who "kindled the land into flame" in April of 1775. The poem tells us little else about the gallant animal, but we know from the record that she was a mare named Brown Beauty, and her forebears included Spanish horses that had disembarked on the Carolina banks in the early years of the conquest. When Paul Revere's ride was over, she was seized by a British soldier, who mounted her and galloped away. She collapsed in mid-run and died later that night — spent, after launching the war for independence.

In the first months of the Revolutionary War, there was no official cavalry; local and regional mounted units began showing up on their own. But it wasn't long before Congress authorized the raising of horses, and the army procured additional mounts as it swept through the countryside. By the time the war ended, in 1783, George Washington himself had been famously painted on his white charger, Jack, leading troops into battle. Sometime later, Washington sold him to a circus, and the four-legged veteran joined a cast of equines touring the new country in its first and very widely attended horse spectacle.

After the Revolutionary War, official cavalry units came and went, becoming more entrenched as the displacement of Indians escalated. In 1829, war hero Andrew Jackson was elected president, and a year later, he authorized the Indian Removal Act, a vicious policy whose implementation required well-organized horse soldiers. Under this law, the so-called Five Civilized Tribes — the Cherokee, Chickasaw, Choctaw, Creek, and Seminole — were taken from their homes in the Southeast in a series of removals and marched by the U.S. Mounted Ranger Battalion to the Great Plains.

The relocations culminated in 1838, when seventeen thousand

Cherokee and their animals and slaves were forced to trek westward for hundreds of miles over a period of months. About a fifth of the Cherokee population died along the way. During the final winter march, a thousand men, women, and children traveled for days with five thousand horses and a number of mules. Many of the animals faltered and perished before the caravan arrived in Oklahoma. Their path became known as the Trail of Tears. Some of the horses that survived it would go on to breed with the horses that had made earlier crossings. Soon, those horses were running on the open range, and they mixed with the herds that were already there, until one day when many were rounded up for other wars.

By 1843, there were two new regiments of American horse warriors — the First and Second Dragoons. The First Regiment had been formed to guard the western borderlands and was based at Fort Leavenworth, Kansas. Its commandant, Stephen Watts Kearny, was a veteran of the War of 1812 and a kind of horse whisperer of his time. Disturbed by the rough treatment of equines in the military, he devised a code for their treatment and laid it out in the *Cavalry Manual,* the first handbook of the U.S. Dragoons. A soldier should always speak to his mount "in a low, even voice," he wrote, and be "very careful to avoid alarming or disturbing his horse." He abhorred the ragtag look of most American outfits; inspired by the French cavalry, he organized each company by horse color because it looked better. Kearny's methods so improved morale that he was asked to lead the newly formed Army of the West in the campaign to seize California and the Southwest from Mexico. He died in 1848 and came to be known as "the father of the American cavalry," officially established in 1855, when Congress passed a bill authorizing the First and Second Cavalry to patrol the new territories.

Stationed at rapidly proliferating forts, this next wave of mounted men were tasked with building roads, accompanying scientific parties, and protecting settlers who were moving into Comanche lands across Texas as well as the Dakota, Wyoming, and Montana territories where the Plains Indians were gaining a tactical advantage with their burgeoning pony herds. But the country was also consumed with other matters. Among them was the question of whether the new states would permit slavery, and across the West, the topic was hotly debated. State after southern state began to secede.

When Abraham Lincoln was elected president on November 6, 1860, a pony express rider galloped westward with the explosive news, racing across prairie and desert from Fort Kearny, Nebraska, to Fort Churchill in Nevada in six and a half days, either switching horses or resting his along the way. On April 12, 1861, at 4:30 in the morning, Confederates fired the first shots of the Civil War, launching a fusillade on Fort Sumter, a Union stronghold in South Carolina. The battle raged for thirty-three hours, until finally the North surrendered. There were no casualties, goes the legend, but that's not really true; amid all the wreckage, a horse had been killed — the first death of the Civil War, an omen of the staggering equine losses to come.

The War Between the States was an era in which horse-based warfare became more sophisticated. It involved campaigns that covered great distances, and battles in which both sides made use of the time-honored mounted charge. It was also a proving ground for generals, whose equestrian theatrics and military skills took them to greater glory in the wars that followed in the West.

As the Civil War unfolded, the South had a distinct advantage. Confederate soldiers were excellent horsemen. There was a fine tradition of horse breeding below the Mason-Dixon Line. Many in the region had their own horses and knew how to take care of them, as well as how to ride. In fact, many officers in the prewar cavalry were from the South, and they resigned to join the new Confederate army. They brought their own horses with them, and so did many other recruits and volunteers — a practice that was encouraged because animals that serve in war are generally well treated by their owners and last longer than those whose riders neither know nor understand them. Many of these horses were used to a quiet life on the farm, and some could not adjust to the sound of gunfire on the front lines. These animals — often big draft horses — were assigned to ambulance duty or to wagons in the supply lines.

Union losses mounted, and the North realized that this was due in large part to reliance on local and regional equestrian units rather than an official cavalry. In 1863, the War Department established the Cavalry Bureau to oversee the acquisition and inspection of horses. But the procurement system was quickly corrupted, with large numbers of horses purchased or taken from everywhere, including frontier herds, and the brokers often camouflaging the animals' age by altering their teeth or painting over gray hairs. Once in the army pipe-lines, the horses were kept in crowded corrals "knee-deep in mud and excreta," an army veterinarian later wrote, "inadequately fed, and watered from a common stagnant trough. With them came every contagion known to the equine world. In such unsanitary remount depots, disease decimated the herds. The only thing that could be said for the system was that survivors were indeed hardy and immune."

Many of the horses that survived the remount depots soon participated in the cavalry charge, facing off against the four-leggeds of the South in the ancient tactic that so thrills the senses. These animals exhibited great fortitude under siege, and some even seemed to come alive for the advance. As one trooper wrote:

> On the skirmish line he will mope back and forth, with his head hanging down and ears lopped, as if very tired. At the sound of the trumpet he will move rapidly to the front or rear at the will of the trooper. When heavy battles are raging, if standing in line, he becomes nervous with the suspense, and will tremble and sweat and grow apprehensive. At any sound that indicates a move, the rider can feel him working the bit with his tongue. As he moves out he seeks to go faster, and when restrained shows his disapproval by feigning to bolt. He will grasp the bit afresh, and dash ahead as if to brave the worst and have it over as quickly as possible.

On the backs of such horses emerged some of the country's greatest cavaliers. One of them, Ulysses S. Grant, went on to become president when the war was over, and faced down constituents who wanted to annihilate the Indian. Another, George Armstrong Custer, was a voracious enforcer of government policies, and because of that he became one of the most notorious figures in American history. Coincidentally, both men were from Ohio. Both attended West Point. But there the similarities end. Grant's lifelong affinity for horses led him to a career in the military. Custer's path was a fluke—and in the beginning, an embarrassment. He graduated last in his class at West Point at the age of twenty-one. Then, because the army needed officers, he was immediately commissioned as a second lieutenant.

He quickly established his battlefield skills, earning a reputation as a dashing, arrogant, and impetuous warrior who lived for the charge.

An advance against a small group of Confederate cavalry was "the most exciting sport I ever engaged in," he later wrote. "I selected [the Confederate commander] as my game, and gave my black the spur and rein." The officer headed for a rail fence and Custer followed. "I reasoned that he might attempt to leap it and be thrown," he wrote, "or if he could clear it so could I. The chase was now exciting in the extreme." Both Custer and his prey cleared the fence. Custer told him twice to surrender. The officer refused, and Custer shot him in the head, seizing his horse and saddle. "Oh, could you but have seen some of the charges that were made!" he wrote. "While thinking of them I cannot but exclaim 'Glorious War!'"

By the time Custer was twenty-four, he had snagged front-page coverage in the *New York Times,* which compared him favorably to Napoleon. He often regaled listeners with tales of horses that had been shot out from under him, and after the battle at Culpeper Court House, he announced, "I cannot be killed."

Custer would go on to serve in the Indian wars with General Phil Sheridan, a Union hero whose famed horse Rienzi carried him through forty-five engagements, including nineteen pitched battles and two cavalry raids. After the war, Sheridan changed Rienzi's name to Winchester, the Virginia town where the pair had begun a famous, grueling trek that was memorialized Longfellow-style in a poem by Thomas Buchanan Read. The horse died in 1878, and was stuffed and sent to a New York museum. He was damaged by fire, refurbished, and moved to the Smithsonian, where he still stands on permanent exhibit in a glass case, about a hundred miles away from Traveller, the beloved gray horse who carried General Robert E. Lee through the war and who is buried in the Lee family crypt on the campus of Washington and Lee University.

As Ulysses S. Grant lay dying in 1885, the former president expressed regret about the path his life had taken. Throughout the Civil War, he had been dismayed by the unkind treatment of animal warriors. Once, he had stripped an officer's ribbons for beating his horse. He had longed for the day when he could retire to a farm and raise horses. But that was not to be, and one of the last things he spoke of were his steeds, Cincinnati, Jeff Davis, and Egypt, who had survived many battles and come with him to the White House.

They were lucky, Grant knew, for behind all the excited cries of "Charge!" there was another story. By the end of the Civil War, one and a half million horses and mules had been killed, wounded, or felled by disease. Their carcasses lay strewn across the battlefields — Antietam, Manassas, Gettysburg (at least five thousand had perished at that battle alone) — and as the reunited country accelerated the war against the Indian, the depleted cavalry now turned to the wild herds of the West, where horses roamed the Great Plains and high deserts by the millions.

When Comanche arrived at Fort Hays in 1868, he joined thousands of horses who were stationed at dozens of outposts across the frontier. The war against the Plains Indian had reached a new height as settlers poured into Montana, Dakota, and Wyoming territory, and Indians fought to keep it. To make peace, General William Tecumseh Sherman (so named because his parents admired the defeated Shawnee chief) had just signed a treaty with Sitting Bull, Red Cloud, and Gall. It said that the army would abandon forts on the Bozeman Trail and in exchange, the Sioux, Arapaho, and Cheyenne would keep certain hunting grounds and move onto a reservation that included the sacred Black Hills. But there was discord in the tribes; many members, including Crazy Horse, did not agree to the deal. In a matter of days, Comanche saw his first action, and later that year, many of his stable mates were part of a brutal winter campaign launched against the Indian holdouts by General Sheridan, who dispatched Custer to help him.

Fort Hays opened its doors in October of 1866, a year and a half after the Civil War had ended. Located at the confluence of two rivers, it was one of eight major forts in Kansas, and one of the most important. Tasked with protecting white settlements and railroad workers who were laying tracks nearby, it was also a supply depot for forts to the south and west. Buffalo Bill and Wild Bill Hickok stopped there as they passed through the region, and well-known cavalry units such as Custer's Seventh and the all-black Tenth (the Buffalo Soldiers) used it as a staging ground for the ongoing wars.

According to chronicles of the time, life at the frontier forts was a monotonous grind interrupted by bouts of extreme weather and aggravated by inferior provisions. "There is nothing of any importance going on and but little to write about," said one soldier at Fort Hays in 1867. The men sat in the tent and played seven-up. Some of them bet on horseraces. Many turned to drink and deserted in great numbers. "Scurvy made an appearance," Custer wrote in his memoir, *My Life on the Plains*, "and cholera attacked neighboring stations."

At nearby Fort Lincoln, horses and cattle were plagued by mosquitoes. The animals would try to hide in thickets of brush. Sometimes fires were lit to drive off the bugs. The cows lost weight because they couldn't graze, were driven mad by the insects, or died of exhaustion after trying to fend them off. Dogs buried themselves in holes. Winter presented other hardships. Once, to keep the horses from freezing to death during a terrible blizzard, they were taken to the nearby town of Yankton, where residents sheltered them in their homes, cowsheds, and stables. Such weather wreaked havoc on the mustangs, because many had just come from a hot climate.

"The sounds of the hoofs of the hurrying horses flying by our cabin on their way to the town had hardly died out before the black night closed in and left us alone on that wide, deserted plain," Custer's wife, Elizabeth, wrote in *Boots and Saddles,* her own frontier memoir. Her servants stopped up the cracks in the windows and barricaded the door. The snow fell in blankets, and she heard feet tramping above the roar of the storm. "A great drove of mules rushed up to the sheltered side of the house," and they pushed and crowded against the little cabin, braying with fear. "All night long," Libbie continued, "the neigh of a distressed horse, almost human in its appeal, came to us at intervals." Finally, the horse approached and pried open the cabin door, peering in for help, and forever haunting her with "strange, wild eyes."

Comanche was trained for cavalry duty as soon as he arrived at Fort Hays. For man and horse, the training process was extensive. Each trooper was issued a copy of *Saddling and Bridling As Taught in the 7th U.S. Cavalry* by Brevet Major General Gibbs, published that year. Like any military manual, it was filled with elaborate instructions that could not be varied, including nearly two hundred words under the heading "To Fold the Blanket": "Seize the blanket by both corners," it said, "bring the hands together so that the fold will come between the U and S, placing both corners in the left hand ..." Veteran steeds were placed near the green ones to make them more comfortable as troopers began the process of teaching the animal how to be saddled and ridden. First, the blanket would be laid across his back while the trainer, ideally, spoke kindly and softly. This went on for a number of days for increasing periods of time each day until the trainer felt the horse was ready for the saddle.

"A trooper is placed on each side of the horse, in position of 'stand to horse,'" the manual said, "holding the horse by the halter strap ... the trooper on the right side of the horse holds him whilst the other executes the manual ..." Over time, if the training had been done properly, the horse would not throw off the saddle and would permit the trainer to leave the saddle on his back; eventually, he'd allow the trainer to tighten it, and soon after that would come the bit and reins. As Comanche was getting used to the absence of freedom—living in a stall, being tied to a picket line, wearing a saddle, bridle, and bit —he was also becoming familiar with the various bugle calls.

A typical day in a cavalry unit involved seventeen calls, starting at 5:50 in the morning for the reveille trumpeters and then reveille it-self at 6:00, followed by calls for the stable, breakfast, fatigues, guard mounting, water, drill, drill recall, dinner, first sergeant's call, boots and saddles, dismount drill, water and stable, retreat, tattoo at 9:00 in the evening, and then, at 9:15, taps. Other calls included to the colors, attention, forward march, trot, gallop, and, of course, charge. The schedule was rigorous, with no room for error. "Woe betide the trooper who through carelessness or intention fails to place himself in his saddle simultaneously with the others," wrote Custer.

After Comanche became accustomed to the daily routine, he was trained to experience the noise of war without running away. To do this, the army used Cook's *Cavalry Manual* of 1861. For instance, to familiarize the horse with the sound of drums that accompanied cav-alry marches, a soldier would introduce him to the drum itself, letting him touch it with his lips. To make sure the horse could run through a line of fire, he was urged toward it, then rewarded as he got closer, and rewarded again when he moved through it.

For his partner-in-arms, Comanche was fortunate; while many horses came into the hands of inept or cruel riders, he had made his

way to Captain Myles Keogh shortly after his arrival at Fort Hays.
"Keogh was the beau ideal of a cavalry commander," wrote historian John S. Finerty, "the very soul of valor." By all accounts, his good
character extended to the treatment of his horses — and they were
important enough for him to talk about them in letters to his family. "I felt [Tom's] loss severely," Keogh wrote to his sister during the
Civil War. "I wish you could have seen the poor fellow how he could
leap and on the Fourth of July he saved my life, whilst riding on a bye
road carrying an order. I suddenly rode into a heavy outlying thicket
of the enemy. 'Tom' saw them as they rose up to deliver their fire and
I jumped sideways over a rail fence into the wood skirting the road.
He carried me safely out of range. I shall never have a horse like that
again." Later, he proudly sent a photograph of a horse named Mark
to his brother.

As is the case for many people, relationships with fellow humans
did not appear to go as well. Myles Keogh was a drunk, like a lot of soldiers of the time, a "swaggering bibulous soldier of fortune," according to a Custer biographer. One man who served under his command
wrote that Keogh was once so blasted that he ordered the sounding
of boots and saddles at midnight and then told his company to charge
across the prairie after an imaginary enemy. The charge lasted for two
hours. "The tramping of the horses and noise of the sabers and carbines as they passed my tent woke me up," the man said. "I was sure
it was the Indians that had made a raid on the post, but soon found
out the cause of the disturbance and went back to bed."

Although Keogh shared an affinity for booze with many soldiers,
there the similarities stopped. Many of the enlisted men were crimi-
nals, fugitives, unwitting wayfarers looking for a government-subsi-
dized trip out west, or recently arrived non-English-speakers with
few skills who had no idea of what they were getting into when army
recruiters met them at the New York docks and said, "Sign here."
Keogh, however, was a war veteran, and a heroic one at that. Before
coming to America, he had left Ireland at the age of twenty; he joined
the pope's army in Italy and then served in the Papal Guards and
Zouaves against the Cossacks for two years. He was awarded a papal
medal, which he was wearing years later at the Little Bighorn — and
some think that when the Indians saw it after they killed him, some-

thing about it made them decide not to scalp or mutilate him as they had done to all of the others except Custer.

In 1862, the year that Comanche was born, Keogh came to the United States and signed up as a cavalryman for the Union, perhaps even meeting Custer at Gettysburg, where he fought and won various commendations. After the Civil War, he was commissioned as a captain in the newly organized Seventh Cavalry. Who knows what draws a man to a particular horse? Was it a wild look in Comanche's eye? Some unspoken message that passes between humans and the animals that have been placed in our service? If deciphered, might it say, *I will carry you into hell and back,* and might not the human emit a scent, a vibration, that says, *I know and I will take care of you always*? The writer Barry Lopez once described the "conversation of death" that happens between two animals when one agrees to let the other kill it. Could there not be an instantaneous "conversation of life," a kind of prayer, that happens between a man and the animal that is not there by choice?

Perhaps Captain Myles Keogh, just back from an encounter with Indians, was walking among the newly acquired mustangs and spotted Comanche. Quite possibly, he looked Comanche over and then looked him in the eye, and most likely Keogh himself was being sized up by the confined animal at the same time. The record tells us that he bought him from the army for ninety dollars — a common practice of reimbursing the government for a desired horse and assuming ownership. From that point on, Comanche joined a steed named Paddy as a favorite mount of Captain Keogh, and when it was all over, like his commander, Comanche had developed a taste for booze.

As the old saying goes, "God protects drunks and children," and so it would seem, for a few years at least, a higher power was with Keogh and Comanche, the innocent wild horse that had become a beast of burden. "The daily intercourse of horse and rider quickened the instinct of the brute, so that he seemed half-human," Libbie Custer wrote. "Indeed, I have seen an old troop-horse, from whose back a raw recruit had tumbled, go through the drill as correctly as if mounted by a well-trained soldier. Many of the soldiers love and pet their dumb beasts, and if the supply of grain gives out on a campaign they unhesitatingly steal for them, as a mother would for a starving child."

In 1868, when the horse received his first wound while fighting Comanche Indians on the Cimarron River near Fort Dodge, Kansas, legend has it that it was Captain Keogh who cradled his head while a farrier removed the arrow shaft that had broken off in his right hind quarter, and perhaps Keogh even suggested the horse's name. In a few days, Comanche was ready to continue carrying Keogh. In 1870, he was wounded again, shot in the right leg in a skirmish with Indians on the Saline River in Kansas. He was lame for several weeks, but "came through like an old soldier," wrote Captain Edward Luce, "and was [soon] ready for duty, good as new." In 1871, Comanche's unit, Troop I, was transferred to Kentucky, where the army was dealing with post–Civil War problems such as moonshiners, carpetbaggers, and the Ku Klux Klan. While taking on a crowd at an illegal distillery, said Luce, Comanche received "a slight flesh wound in the right shoulder, but as usual he quickly recovered." In 1873, Troop I received orders to return to Fort Abraham Lincoln in the Dakota Territory, to rejoin Custer in the Indian wars.

For George Custer, a Civil War hero, life at Fort Lincoln was not monotonous at all. Weather permitting, he and Libbie, an avid rider, would sojourn across the prairie on horseback, dogs nipping at their heels, and an entourage carrying the day's picnic behind them. Well versed in wildlife, Custer often accompanied academics from New England as they scoured the plains for fossils and animal specimens, negotiating with Indian parties as the scientists rode through on their expeditions. Known for his ravenous hunting expeditions, Custer frequently headed out with his dogs to join Buffalo Bill and visiting European archdukes as they bagged scores of bison, antelope, elk, and bear. At the fort, he had a menagerie of badgers, porcupines, and bobcats, cared for by his devoted orderly John Burkman, an army hermit with a Klondike beard. "Custer loved animals," a biographer said, "including those he killed and stuffed."

At the time of Comanche's return to Fort Lincoln, the Indian wars were about to enter their final phase. Many tribes were already decimated, with some stripped of their ponies. Often the animals were confiscated, such as in 1869, when the army defeated Cheyenne dog soldiers at the Battle of Summit Springs in Colorado and took their four hundred horses and mules. But sometimes the large herds were killed. This was a tactic first carried out in 1858 by Colonel George

Wright, who ordered the massacre of eight hundred horses that belonged to the Palouse tribe, east of what later became Spokane, Washington. The site is now known as Horse Slaughter Camp, and it has a stone marker. On Thanksgiving night in 1868, Custer repeated the deed when he attacked Black Kettle and his small tribe of Cheyenne, the sole survivors of the brutal Sand Creek Massacre in Colorado four years earlier, at their camp along the Washita River in Oklahoma. It was so cold that when the band struck up "Garryowen" in the dead of night, the musicians' saliva froze in the instruments. On they played as the cavalry advanced on the sleeping Indians; most of the tribe was wiped out in the surprise attack, including Black Kettle and his wife, who were shot as they fled on horseback. When it was over, Custer told his scout California Joe to round up the herd of 875 ponies and mules on the riverbanks nearby and drive them into the smoldering village.

In a little while, about three hundred ponies came trotting in, followed by two mounted Cheyenne women who had been captured by Joe and forced to bring in the horses while he rode behind twirling his lariat. Soon the remaining animals followed, and the women tried to gentle the agitated ponies, while others were still singing their Indian death songs in the ruins. As they herded the horses to their doom, the women talked to them softly. Officers and scouts took the best ones for themselves, and then Custer told Lieutenant Godfrey to take four companies and kill the rest. Here is what Godfrey recalled:

> We tried to rope them and cut their throats, but the ponies were frantic at the approach of a white man and fought viciously. My men were getting very tired so I called for reinforcements and details from other organizations were sent to complete the destruction of about 800 ponies.

And so the rest were shot, and the Cheyenne woman Moving Behind, who was fourteen at the time, would later remember that the wounded ponies passed near her hiding place, moaning loudly, just like human beings.

There would be other horse massacres, as if prefiguring the coming government war against the horse itself, including Colonel Ranald Mackenzie's in 1874. During the Red River War against the

Kiowa and Comanche on the Staked Plains of Texas and Oklahoma, he ordered the killing of fourteen hundred Indian ponies. This was one of the last threats in that region of the country.

By then, there were more than 130 forts, posts, camps, and quarters across the frontier, as well as more than a dozen armories and arsenals. The tribes were surrounded by what *Army and Navy Journal* called "a contracting circle of fire." It consisted not just of military power but also settlers, ranchers, miners, missionaries, and corrupt government agents with an interest in fomenting discord, and its flames were stoked by the government itself. Although most of the tribes had been vanquished, and some were allied with the army, there still remained holdouts on the plains, including the Lakota and the northern Cheyenne. In 1876, gold was discovered in the Black Hills. The government seized the land, and the Indians who had not yet agreed to live on reservations continued their raids on settlers. Angered that the treaty of 1868 had been violated, Sitting Bull allied with the holdouts.

"Give them whiskey," suggested General Sherman. "Kills them like flies." General Sheridan had another idea — "obliterate" the red man. From that point on, Indians who refused to surrender were known as hostiles, and they would be quelled with a massive, three-pronged attack. The plan was this: At Fort Lincoln, Custer would be met by General Alfred Howe Terry's column, leading the Seventh Cavalry west and then south toward Montana Territory. There, they would hook up with General George Crook's column from the south and General John Gibbon's column from the west — and wipe out the enemy encampments of Sioux and Cheyenne led by Sitting Bull and Crazy Horse.

Sometimes, in the morning on the plains, there comes a moment of great promise, just after daybreak in the springtime, when the rivers and streams are running free and at the banks the water is warm to the touch and neither beast nor human appears to want for anything, when all of nature itself is a kind of prayer — the meadowlark trills a quick symphony of notes and the wind that is always moving across this land caresses the leaves on the cottonwoods, and prairie dogs pop up from their subterranean cities and chatter across the grasses and paintbrush and sage. Such was the morning that greeted

George Armstrong Custer on May 17, 1876, and once again, it was time to march off to war.

As the Seventh Cavalry prepared for the journey, excitement swept through the ranks. "When you were on a good horse," wrote Sergeant Charles Windolph in a memoir, "with a Colt revolver strapped to your hip and a hundred rounds of ammunition in your belt, you felt like you were somebody. You belonged to a proud outfit and you were ready for a fight."

Soon the column departed, and the guidons of each regiment snapped in the breeze. Custer was riding one of his favorite horses, Vic, and he was dressed in his signature buckskin pants and jacket (this time, the one he had worn at the Battle of the Washita). He also wore his trademark red silk cravat, which many men in his outfit sported in imitation. Libbie joined her husband on horseback at the head of the column. When they passed the Indian quarters, where their allies from the Crow tribe were living, the squaws, old men, and children sang death songs, the red-man equivalent of "Garryowen." The Crow scouts also sang and beat their drums — long after the parade had left the garrison. When the column passed Laundress Row, wives and children of soldiers lined the road, and mothers held their babies aloft for a last look at their departing fathers.

After fourteen miles, the column separated from camp followers and Custer leaned down from his horse to embrace his wife. "Watch for our return," he said, but for now she stopped and watched the departure, "a scene of wonder and beauty," she later recalled. But leave it to mules to suggest that all was not right — as the parade had passed General Terry's reviewing stand, a few in the train had broken formation and thrown their packs, and a little while later on that fine spring morning, just five weeks before the most famous cavalry and Indian battle in American history unfolded, Libbie Custer had an omen. Just as Sitting Bull would soon dream of soldiers falling upside down from the sky, a good omen for the Sioux, the wife of the warrior with the long golden locks saw something that disturbed her as she watched the line of pack mules, ponies, cavalry, artillery, infantry, soldiers, orderlies, cooks, Indian scouts, veterinarians, and surgeons that stretched for more than two miles march off into the morning mist. As it vanished, Mrs. Custer later recounted, there appeared a mirror image of the procession in midair, halfway between heaven and earth — a ghost train of horses and riders, swallowed by the sky.

The march from Dakota to Montana Territory took the Seventh Cavalry across Miocene cliffs and down banks of sandstone and granite, over hills and down into the gullies of time; past walls of ancient petroglyphs that perhaps served as portals to another dimension, over fossil quarries of prehistoric plants and horse bones, through starry nights where the constellations shimmered close and bears and wolves hunkered on outcroppings and licked their chops at the sight of a faltering mule, and the cavalry marched on, through valleys of Ice Age kills and frontier echoes of pagan warrior rituals — "we passed a sundance lodge," a soldier later wrote, "and inside there was a white scalp."

Comanche and the other horses must have sensed surrounding danger, and it is very likely that Captain Keogh, out in front of the unit, watched Comanche's ears for telltale twitches, noting in what direction they turned, and perhaps in response he looked to his right or left to see if anything or anybody lurked, and his men, their hands on their guns, would have looked too, warned by a horse to stay alert. But the march was not easy on the animals, starting with the four condemned cavalry horses who hauled the Gatling guns on the first leg and were probably treated accordingly. By many accounts, a number of horses and mules fatigued or broke down en route — some had not been in great shape when they began. Many soldiers feared that the horses would be no match for the Indian ponies, master survivors who lived on the run, eating tree bark if they had to and accustomed to rough conditions. Sometimes the river water where the cavalry stopped for rest was too alkaline for the animals to drink, and toward the end, the rations of feed were not equal to the task at hand, which was carrying not just a rider but other weight as well.

As Captain Godfrey reported in *Custer's Last Battle,* in addition to the rider, each horse carried between eighty and ninety pounds of equipment, including a hundred rounds of ammunition. The two-horse wagons in the pack train, hired by contract, each hauled about fifteen hundred to two thousand pounds. The six-mule government wagons each carried from three to five thousand pounds, depending on the size and condition of the mules. In addition to tents, food for men and animals, kitchen gear, and farrier equipment such as horse-shoes and nails, the pack train carried axes, shovels, pickaxes, pine

boards, and scantling in order to make bridges along the way. Sometimes such crossings delayed the train for several hours. "During this
time," Godfrey wrote, "the cavalry horses were unbitted and grazed,
the men holding the reins ... the officers usually collected near the
crossing to watch progress, and passed the time in conversation and
playing practical jokes."

En route, Custer went hunting with his staghounds — Bleuch,
Tuck, and Lady — who had followed him out of Fort Lincoln and
caught up with him hours after the column had left. They ran along
with the horses, and at noon when the haversacks were opened and
the men had lunch, the horses would stop grazing, "put their noses
near their riders' faces and ask very plainly to share the hardtack,"
and look on as the dogs gnawed on the bloody flesh of a fresh bison
kill. If the men would not share their meals with their mounts, "they
would paw the ground and even strike their riders," Godfrey remembered, at which point "the old soldier was generally willing to share
with the beast."

There are no records of Comanche on the march, but from Godfrey's account, we know that when stable call was sounded, about
an hour after sunset, the men would march to the herds just outside
camp limits where Comanche and the other horses were kept in hast-
ily made corrals. There they would remount, assemble, and march to
a watering place, "usually selected," Godfrey said, "with great care
because of the boggy banks and miry beds of the prairie streams."
After watering, the horses were tied up closer to camp, and the men
got their currycombs, brushes, and nosebags, and went to the troop
wagon, where the quartermaster sergeant and farrier took tin cups
and measured forage to each man. Then the soldiers would return
to the line of horses and feed and groom them as an officer examined each one's back and feet. When a horse's back was sore and its
rider was to blame, that man would have to march on foot and lead
his horse until the sore healed.

After the horses were fed and groomed, they were unsaddled and
returned to the area outside of camp until retreat was sounded, at
which point most were brought inside and picketed in front of the
men's tents to protect them from animals and Indian raids. Comanche would have spent the evening outside Keogh's tent, and it's not
inconceivable that under a starry night on the plains, as the last of

the campfires flickered out, the captain might have opened the *Key of Heaven,* a popular Catholic prayer manual at the time (one would later be found on the battlefield), and selected the incantation for the time of conflict.

And Comanche may have nickered or been a comfort in the shared silence, for he was a partner in almost every way, and, like many troopers, Keogh used his horse's saddle as a pillow, which heightened the link between man and animal by way of scent and sweat so that in the morning, when boots and saddles was sounded and the horse was prepared for the march, he would recognize the gear that was being placed on his back and register acceptance. Perhaps this is why, when the battle was over and Comanche had a chance to desert the army, unlike other horses that day, he did not.

On June 16, the Seventh began to encounter what some would later view as portents. They passed an Indian burial ground — an orchard of corpses on scaffolds in trees, including the body of an infant whose face was painted red. Three days later, where the Tongue and Yellowstone rivers joined, the Dakota column spent the night at an abandoned Indian camp. The driftwood pony shelters were still there, and troops used the wood for fires. Again, there was an airborne cemetery, and some of Custer's men stole beaded trinkets from the bodies in the cottonwoods and as the Seventh resumed its march the following day, they brandished the souvenirs from their saddles, not just whistling past a graveyard but taunting the dead to come and get them.

On June 21, Custer arrived in Montana Territory, at the confluence of the Yellowstone River and Rosebud Creek. The unit stopped there and spent the night, during which Custer and Gibbon, arriving with his Montana column, met with General Terry on board the steamer *Far West* for a final strategy conference. It was here that Custer got the orders that would send the Seventh to their doom:

> As soon as your regiment can be made ready for the march, you will proceed up the Rosebud in pursuit of the Indians ... It is, of course, impossible to give you any definite instructions in regard to this movement, and were it not impossible to do so the Department Commander places too much confidence in your zeal, energy, and ability to wish to impose upon you precise orders which might hamper your action.

Now completely unfettered (as many have interpreted the phrase "orders which might hamper your action"), Custer began to plan the charge and told the bugler to sound officers' call as soon as the conference was over. Late that night, the officers gathered outside his tent, and as Custer laid out his plan, commanders were immediately struck by how hard it was going to be on animals: the pack mules would carry fifteen days' rations of hard bread, coffee, and sugar, Custer said; twelve days' rations of bacon and fifty rounds of ammunition per man. Each man would carry additional rounds on himself and in his saddlebags, as well as twelve pounds of oats on his horse.

Although the pack mules sent up the trail on an earlier scouting expedition had been badly used up, Custer now suggested that they carry even more weight, in the form of extra forage. Warned that the mules would break down, he became agitated, according to Godfrey, and said, "Well, gentlemen, you may carry what you please; you will be held responsible for your companies. The extra forage was only a suggestion, but this fact bear in mind, we will follow the trail for 15 days unless we catch them before that time expires, no matter how far it may take us from our base of supplies; we may not see the supply steamer again." Then it was off into his tent for the evening, but not before wheeling around with one more order. "You better carry along an extra supply of salt," he said. "We may have to live on horse meat before we get through."

That night, with Comanche picketed outside his tent, Captain Myles Keogh made out his will.

On noon of the following day, June 22, forward was sounded, and the Seventh marched out of camp in a column of fours, with each troop followed by its pack mules. Custer appeared to be stripping down to essentials. The condemned horses and the Gatling guns they carried had been left behind at the Powder River depot — on the upcoming march through rough terrain, Custer feared, they would hamper troop movements. So too was Custer's beloved regiment band jettisoned — there was no music accompanying this departure, but perhaps the parade found urging in the calls of hawks or eagles, and surely they were encouraged by the steady clip-clop of hooves on the hard dusty trail, and then by the reassuring thunder of the gallop as the parade picked up steam and began its southerly and fateful move along Rosebud Creek.

Trouble came early: the mules straggled badly on that first after-noon, losing boxes of cargo, and that night, Custer started acting strange, outlining his concerns for the march instead of showing his customary bravado. The pace of the marches would increase from twelve miles a day to twenty-five to thirty-five miles a day, he said, lest the Indians who were thought to be in the vicinity break up into small bands and escape. Officers were warned to trim down their ra-tions for themselves and the horses and mules because they might be out longer than expected. "His manner and tone," Godfrey wrote, "usually brusque and aggressive, or somewhat rasping, was on this occasion conciliating and subdued. There was something akin to an appeal, as if depressed, that made a deep impression on all present."

As several lieutenants walked to their bivouac in the dark, one of them said he thought Custer was going to be killed. The Crow scouts—Mitch Bouyer, Bloody Knife, and Half-Yellow-Face—also had a bad feeling. The next morning the cavalry hit the trail and pressed on, amid clouds of choking dust.

Several horses broke down, and their riders proceeded on foot. By nightfall on the twenty-fourth, the Crow scouts gave Custer some new intelligence—they had been following the tracks of Indian po-nies and travois poles; the tracks veered to the west of Custer's en-campment and then climbed up a divide between the Rosebud and Little Bighorn rivers. Facing into the setting sun, the scouts couldn't see what lay beyond. Custer decided to speed up the attack. Over a flickering candle in his tent, he told his officers it would happen in two days.

The cavalry would have to move right now, he said, at midnight. The troops were rousted in the dark, and the men and horses—al-ready fatigued from a relentless trek over the previous forty-eight hours—waged a six-mile march up rough and rocky terrain until they reached a place now known as the Crow's Nest, in the mountains looking down into the valley of the Little Bighorn. One of the Indian scouts spotted Sioux pony herds grazing in the distance down below. A Ree warrior named Red Star mounted his horse and raced toward Custer's encampment, zigzagging his animal as he approached to sig-nal that the enemy had been sighted. When Custer heard the news, he cut his meal short and told Burkman to saddle Vic. "Take good care of the horses," he said, referring to the animals in the pack train.

"We may need them before morning." Then he mounted Vic, tipped his hat, and signaled to his men to fall in line.

Keogh, perhaps polishing off a pint of whiskey, boarded Comanche, and the men of the Seventh Cavalry hoisted themselves up and over their horses into the well-worn saddles, adjusting their stirrups, and then they all, as one, marched on their dancing steeds into the valley below.

Unbeknownst to Custer, scores of Indians had been assembling in the Valley of the Little Bighorn, coming together as they often did just before summer began, in May, the Month When the Ponies Shed, for the annual sun dance. In previous years, they would meet elsewhere, but in 1876 things were different—Sitting Bull wanted the tribes to gather in a remote place while they discussed how to respond to the latest developments. They had camped at nearby Ash Creek, but their horses—perhaps as many as fifteen thousand—had grazed the grasses down, and a few days before the troops arrived, they moved into the valley where the forage was lush and as high as a horse's belly.

It was the biggest encampment the tribes had known, with ten thousand Indians stretching for two miles along the western side of the Little Bighorn River. The site—as it turned out—was a protective shield. Across the river, "the land rose suddenly and formed a line of ridges that undulated sharply as they followed the river," wrote Lakota historian Joseph M. Marshall III. "Long slopes, deep gullies, and steep sides made the ridges formidable obstacles to easy movement, except for the likes of deer and antelope. Within the protective canopy of young and old cottonwood groves, the people pitched their lodges."

Shortly past noon, Custer arrived at the divide between the Rosebud and Little Bighorn watershed. He stopped and split the Seventh into three battalions—one led by Major Marcus Reno, composed of 140 mounted men, another by Captain Frederick Benteen, which included about 125, and the third led by Custer himself. Custer's battalion included 225 men and their horses, and he divided it into two more distinct units, one led by Captain George Yates and the other by Captain Keogh. From this spot, a line of ridges blocked his view into the valley, and he was unable to pinpoint the location of the Indians. He sent Benteen into the hills to scout for hostiles. With Benteen wheeling to the left, Reno and Custer led their commands on a parallel path along either side of what was later named Reno Creek, heading westward. A Lakota boy saw the dust kicked up by the cavalry horses and raced back to warn the others. At 2:15, army scouts discovered an abandoned Indian campsite and flushed about forty warriors north toward the river. Custer ordered Reno to pursue them, promising to follow soon. Reno's men took off on a fast trot along the creek. At 2:55, the thirsty and tired horses stopped at a ford for a drink, upsetting the formation.

Within minutes, the battalion was surrounded, and Reno ordered the soldiers to dismount for the fight. Following custom, every fourth man took the horses and headed for ravines as the others skirmished on foot. The men were quickly overwhelmed, and Reno told them to abandon their position. They tried to head up a riverbank as warriors converged, firing off a hail of bullets. Some of the horses were spooked and broke from their holders, running back toward the water, where soldiers by the twos and threes grabbed on to their tails and used them as life rafts. Others were run off by Indian women who waved buffalo hides. "Our ponies were well-rested and fast runners," Sioux chief Gall later said, "but the soldiers' horses were tired out before the battle began. These horses were so hungry that they were eating grass while the battle was going on."

With Custer failing to arrive with support and his battalion rapidly dwindling, Reno told his men to remount and abandon their position. The Crow scout Bloody Knife was next to him on his horse. As they prepared to flee, a bullet ripped through Bloody Knife's skull and his brains splattered across Reno's face. Reno issued a flurry of commands, some not even heard, and then quickly ordered a retreat. The battalion headed for the bluffs on the east side of the river and was soon joined by Benteen and his men as Custer headed north. The beleaguered soldiers of Reno's and Benteen's battalions spent the night on the bluffs, with their wounded in a hollow, tended by the only surviving doctor and surrounded by horses and mules for protection. At about 3:30 P.M., Custer passed through the Medicine Tail Coulee on the east side of the river and approached what would soon be called Last Stand Hill.

From the southeast, Crazy Horse was approaching. He stopped at a wall of sandstone near Ash Creek and carved a petroglyph. It depicted a horse — undecorated and on the move — with a snake hovering above. We do not know which of his prized horses, the bay or the sorrel, he was riding that day. Nor do we know how long he lingered at this site, but somewhere en route, he must have prepared for the task at hand, anointing himself and his animal with gopher dust and paint and wearing his special stone pendant over his heart. As for when exactly he arrived at the fight, that is also a mystery; perhaps, as per his vision, the dust made him disappear until he was sighted on the field.

Custer was now leading his column north, followed by Keogh's. The battalion led by Yates headed east from the coulee to the river. There they were met by thirty Indians, who were soon joined by others with fresh ponies from the herd, along with Sioux chief Gall and the warriors who had just finished off Reno's brigade. "Our young men rained lead across the river," Sitting Bull later recounted, "and drove the white braves back." Yates's companies were quickly repelled. "The horses were so frightened that they pulled the men all around," Low Dog recalled, "and a great many of their shots went up in the air and did us no harm."

Keogh led his men up a nearby ridge with Gall's band in pursuit. He gave orders to dismount and form a skirmish line; the battalion kept the Indians at bay for half an hour, then withdrew and headed up another ridge. Keogh again told his men to dismount and form a line. The Indians ran off a number of horses; with soldiers now on foot and without ammunition, they began fighting with pistols and retreated to the south, linking up with Yates's band on top of what came to be known as Calhoun Hill.

Meanwhile, Custer's flank was hit in a lightning raid led by the Cheyenne warrior Lame White Man, forcing the survivors back to Calhoun Hill, where they joined Keogh as he tried to hold it. Yates and his men were now moving north on nearby Battle Ridge. As many have conjectured, they were probably joined by Custer, still looking for a way to penetrate the village. Within minutes, they were surrounded by Indians, who launched arrows and blasted them with rifles, carbines, muskets, and pistols, felling dozens of troopers and horses in the attack.

Now, from the north, came Crazy Horse, heading toward Battle Ridge. Leading a large force of Cheyenne, he attacked Keogh's battalion head on; from either side of the ridge, the Sioux raced in at the same time. The shooting was quick—"pop-pop-pop very fast," according to Cheyenne warrior Two Moon in a pictograph drawn after the battle. "The smoke was like a great cloud. Soldiers drop, and horses fall on them." Throughout the attack, one man was galloping back and forth in front of the skirmish line, drawing fire until he was blasted from the saddle. "The Sioux say this officer was the bravest man they ever fought," said Chief Red Horse in 1881.

By 4:30 in the afternoon, Custer was waging his final fight, at the northern end of Battle Ridge, where he had planted his banner. He was joined by survivors of the other battalions as Crazy Horse and his men and warriors from the various tribes closed in. A large group of cavalry soldiers broke away, running down a gulley toward the river. "We finished up this party right there in the ravine," Red Horse said later. About forty men remained on the hill, including Custer. They too were soon killed.

Exactly how Custer died is a question for the ages. Some say that Crazy Horse himself finished him off. According to various Native American accounts, he never really had a last stand but was killed in the river before his battalion made it to the hill, then was later dragged there by the army to readjust the scene. Others contend that he killed himself.

When the battle was over, Cheyenne participant Wooden Leg said that a crowd of old men and young boys rushed their ponies onto the field and began to move among the bodies. A wounded captain, dazed, raised himself on an elbow and glared wildly at the Indians. They thought he had returned from the spirit world. A Sioux warrior wrested the revolver from his weakened hand and shot him in the head. And so passed the last soldier to have fought with Custer, his identity unknown—although he's believed by many to be Captain Myles Keogh, the dashing, stouthearted warrior from Garryowen who had raced in front of the skirmish line to protect his men earlier in the day. A few years later, when Sitting Bull joined up with *Buffalo Bill's Wild West* show, one of the things he wore was a papal medal.

Like Keogh's, Custer's body was left intact, save for a stick in the ear. According to Native American accounts, he was spared because one of the women on the field was a Cheyenne who had a child conceived by Custer in the heat of his attack on Black Kettle's tribe ten years earlier. A few hours after the battle, the Indians of the Great Plains dispersed, dressed in cavalry gear. They struck their vast impromptu village that had covered miles of prairie and faded into the wilderness, followed by thousands of Indian ponies whose ranks were now swelled with army horses.

When General Terry and his battalion arrived two days later, the field was baking in the summer furnace and strewn with bodies — the dead, mutilated, and scalped bodies of men and the bodies of dead

Custer's Last Charge by Feodor Fuchs, 1876. Within minutes of the attack, the gray horse unit of the Seventh Cavalry would be decimated.

and dying mustangs. The service of the men in this battle has been recounted in many places, from every point of view, exploring at length who may have died on what ridge, how long they may have fought after suffering the first wounds, the possibility that Custer's last recorded message — "come quick — need help" — may have been improperly written down by the Italian bugler who did not speak very good English, what impetuous or self-destructive or inevitable plan of Custer's the men of the Seventh may have been following. Scraps of their clothing, their riding gear, mementos they carried into battle were long ago gathered and held on to forever by the legions of people who have swarmed across these grounds looking for answers — soldiers, widows, sons, great-granddaughters, politicians, archaeologists, students of forensics, historians, citizens who partake of the Little Bighorn like the blood of Christ on a wafer.

The service of the horses has also been recorded, but to find it, one must look deep inside the broader accounts. Mule packer Private William H. White was one of the first on the scene after the battle. While the entrance to Custer's tent was marked by Dante's famous warning, "Abandon hope, all ye who enter here," what White walked into was a modern echo of the inferno: all of Custer's men were dead — naked, gashed, and dismembered. Except for one trooper — whose last few moments of grace were found under the belly of a horse, where he died. He must have been thirsty, for he had sliced open a haunch and held his tin cup below to catch the blood. When White found him, his knife was next to his right hand and his left had stiffened around the cup. In *Son of the Morning Star,* Evan S. Connell reports another wrenching episode:

> Captain Walter Clifford of the Seventh Infantry rode up into the hills for an elevated view of Reno's defensive position and there he happened to see an Indian pony with a shattered leg — the leg swinging hideously each time the little animal moved. Flies swarmed on the wound. The pony came hobbling over and rested its head against the flank of Clifford's horse. Clifford pulled away because nothing could be done, but when he looked around he saw the pony trying to follow. He rode back and again the pony approached, "this time laying his head on my horse's rump, looking straight at me, as if pleading for help." Clifford held his pistol against the pony's head and fired. "Lightning could not have finished him sooner."

The equine carnage grew worse as men approached Custer or Last Stand Hill. On top of it, "there were 42 men and 39 dead horses," observed Lieutenant Edward S. Godfrey, who had participated in the Washita pony massacre. They were in a circle with a thirty-foot diameter, and had been used as a breastworks around Custer and his men. Colonel John Gibbon noted that there were "numerous dead horses lying along the southwestern slope ... On the very top were found four or five dead horses which were swollen, putrid, and offensive, their stiffened legs sticking straight out from the bodies. Close under the brow of the hill several horses are lying together, and by the side of one of these Custer was found."

In fact, it would appear that Custer himself was not only protected by a ring of horses before he went down, but also in death could not be separated: when found, according to one account, his left leg was extended across the grass, and his right leg stretched across a dead soldier and rested on the carcass of a horse.

Other than the fact that many of these horses once lived in the wild, what else can be gleaned from the record? In 1923, after poring over many accounts of the battle and interviewing survivors from Reno's and Benteen's companies, Walter Camp compiled his famous muster rolls in which he named and enumerated the fates of every member of every company in the Seventh who battled that day. Buried in his lists are the names of some of the horses who were shot in the jaw, the shoulder, the flank, the knee, the leg, the tail, the head, with arrows, with bullets, sometimes two or three times, in service at the Little Bighorn. There was Dandy Jim, a large gray named Badger, Silverheels, Shakespeare, the government horse Puff, Goat, an unnamed bay, a black pinto, one that was big, black, and unruly, a gray that was "one of the best buffalo horses," Blue Streak, Tip, Pete, Stumbling Bear, Old Dutch, General Custer, Phil Sheridan (after the famous general), an iron-gray mare named Molly, Steamboat ("a dilapidated horse which should have been condemned"), Wild Bill, Dick, of course Custer's horses Vic and Dandy, and all the mules with no names, burdened with ammunition, supplies, and hardtack, who had stood with the pack train lashed to wagons, unable to move as bullets and arrows hissed over and around them, and through their flesh.

The horse cavalry had become a horse Calvary, the fate of the equines sealed long ago in the moment nail was driven to hoof, brand burned to flank. But out of the carnage, as Last Rites were being said for the fallen men, along the banks of the Little Bighorn River under the shade of a cottonwood tree, there came a valiant war veteran, a horse with a big heart and a will to live. It was Comanche, his head hung low, blood oozing from his seven bullet wounds — or perhaps it was ten or even twelve, the record varies — and his saddle now upside down and hanging from his belly.

This drawing of horses killed at the Little Bighorn was part of a series made by the Minneconjou chief Red Horse in 1881 when the army asked for a pictographic account of the battle.

"Better cut his throat," someone said, for it appeared as if the horse was well beyond the point of return, and if the bullets hadn't yet killed him, his broken heart would; according to one soldier, he kept looking for someone and was disappointed when it turned out that none of them was that person. Where's my rider? Comanche seemed to say, plodding the killing fields. Later it was determined that Keogh and Comanche had been shot together. "Keogh's left leg and knee were badly shattered by a gunshot wound," observed Luce on the scene, "and Comanche had suffered a severe bone-hit, the bullet entering the right shoulder, and emerging from the left — exactly where Keogh's knee would have been. This would indicate that Keogh rode Comanche to the last" — and perhaps both horse and rider were knocked down, or perhaps Keogh was knocked out of the saddle and then killed as Comanche lingered in the brush, waiting for his captain to rally.

Custer's famous luck had run out, but really all along it was Comanche who was the lucky one, Comanche, the four-legged survivor of countless charges, and now, once again, the Fates — in the form of one man — no one knows exactly who — decided to spare Comanche. "No, don't kill him," the man said (which man, we do not know, but at least ten later claimed credit), and what happened next is also a matter of truth-inflected myth. Some say he was given a drink of water, others say that a doctor "sacrificed the larger part of a bottle of Hennessy" to make a mash and poured it into a hat, from which Comanche took a mighty swig, thereby beginning a taste for the hard stuff that would last for the rest of his life.

From that point on, the various stories are in general agreement: his wounds were dressed, probably with a zinc wash, and he was led for many hours across the fifteen or sixteen miles to the *Far West* at the confluence of the Little Horn and Bighorn rivers, joining a caravan of wounded men carried on stretchers by mules and horses. On board the steamer, an area in the stern between the rudders was turned into a stall for Comanche — the men bedded it with prairie grass, and "his care and welfare became the special duty of the whole boat's company," according to Captain Luce. The *Far West* made the 950-mile journey up the Bighorn River, down the Yellowstone, and then down the Missouri to Bismarck in the Dakota Territory in the record-breaking time of fifty-four hours, and then, wrote Luce, "the badly wounded animal was tenderly conveyed by wagon to Fort Lincoln, the same garrison which it had left only eight weeks before."

It was almost July 4 in the year of the country's centennial. As word of the Custer disaster filtered back east, the celebrations began to take on a somber tone. But the country found hope in Comanche, who was almost literally hanging by a thread — a bellyband sling, actually, where he would remain for nearly a year. He was assigned three personal attendants — the Fort Lincoln veterinarian Dr. C. A. Stein, the blacksmith Gustave Korn, and Custer's orderly John Burkman. By 1878, he was able to move freely, and Colonel Samuel D. Sturgis decreed that Comanche was the second commanding officer at the fort, after him. On April 10 of that year, he issued General Orders No. 7, believed to be the only such order ever issued by the cavalry. It stated that Comanche was "the only living representative of the bloody tragedy of the Little Bighorn" battle and that, "though wounded and scarred, his very silence speaks in terms more eloquent than words of the desperate against overwhelming odds." From that day on, he was to be kept in a comfortable stall, never to work or be ridden under any circumstances. His only assignment was to appear in parades.

Various survivors of the Little Bighorn had lost their minds; by the time Comanche's sling was removed, he was a drunk: he had been given a whiskey bran mash like the one he got when he was found on the field every other day for his one-year convalescent period. Free to roam at will, he became a regular at the enlisted men's canteen, where men treated him on paydays to buckets of beer. When the men were short on cash, he would head over to the officers' lines and beg for sugar lumps. "If these were not sufficient to satisfy his peculiar tastes, he would visit the company garbage cans, kick them over and select what articles of food he craved, and then return to his stall for a quiet night's rest," wrote Luce.

When it was nice out, Comanche would wander around the post, sometimes roll around in a wallow, and then come in for stable call covered with mud. "Often," reported a major at the fort, "he would be covered from nuzzle to ears with coffee grounds and other garbage which he would get from searching company garbage cans." He loved tramping across lawns and browsing in flower gardens, and he especially liked sunflowers. On summer evenings when the regimental band performed a concert, he would nibble grass around the bandstand, and he would often answer the bugler's call, taking his former position at the head of his old troop and going through the various drills as though Captain Keogh were leading him.

On June 25 of every year, the regiment remembered the Battle of the Little Bighorn. Comanche would lead Troop I, dressed in a black mourning net with saddle and riding boots reversed, in honor of the fallen troopers and his rider, the man who had picked him out of the herd of mustangs that day in the corrals of St. Louis.

Although Comanche was never ridden again, he seemed to find a new friend in Gustave Korn. Wherever the blacksmith went, so did Comanche, following him all over the garrison, and when he could not find him, he would trot down the Junction City road, Luce said, "to a certain house where Korn's lady friend lived and neigh his presence until his attendant would appear and lead him back to the post." In 1890, after Korn's transfer to Fort Riley in Kansas, Comanche accompanied Korn to Wounded Knee as part of the pack train. Korn was killed, along with scores of Indians in the terrible episode that put out the last flame of Native American hope.

Crazy Horse had been murdered in 1877, shortly after a trip to his old stomping grounds, where he had fasted and ridden to the top of Beaver Mountain on his war pony and then decided to surrender. Weeks before he embarked on the sad mounted procession to Fort Robinson, he ordered his men to shoot ponies that belonged to several families that had left camp and were heading for the Red Cloud Agency. "The whole sad business must have caused Crazy Horse great pain," Stephen Ambrose wrote in *Crazy Horse and Custer*. Perhaps he believed that the families would have been shot once they surrendered. Or perhaps it was the only way to prevent his weary band from coming apart in the dead of winter with nowhere to go but the reservation. As always, it was the horses that suffered. Most of the four-leggeds belonging to the Horse Nations had already been seized and sold at frontier markets; later, the tribes filed a series of pony claims that were paid out in World War II for a paltry sum.

As Crazy Horse and his band approached the agency, the Lakota warriors who had already surrendered greeted him with songs of peace. The Cheyenne White Hat told him to relinquish the rest of the horses. He dismounted and gave his yellow pinto to a soldier. Then he entered the fort, where a few days later he was stabbed in the back and died in the arms of his father. But his spirit lived on, and dwindling numbers of various tribes remained on land that hadn't been appropriated, hiding from the army in the dead of winter with little food, supplies, or protection until they were sacked and killed at Wounded Knee.

Comanche may have viewed the attack from a distance, may have once again heard the cries of people and horses, may even have seen Korn, his companion of fourteen years, go down. When he returned to Fort Riley in early 1891, he had lost interest in life. He just "didn't care," observed one of his longtime caretakers. He made more frequent trips to the garbage cans and visited the canteen so often that he became known as a panhandler. After these panhandling sprees, he would lie in his stall or mud wallows for hours. By June of that year, First Lieutenant Henry J. Nowlan, who had been among those who found Comanche in the greasy grass, said, "I fear the famous horse will not last much longer." Farrier Samuel J. Winchester had vowed to take care of him until the end, and finally, on November 6, 1891, Comanche died, at the age of twenty-nine. Winchester and Comanche appear to have had a variation of the conversation of death described by Lopez, as recounted by the blacksmith in this brief summary:

> Fort Riley, Kansas, Nov. 7, 1891 — in memory of the old veteran horse who died at 1:30 o'clock with the colic in his stall while I had my hand on his pulse and looking him in the eye — this night long to be remembered.

In 2004, on the 129th anniversary of the Battle of the Little Bighorn, I headed to the battlefield — a national monument since 1946 — for the annual commemorations. As I was traveling east out of Billings along Route 90, one of the first things I noticed was a feedlot filled with cows and horses near a big stadium advertising the next livestock auction. Some of the horses were probably spent rodeo mustangs en route to the slaughterhouse and others could have been waiting to be picked up for service on the range. Soon, mighty rivers of equine history began to thunder past on all sides.

To the south, in the mountains, there was the Pryor Mountain Wild Horse Range, where a small herd of direct descendants of horses brought by the Spanish still roams. To the north was the Lewis and Clark Trail, where the explorers purchased horses from the Shoshone Indians so they could cross the Bitterroot Mountains. To the west, there was the Nez Perce National Historic Trail. Along this path in 1877, Chief Joseph, Chief Looking Glass, Chief White Bird, Chief Ollokot, Chief Lean Elk, and others led nearly 750 men, women, and children and twice that many horses over 1,170 miles across Nez Perce homelands as they fled the U.S. Army. Many of the Indians and their animals perished.

When Chief Joseph surrendered, the surviving horses were confiscated, and the Indians were herded into cattle cars and shipped to a reservation. Chief Joseph was confined to a small parcel of land near the Columbia River. An army lieutenant sent his son to stay with the chief. When the sojourn was over, the lieutenant told his son to ask Joseph what he would like as a gift. "A horse," he said. But the boy did not think the request significant and he did not pass it on. Chief Joseph died in 1904, and a hundred years later, the Nez Perce resumed breeding their famous Appaloosas. Today you can see them running on their reservation.

After a long stretch of interstate heading straight into big Montana sky, I turned off on the 212, a two-lane blacktop, and found myself mired in the present, a long line of cars, Harleys, SUVs, RVs, pickup trucks, and tour buses packed with people from Japan, France, and Germany inching toward the battlefield. It was an hour or so past dawn, and I parked and followed the park service map to the Indian memorial where the first of the day's ceremonies was about to begin. There would be much to mark over the next two days — the park had several events planned, the nearby town of Hardin had a Chamber of Commerce–sponsored reenactment of the battle (not endorsed by any of the tribes because of its emphasis on the cavalry), and the Crow (who fought with Custer) had their own reenactment on the reservation (playing all the Indian parts, including Sioux and Cheyenne; because of the ongoing rivalry with the Sioux and Cheyenne over the sides each tribe took in the battle, the Sioux and Cheyenne will not participate in the Crow reenactment). But such blood feuds were not my concern; mainly, I was there to pay tribute to Comanche and to visit the park's little-known horse cemetery.

On the way into the battlefield, there was a long line of Indians on war ponies. They were in breechcloths and some wore feathered war bonnets and were barefoot. They rode bareback, and their beautiful compact ponies were painted with symbols — one had red circles around the eyes and nostrils for vision and sense of smell; another had a pair of red thunder stripes on the forelegs to please the god of war; there was one with a downward-facing fire arrow indicating trouble for the enemy; a bay mare had a pair of white hoof prints, meaning that two horses had been captured in a raid; and a sleek black pony had a blue left hand drawn on his right hip — because he had brought his rider home unharmed from a dangerous mission.

The Native American memorial — or circle of unity, as it's called — was a large sunken circle with a weeping wall of stone ringing two-thirds of its circumference, lined with plaques honoring the Indians who fought Custer. Along an outer perimeter, there was an iron-cable sculpture of Indian warriors on galloping horses; you can look through it, across the battlefield and all the way to the horizon. A visitor had tied some ceremonial feathers to the sculpture, adding to the scarves and strings of beads and small American flags that rippled in the stiff prairie breeze. A cloud of dust rose from the south, and the Indians on their ponies raced across the field, shouting war cries. They had been traveling for ten days, leaving from reservations in South Dakota, making their way to the canyon where Crazy Horse had carved a petroglyph on his way to the battlefield, and then resuming their ceremonial ride.

Just outside the circle, they stopped, forming a line of horses that separated now from then. As they stood in for their ancestors, a pow-wow circle came together inside the shrine, and Sioux and Cheyenne tribesmen beat their drums and sang songs of war, and native warriors across several generations stepped into the circle and surrounded the men pounding their drums. There were veterans of World War II, the Korean War, the war in Vietnam, the Gulf War, all dressed in their

army fatigues or Marine finest, and wearing war bonnets or feathers in their military caps — fighters all, men and women whose ancestors fought for the Horse Nations and who themselves fought in
twentieth- and twenty-first-century wars for the nation that had conquered them.

With the war ponies flanking the memorial circle, the sun rising
higher in the east, and the powwow drummers and singers chanting
for the ages, two Indians joined the circle, and the drums and singing stopped. One of them was Donnie Red Thunder, a former Navy
SEAL and great-great-grandson of Crazy Horse. He had traveled the
365 miles from the Cheyenne River camp in South Dakota on horseback. "We're the only country that can say they defeated the United
States," he said, referring to the Little Bighorn. "Indians."

Across the way, near the cavalry cemetery, there was a burial in
progress. It was for an unknown soldier whose bones had recently
been discovered. There are always discoveries of bones on the Great
Plains, from dinosaurs in the Badlands to prehistoric horses in Wyoming to cavalry soldiers in riverbeds and gullies. This particular
soldier was said to have been killed at the Fetterman incident, a surprise Indian rout of an army troop that was a prelude to the Little
Bighorn. As the sad notes of taps sounded across the killing field, another cloud of dust rose in the distance. There were more ponies approaching, also gaily decorated, their manes and tails braided with
beads and feathers. Now, they carried members of the northern
Cheyenne reservation in Wyoming, who had also been traveling for
days. The ponies slowed to a canter and then a walk, and the warriors joined the Lakota at the prayer circle.

Later that day some park rangers mentioned in passing that the
bones of a horse had also recently been discovered, right here in the
park. What else was known about the horse? I inquired. Nothing else
so far, I was told. There would be no ceremony marking the burial of
the unknown horse, and in fact, it was not known if he or she would
ever be buried under the small horse tombstone that marked the
horse cemetery in the park.

The horse cemetery is about halfway between the Indian memorial, finally installed in 2003, and Last Stand Hill, with its huge tombstone, erected three years after the battle. It's shown on the park map,

but on foot was easy to miss because the stone that marked it was small, perhaps a couple of feet high. It said:

> 7th CAVALRY
> HORSE CEMETERY
>
> In memory of
> 7th Cavalry horses
> Killed during
> Custer's last stand
> June 25, 1876
> And later buried here
> In July 1881
> Under supervision of
> Lt. Charles F. Roe
> Of the 2nd Cavalry

This stone was placed in 2002, after a long controversy involving the question of whether it would impede wheelchair access between the Indian memorial and Last Stand Hill. Also, Native Americans were concerned that if there was a well-marked horse graveyard in the park, more people would visit it than their own memorial, for which they had waited so long. In fact, people had lost track of the horse grave until 1941. "While digging an excavation, the East End of the wooden trench or 'horse cemetery' on Custer Hill was encountered," wrote Edward S. Luce, then the park superintendent. "The wooden end of the trench gave way and about ten horse skeletons fell out. Among these bones were human bones. They were the leg and arm bones, but no skulls. There was also a pair of cavalry trooper's boots with a few toe bones inside. The tin cracker boxes: 'C.L. Woodman & Co, Chicago,' with bullet holes through the tin were found. These at one time contained 'hardtack' and were used for protection as breastworks during the fight on Custer Hill, at the time when General Custer ordered all the horses shot to form protection."

When the horse cemetery was found, park administrators began a search through the records to find out how it got there. They knew from a famous photograph taken on Custer Hill in 1877 and another one taken in 1879 that there were huge mounds of horse bones all over the knoll. Further investigation revealed that in 1879, the remains of the cavalry horses were collected and placed inside a temporary monument on Last Stand Hill, very near where Custer's body had been found. As Captain G. K. Sanderson, Eleventh Infantry, wrote at the time:

> I built a mound ... out of cordwood, filled in the center of the mound with all the horse bones I could find on the field ... This grave was then built up with wood for four feet above ground, well covered, and the mound built over and around it ... Newspaper reports to the effect that bodies still lay exposed are sensational ... I believe the large number of horse bones lying over the field have given rise to some of such statements, and to prevent any such statements being made in the future, I had all the horse bones gathered together and placed in the mound where they can not be readily disturbed by curiosity seekers.

In July 1881, the cordwood horse monument was dismantled and a massive thirty-six-thousand-pound granite memorial was erected at the same place, in honor of Custer and the soldiers who had died in the battle. The animal bones were probably re-interred just to the northeast of the monument, according to the Friends of the Little Bighorn, whose members devote much of their lives to poring over and analyzing all manner of battle history and details. Further excavation had been planned, but then was scuttled because of World War I and then II, and it was not until a few years ago that it resumed.

I sat with the horse spirits for a while, as the music of the commemoration floated by — drumming and singing from the Indian shrine and from elsewhere, bugle calls demonstrated by a ranger. After a time, I began a long walk to an incline on the field where Myles Keogh's body had been found. "Stay on the path," a ranger had told me. "Watch for snakes." I walked a bit along the paved path, and then, spotting a crop of marble slabs, stepped off into the prairie grass and sage and made my way toward Battle Ridge. Every battle, especially this one, has its scholars and devotees, and one of them was sitting among the stones, drawing pictures. "I've been coming here for twenty years," he said. "For the memorial?" I asked. "No, all the time. I can't stay away."

I asked him what he knew about the cavalry horses. "See that place over there?" he said, pointing to a depression in the grasses. "That's Horseholder's Ravine. It's where the soldiers would hold the horses while three or four of the men would dismount and fight on foot." I walked into the ravine and imagined the scene when the grass was three feet high and touched the underside of a horse's belly and then asked him if he could point me to Keogh's marker. "Oh, yes," he said, indicating the stone. "Watch for snakes. Let me know if you need some drawings. I'm working on Comanche."

Not too far away from the captain's stone, some cavalry reenacters had set up a period camp, living just the way the Seventh had 129 years earlier, dressed in the garb of the time, each according to rank, covered in dust to simulate days of marching, and feeding their horses from bags strapped around their noses, just like in the old days. Some had trucked in their horses from points east, west, north, and south—wherever they lived—to the battlefield. Others borrowed horses every year from the Crow. "Where's the guy who plays Captain Myles Keogh?" I asked some men who were bivouacked with their horses along the banks of the Little Bighorn. "Is he here this year?" one said. "I haven't seen him." "I just saw him," said another. "I think he's over there with a film crew from Germany."

I headed deeper into the encampment and kept asking. A guy dressed as an orderly directed me toward a tent. "Hello?" I called out. "Captain Keogh?" Out came junior high school history teacher Bill Rino, dressed just like all the pictures of the cavalry captain. He didn't really look anything like Keogh though—he was short and Italian. He had been coming all the way from Queens every year since 1995. Like many reenacters, he was very certain about what happened that day. "Actually, there were four last stands," he said. "Custer's, Keogh's, Weir's, and Calhoun's. Once Reno ran, Custer was in trouble. Did you know Custer's bugler is buried in Queens?" Of course, I asked him about Comanche. "Comanche was identified by Keogh's best friend, Lieutenant Nowlan. He was shot ten times, not seven. Probably by Crazy Horse. By the way, do you know how horses gave the Indians an advantage? When they surprised Custer in the morning, they ran their horses up and down the perimeter to make a dust cloud. The cavalry couldn't see where to shoot. And one more thing. Captain Keogh did not die while crouching under Comanche between his forelegs and getting off a few final shots. He was definitely shot out of the saddle. You can tell from the wound in his knee."

The bugler sounded dinner, but before Captain Keogh disappeared, I took his picture. The horse playing Comanche had been taken back to the rez by the Crow, so it was a solo shot of Bill standing near the river. It was dusk, and as the sun set in the west, he straightened out his buckskin shirt, stood erect in his cavalry boots, and his chest swelled. With his body stretched to the sky and his eyes looking off to the future, behind him the Crow ran some ponies through the Little Bighorn River.

The next day, I attended a press conference at the Custer Battlefield Museum in the town of Garryowen, where the first skirmish of the battle took place. Outside the museum, a recording of "Garryowen" played, sung by a piercing high-pitched Celtic voice, the very siren that had lured many across the prairie to their doom. Inside, Joe Medicine Crow, ninety-seven, the grandson of Custer scout White Man Runs Him, consultant to the 1941 Errol Flynn movie about Custer, *They Died with Their Boots On,* was talking story. Alas, not many were there — some members of the European press, a few academic types, a couple of local reporters. The Crow elder wore a full war bonnet, jeans, a denim shirt, and cowboy boots. He spoke of how the Crow got horses — it was before the white man found the tribe. "Intertribal warfare started over horses," he said. "The horses reached the Crow in 1730." As with all the Horse Nations, the Crow quickly partnered with the horse, and today they have one of the country's premier annual rodeos.

Earlier that day they had presented one of the finest horse spectacles I've ever seen, their grand reenactment of frontier history from the arrival of the four-legged to the Little Bighorn battle. It began with the national anthem, then the Crow anthem, and then there was a prayer in Crow. A horse whinnied as the prayer finished — perhaps on cue, perhaps not — and then the Crow narrator told a joke: "Custer and his brother Tom are on the battlefield. Tom says, 'I've got some good news and some bad news.' George says, 'What's the bad news?' Tom says, 'We're gonna die here.' George says, 'What's

the good news?' Tom: 'We don't have to go back to North Dakota.'"
And then the panorama unfolded, accompanied by dancing, decorated ponies, and corresponding commentary: "You won't hear this
at the other reenactments, but when Custer and his troops came
down the Little Bighorn River, he was captured by the Cheyenne and
they cut out his heart. That's the way Spotted Wolf tells it."

At his press conference, Medicine Crow picked up the story of
the Crow after Custer, when the Indians had been vanquished and
stashed away on reservations. The Crow — with the largest reservation in the country — were allowed to keep their horses. "By 1920,"
he said, "Crows had thousands of them. In 1922, non-Indian cattle
ranchers started to complain about Indian ponies eating their grass.
So the government ordered the killing of all the horses, with a bounty
per horse. After a while, local cowboys got disgusted and a contrac-
tor was brought in from Texas to do the job. That summer, you could
smell the dead ponies everywhere." By the time it was over, the government said that 45,000 horses had been killed. "But really," said
Medicine Crow, "it was worse."

The army will tell you how much it loved its warhorses. Souvenir
hunters cut the hooves from Custer's horse Vic when they found him
dead in the greasy grass. The hooves were made into inkstands and
sold back east. No one knows where they are now. When Comanche died, he was sent to a taxidermist at the University of Kansas to
be stuffed and mounted. In 1893, he was sent to the Chicago World's
Fair and displayed, not along the rotunda with other living participants of the Little Bighorn such as Chief Rain-in-the-Face (billed as
"A Professional Scalper") or Sitting Bull (who appeared across the
way with *Buffalo Bill's Wild West Spectacle*), but in the Kansas State
building, with stuffed wildlife from the Great Plains — one of the
fair's most popular exhibits.

When the fair was over, Comanche should have been returned to
Fort Riley. But the army had never paid the taxidermist's four-hun-
dred-dollar bill, so he was returned to the natural history museum at
the University of Kansas, where he was placed in a glass case on the
main floor. In death, as in life, he has gone on many a march and has
also had several close calls. "Comanche Moved Today," announced a
Kansas newspaper in 1934. "This morning, workmen took him from

his cage, placed him on a truck, and drove carefully across the campus to a temporary resting place under the floor of the auditorium until the Dyche Museum can be built. Few of the students arriving for their eight thirties even turned to look. It was just a stuffed horse on a truck."

Comanche stayed in that basement until 1941, when the museum was reopened, and after being treated for mildew, he was returned to the most prestigious spot in the museum, just inside the front door. In 1947, Fort Riley mounted a nationwide campaign to have Comanche returned to them, and then the town of Deadwood made the same request, as did Miles City, Montana — named after Colonel Nelson A. Miles, who "completed the task" of defeating the Sioux and Cheyenne — making a case that Comanche should be displayed at its Range Riders Museum. Locals in Lawrence, Kansas, mounted a vigorous countercharge against the appeal from the now-mechanized Fort Riley, and the controversy grew so heated that Robert E. Haggard wrote a poem called "Comanche," published in the *New York Herald Tribune* in 1948:

> His was the day of fair-haired reckless Custer
> Of Sitting Bull and wild Rain-in-the-Face
> Of yelping Sioux and troopers quick to muster
> For fun or fight, and these were out of place
> Where no fast horses were, nor bugle peals . . .
> What tie has he with cavalry on wheels?

Requests to house and exhibit Comanche continued for the next thirty years, until, like most obsessions and crusades, they ran out of steam. But the horse was besieged in other ways: even when he was alive, people would pluck his hair, and over the years, while on display, he was nearly stripped of mane and tail. In 1936, a museum employee confessed that "since his death, Comanche has had seven tails," all of which came from other defunct horses. A few years ago, a pipe burst while Comanche was being refurbished in the basement, and his coat was reportedly blow-dried in order to get him ready for a conference of the Friends of the Little Bighorn, who were scheduled to spend time with him the following day.

Today, Comanche resides in a glass case in his own room on the fourth floor of the museum, next to the panorama of North American mammals. He has a cult following among military history buffs, and people drive for hundreds of miles to see him. In an age when many claim to whisper to horses, perhaps it's time to hear from Comanche himself, the great silent witness who is whispering back, across the centuries and through his transparent walls where treasure hunters can no longer take relics from the mane and tail that once flew in the wind of the Great Plains and, before that, on the Great Horse Desert, where the call to boots and saddles was never heard. Can I have a beer? he's saying. Anyone got a drink?

PART II

CENTER STAGE

5

All Roads Lead to Buffalo Bill

I N 1887, ABOUT 350 YEARS after the horses had come home, they crossed the Atlantic once again, sailing out of New York Harbor as excited crowds looked on and a cowboy band played "The Girl I Left Behind Me"—a tune that some of the horses who were cavalry veterans may have recognized. But they were not heading off to war this time. They were going back to the Old World, to reenact scenes from a war they had helped to win. They were part of *Buffalo Bill's Wild West* show, nearly two hundred of them, along with eighteen buffalo, various mules, elk, Texas steers, donkeys, and deer, as well as Buffalo Bill himself, Annie Oakley, King of the Cowboys Buck Taylor, and nearly a hundred Lakota men, women, and children. The passage, although rough, was not as difficult as those that the horses of the conquest had endured. The three- and four-masted sailing ships of the sixteenth century had been replaced by ships that were powered by wind and steam. There was no danger of a vessel becoming becalmed and the crew having to jettison living cargo in order to lighten the load; now the horses stood a much better chance of surviving ocean crossings.

Still, even the great horseman Buffalo Bill had not fully figured the needs of the equine stars of his show on this, his first sojourn overseas. Below decks, the ventilation was poor, and the horses—the wind-drinkers, as Native Americans called them — had trouble breathing. In a last-ditch effort to save them, the crew of the *State of Nebraska* cut holes through the timber hull. Imagine the moment as their nostrils flared and the first life-saving streams of air filled their starving lungs; although replenished, the horses' instinct would have been to flee, as the information they received, the scent, would have been one of no land, no grasses on which to feed. Of course, their escape route was blocked, and so they remained, breathing somewhat easier now, but still frightened. Several buffalo and elk did not survive the crossing and were thrown overboard. Some of the human passengers did not fare well either, at least in the beginning of the voyage. As Buffalo Bill wrote in his memoir:

> On the day following our departure from New York the Indians began to grow weary and their stomachs, like my own, became both treacherous and rebellious. Their fears were now so greatly intensified that even Red Shirt, the bravest of his people, looked anxiously towards the hereafter, and began to feel his flesh to see if it were really diminishing. The seal of hopelessness stamped upon the faces of the Indians aroused my pity, and though sick as a cow with hollow-horn myself, I used my utmost endeavors to cheer them up and relieve their forebodings. But for two days nearly the whole company was too sick for any other active service than feeding the fishes, in which I am not proud to say that I performed more than an ordinary share. On the third day, however, we all began to mend so far that I called the Indians together in the main saloon and gave them a Sunday address, as did also Red Shirt, who was now recovered from his anxiety about the future. After the third day at sea we had an entertainment every afternoon ... On the seventh day a storm came up that raged so fiercely that for a time the ship had to lay to, and during which our stock suffered greatly, but we gave them such good care, and had such excellent luck as well, that none of our animals, save one horse, died on the trip.

Another horse, nineteen-year-old Charlie, a favorite of Buffalo Bill's, was about to put on his last show. And Cody himself was about to unfurl the glory of his upstart country before an astonished motherland, becoming the first of that strange American offering: the superstar.

Like America, Buffalo Bill is a riddle inside an enigma wrapped in a saddle blanket. Every American worth his or her birthright has heard the story of this fearless horseman — he of the flowing white mane, the daring maneuver from the saddle in which he took aim with his Winchester and blazed into vast herds of buffalo to carry out his massive kills. To this day, the tall tales about his life endure — he scalped the Indian Yellow Hair to avenge Custer, just hours after the massacre! He was the best Pony Express rider ever, tearing through Indian territory and dodging arrows all the way! He was the only *wasichu* the Lakota respected!

But more importantly — and more accurately — he was a one-man frontier trinity. In Buffalo Bill the three totems of American wilderness came together and now live together forever — man, buffalo, and horse. Viewed through this kaleidoscope, the tales fade and a truth appears: Buffalo Bill was one of the greatest equestrians the world has ever known, often referred to during his time as the Peerless Prince of Horsemen, the show-biz answer to Charles V's Prince of Light Cavalrymen. Of course, he owed it all to the animals that carried him — and unlike many celebrated horsemen before him, he happily shared the spotlight with his horses and considered them his partners.

According to his own documents and the accounts of others, there were twenty-two that were a significant part of his life; unlike his friend Custer, for example, who boasted about having had horses shot out from under him, Buffalo Bill had a deep kinship with the animals he rode — although, strangely, he had no such feelings for the mighty buffalo from whom he derived his claim to fame. But like Custer, Buffalo Bill was born to ride. And as we shall see, in the act of being a horseman, of bringing wild horses back to Europe, he did something far greater than simply entertain his contemporaries on both sides of the pond; he ensured that some part of the American West would be preserved far into the future, even as Americans themselves continued to destroy it.

And what of the horses? A hard-working parade of wonderful steeds carried Buffalo Bill to glory, displaying the very essence of freedom as they crisscrossed the United States and then England and Europe, performing in marvelous spectacles that portrayed the national scriptures. During their time, some of them were famous throughout the world. Like other horses central to the American story, these animals and their hoof prints have nearly disappeared from the record. Now we will dust off the trail, travel back in time, and meet them on their paths.

William Frederick "Buffalo Bill" Cody was born near LeClaire, Iowa, on February 26, 1846. Horses were part of his life, as they were for many in his time. His father, Isaac Cody, managed large farms for absentee owners and ran a stagecoach business between Davenport and Chicago. With his six siblings, Cody would stand on the riverbank and watch his father's horse-drawn coach pass by — perhaps an early seed for a scene he would later re-create in a much more dramatic fashion. "It was at LeClair that I acquired my first experience as an equestrian," Cody later wrote. "Somehow or other I had managed to corner a horse near a fence, and had climbed on his back. The next moment the horse got his back up and hoisted me into the air. I fell violently to the ground, striking upon my side in such a way as to severely wrench and strain my arm, from the effects of which I did not recover for some time. I abandoned the art of horsemanship for a while." But of course that was a joke — a year later his father let Bill ride one of his horses.

In 1853, his oldest brother, Sam, who was twelve, was killed by a bucking mare. In 1854, the family moved to the Kansas Territory, taken by their six horses — four pulling a wagon filled with the family's goods and two pulling the stage that carried the family. A relative named Horace Billings continued Cody's education in things equestrian, teaching him to ride a small, fast horse named Little Gray that the family had purchased along the way. "I made rapid advances in the art of horsemanship," Cody later wrote. It was a skill the young man immediately put to good use. When the Codys arrived in Kansas, the territory was roiling with the question of slavery. Like many new settlers, Isaac Cody was against it — and spoke out. He incurred the wrath of ferocious pro-slavery neighbors in Missouri. "One night," recalled Buffalo Bill, "a body of armed men, mounted on horses, rode up to our house and surrounded it." His father — who months earlier had been attacked with a knife for his views — escaped by dressing in his wife's clothes and making his way through a pack of mounted vigilantes, then hiding in a cornfield. Later, gangs from Missouri torched the Codys' hay field and stole their horses, including Prince, a sorrel horse that Billings had helped Bill train when he was nine. "The loss of my faithful pony nearly broke my heart and bankrupted me in business, as I had nothing to ride," he said later.

Soon, with John Brown and his abolitionists carrying out their infamous raid, Isaac Cody's house became a site of Free Kansas rallies, and Isaac won a seat in the Topeka legislature. His enemies continued to threaten his life, and there were periodic raids on the Cody property. One night as ten-year-old Bill lay in bed with the flu, his mother roused him and told him of a plot to kill his father. "The boy arose and clambered onto a horse," Louis Warren reports in *Buffalo Bill's America;* Cody carried a letter about the plot to Isaac, who was several hours away in the town of Grasshopper Falls. After riding eight miles, Bill realized he was being followed. "The boy put his heels to his horse, and for nine more miles the men chased the sick and terrified child," Warren recounts. "He finally reined up at the home of a family friend ... the would-be assassins turned and fled ... The animal was covered in lather, and flecked with the boy's vomit." Both boy and horse rested that night and delivered the message the next day.

It was an experience that certainly prepared Cody for his brief and notorious career with the Pony Express — one of the key elements of the showman's official biography, as well as of the show itself. Various investigators of Buffalo Bill's life have suggested that the Pony Express part of his story is a lie. I disagree. But his accounts have the ring of truth, unlike some of the more florid tales, and being a Pony Express rider was certainly a likely vocation for someone with Cody's background. His father died when he was ten, and Cody immediately went to work herding cattle with a small mule for a mount. He quickly became a wagon master, and by the age of fourteen, he was a highly skilled equestrian. He signed on as a Pony Express rider ("orphans preferred"), and later claimed that he made a 322-mile ride — the third longest in the history of the mail service. The longest ride was 384 miles and was made by Bob Haslam, whom Buffalo Bill would later hire for his *Wild West* show. "The second longest, 330 miles, was made by one Howard Eagan," writes Larry McMurtry in *The Colonel and Little Missie.* "Buffalo Bill's ride took twenty-two hours and was accomplished with the help of twenty-one horses, which suggests that he got about an hour's hard work out of each horse." Cody often spoke of his mounts, and in his memoirs, he recounted the following episode:

> One day, when I had nothing else to do, I saddled up an extra Pony Express horse, and arming myself with a good rifle and a pair of revolvers, struck out for the foothills of Laramie Peak for a bear hunt. Riding carelessly along, and breathing the cool and bracing autumn air which came down from the mountains, I felt as only a man can feel who is roaming over the prairies of the far West, well armed and mounted on a fleet and gallant steed. The perfect freedom he enjoys is in itself a refreshing stimulant to the mind as well as the body. Such indeed were my feelings on this beautiful day, as I rode up the valley of the Horseshoe.

There's always a point, or several, at which a person passes from merely human to legend. Certainly, for William Cody, acquiring the name Buffalo Bill was key. But of course, first he had to do the thing that got him the name. After his career with the Pony Express, Cody was chief of army scouts for the Fifth Cavalry, "mastering the accomplishment of riding bareback and leaping off and on his horse while the animal was galloping at full speed," reports Agnes Wright Spring in *Buffalo Bill and His Horses.* In 1866, he met the woman he would marry, Louisa Frederici, through a runaway horse. "More than once," wrote his sister Helen Wetmore, "while out for a morning canter, Will had remarked a young woman of attractive face and figure, who sat her horse with the grace of Diana Vernon . . . He desired to establish an acquaintance with the young lady, but as none of his friends knew her, he found it impossible. At length, a chance came. Her bridle-rein broke one morning; there was a runaway, a rescue, and then acquaintance was easy."

Now came a new form of employment — the railroad was coming through, and in 1867, he began hunting buffalo to feed construction crews who were building the Kansas Pacific. Of course, he couldn't have done it without a horse, and the one he rode during this time was named Brigham, after the Mormon leader Brigham Young, and purchased from a Ute Indian. Cody often said Brigham was the best horse he ever had for chasing buffalo, referring to him as "King Buffalo Killer." Riding Brigham, he wiped out buffalo by the hundreds. Eighteen months later, he boasted that he had killed 4,280 buffalo; around this time, people started calling him Buffalo Bill. On January 11, 1868, the *Leavenworth Daily Conservative* reported that "Bill Cody and Brigham started on a hunt Saturday afternoon, and came in Tuesday. The result was nineteen buffalo. Bill brought in over four thousand pounds of meat, which he sold for seven cents per pound, making about $100 per day for his time out."

Around the same time, a prolific hunter named William Comstock was also referred to as Buffalo Bill. To determine "the owner" of the name, they had a contest to see who could kill more buffalo. Here is how Buffalo Bill himself described the grim dance of death and the role of Brigham:

> Comstock and I dashed into the herd, followed by the referees. The buffaloes separated; Comstock took the left bunch and I the right. My great forte in killing buffaloes from horseback was to get them circling by riding my horse at the head of the herd, shooting the leaders, thus crowding their followers to the left, till they would finally circle round and round. On this morning the buffaloes were very accommodating, and I soon had them running in a beautiful circle, when I dropped the thick and fast, until I had killed thirty-eight; which finished my run. Comstock began shooting at the rear of the herd, which he was chasing, and they kept straight on. He succeeded, however, in killing twenty-three, while mine lay close together. I had "nursed" my buffaloes, as a billiard player does the balls when he makes a big run.

After eight hours of shooting, Cody won — 69 to 46. Then, he removed Brigham's saddle and bridle and rode bareback into the herd. "Shooting from the horse's back with his needle-gun," reports Warren, "a breech-loading 50-caliber Springfield, which he called 'Lucretia Borgia,' Bill Cody killed an additional 13 animals." Unto us, a superstar was born. But soon Buffalo Bill was jobless. The Kansas Pacific suspended work, so his most valuable possession had to go: he raffled off Brigham, who spent the rest of his life on the speed-and-endurance contest circuit. In 1868, Buffalo Bill resumed his scouting duties for the army and soon met the writer Ned Buntline, who was trolling the West for material.

Although Buffalo Bill had invented himself, it was Ned Buntline, another adventurer with a flair for promotion, who took Cody's career to the next level. Buntline was born in 1823 in upstate New York. His father was a writer. He ran away from home as a young teenager and fought in the Seminole wars; then he returned to the East Coast, where he picked up the pen and began spinning tales. In 1845, he launched *Ned Buntline's Own,* a magazine that published his sensational stories about pirates, outlaws, and frontier romance. In 1846, he was lynched for murder, but he was cut down while still alive. The incident fueled his own notoriety, and he went on to write hundreds of short novels, forerunners to the era's popular dime novels about the Wild West. When he journeyed west and met Buffalo Bill, the pair of self-promoters formed a natural partnership. Buntline returned to New York and penned the serial *Buffalo Bill, the King of Border Men* for *New York Weekly.*

Cody was every writer's dream — a true-life megacharacter whose story could be magnified, recast, and cashed in. He soon joined other frontier characters such as Daniel Boone, Davy Crockett, and Deadwood Dick and became one of the country's most popular figures as epic tales of buffalo massacres and battles with Indians captured the fancy of both high- and lowbrow readers across the land. Capitalizing on the series' popularity, Buntline went on to write *The Scouts of the Plains,* a play that opened on Broadway in 1872. It starred Buntline and famous scout Texas Jack Omohundro as themselves. It also featured Buffalo Bill, who periodically dropped in to play himself, literally "just in from the Indian wars." The critics loved him, and he appeared in the play for eleven seasons.

For the next few years, he continued his work as a scout, riding an Indian pony that he named Buckskin Joe. Although Brigham was the horse who had helped Cody blaze his way to nickname status, in a curious way, it was Buckskin Joe who figured most prominently in the rapidly expanding Buffalo Bill myth. Bill had first spotted the horse when he was hunting on the plains. "Presently a Pawnee shot by me like an arrow," he wrote in 1879, after Buckskin Joe had died, "and I could not help admiring the horse that he was riding. Seeing that he possessed rare running qualities, I determined if possible to get possession of the animal in some way. It was a large buckskin or yellow horse, and I took a careful view of him so that I would know

him when I returned to camp." Soon afterward, he traded his govern-
ment-issue horse and some gifts to the Pawnee in exchange for the
yellow horse. Buckskin Joe "was not a very prepossessing 'insect,'"
wrote Bill's sister Helen Cody Wetmore and the western writer Zane
Grey in their book *Last of the Great Scouts*.

In fact, he was "rather a sorry-looking animal. But he was known
all over the frontier as the greatest long-distance and best buffalo
horse living." When it came to dangerous tasks, Buckskin Joe was
Cody's first choice. Anticipating a war party out on the trail, he would
generally ride another horse and "let Buckskin Joe follow along to be
used for reserve in case he had to make a run for his life," as Agnes
Wright Spring reports. "Buckskin Joe instinctively scented danger
and showed his fear at once. He was almost human in thrusting his
head into the bridle and in standing still to be saddled. The longer
the chase, the better the pony seemed to like it."

In 1872, Cody served as the guide for Grand Duke Alexis from
Russia and his hunting party, and that's when he was catapulted into
the stratosphere of international celebrity. By then he was much more
than a notorious buffalo hunter — he had become the country's most
famous frontier guide. A year earlier, he had escorted a hunting party
organized by General Philip Sheridan. It included prominent finan-
ciers, lawyers, reporters, and newspaper publishers. "One of the
most glamorous hunting parties in the history of the Plains," Warren observes, "it expressed the confluence between the urban power
elite of the East and Midwest, the U.S. army, and sport hunting on
the Great Plains." For the occasion, Buffalo Bill selected his clothing carefully. It was "a nobby and high-toned outfit which I was to accompany," Cody said, and he vowed to put on a little style.

The frontier was his stage, and he made a grand entrance. On
the first morning of the hunt, he rode down from the fort on a white
horse, "dressed in a suit of light buckskin," recounted Henry Da-
vies, an assistant district attorney from southern New York who was
a member of the party, "trimmed along the seams with fringes of the
same leather, his costume lighted by the crimson shirt worn under
his open coat, a broad sombrero on his head, and carrying his rifle
lightly in one hand, as his horse came toward us on an easy gallop."
Because Buffalo Bill embodied the American West so effectively, Gen-

eral Philip Sheridan wanted Grand Duke Alexis to meet Cody when the grand duke came for a visit — the first ever for a Russian royal.

In fact, Sheridan was on his way to Arizona to deal with the "Apache problem" when he got word that the grand duke was coming and quickly changed plans to accommodate the visiting dignitary. As it turned out, not only was Alexis en route, but he also wanted to kill buffalo, ride horses, and, if possible, meet some real live Indians. Plans were quickly arranged. First, Buffalo Bill and his crew constructed what came to be known as Camp Alexis on the banks of the North Platte River in Nebraska. Then — although war with the Plains Indians was raging — Cody set out to find the Sioux chief Spotted Tail and persuade him to provide entertainment. As Cody dramatically wrote in his own book *Buffalo Bill's Life Story:*

> Although Spotted Tail himself was friendly, I was afraid I might have difficulty in getting into his camp. I was liable at any moment to run into a party of his young men who might be out hunting, and as I had many enemies among the Sioux, I would be running considerable risk in meeting them ... At the end of the first day I camped on Stinking Water, a tributary of the Frenchman's fork, where I built a little fire in the timber; but it was so very cold I was not able to sleep much. Getting an early start in the morning I followed up the Frenchman's fork and late in the afternoon I could see, from the fresh horse tracks and from the dead buffaloes lying here and there, recently killed, that I was nearing Spotted Tail's camp. I rode on for a few miles further, and then hiding my horse in a low ravine I crawled up a high hill, where I obtained a good view of the country. I could see for four or five miles up the creek, and got sight of a village and of two or three hundred ponies in its vicinity. I waited until night came and then I succeeded in riding into the Indian camp unobserved.
>
> ... As I entered the village I wrapped a blanket around my head so that the Indians could not tell whether I was a white or a red man. In this way I rode around until I found Spotted Tail's lodge. Dismounting from my horse I opened his tent door and looking in, saw the old chief lying on some robes. I spoke to him and he recognized me at once and invited me to enter ... I told him that the warriors and chiefs would greatly please General Sheridan if they

would meet him about ten sleeps at the old Government crossing of the Red Willow. I further informed him that there was a great chief from across the water who was coming there to visit him.

Spotted Tail replied that he would be very glad to go; that the next morning he would call his people together and select those who would accompany him ... He directed his squaw to get me something to eat, and ordered that my horse be taken care of and upon his invitation I spent the remainder of the night in his lodge.

On the morning of January 12, 1872, the grand duke and his party arrived by special train, accompanied by General Sheridan. They were met by Buffalo Bill, about twenty saddle horses, and a cavalry company. After General Sheridan introduced the grand duke to Buffalo Bill, "the whole party [dashed] away towards the south," Cody wrote, "across the South Platte and towards the Medicine, upon reaching which point we halted for a change of horses and a lunch. Resuming our ride we reached Camp Alexis in the afternoon." They were joined by no less than George Custer, who certainly would not pass up a chance to hunt, especially with a visiting royal. "General Sheridan," reported Buffalo Bill, "was delighted to find that Spotted Tail and his Indians had arrived on time," in war paint and feathers. On cue, they enacted a war dance, with "outlandish contortions and grimaces, leaps and crouchings," according to Cody's sister and Zane Grey, "their fiendish yells and whoops making up a barbaric jangle of picture and sound not soon to be forgotten."

Unbeknownst to even Cody himself, it was a preview of his forthcoming traveling spectacle — and the grand duke's sojourn was just getting started. That night at Camp Alexis, both the grand duke and Custer "flirted with red-skinned maidens," as Cody reported, and the following morning it was time for the buffalo hunt. Could you pair me with a good horse? the grand duke had asked; Bill offered him one of his favorites, Charlie, aka Charlie Almost Human, a half-blood Kentucky horse purchased as a five-year-old in Nebraska. "Charlie was an animal of almost human intelligence, extraordinary speed, endurance and fidelity," Cody wrote. When the horse was young, Cody rode him on a wild horse hunt, running the herd down after a fifteen-mile chase. Once, someone bet Cody five hundred dollars that he couldn't ride Charlie across a hundred-mile stretch of prairie in ten hours. Charlie went the distance in nine hours and forty-five minutes. "All you have to do is sit on his back and fire away," Cody said when he handed the horse over to Grand Duke Alexis. They tore down a hill and into a herd; the duke fired and missed. Then, as Cody recounted:

> I now rode up close beside him and advised him not to fire until he could ride directly upon the flank of a buffalo, as the sport was most in the chase. We dashed off together and ran our horses on either flank of a large bull, against the side of which the Duke thrust his gun and fired a fatal shot. He was very much elated at his success, taking off his cap and waving it vehemently, at the same time shouting to those who were fully a mile in the rear. When his retinue came up there were congratulations and every one drank to his good health with over-flowing glasses of champagne. The hide of the dead buffalo was carefully removed and dressed, and the royal traveler in his journeying over the world has no doubt often rested himself upon this trophy of his skill on the plains of America.

There was one more experience that General Sheridan wanted the grand duke to have—a stagecoach ride. "Shake 'em up a little, Bill," Sheridan said as the party headed back to the train depot, "give us some old-time driving." Buffalo Bill cracked the whip, and the horses broke into a run. With a light load to pull, they increased their speed at every jump, and it was difficult to hold them. "They fairly flew over the ground," Cody wrote, "and at last we reached a steep hill, or divide, which led down into the valley of the Medicine." There was no brake and Cody couldn't stop them. "All I could do," he said, "was to keep them straight in the track and let them go down the hill, for three miles." They made it in six minutes, the hind wheels periodically striking a rut and then not touching the ground again for fifteen or twenty feet. "The Duke and the General were kept rather busy in holding their positions on the seats," Cody said, "and when they saw that I was keeping the horses straight in the road, they seemed to enjoy the dash which we were making. I was unable to stop the team until they ran into the camp where we were to obtain a fresh relay, and there I succeeded in checking them." The grand duke asked Cody to take it easy on the rest of the drive. Back at the station, Alexis invited Buffalo Bill into his private car and showered him with gifts. General Sheridan invited Cody to New York.

In 1873, with most of the buffalo gone, a circuit-riding physician and homesteader named Brewster Higley wrote a poem that became the unofficial national anthem. It was called "My Western Home," and it was published in a Kansas newspaper called *The Pioneer*. A year later a friend convinced Higley to turn it into a song. A fiddler was rounded up, a tune conceived, and as cowboys came through Kansas Territory, they picked it up and carried it into history. Somewhere along the trail, it became known as "Home on the Range." Today, many people are familiar with it because they know the refrain about the range being the place where the deer and the antelope play, a discouraging word is rarely heard, and the skies are not cloudy all day. But the famous anthem actually expressed a darker truth, a yearning for the life that Americans, by way of Buffalo Bill, were extinguishing as they turned it into theater. A lesser-known part of the song goes like this:

> *The red man was pressed from this part of the West,*
> *He's likely no more to return*
> *To the banks of Red River where seldom if ever*
> *Their flickering campfires burn.*

For the next few years, the country's most famous hunter shuttled between the frontier and the world of greater sophistication — an actor in both the destruction of the American Eden and the mythologizing of it, a progenitor of every kind of "ripped from the headlines," "based on," "inspired by" adaptation of reality that has ever come down the pike.

Back on the plains, he continued his work as an army scout, still riding Buckskin Joe. On one legendary ride, the little mustang helped Cody escape a hundred mounted Indians, leading them on a wild 195-mile chase from the Republican River to Fort McPherson. When it was over, most of the Indian ponies had been left in the dust — and Buckskin Joe had gone blind. Bill kept him until he passed on and buried him at his ranch on the North Platte in Colorado Territory.

"Old Buckskin Joe," it said on his tombstone, "the horse that on several occasions saved the life of Buffalo Bill by carrying him safely out of the range of Indian bullets. Died of old age, 1882."

A year later, on May 19, 1883, he launched his equine extravaganza in Omaha. The progenitor for the spectacle that he would take abroad, it was called *The Wild West, WF Cody and WF Carver's Rocky Mountain and Prairie Exhibition*. Interestingly, the title did not include the word *show* — it was not presented as something removed from the frontier, but rather as the Wild West itself. Anticipation of the event was keen, as this newspaper account of a dress rehearsal at Buffalo Bill's Nebraska ranch chronicles:

> In the afternoon in company with Mr. [James] McNulty and Hon. W. F. Cody we visited the germ of the great show which is to spring into existence the latter part of this month at Omaha and which will sweep all before it when once fairly started ... On a piece of level meadow land was pitched the tents for the men while the buffalo and a large number of horses were grazing in an adjoining pasture. A number of elk were expected in a day or two and men were engaged purchasing the most famous bucking horses that Nebraska afforded. "Buck" Taylor, who is to be one of the star riders of the combination, gave an exhibition on a wall-eyed calico horse that would astonish the effeminate easterners, and if he lives long enough the performance will be repeated for their benefit during the summer. Another wing of the show is getting under way at Omaha, where the Indians will join it, and about the 17th of the present month the western Nebraska wonder will give its opening exhibition at the state's metropolis.

The actual production was a huge hit, although not as polished as it eventually became. And just as one of their kind had interfered with the advance on Little Bighorn, mules deranged the premiere. As Larry McMurtry reported, "A number of Omaha dignitaries, including the mayor, were invited to ride in the Deadwood stage while it came under mock attack from a party of Pawnees ... As soon as the Indians started whooping and hollering, the mules panicked and made several bouncy circuits of the arena before they could be stopped." Once the kinks were worked out, Cody and his partner took the show on the road, staging it around the country to packed houses, including Madison Square Garden.

Along with the Indians and representatives of other horse cultures such as Turks, Cossacks, and Arabs, hundreds of mustangs, buffalo, and burros were featured. When the *Wild West* show opened in St. Louis in 1884, a friend of Cody's sent him "five of the ugliest, largest, and most vociferous burros around, for which they paid an average of $30 each," wrote Agnes Wright Spring. "One of them was reported to be the burro Kokomo Jim," who evidently had become famous in Kokomo because of the way he sounded when he brayed. By the time the show opened at Madison Square Garden in 1886, Buffalo Bill and W. F. Carver had gone their separate ways for a number of reasons, including the fact that Carver was volatile and unpredictable; in a moment of rage some time after the partnership ended, he broke a rifle over a horse's head.

Advertising poster, c. 1895. Buffalo Bill's show, with its cowboys, Indians, gauchos, and bedouins, drew packed houses around the country.

The *Wild West* show now had at least eighteen railcars to transport its condensed version of the frontier—including performers, work crews, animals, and equipment such as Gatling guns, stagecoaches, tepees, and fire-making machines. There was enough food to feed seven hundred people three times a day (including nearly six thousand pounds of beef, six gallons of mustard, and five hundred pies). Sandwich boards all over the city promoted Buffalo Bill's *Drama of Civilization,* which played to packed houses for weeks. "It is often said on the other side of the water," Mark Twain wrote after attending the show, "that none of the exhibitions which we send to England are purely and distinctively American. If you take the *Wild West* show over there, you can remove that reproach." A few months later, the organizers of the American exhibition at the London World's Fair invited Cody to participate in the upcoming extravaganza. He agreed, and soon became the toast of the motherland — and then of Scotland, France, and Italy; royals and commoners alike all wanted to meet the man who had given Grand Duke Alexis the ride of his life.

Queen Victoria had already been introduced to the Wild West in 1839. The American artist George Catlin was trying to save the Native American — vanishing even then — with the very first show about the Wild West, consisting of his stunning artwork and live reenactments of frontier scenes with actual Ojibwa Indians whose portraits he had painted and live grizzly bears he had captured on a trip up the Missouri River and transported across the Atlantic. Blazing the trail for Buffalo Bill, he took his troupe to Brussels and Paris after London. But in the nearly half a century since Catlin's visit, the world had changed dramatically. As Buffalo Bill sailed into port in 1887, Spain was about to lose Mexico to the United States, the West had been fenced in, and the Indian was not just vanishing but nearly purged from his homeland. The children of England had accomplished much since the Boston Tea Party, and now on board the *State of Nebraska,* they were met by a tug flying American colors. The passengers cheered and the cowboy band struck up "Yankee Doodle." Cody recorded the moment in his memoir:

> A certain feeling of pride came over me when I thought of the good ship on whose deck I stood, and that her cargo consisted of early pioneers and rude, rough riders from that section, and of the wild horses of the same district, buffalo, deer, elk and antelope — the king game of the prairie — together with over one hundred representatives of that savage foe that had been compelled to submit to a conquering civilization and were now accompanying me in friendship, loyalty and peace, five thousand miles from their homes, braving the dangers of the to them great unknown sea, now no longer a tradition, but a reality — all of us combined in an exhibition intended to prove to the center of old world civilization that the vast

region of the United States was finally and effectively settled by the English-speaking race.

At the Albert Dock, the astonishing traveling version of the Horse Nations debarked—including Mustang Jack and Cherokee Bill and Mr. and Mrs. Walking Buffalo, Mr. and Mrs. Eagle Horse, Moccasin Tom, Blue Rainbow, Iron Good Voice, Mr. and Mrs. Cut Meat, Double Wound, the visionary Black Elk, and the sea-weary animals—and they all headed to London, where they would reside for the next several months in a huge camp next to a specially built arena. The encampment was frequently visited by royals, regular citizens, and reporters—all thrilled by the noble savages of the American frontier, red and white man alike. Of the cowboy Buck Taylor, a London reporter was moved to write in rhyming couplets:

> *The Cowboy King, Buck Taylor*
> *Is quite an equine Nailer*
> *What man dare he will dare O*
> *Pick up his wide sombrero,*
> *From off the ground*
> *While at full bound*
> *His steed away does tear O!*

The Indians too received much coverage in this nineteenth-century media circus, with gallons of ink spilled over their novel appearance and barely a trickle exploring the story behind the show. Many had joined the production as a way to make money—at twenty-five dollars a month, it was more lucrative than reservation jobs but paid less than a cowboy's salary. Others, such as Black Elk, had joined up for the adventure and for the knowledge. "I wanted to see the great water," he would say later, "the great world and the ways of the white men; this is why I wanted to go . . . I made up my mind I was going away . . . to see the white man's ways. If the white man's ways were better, why I would like to see my people go that way." Equally popular among spectators and reporters were the horses, especially the bucking broncos, including a gray horse from Wyoming named Pat Crow who came to be known as the "horse that bucked around the world."

But perhaps most of all, everyone came to see Charlie, who had been the star of the *Wild West* show since it opened in 1883. At the *Wild West* camp, Buffalo Bill would race Charlie across the grounds, shooting glass balls that had been tossed up as targets. The Prince of Wales was evidently so taken with Charlie that while visiting the *Wild West* camp, he asked for the saddle to be removed so he could make a closer inspection. Grand Duke Michael of Russia, cousin of Alexis, showed up to ride Charlie and chase buffalo. And the *English Metropolitan* welcomed the frontier horses with breathless prose in an article titled "Mustangs, Horses, Mules, Some 250 Animals, 166 Horses":

> These are not remarkable for height or the ordinary points of thoroughbreds, but they possess staying powers that an English racer does not. They are suitable for riding unshod over rough country for many miles together . . .
>
> Bronco horses, mustangs, or buck jumpers are to be seen here — animals that have never been, and never can be tamed; whose kick is death, and upon whose back no man could remain for a moment. The horses, though they have no direct pedigree, nevertheless have a history. They are descendants of the Berber horses, taken in Central America by the Spaniard Cortes, and getting loose became wild, and produced a race of fierce and sturdy animals.

The whole unsophisticated and rough parade was starring in theater American-style — not Shakespearean actors coming to the West to perform for cowboys and miners, but the reverse, Americans themselves exporting their own kind of theater, our theater, our magic, our fable, featuring the people who had made it — our own stars, playing themselves — and of course the greatest celebrities of all, the wild horses of the West, in whose flying manes and tails and rippling muscles was writ the whole saga. Still, Shakespeare was owed a debt, and Buffalo Bill always played to his audience. On the front page of the program for his show, he quoted from Shakespeare's "Venus and Adonis," a poem that illustrated the bard's passion for horses:

> *Imperiously he leaps, he neighs, he bounds,*
> *And now his woven girths he breaks asunder;*
> *The bearing earth with his hard hoof he wounds,*

Whose hollow womb resounds like heaven's thunder;
The iron bit he crushes 'tween his teeth,
Controlled what he was controlled with.

His ears up-pricked, his braided hanging mane
Upon his compassed crest now stand on end;
His nostrils drink the air, and forth again
As from a furnace, vapors doth he send;
His eye, which scornfully glisters like fire,
Shows his hot courage and his high desire . . .

In the past, when Queen Victoria had asked for a command performance, the theater came to her. Now, Grandmother England, as the Indians called her, came to the theater — to Buffalo Bill, although even he acknowledged that the *Wild West* show was too big to bring to Windsor Castle. As Cody recounted in his memoir:

With the punctuality that is conventional with royalty, this great sovereign and suite came upon the tick of time and their carriages entered the arena and were driven around to the entrance of the box that had been prepared.

With her Majesty came . . . a collection of brilliantly uniformed military attendants and exquisitely gowned ladies, forming a veritable portiere of living flowers about the temporary throne.

Then another very remarkable incident occurred. Our entire company of performers having been introduced in the usual manner and the American flag sent around the arena at the hands of a graceful and well-mounted horseman, the statement preceded it that this was an "emblem of peace and friendship to all the world." As the standard bearer passed the royal box with "Old Glory" her Majesty arose, bowed deeply and impressively to the banner, and the entire court party came up standing, the noblemen uncovered, the ladies bowed and the soldiers, generals and all, saluted.

The incident thrilled, unspeakably, every American present, and with the impulse of the West our company gave a shout such as had never before been heard in Britain . . .

For the first time in history a British sovereign had saluted the Star Spangled Banner, and that banner was carried by a delegated and exalted attache of Buffalo Bill's Wild West.

Queen Victoria also paid homage to the Native American members of the show, and in return, as Black Elk later recounted, they "sent out the women's and men's tremolo and all sang her a song — it was a most happy time!" The company proceeded to put on its dazzling show, which always began with Buffalo Bill galloping into the ring, dressed in buckskin and sombrero, bringing his horse to a halt, doffing his sombrero, and announcing: "Ladies and gentlemen, permit me to introduce to you a congress of rough riders" — and then the mounted cast would parade through. The show consisted of five "epochs," each one representing a particular period in American history. The first epoch was "The Forest Primeval," and it portrayed Indians and animals living together before the arrival of Columbus. It took place at dawn. The animals were sleeping, and so were the Indians in their tents. As the sun came up, a friendly tribe arrived for a visit, awakening the sleeping natives. A friendly dance followed. Then a hostile tribe arrived and a battle ensued. The winners celebrated with a wild war dance, at which point the Pilgrims landed, and Pocahontas arrived to save John Smith. The second epoch was "The Prairie." The scene unfolded at a buffalo lick. The animals were driven in, followed by Buffalo Bill on Charlie, leading an emigrant party, which set up camp for the night. In the morning, a red glow illumined the horizon. Then the glow widened and filled the sky — a prairie fire. The emigrants rushed out and tried to stanch the roaring flames. An animal stampede followed. The third epoch was "The Cattle Ranch," featuring pioneers under attack by Indians and Buffalo Bill coming to their rescue. "Mining Camp" was the fourth epoch and included the Pony Express, an Indian attack on the Deadwood stage, bucking broncos, and other cowboy diversions. The fifth epoch was "Custer's Last Stand," which featured some of the Indians who had been in the actual battle and then Buffalo Bill galloping onto the scene with the words *Too Late!* projected onto a screen behind the giant mural of the battle.

The presence of the queen inspired the cast to put on its best performance, Cody reported, "even the bucking bronchos seemed to be under the influence of the contagious enthusiasm." At the conclusion of the performance, Bill presented Red Shirt to the queen, followed by two Indian women whose papooses were strapped to their shoulders. "The red babies were passed up and petted," Cody wrote later. Queen Victoria was so taken with the show that she soon ordered another command performance.

At this performance, the rulers of Denmark, Saxony, Greece, and Austria wanted to sit on the Deadwood stage while it was attacked. The Prince of Wales wanted to ride up front with Buffalo Bill. "The Indians had been secretly instructed to 'whoop 'em up' on this interesting occasion," Cody's sister wrote, "and they followed energetically the letter of their instructions. The coach was surrounded by a demoniac band, and the blank cartridges were discharged in such close proximity to the coach windows that the passengers could easily imagine themselves to be actual Western travelers. Rumor hath it that they sought refuge under the seats, and probably no one would blame them if they did."

As the story goes, when the ride was over, the Prince of Wales turned to Cody and said, "Colonel, did you ever hold four kings like that before?"

"I have held four kings more than once," Cody replied, "but, your Highness, I never held four kings and the royal joker before."

It was a joke that played well everywhere, and by now, Buffalo Bill was enshrined as an emissary of national good will on the international stage. When General Sherman got word of the episode, he sent Cody the following letter. Actually, it wasn't a letter but a strangely deluded thank-you note, expressing gratitude for the acclaimed horseman's reenactments of the wars that tamed the West and lamenting the end of the Native American and buffalo, even as it suggested that the white man had walked the moral high ground:

Dear Sir,

In common with all your countrymen, I want to let you know that I am not only gratified but proud of your management and success. So far as I can make out, you have been modest, graceful, and dignified in all you have done to illustrate the history of civilization on this continent during the past century. I am especially pleased with the compliment paid you by the Prince of Wales, who rode with you in the Deadwood coach while it was attacked by Indians and rescued by cowboys. Such things did occur in our days, but they never will again.

As nearly as I can estimate, there were in 1865 about nine and one-half million of buffaloes on the plains between the Missouri River and the Rocky Mountains; all are now gone, killed for their meat, their skins, and their bones. This seems like desecration, cruelty, and murder, yet they have been replaced by twice as many cattle. At that date there were about 165,000 Pawnees, Sioux, Cheyennes, and Arapahoes, who depended upon these buffaloes for their yearly food. They, too, have gone, but they have been replaced by twice or thrice as many white men and women, who have made the earth to blossom as the rose, and who can be counted, taxed, and governed by the laws of nature and civilization. This change has been salutary, and will go on to the end. You have caught one epoch of this country's history, and have illustrated it in the very heart of the modern world — London, and I want you to feel that on this side of the water we appreciate it . . .

Halfway back to America, twenty-one-year-old Charlie became ill. Plenty of horses live well past that age, and the record indicates that no one knows what befell the equine superstar. With the frontier tamed and the country having less use for the horse, hundreds of thousands of Charlie's own kind would soon be rounded up and sent to the front for the first wars of the twentieth century. While the Atlantic crossing did not take Buffalo Bill's ship as far south as the horse latitudes, the halfway point would have placed the ship due north of that deadly region, and perhaps, in the same way that sailors report hearing the moans and wails of those who have been claimed by the seas, Charlie too heard a distant nicker on the wind, the last notes of a panicked whinny, calling from the lower depths, echoes of another era. In any case, it happened quickly. Buffalo Bill had gone below decks on the morning of May 14, 1888, to give him some sugar. Less than an hour later, the groom reported that Charlie was sick. Cody went down again and noticed that he had a chill. "In spite of all we could do," Cody wrote, "he grew rapidly worse and at two o'clock on the morning of May 17 he died." The crew took him to the main deck, wrapped him in a canvas shroud, and covered him with an American flag. He lay in state that day, and everyone reminisced about their times with the horse. Cody stood alone near Charlie and was heard to say the following:

Old fellow, your journeys are over ... Obedient to my call, gladly you bore your burden on, little knowing, little reckoning what the day might bring, shared sorrows and pleasures alike. Willing speed, tireless courage ... you have never failed me. Ah, Charlie, old fellow, I have had many friends, but few of whom I could say that ... I loved you as you loved me. Men tell me you have no soul; but if there is a heaven and scouts can enter there, I'll wait at the gate for you, old friend.

At eight o'clock that evening, candles were lit and with all hands and members of the *Wild West* show assembled, the band played "Auld Lang Syne." Charlie was lowered into the water — his bones to be laid bare over time and perhaps borne by currents toward the graves of his ancestors — and the ship's cannon boomed farewell.

Buffalo Bill — now a man who had charmed the queen — was met with a great tumult when he returned, not unlike the kind of fanfare given to military heroes. In a way, he was one. Although America had defeated England more than a century earlier, the rivalry between the two countries had still been simmering when Cody arrived in London in 1887. "We felt that the hatchet was buried," he said later, referring to the moment when Queen Victoria stood and bowed to the American flag and the thousands of spectators in the arena followed suit. Now, as the ship carrying the *Wild West* show steamed toward Staten Island, Buffalo Bill stood on the bridge, his long hair waving in the wind, said the *New York World*, the "gaily painted and blanketed Indians" leaning over the rail, and the flags of many nations fluttering from the masts. The show's band played "Yankee Doodle," and when Cody debarked, he proclaimed: "I cannot describe my joy upon stepping again on the shore of beloved America ... There is no place like home."

He spent the next year crisscrossing the country putting on his show, adding new acts, new effects, new tricks, new horses. In 1889, the *Wild West* show headed back across the Atlantic. A major American star had been added to the cast — Sitting Bull, who had turned himself into the reservation soon after the Little Bighorn. Now that the famous war veteran was part of the spectacle, it became even more extraordinary. Could this be the man who killed Custer? What secrets did he bring from the battlefield? Newspapers buzzed about the show for days, and reporters documented the lives of Native Americans in detail, following them around town and marveling as they climbed the Eiffel Tower. French couples even took to touching the Indians; according to newspapers, contact assured fertility. And children were so enchanted that they set up their own encampment in the Bois de Boulogne. To pay homage to the French exploration of the American frontier, Buffalo Bill added fur trappers to the show. More than ten thousand people, including French president Sadi Carnot, turned out for the show's opening at the Paris Universal Exposition. It ran all summer, and when it was over, Buffalo Bill presented President Carnot with a nine-foot-tall lamp topped by a preserved buffalo head and a red lampshade — a gift that he declined because it was too rugged.

But Buffalo Bill would still leave a legacy in France. The celebrated artist Rosa Bonheur had come to paint him. Even before he arrived, she was part of his show — though not in the flesh. In 1853, her painting *The Horse Fair* had debuted, to much fanfare and acclaim. It portrayed an auction of Percheron horses, "the animals' bobbed tails and gigantic muscles bathed in sunlight," as Louis Warren observes. "By 1859, the *United States Journal,* an American magazine devoted to middle-class readers, was offering a free lithograph of the work with every subscription." Now, on his current tour, Buffalo Bill included the beloved Percherons in his troupe; there were 160, brought along to haul his moving city across land. At the Paris Expo, Rosa Bonheur — the woman who had mythologized the big draft horse for the American public — arrived to do the same for the *Wild West* show. She painted various scenes of buffalo and Indians. She also painted a portrait of Buffalo Bill on his favorite white charger, Tucker, and — unlike President Carnot, who wanted no such frontier relic — she asked to have the horse's head when he died. Back in the States, the portrait of the showman on his horse quickly became must-have art, with countless prints purchased and displayed in pubs and parlors across the land. Cody himself hung the original at his home in Nebraska. One day, he reportedly got word that his house was on fire. Save Rosa Bonheur's picture, he telegraphed back, and the house may go to blazes. The painting has been passed from collection to collection over the decades, and is now on permanent display at the Buffalo Bill Historical Center in Wyoming. As for Tucker's head, as legend has it, Buffalo Bill sent it to Rosa Bonheur when the horse passed away.

Over the next few years, the *Wild West* show put on performances in Italy, Spain, Scotland, and again in England. In Florence, a newspaper chronicled the scene that unfolded as the show arrived one clear and beautiful morning at the station of Porta della Croce. "The horses were gotten off by a very simple means," it said. "Four cowboys held a small iron platform and the horses ran down it from the wagons onto the street. Then the Indians each took away one, two, or three horses. The horses are small, young and unshod." The Indians, the paper said, wore multicolored clothing and strange necklaces. At first, they all appeared to be women, with their long black hair parted in the middle and falling over their shoulders or in braids tied with ribbons and little mirrors. Once the horses were unloaded, the Indians jumped on their horses, followed by Mexican vaqueros and cowboys, and began the parade across the Piazza Beccaria toward their encampment. Among the mounted horses were buffalo and "groups of cowboys on foot ran and yelled some words of American slang," the article noted. In Scotland, spectators said that the grand entrance alone of the *Wild West* performers—which at one point included Cossacks, Cubans, Bedouins, and Japanese cavalrymen, in addition to the frontier cast—was worth the price of admission. One newspaper reported that the opening review was "rendered all the more extraordinary by the curious singing of the Indians and the wild whooping of the cowboys," sounds that reverberated across Scotland and England and lands beyond and continue to echo to this day. "The Indian battles featured the crack of a hundred rifles," reports Tom F. Cunningham in *The Diamond's Ace: Scotland and the Native Americans,* "as well as blood-curdling cries. The covered wagons of the immigrant train came lumbering across the field and formed camp for the night, before men and women on horseback performed a quadrille." The toll it took on the horses to perform two *Wild West* shows a day, six days a week, for months on end was rarely recorded. But there is this obscure report, from the British newspaper the *Weekly Budget,* that eulogized one of the show's horses, Ta-ra-ra-boom-de-ay, in the article "Wild West Bucking Horse," published on June 4, 1892:

Ta-ra-ra-boom-de-ay is dead — dead as a door-nail — and not all the king's horses, not all the king's men, will put it on its legs again. Not the song that goes on as merrily as ever, notwithstanding the tale told by the thermometer of 135 degrees of sunshine; but the fiery untamed steed of that name, which formed one of the attractions of the Wild West. The animal was one of the best hoop jumpers, and while going through its performance on Monday afternoon, jumped and pirouetted to such an extent that it kicked itself heels over head and fell heavily with its rider. The cowboy saved himself by admirable agility, but Ta-ra-ra-boom-de-ay broke his neck and kicked no more.

Yet the *Wild West* show reached greater acclaim in repeat trips across the Atlantic, even as the thing it portrayed was nearly gone. Was the death of Ta-ra-ra-boom-de-ay an omen, like Charlie perishing on his way home to an America whose frontier was nearly gone? There are many horses who would rather die than be locked up. Perhaps the hoop jumper, like his predecessor, sensed a change in the air, perhaps he knew that back home his own kind was in trouble, and so he said, To hell with it, I'll show 'em freedom one more time, then kicked up his heels and died.

The *Wild West* spectacles were also taking their toll on the Native American stars. After the 1889 tour, Sitting Bull returned to America, drawn by the call of his homeland. According to legend, Buffalo Bill gave him the beautiful white horse that he rode in the *Wild West* show as a farewell gift. Other Indians went home as well, including Black Elk, who had become separated from the troupe in 1886; he wandered the streets of London before hooking up with a rival Wild West show and was later arrested and interviewed as a suspect in the Jack the Ripper killings. True to his plan, he had seen the white man's ways, and it was time to go.

Back on the plains, shortly before the 1890 massacre at Wounded Knee, Sitting Bull had a vision. He had once seen the destruction of the U.S. cavalry at the Little Bighorn; now he saw his own death. This time, the vision came by way of a meadowlark, the sweet songster of the Great Plains, who sat down beside him and said, "Your own people, Lakotas, will kill you." Fearing that the influential warrior was about to join the Ghost Dance, the last-gasp revival move-

ment that promised salvation to the defeated Native American population, the government had dispatched forty-three tribal policemen
to arrest him. When Sitting Bull got word, he asked for his horse to
be saddled. Outside his cabin, resisters had gathered.

His jailers arrived, and another frontier drama quickly unfolded
— one that would never be acted out in a Wild West show. Live
rounds, not blanks, were fired into the crowd, and when it was over,
fifteen Lakota had been killed, including Sitting Bull, who had been
shot in the head. As the battle at Sitting Bull's cabin played out, it
is said that his white horse heard the shooting. He recognized the
sound, having heard it many times in the *Wild West* show and perhaps even in other battles. Just as Comanche had responded to boots
and saddles and trotted from his stall to join formation, Sitting Bull's
horse began to dance. He drew himself up and snorted, the legend
goes. He arched his neck and pranced in a circle. He bowed and then
stood up and shook his long mane and pawed the ground, and reared
up and leaped into the air. He cantered around and around in a circle, stopped and backed up, and then cantered some more. He did all
of this while the battle was raging around him, and the bullets never
touched him. When the noise stopped and the battle was over, he
danced until he was exhausted.

About two weeks later, just after Christmas in 1890, one last cavalry charge was waged on Indian holdouts at Wounded Knee, South
Dakota. It was led by General Nelson A. Miles, who closed in on the
band of 350 Lakota, mostly women and children, and ordered their
destruction. They were cut down as they ran for cover. Miles was
riding a horse named Duke, a veteran of the Pine Ridge campaign.
Like Comanche, Duke surely noted the anxiety of the pack train as
the army closed in, surely took in all the cries and screams. Soon after the massacre, Miles gave Duke to Buffalo Bill, as a token of his
appreciation for the horseman's contribution to the Indian wars (although it should be noted that Buffalo Bill had been asked to participate at Wounded Knee and had declined — and always regretted
it, figuring that if he'd intervened earlier, he might have been able to
forge a truce with his old friend Sitting Bull, preventing his death).
Duke became a wildly popular member of the *Wild West* show, probably appearing in scenes with Native American survivors of the same

battles, and remembering their scent and all the sad and terrible information it carried. A few years after Wounded Knee, in an article called "Colonel Cody's Splendid Charger and His Graceful Performance," the *Chicago Herald* praised the horse who was famous for his quadrilles:

> This splendid chestnut sorrel, admired by everybody, as he gracefully backs the length of the Coliseum, is probably the most admired horse that ever lived. More persons have seen Duke do his act than ever saw any other horse perform. And even then what Duke does can hardly be called a performance. It seems rather to be an act of unconscious grace, but of course it isn't. Duke is so well trained, however, that he acts naturally ... There were 12,000 pairs of eyes focused on Duke last night when he did his pretty act. Duke seemed to know it too, for he never was more graceful.

But behind the beauty of the performing horses, the terror continued. In 1899, the government gave the railroad the right of way through Indian reservations, slicing up what remained of the wide-open space of the frontier. In 1902, the Department of the Interior ordered Native American men to stop painting their faces and wearing traditional Indian clothing, and to cut their hair. That same year, a terrible accident befell the *Wild West* show, sounding the beginning of the end. One night in April, the show was traveling by train through North Carolina, en route to Danville, Virginia. There was a mix-up in signals, and the show train collided with an oncoming freight train.

According to an eyewitness, the engines appeared to devour each other. "One had run halfway inside the other and then they reared up on the tracks like two giant beasts in deadly combat," said an account in the *Salisbury Post*. The cars of both trains were made out of wood and shattered into thousands of pieces on impact. Nearly five hundred horses and scores of cattle and buffalo were strewn through the wreckage, "with timbers run through them like knives." Residents converged on the scene, carting off saddles, bridles, and costumes. Cowboys and Indians began shooting animals that were badly injured but were stopped by insurance officials from the railroad. One of Buffalo Bill's horses was found dead, mangled in the tender. Two stallions that Queen Victoria had given to him also died in the crash. Annie Oakley's back was broken, and she would never shoot straight again. When Buffalo Bill arrived at the wreck, he sat down and cried.

With most of the animals and equipment lost, Buffalo Bill was out of business. A suit against the railroad helped recoup much of the loss, but the *Wild West* show was never the same. It struggled along for another decade or so, but by 1913 it had gone bankrupt, and everything—horses, buffalo, cattle, stagecoaches, tepees—was turned over to creditors. One would think that the army or the Department of the Interior or even the president might have come to the aid of the one man who had carried and exalted the American way to "the rulers of republics and mighty potentates of foreign lands," as one newspaper put it. But such was not the case; there wasn't even

Buffalo Bill in full dress with his beloved horse Isham. The photograph was probably taken at his TE Ranch in Ishawooa, Wyoming, around 1916.

a bailout from a Russian duke, and in the end, Buffalo Bill, like everyone, was down to a few good friends. They could not bear to see his horses sold off, and, along with the country's newspapers, they rallied around the sale of one horse in particular. This was Bill's beloved Isham, a horse he had ridden since it was given to him in 1888.

"Buffalo Bill Must Sacrifice Famous Horse on Auction Block," screamed the headlines in August of that year. "Isham belongs to the company," Cody, holding back tears, said to the reporters who had gathered for the sad announcement. "We were together a long time, and we know each other better than brothers . . . I would not want to even estimate the number of shots I have fired from Isham's back. I do know that he has taken as much interest in my exhibitions as I myself have. And at any time I scored more misses than I was entitled to make, Isham showed his sympathy by his looks and actions. And when I made full scores, he would prance off the grounds like a conquering hero."

A few days later an auctioneer took the podium at the Overland Park arena in Denver. "We will now offer Isham," he called, as many in the packed house choked up. "Colonel Cody is unable to save his side partner. His means are insufficient. There is a man here all the way from Nebraska to buy this faithful animal for the purpose of presenting him to his owner."

Then Carlo Miles, an Indian aide to Buffalo Bill, rode into the arena leading Isham. The crowd fell silent. "Ten dollars," the Nebraska man called, opening the bidding.

"Twenty dollars," called the Indian. Unbeknownst to Cody, each bidder was planning to give Isham back to Buffalo Bill, but none of them knew that each was bidding for the same reason. Other bids came quickly, almost simultaneously — twenty-five dollars, thirty-five, fifty. Carlo Miles called out, "Seventy-five dollars." "Eighty dollars," called someone else, then a hundred dollars from "the man from Nebraska" — Colonel C. J. Bills, an old friend who had fought with Buffalo Bill in the Indian wars. "I would sooner lose my life than see Buffalo Bill lose that white horse," he had told a reporter before the sale. "It doesn't make any difference who bids, or how many want the horse. I am going to buy it and the next minute turn it over to my old friend. I know how he loves the animal, and I know how I love

Colonel Cody. It would hurt me even worse than it would him to see the horse fall into the hands of others."

Carlo Miles upped the bid to $110. And so the bidding continued, and finally Miles started to cry, not knowing what Colonel Bills was up to and concerned because he couldn't go much higher than the current bid of $150. "If the man who buys that horse don't give him back to Colonel Cody, I'll steal the horse tonight and take it to him," he said, and he swore an oath. Isham went to Bills, and then Bills turned him over to Cy Compton, a *Wild West* cowboy who had cared for the horse for years. Compton sat down and wept. As for Buffalo Bill, there is no mention of him in the coverage of the auction — most likely he had decided not to attend.

Over the next few years, Buffalo Bill traveled with other Wild West shows. There is nothing in the record that indicates he was tired of the act, weary of the jokes that must have come — "Hey, Bill, how about a trick? Hey, Bill, will you take me hunting? Hey, Bill, you're not gonna buffalo me, are you?" In fact, by all accounts, he seemed to maintain his happy demeanor, that quintessentially cheerful and self-effacing American façade that masked the heart of a killer, even though he himself was either competing with or starring in spinoffs and knockoffs of himself and his original show. Of course, the proliferation of shows meant a greater consumption of horses, and in 1914, the 101 Ranch troupe — a famous spectacle of the era — traveled to England with a number of half-broken Mexican steeds. Soon after they arrived, they were requisitioned by the British for the war and shipped to the western front. There they most likely perished, along with thousands of others who had been pressed into service from the range.

With the film industry beginning to flourish, sooner or later most of the surviving frontier characters converged in Hollywood. Trapped in their personas, they had nothing else to do except get paid to be some version of themselves. Some of the Earp brothers had moved to Los Angeles to cash in on their fame. The bright Southern California sun would not keep the demons away from Frank James, Jesse's brother, and one day in the Hollywood hills he blew his brains out. Like the others, Buffalo Bill came to Hollywood near the end of his life. He had arrived in Los Angeles to participate in the new mythmaking machinery, and produce a movie called *The Indian Wars*. Among other things, it featured General Miles and the cavalry acting out the massacre of Indians at Wounded Knee, with the participants playing themselves. The film fared poorly, criticized by Indians for excluding women and children from the massacre scene and not appreciated by whites, who were unimpressed by the anticlimactic ending in which Indians were assimilated and went to school, instead of going on the warpath. The strange relic is said to have disappeared, although a few remnants are rumored to exist somewhere—a celluloid anti-Grail that bears nothing transformative or magical.

With the failure of his film and the vanishing of the Wild West show, Buffalo Bill got sick, and he prepared for his final scene, calling in his friends for a last round of poker just before he died, in 1917. Although Cody had wanted to be buried in Wyoming, the *Denver Post* paid his wife ten thousand dollars to bury him in Colorado, so that's where he was eventually laid to rest, on Lookout Mountain in the town of Golden, overlooking the plains. Months earlier, so many people had gathered for Buffalo Bill's funeral that the country had its first traffic jam—or so newspapers reported. His body was carried by caisson past a sea of spectators, escorted by fellow members of an Elk lodge, all wearing top hats. One of his favorite horses, McKinley, followed the caisson. When the casket was lifted and carried into the lodge, according to a witness, McKinley tried to break free from his handler. As the lodge doors closed, the horse whinnied, bolted, and ran to the caisson—like Sitting Bull's horse, and Comanche before him, looking for his rider. Then he sniffed and whinnied again. The handler grabbed his reins and led McKinley away. But he turned his head and stared at the doors, longing for Buffalo Bill.

Decades after Buffalo Bill took his *Wild West* show to points near and far, his legacy reverberates, preserved most adamantly by people who are not from America. A French Canadian equine spectacle called *Cavalia* presents the history of the world from ancient times through the blazing of the American frontier by way of man's relationship with the horse, a script whose progenitor was Buffalo Bill. When the painted ponies thunder across the stage for the Wild West scene, manes and tails flying, their gaily festooned riders whooping on their sleek bare backs, something changes—the ions in the air maybe, some sort of energy rearrangement that stirs the blood — and spectators are thrilled to the quick, literally gasping out loud, mouths dropping, eyes glowing, just like Buffalo Bill's own audiences over a century ago when Duke and Tucker and Isham and Old Charlie recreated the American Dream.

Wild West camps flourish in Germany, the Czech Republic, and England, and European tourists come to the States and pay homage to American shrines such as the Little Bighorn battlefield, Monument Valley, Deadwood, the Grand Canyon, the OK Corral in Tombstone, Arizona, more frequently than we visit those shrines ourselves. Often tourists visit Buffalo Bill's grave, where they stand in front of a mural and have their pictures taken with the famous buffalo killer and some of his costars — Champion Lady Bucking Horse Rider of the World Lulu Parr, Red Cloud, and Sitting Bull — or on top of a life-size fake horse. Back in their home countries, such visitors seem to have a reverence for America's past that is often lacking in our own land, a respect that adds another dimension to their curious obsession with a history that belongs to someone else: they subsidize various Native American causes, and some have been moved to return long-lost or pilfered Indian relics from the days of Buffalo Bill.

Because of such concern, the bodies of two long-deceased members of the *Wild West* show were finally returned to the place where it all started, the Great Plains. One was a man named Long Wolf, who had come down with pneumonia after a performance in London in 1892. Not wanting to be buried at sea, he asked his wife to leave him behind. Buffalo Bill helped them find a plot, and then the show left port. Buried along with Long Wolf was an Indian girl named Star, who had fallen from her mother's arms when they appeared on horseback in the show. In 1997, a Worcestershire housewife named Elizabeth Knight read a story in an old book about Long Wolf's life, death, and burial "in a lone corner of a crowded London cemetery, just at the end of a smoke-stained, Greco-Roman colonnade, under a poplar tree." She located the plot by visiting local cemeteries and looking for a wolf emblazoned on an old tombstone. When she found it, she vowed to return the Native American to the Great Plains, and she tracked down Long Wolf's descendants in South Dakota. Granted permission from Queen Elizabeth to have his body exhumed, Long

Wolf's people came to bring him home. To their surprise, the bones of a young girl were also found in the grave. These, they realized, belonged to Star, long rumored to have been buried in England.

A century after the two Indians had perished in a strange land, their descendants carried off their remains in a ceremonial procession. In red satin and white feather headdresses, the three Lakota led mourners through the foreign burial ground, followed by a pair of black horses pulling a wagon with a casket draped with the Sioux and American flags. A few weeks later, Long Wolf was reburied at Wolf Creek, east of Pine Ridge, and a herd of buffalo came to a rise and watched. These were buffalo that had been repatriated from elsewhere, to make the Lakota whole again.

In 1999, there was another return. This time, a ghost shirt was given back. It had bullet holes and bloodstains and had been taken from a warrior at Wounded Knee, carried to Glasgow in 1891, and offered for sale, along with a baby carrier and a pair of boy's moccasins, by a man who said he was in charge of Indian relics in Buffalo Bill's show. A century later, a Cherokee Indian who was visiting Scotland saw the shirt in an art gallery at an exhibit called "Home of the Brave." He told the Wounded Knee Survivors' Association, and after lengthy negotiations, the shirt was finally handed back to the Lakota, in a ceremony at the massacre site on a summer afternoon. There was chanting and drumming and the sound of Scottish bagpipes as more than two hundred people assembled to receive the relic. An Indian named Goldie Iron Hawk sprinkled tobacco on the mass grave, and then another Great Plains totem, this time a bird — a hawk, some say, others a spotted eagle — soared over the gathering, riding the currents. Once again, on a ridge nearby, some buffalo watched the ceremony from the moment it began, responding to the cue that we all know, the one that is in the hearts of all living things. A few years later, they would gather in the same place to watch the return of wild horses, and a few years after that, at the very moment some mustangs were sent to the slaughterhouse, others of their kind would escape from a corral on the far side of the country and tie up traffic.

6

Rawhide

Of Cow Ponies and Bucking Broncos

FTER THE WEST WAS WON but before Buffalo Bill took it on the road, there was a brief moment in American life that superseded all the rest and has forever defined us. It was the time of the cattle drive, when men and horses herded endless parades of beef on the hoof up the rugged trail to markets thousands of miles away. The era began around 1864, when the range was wide open, and ended a little more than twenty years later, when the Indians and buffalo were gone and the range was crisscrossed and zigzagged with barbed wire. Those years brought us one of our greatest icons, the cowboy, and edged another one, the mustang, toward the end of its own trail.

How that happened is a tale that's tied up not just with social forces but with the cowboy himself, a character we all know and admire. He is a man's man and a woman's man; he's tall, handsome, simple, bighearted, and brokenhearted; he's straightforward, doesn't say much, has a code, follows the code, and follows the stars; he says yes ma'am and please and thank you, lives out there on the bluffs with the wolves and coyotes, makes good coffee, sings calves to sleep, and has only one friend in the whole world, and that's his horse. But as we shall see, the man who loves freedom also hates it when his horse goes its own way, laying bare the schizophrenic heart of the American West in a strange and never-ending dance with demons. This shadow dance reached a fever pitch out on the plains of the late nineteenth century, where extreme temperatures and desperation and the winds howling across empty space combined with a certain American recklessness to make many a man turn against his four-legged partner.

Like horses, cattle — specifically longhorns — came to the New World with the conquistadors. Unlike horses, they were not heading home, although it did not take long for them to go wild. The first cow to cross the Rio Grande was part of the Coronado *entrada,* and here is how Mari Sandoz imagined the historic moment in her elegant book *The Cattlemen:*

> She came first in a mirage, behind a long string of glorious although worn and impatient horsemen, moving out of the heat and shimmer of the west. By comparison she and the rest of the cattle herd seemed without significance, a little like the great humpbacked wild cows of the Plains, but smaller, longer of horn, and almost lost in the plume of dust raised by the riders up ahead ... Those in front [were] still the stronger young cows, their leader a long-bodied, well-horned four-year-old, her coat the color of sun on heat-bleached earth.

It was fitting, Sandoz noted, that the arrival of cows in America was associated with missionaries, because they have been deified for thousands of years. Long before the Egyptians prayed before animals of precious metal, long before the Chicago stockyards or rodeo days in Cheyenne, Wyoming, someone was painting the cave walls at Lascaux, invoking a cattle cult that prefigured our own version. Across the ancient sandstone ceilings, Neolithic hunters inscribed a magical world of horses, cows, and stags, in slashes of red and black, with dots and dashes, flowing manes and tails, flaring nostrils and muscled flanks. In the Great Hall of Bulls, the largest cave, there is the eternal dance: a unicorn guards or chases a herd of horses and a giant bull, and running toward the horses is a trio of aurochs, or wild ox. In the famous Painted Gallery, a prehistoric Sistine Chapel, a stag guards the entrance and a bison stands at the end, and in between is an astonishing parade of ibex, horses, and aurochs; in the middle, the elegantly rendered horses in full extension are surrounded by large red cows. In the Main Gallery, there is the Black Cow panel, a series of cows before a background of horses, bison, and quadrangular signs. Just as the horse and cow are linked at Lascaux, so too do they remain a pair in the American West, but in terms of monetary value, the cow ascended long ago. So we worship at its altar, wear its horns on our belt buckles, participate in strange backyard festivals with burnt offerings and libations, and, in the early days of this country, built towns around it.

Before the Civil War and the great cattle drives, longhorns flourished in the deserts of the Southwest and Texas, having escaped, like horses, from expeditions and rancheros. Cowboys rounded them up and drove them across trails running every which way, selling beef to Indians, the cavalry, settlements. The primary trail at that time was the Shawnee, which ran from central Texas to markets in Kansas City and St. Louis, overshadowed in lore by trails that were blazed later.

When Confederate soldiers returned to Texas, they found that their herds had doubled in size and were roaming the range, unbranded. Texas ranger Charles Goodnight was one of those soldiers; when he came back, he joined a massive roundup of the fugitive cattle and recovered his herd. With immigrants now flooding the North, there was an untapped beef market. The problem was how to get it through the war-torn South. The solution marked the beginning of the great drives.

Goodnight decided to circumvent the devastation and head west, toward New Mexico and Colorado, although that meant crossing a great parched region of Texas. He partnered with cattleman Oliver Loving, and on June 6, 1866, they, their horses, their eighteen hired hands (including a classic character named One-Armed Bill Wilson), and their two thousand cows left Belknap, Texas, west of Fort Worth, and followed the old Butterfield stage route in a southwesterly direction, losing three hundred head before they hit the Pecos River at Horsehead Crossing. This crossing was named by an early explorer who had found horse skulls in the mesquite trees along the riverbank. It was a treacherous point littered with the bones of cattle, mules, and mustangs that had reached the end of the line; they had raced down to the water for a drink only to find themselves mired in the violent swirl and muck of this legendary river.

Years later, in his seminal account called *Riding the Mustang Trail,* Forrester Blake described what happened when his crew found one of their fillies stuck in the sand at a similar location, lying on her belly with her forelegs stretched out and her left hind leg trapped in the bog. "We were quick," he said. "Sinking to our ankles, we grabbed the filly's head and tail and heaved, grunting and bursting into a heavy sweat ... The quicksand was like an octopus, its suction so strong we could not free the mustang." The men extracted themselves, considered shooting the filly, then decided to drag her out with a saddle horse. The buckskin fought to stay away from the quicksand but he was whipped hard, and horse and rider slogged their way to the stranded horse. The cowboy threw a rope around her neck and the work began; the pair tried to haul her out of the muck, and the buckskin strained and grunted and broke out in a foamy sweat, his mouth wide open, sucking air. The little black filly was gasping and choking from the burning lariat, and a coat of quicksand glistened on her hide. Finally she was torn loose from the bog, and she fell on her back and they hauled her to a dry bank, where she wheezed and gulped in air. "Give her a little time to get her wind," one of the men said, "and she'll be crazy as ever." Blake didn't think so and patted her nose, and in a little while she got up and stumbled off to join the other mustangs in their long trek to the market, away from the place known as Skull Valley.

The same cannot be said for many of Goodnight's water-starved cows. "When they reached the river," he later recalled, "those behind pushed the ones in the lead right on across before they had time to stop and drink." One hundred cows met their doom, stranded in quicksand or drowned in the stampede for water. After three days' rest, the battered caravan continued, north along the Pecos and through the domain of the diamondback; then, at the border of Texas and New Mexico, the drovers themselves contributed to the rangeland bone orchard, shooting newborn calves because they couldn't keep up with the herd. "I always hated to kill the innocent things," Goodnight recounted near the end of his life.

Three months later, after driving for another three hundred miles and inventing the chuck wagon en route, the men arrived at Fort Sumner, New Mexico, home to at least ten thousand incarcerated Navajo and Apache. They were hungry. Goodnight and Loving immediately sold their steers for the then-exorbitant price of eight cents per pound, making a total of twelve thousand dollars — a frontier jackpot.

That was the first great cattle drive, and there soon followed more drives along the path that Goodnight had described as "the most desolate country I had ever seen"; within a year after it was blazed, the Goodnight-Loving Trail became one of the most heavily trafficked trails out of Texas, with tributaries branching off to the north and west. By the end of the cattle-drive era, it was a station of the cross in the annals of cowboy history, a geographic touchstone spawning songs and stories about cattle that bawled and were swept away and the men who could only stand by and watch and then move on, cursing thirst and the weather.

Before Charles Goodnight and the men who pioneered the cattle drive, there was a different kind of cowboy, and his descendants were among the many drovers on the great trails, perhaps part of Goodnight's own crew. These cowboys did not have red hair or blond beards, and they did not call themselves Rowdy, Dad, Ike, Wyatt, Zeke, Deke, and Chance. They were named Juan and Isaac and Ismael, although they may have kept that to themselves. Like the horses they rode, these cowboys had come with the conquistadors, who did not want to dirty their hands once the land was taken and so had given the job of running the ranches, taking care of the cattle, and raising the horses to the secret Jews and the Moors and, later, when they were allowed to ride, the Indians of Mexico and Peru and Argentina.

The first man to appear in the official *conquista* records as a vaquero was Sebastian de Mendoza, a Jewish passenger on the *Diego Garcia,* which left Seville in 1513 and landed in the West Indies. In fact, de Mendoza may have been the first cowboy in the New World, although there could have been others who eluded the records. Later, in 1549, the documents list a nameless Morisco, or half Moor, as "the vaquero" on a census for a slave farm in Mexico that was owned by

Cortés — the first such official job designation on the mainland of the New World. By 1545, according to a royal census of that year, a quarter of the Spaniards in Mexico City were Jews, most of whom were Conversos fleeing the Inquisition. Many of them made their way to the outback, as far away from Church officials as possible. By the 1650s, so many secret Jews had fled to Mexico that there were fifteen synagogues in Mexico City, three in Puebla, two in Veracruz, two in Guadalajara, and one each in Zacatecas, Campeche, Mérida, and Monterrey — all ranching centers, with the exception of Mexico City.

As the Spanish Inquisition became the Mexican, Jews who hadn't been arrested and executed abandoned their settlements and headed north, another exodus through arid lands, crossing not the Jordan but the Rio Grande, along with the other new pioneers — the longhorn cattle and mustangs — and the half-breeds and the Indians, now rootless and nomadic, all forming a long-forgotten caravan. The cattle that the Spanish had brought multiplied so quickly that in 1555 the need for Indian cowboys was recognized, and slaves were permitted and encouraged to ride and own horses. "Even the humblest mestizo and the poorest Spaniard possesses his own horses" went the saying, referring to the large numbers of mustangs that were flourishing on the rugged terrain.

These numbers gave Indians mobility; if they didn't like the jobs on a particular ranch, they would ride off to the next ones, and if they needed a few extra cows for themselves, they would rustle some up. For entertainment, they played games with horses and steers — the first rodeos — some of which were very cruel, involving unspeakable terror for the animals of the kingdom, a new take on ancient Roman entertainments that gringos later refined again. These Indians were drifters and vagabonds and often traveled in what might today be called gangs. They polished their riding style, appropriating the Spanish saddle with its pommel and cantle to suit themselves; they coined a new uniform, of the wide sombrero to protect from the blistering sun, and chaps (from the Spanish *chaparro*) to protect from cactus and mesquite.

Since many were fugitives and had secrets, their affect was not at all like that of the expansive and grandiose dons who had driven them from their own land; they generally didn't have much to say, and in that way they had much in common with the Hebrews who were on the run and who made the sign of the cross in public but observed the Jewish Sabbath beyond the eyes of mission priests and their spies. Thus was the first cowboy born — a mysterious stranger who wouldn't be fenced in, who reinvented himself on the plains of the Southwest. Years later the descendants of these early cowboys would discover a menorah stashed behind the crumbling stucco of a bunkhouse, a tattered scroll with strange glyphs rolled up inside an old saddle blanket — remnants from a forbidden world about which they knew nothing — and they would wonder about their family histories, and some would make inquiries and join synagogues, and others would wall everything back up.

After all, everyone thought he or she had come from "an old Spanish family," as the early twentieth-century vaquero Arnold R. Rojas wrote in his beautiful memoir, *California Vaquero*. But that was a lie. "The blood of *caballeros,* bullfighters, Jews, Moors, Basques and Indian heroes ran in the *vaquero*'s veins," Rojas said. "He was a strange mixture of races … He admired his Iberian father, but sided and sympathized with his raped Indian mother. If food was short he fed his horse before he fed his wife. Though often a strange contradiction he was, without doubt, the most interesting man in the New World." By the time the drives ended, the vaquero had become an anomaly of the West. Like the gringos who had appropriated his style, affect, and very name (*vaca* translates as "cow"), he was out of a job, and worse, disappeared from the record and lore, soon to be found under a sombrero as a cowboy's sidekick in the new form of entertainment called the Western.

From the close of the Civil War through 1888 or so, a million horses, six million cattle, and thirty-five thousand men traveled from deep Texas, through the Indian Nations' territory that later became Oklahoma, and into Kansas on the rocky roads that formed the cattle-drive trail system. The figure of a million horses refers to those that were taken from what is still called the Wild Horse Desert (although long bereft of the animal). An unknown number of horses did not even survive the cullings. In his memoir, *A Vaquero of the Brush Country,* John D. Young recounted an incident in which some mustang hunters built a corral for two hundred horses along the Cibolo Creek in Texas. They drove in a thousand on a dead run, and as the path of entry narrowed, the horses ran harder. The corral quickly filled up, but the animals kept running, climbing over horses that had gotten there first. "Hundreds of the mustangs were smothered and trampled to death," Young wrote. "In some places around the fences, the dead and maimed were piled up so high that the plunging horses on top of them climbed over and got away . . . I often passed by the ruins of the old pen and saw the whitened bones of its victims."

The survivors joined countless others on the trail and were driven to market themselves. But some did not get that far, because of accidents and killings. Mustanger Blake recounted an episode in which one of the horses on his drive became so uncontrollable — or wild — that instead of letting it go, the men shot him: One day, they came across a lake and let the horses stop for a drink. There was a roan that waded in and kept going. One of the men picked up a gun and fired. He hit him behind the ear and the roan quivered and began walking in circles. The shooter fired again, hitting him between the eyes. The roan fell, struggled to his feet, and resumed walking. Again the man fired, hitting him in the brain. Still the roan kept walking. Disgusted, the shooter retrieved a bigger gun. "At the loud report," Blake wrote, "the roan lifted off all four feet and sailed through the air. He never got up to start the circling. A big hole had opened between the eyes and blood poured out of it. Pretty soon we began to hear noises in the belly region. We left the little roan to the buzzards."

The historical record does not tell us how many horses were used in the actual drives. But considering that most of the thirty-five thousand men on the trails had not just one horse but several (a remuda, supplied by the owner of the cattle), and given that many of these horses died along the drives and had to be replaced, then, in addition to the million mustangs that were driven to market, there must have been at least half a million horses running up and down the old cattle trails of the central Great Plains.

Exactly who were the horses that traversed these trails? The most famous cow horse of them all was Smoky. Although his story was a fiction, told in the novel of the same name, it serves as the only full account we have of the life of a cowboy's best friend.

It was written in 1926 by the cowboy author and artist Will James, a devotee of Charles Russell and Frederic Remington. As a young boy, James was lured from Canada to the American West by pulp novels. He became a ranch hand and found salvation in mustangs. Soon he began drawing and writing about range life in Montana and submitted his stories to *Scribner's Magazine,* where Maxwell Perkins gave him his first professional boost, publishing his work alongside Faulkner's and Hemingway's.

But he achieved his greatest acclaim with *Smoky.* Written in cowboy vernacular and accompanied by the author's wonderful line drawings, *Smoky* told the tale of a wild horse whose life paralleled the rise and fall of the cattle-drive era. He was captured by a cowboy named Clint and became his best friend as they traversed the trails herding longhorns. Then he was lost, fell into the hands of a cruel owner, was passed to another one, nearly got sold for chicken feed, and then was found again years later by the long-heartbroken Clint and finally returned to the wild. *Smoky* was one of the bestsellers of all time, generating not one but two movies and calling many a young boy to the range.

By today's standards, it is certainly a literary curiosity. But it has never gone out of print, remaining a favorite among devotees of early Western fiction, a classic story of a great horse from his first breath to his last days. This is how it begins:

> It seemed like Mother Nature was sure agreeable that day when the little black colt came to the range world and tried to get a footing with his long wobblety legs on the brown prairie sod. Short stems of new green grass was trying to make their way up thru the last year's faded growth and reaching for the sun's warm rays. Taking in all that could be seen, felt, and inhaled, there was no day, time, nor place that could beat that spring morning on the sunny side of the low prairie butte where Smoky the colt was foaled.

Of course, Smoky was not yet named Smoky and his black coat would become the color of smoke by the time he was captured by Clint a few months later. Within a couple of years, he would be working the famous Chisholm Trail — although not named in the book, that's the trail that all the lesser paths fed into, and sooner or later, every trail-broke cow pony traversed it. The Chisholm was a wide avenue, ranging from two to four hundred yards across, "a chocolate band amid the green prairies, beaten into the bare earth," according to one traveler. Along its flanks were the bleaching skulls and skeletons of tired animals that had died along the way. "Here and there," said the traveler, "was a low mound showing where some cowboy had literally died with his boots on." The trail was also pockmarked with vast barren circles, where massive herds had bedded down for a night before they were urged on.

Although the Chisholm was primarily a cattle trail, it was also much more. Like Route 66, the highway that later carried Dust Bowl exiles to California for the golden dream, the Chisholm was a great river of humanity, ferrying all manner of post–Civil War wayfarers to the promise of a better life. Freed slaves headed to Kansas for the mules and plots of farmland promised them by the government, and they were joined by sodbusters heading for federally granted homesteads. "Some of these negroes were afoot," wrote cowboy Charles A. Siringo at the time, "while others drove donkeys and oxen. The shiny black children and half-starved dogs were plentiful."

Cowboys celebrated the well-worn path in the epic ballad called "The Old Chisholm Trail," and over the years it was embellished and refined many times, recounting various escapades and characters of the drive, with possibly the most well-known refrain in the annals of the West — "Come a ti yi yippee, come a ti yi yea."

A drive up the Chisholm was organized with great precision. As *History* magazine tells it, here's how it worked:

Ahead of the herd rode the trail boss, searching for the best route, grass, water, river crossings, and campsites. Next came two point riders, who guided the lead steers, old and experienced animals trusted by the rest of the herd ... About a third of the way back from the point riders, a pair of swing riders rode on either side of the herd. They zigzagged back and forth, keeping cattle from straying from the herd. About two thirds of the way toward the rear rode two flank riders with similar duties.

The toughest job of all on the drive was riding drag, watching the rear of the herd. Drag riders had to watch out for steers bolting away from the herd, but also had to push and prod straggling animals. All the while, the dust kicked up by 10,000 hooves enveloped, choked, and nearly blinded them. A bandana worn over the nose and mouth filtered a little of the dust.

Generally, drives would begin in the spring to avoid bad weather, and usually the trip from Texas to points north took about four months, covering about ten to fifteen miles per day. On the first few days, they went farther, to make sure the cattle were too tired to stampede at night. Cowboys were paid about thirty dollars per month, plus all the game they could find on the drive. But they were not allowed to take cows from the plentiful herds, which ranged from 1,000 to 2,500 animals. Sometimes there was just one cowboy for every 250 to 400 cattle. The convoy often moved in a long single column that stretched out for a mile or two on the trail.

Cowboys on the trail communicated by sign language, a system derived from Plains Indians, or by moving their hats. Hat in the left hand and reins in the right meant break camp and move up the trail. The hat would be angled toward the route, and the signal would be passed down the line. At around eleven in the morning, the leader would wave his hat to either the right or the left, indicating on which side of the trail they should stop and let the cattle graze. When the cattle lay down, it was time to move on, for they had clearly had enough to eat.

Some members of the herd were considered good lead steers, and they would make the trip up and down the trail several times, winning them a reprieve from slaughter. A lead cow was called the Judas steer (a sad name that would later be passed on in both label and task to a "lead" wild horse when mustangs became subject to mass government roundups). Some trail veterans became famous, including Charles Goodnight's steer Old Blue. According to legend, he lived out his final years at Goodnight's ranch, where he eventually passed away with dignity, and a shrine was made of his horns.

On May 10, 1869, the golden spike was hammered into the ground, commemorating the joining of the Union Pacific and Central Pacific railroads at Promontory, Utah, which completed the first cross-country rail line. With much fanfare, the two coasts were now linked by the iron horse, and the great wide open was on its way to being a smaller place. Time began to overrule space, and by 1883, the country had been divided into time zones to accommodate railroad schedules. Yet the trails were still an echo of ancient civilizations, with mounted nomads shepherding meat through rugged terrain, not concerned with artificial zones, tracking time and direction by way of the Big Dipper. "Only one man in our particular outfit started out with a watch," cowboy John D. Young wrote, "and he got it so full of water when we crossed the Brazos that it quit running." The Mexican vaqueros in Arizona referred to the Big Dipper as *el Reloj de los Yaquis* — the Clock of the Yaqui Indians. "It was more clearly and beautifully illuminated than the dial of any hour plate that ever looked down from cathedral or statehall tower," Young said. "We could not hear its chimes as it revolved around the North Star, but in clear weather we changed guards according to its position as accurately as the Moslems of the East bow at sunset to the muezzin's call to prayer."

As always in the wilderness, the beautiful starlit trails could also kill, dealing blows that neither man nor beast could answer. "Out on the range," said *Prose and Poetry of the Livestock Industry,* a lively nineteenth-century encyclopedia documenting the role of various animals in ancient and modern cultures, "there was a trinity of evils." Each of them created conditions in which "horses were crippled or gored daily," said one cowboy. For instance, if a drive slowed down or left late in the year, there was the blizzard. It could bury man and beast alike, and sometimes did. A plains trail veteran recounted the story of what happened to "a negro cowboy named George" during a severe winter storm. "We all had colds and coughs till it was like a bunch of Texas pot hounds baying a 'possum when we tried to sleep. One bitter night I was near George on herd and tried to get him to go to the chuckwagon and turn his horse loose. His teeth were chattering as he said to me, 'I can stand it if the rest of you all can.' Presently I saw him lean over his saddle horn, coughing, and he looked like he was losing his breath. By the time I got to him he was off his horse, as dead as a mackerel and as stiff as a poker."

One of the saddest cowboy songs ever written, "The Blizzard," tells the story of a cowboy returning on his pony, Dan, to his sweetheart, Mary Anne, with a treacherous winter storm coming on. Dan is lame, "can't hardly stand," the cowboy's hands are froze, and there's a numbness in his toes. But it's "only seven miles to Mary Anne," as the chorus goes, subtracting miles with each new stanza. Now it's suppertime and the cowboy imagines biscuits in the pan but "the wind's howlin' and we'd best be movin' faster if we can." He tells his pony to think about "that barn, with hay so soft and warm," but Dan falls, and then comes the line, "get up you ornery cuss or you'll be the death of us." With three miles to go, the cowboy relents, and agrees with Dan that maybe it's a good idea to stop and rest, now with just one mile to go. The storm passes that night, and at dawn, horse and rider are found. Dan could have made it, the song says, but the cowpuncher didn't want to leave his pony and so "they found him there on the plains, his hands froze to the reins, he was just a hundred yards from Mary Anne."

Unlike cowboys and their ponies, wild horses on the trails weathered severe storms just fine. Forrester Blake — the man who had coldly recounted a mustang killing in his book — wrote with admiration about the great survival qualities of wild horses. He recalled a storm in which the thunder "had come close, sounding hollow and

Drifting Before the Storm by Frederic Remington, 1904.

deep as if someone were beating on a kettle drum" and the lightning "came straight down in smooth and solid bars." The mares were up with their colts at their sides; "the herd had bunched, tails to the rising wind." The horsemen circled the herd, talking to the mustangs, watching for signs of stampede. "But the wild ones from the Mescalero stood together on the prairie," Blake wrote. "Necks low, bodies pressing close together and always tails to the wind that ripped their hides with rain and hail, they stood and made no trouble ... Too long had they lived in the high mountains where storms are as common and sharp as the pine trees on the ridges. When morning came, with a red clear dawn lighting up a prairie smelling clean and fresh, they scattered out to graze. Night watch was done. The prairie storm had passed away."

The next evil along the trail was drought. Many a steer on the Chisholm went crazy or blind due to lack of water, and countless horses and men faltered. "The science of the trail was in grazing and watering the cattle," said one observer. "I have met but few men who know how to water cattle properly ... the last half of the day's travel was accomplished much easier than the first half, for the cattle would be growing thirsty and becoming eager to get to water." Sometimes the water source they reached was too alkaline, but there was no stopping the cattle from drinking, and they would poison themselves and die. Sometimes they ran over one another to get to a stream. Sometimes wildfires raged through the prairie tinder, and the cattle themselves were used to stanch the blaze; one cowboy recounted an incident in which he and other hands shot dozens of cows and heaved their wet and bloody carcasses onto the encroaching, wind-driven flames.

The third evil of the trail was the stampede, an event cowboys were so concerned about that during the first few days of the drive, they often slept with their boots on, their lariats wrapped around their wrists, and their horses close enough to mount quickly if the herd took off. Things were so tense at this stage of the drive that it was forbidden to touch a sleeping compadre without speaking to him first, lest the sleeper awake and fire his gun — perhaps killing someone and starting a stampede at the same time. If that happened, the cows could run for thirty miles before they were stopped or became too worn out to continue. "If the herd were not quickly brought un-der control," said the livestock encyclopedia, "there would be plenty of beef wreckage at the first bluff."

One way of subduing the cows was to shoot them through the horns. According to John Young, a center hit caused enough pain to calm the steer. If the pith of the horn was punctured, the sore-ness kept the steer on his best behavior for weeks. Sometimes a shot would ricochet off the horn, back toward the man who shot it. Oc-casionally a missed shot killed a steer. But the cows were cheap, and it was an advantage to get rid of the rebellious ones so they wouldn't cause more trouble.

But all too often on the Chisholm, both man and horse were in-jured or killed by runaway cattle trains. If the ground was rough, the horse could stumble and fall while chasing down the herd. If the horse got too close to the cattle, both horse and rider could get mowed down by the barreling hooves. On the leeward side of a herd, so much heat was thrown off during a stampede that a man's face might blister, "as if he had been struck by a blast from a furnace," a cowboy recalled. Blisters may well have erupted under a horse's sad-dle, and a horse may have been knifed by the horns of a careening steer. The clashing of horns and hooves created a terrible odor, and the horse — the wind-drinker — would have gulped in great waves of it, tasting the fear of the renegade animals, swallowing the despera-tion as he charged on, responding to his rider's calls and physical commands as he tried to contain the herd.

The most perilous moment came when horse and rider found themselves in front of a stampeding herd — a situation that spelled doom on the trail. Such was an incident recounted by legendary cowpuncher E. C. "Teddy Blue" Abbott in his famous memoir, *We Pointed Them North.* One night, while taking a herd of cattle from Ne-braska to Colorado, Abbott and three other cowboys camped along the Blue River close to a prairie dog town. A terrible storm came up, and all four men tried to hold the cattle, but they could not and there was a terrible stampede. In the morning, one man was missing. "We went back to look for him," Abbott said, "and we found him among the prairie dog holes, beside his horse. The horse's ribs were scraped bare, and the rest of the horse and man were mashed into the ground as flat as a pancake. The only thing you could recognize was the handle of his six-shooter."

When the crew wrote to the cowboy's family about the accident, they blamed lightning—which also took its share of earthly sacrifice along the trail. But what had really happened was that the horse had stepped into a prairie dog hole, and both man and animal fell before the onrushing cattle. And all night long, as the three men tried to contain the cows, the frightened animals had been running back and forth across their friend and his steed. They buried the cowboy on a hillside, on top of his saddle blanket, and covered the grave with rocks. As for what happened to the horse's remains, there is no mention. Perhaps a coyote emerged from a den at dusk, noted the carcass, called to her cubs, and they converged to pick it clean. Or perhaps the stampede left nothing in the way of meat or sinew. As for the longhorns themselves, we do know this: those that survived would have lost considerable weight; if they were not fit for the market, or not able to make it that far, they would have been shot, stripped of their hides, and eaten.

In dangerous situations, a cowboy was only as good as his remuda. Every cowboy had a favorite horse that performed a particular task with great loyalty and finesse. For instance, the Will James stand-in Clint said Smoky worked cattle so well that riders from other outfits would come to watch, and soon he became the talk of all the cow camps and many suitors offered to buy him. But Smoky was Clint's one true love—and he returned the devotion:

> Once in a while . . . Clint would get sort of selfish and want Smoky's company on that long half a day's herding, and it was during them spells that the two got to be more understanding . . . Neither was so rushed for work then, and there was times when the big herd of beef steers and cows and weaners would want to graze and not to drift away or scatter. At them times Clint would rein Smoky up a knoll, and where both could see the whole of the herd. He'd get out of his saddle and stretch out in the shade Smoky made, and take it easy, and there, with one eye on the cowboy, the other on the herd, and swishing flies, Smoky would stand.

For drover John Young, his heart belonged to Payaso, a gentle six-year-old with a mottled face. Payaso was good on the road and in the brush. He never stumbled. He came to Young's call or whistle. He was fond of sugar, which Young often gave him, but that "never impaired his wonderful foraging abilities." He was such a good cutting horse that Young could ride him into a herd, show him the cow that he wanted cut out, take off the bridle, and let Payaso act alone. "Sometimes I actually felt ashamed of myself in his company," Young said. "He knew so much. Indeed he was a kind of equine genius in the business of handling cattle." Young never hit Payaso, and he barely touched spurs to his flanks. At night, Payaso would not leave his side. "I loved him," the cowboy declared.

J. Frank Dobie's favorite was a cutting horse named Buck, not just for his skills and loyalty and generosity, but also because he was Buck. And Dobie was not ashamed to declare his passion on the page. One of the cowboy's great pleasures was listening to Buck drink water, and he loved to watch him after he had had his fill, when he would "lip the water's surfaces and drip big drops back into it." Reminiscing about Buck made him recall the girls of his youth. Oh, he had loved four or five but had told only one, he said. She thought it was a joke, and Dobie moved on, later considering the rejection a favor. "All those rose-lipt maidens and all the lightfoot lads with whom I ran in those days have receded until they have little meaning," he said. As the years passed, Buck became more important, forever connecting Dobie with the land. "To remember him," Dobie wrote, "is a joy and a tonic."

Among all the horses in a remuda, it was the night horse who was perhaps the most valued, often making the difference between life and death for the cowboy. A good night horse could find his way home during a dark and stormy evening, would not spook at the sounds and sights of the wilderness nocturne, and would know exactly what to do in the case of a midnight stampede. Up and down the trails, cowboys gathered at the fire and swapped tales about the legendary night horse Sid (named for the CID brand) as if reciting a prayer. He was a brown Spanish horse working out of a ranch on the lower Texas plains. When dawn broke and the stampedes had ended and the fanged and fur-covered stalkers that licked their chops at the sight of the passing and captive meat began to recede, Sid knew that his shift was over and would start to head home. But where was home? Sometimes the camp had moved to avoid bad weather or the runaway train of cattle. That's when Sid really proved his worth: he would take his bit in his teeth and head for the chuck wagon.

Then there was the famous night horse — unnamed in the record — who saved the life of cowboy Uel Livingstone. The longhorns had grazed, the sun had gone down, and the cattle were sleeping. In fact, the herd had gotten so quiet that Uel took his horse aside, dismounted, and caught a nap. But the earth rumbled and vibrated, and he woke up. The cattle were running, a roiling mass, with little blue flames flickering at the tips of their horns — electricity caused by the friction of their hides as they rubbed up against one another in the jam. What had set them off, we do not know. A horse's nicker perhaps. A drop of rain. The beat of an owl's wings. Uel awoke as the crazed mass closed in. He started to get up, but something stopped him — his horse, who was standing over him, front feet on one side of his body and hind feet on the other. When the stampede was over, he was alive, and so was his horse. He was convinced that his night partner had saved him. "In a stampede," a cowboy observed, "a man was not himself, and his horse was not the horse of yesterday."

Over time, cowboys learned what would and would not disturb the driven cows, and they began to sing to their herds at night, or play calming melodies on the fiddle, to soothe them as they rested on the plain. These cowboy lullabies are a great legacy of the cattle-drive era, and who can say that they did not quiet the animals in their last days, as well as the anxious riders who longed for sweethearts or safe passage through wind and sleet?

"One lazy old brindle steer that always stayed in the drag by day and slept on the south edge of the herd at night seemed particularly fond of 'One Evening in May' — a waltz tune," recalled John Young. "More than once I stopped to see him wriggle his ears and kind of blow in an appreciative manner. Pleasant it was on a warm, clear night to circle slowly around a herd of cattle that were bedded down quiet and breathing deep and out there to catch the strains of song or fiddle coming from camp, where the fire was like a dim star."

Certainly, over time the horses would recognize some of these songs and perhaps, like their riders, would find comfort in the hearing, for they are creatures of habit as well as of instinct. And so when the thunderheads would crack and explode and the horses would want to bolt but could not, who can say that the vibrations of a particular note or series of notes, sung, for instance, in a strong and confident tone by someone whose voice they recognized, would not in fact resonate in the very cells of the horses, and help them go about their nighttime tasks, keeping all hell from breaking loose?

In fact, there are tales of such episodes, of range animals drawn to the singing of men at night, listening to a particularly compelling voice. In his account of a journey across the Colorado River in Texas in 1849, the French missionary Abbé Domenech told of his party's last night on the plain before returning home:

> Pipes were lighted, conversation became animated, we wrapped our cloaks about us, looked up to the heavens, and sang in concert such as memory recalled of the hymns and melodies which had been familiar to us in our childhood. At two o'clock in the morning, we ceased singing, but what was our surprise on finding that we were surrounded by Americans, Irishmen, and Mexicans, who had drawn near to hear us sing; behind them we saw a regular troop of horses and cattle, forming a circle around us.

In 1867, the Kansas Pacific railroad built a depot in Abilene, Kansas, for the purpose of shipping cattle that were being run up the Chisholm from Texas. The first longhorns arrived that same year, and Abilene became the original cow town on the prairie. A year later, it was a thriving and rowdy prairie crossroads, filled with businessmen, gamblers, pimps, prostitutes, and outlaws. "At this writing," proclaimed the *Topeka Commonwealth* two years later, "Hell is now in session in Abilene." Meanwhile, homesteaders had been streaming across the plains, taking advantage of the Homestead Act that Abraham Lincoln had signed in 1862. For a small filing fee and five years of continuous residence, settlers were given 160 acres of surveyed public land, which they promised to farm. As soon as the settlers arrived in the West, they built fences — they didn't like free-ranging cattle running across their fledgling crops, and even toward the end of the cattle-drive period, one Nebraska pioneer complained of being unable to step out of her front door and into her yard because there were too many longhorns.

Bereft of trees that could be chopped down for wood, land on the plains provided a different kind of fence — a thorny bush called Osage orange, which settlers planted on the edges of their fields to keep cattle out. It didn't work that well, and some citizens of Abilene wanted the ranch hands gone for reasons other than their trampling cattle — cowboys were simply too violent. The settlers brought in a different kind of fence, the town marshal, but that didn't work either. In 1872, they tried one more approach: circulating a countywide petition that asked cowboys to leave. "We, the undersigned, members of the Farmers' Protective Association, and officers and citizens of Dickinson County, Kansas," it read, "most respectfully request all who have contemplated driving Texas cattle to Abilene the coming Season to seek some other point for shipment, as the inhabitants of Dickinson will no longer submit to the evils of the trade." It was signed by 80 percent of the county's citizens. And thus the first cow town became the first victim of the new wagon in the American parade; wheat was taking over, and the drovers moved on up the trail.

The pattern in Abilene would be repeated in towns up and down the trails, from Ellsworth to Hays City, Newton, Wichita, and Dodge City, the last of which acquired the label of Cowboy Capital and became the most infamous of them all. As the prairie began to fill up with farmers, tensions between homesteaders and cattlemen increased, and there soon came the demand for better fencing. On November 24, 1874, the federal government issued patent number 157124 to Joseph Glidden of DeKalb, Illinois. At the time, Illinois was a crossroads for the problems of the day. "It looked to the East and to the West," as one observer said. "It was of the frontier and not of the frontier, a meeting ground for the past and future." While strolling through the DeKalb County fair a year earlier, Glidden, a farmer, had been intrigued by an exhibit that featured a new kind of fencing. It was designed by another farmer to control a wayward cow, and it consisted of a wooden rail with short wire points that extended out in sharp projections. The rail could be attached to an existing fence.

At home in his kitchen, with the help of his wife, Glidden began to improve on the idea. He attached twisted barbs to a smooth wire but quickly realized that they did not stay in place. A modified coffee grinder solved the problem; he bent a short wire around a longer one, then placed the short wire between the pins of a coffee mill; with each turn of the mill's crank, he tightened the loop around the long wire. Then he clipped the short wire to about an inch long, cutting at an angle so that the ends formed sharp points. He then wrapped a second long wire around the first long wire, twisting them together so that there were two lengthy strands of entwined wire with barbs along the entire length. He tested the invention in his barnyard, and it worked. Glidden registered the patent, calling his barbed wire "the Winner" (although within a couple of years, many referred to it as "the devil's rope" because of the damage it did to cows). Glidden began selling it to neighbors. Word of the wire spread quickly, sales increased, and Glidden sold his company to a competitor.

Behind almost every cataclysmic change, there's an advance man, beginning with John the Baptist. For barbed wire, that man was John Warne Gates, hired to make the pitch in Texas where cattlemen had shunned the new gimmick from the North. Moreover, they remained firm in their desire to preserve the open range, and they also feared that the wire would hurt their cows. In 1876, the year that Custer was routed at the Little Bighorn, Gates, the twenty-one-year-old farm boy with the gift of gab, was sent to San Antonio, a center for the cattle trade. As the story goes, a rancher told Gates about a stubborn bull named Ol' Blue who could "go through anything" and would probably not stop at barbed wire. "I've worked something out," Gates replied. "We'll sell more barbed wire than you can shake a stick at. Get the wildest damn cattle in Texas. Corral 'em here with barbed wire and then let 'em try to get out. That'll show 'em."

The rancher agreed to the plan, and a large corral in front of the Alamo in downtown San Antonio was constructed. Cattlemen gathered with their longhorns and drove them into the pen. Taunted by spectators, the cows repeatedly charged the wire. The barriers held, and a fencing frenzy erupted across the West.

Initially, the railroad had been the biggest buyer of barbed wire, using it to keep cattle from roaming across the tracks and getting hit by trains. But now cattlemen, particularly those who owned the biggest spreads, purchased the wire; fearing that there wasn't enough grass and water to feed the coming herds, they began to fence off the range themselves, lest they be closed out by others.

In 1881, a book called *The Beef Bonanza: How to Get Rich on the Plains* was published, and it drew yet more people to the changing frontier. "The West! The mighty West!" proclaimed its author, the Civil War hero General James S. Brisbin. "That land where the buffalo still roams and the wild savage dwells . . . where the poor, professional young man, flying from the overcrowded East and the tyranny of a moneyed aristocracy, finds honor and wealth." The book was hugely popular in Scotland and England, where many read this early and overblown self-help guide and became determined to strike it rich in America by parlaying a few cows into a fortune. Whereas many previous accounts of the Great Plains had described the region as a desert, Brisbin had experience driving cattle across the arid region to Indian reservations and knew that the animals could thrive there, suggesting that the prairie grasses rendered the land perfect for producing meat. In typical American style, he omitted any mention of difficulties such as catastrophic weather, and he presented an enticing formula:

> If $250,000 were invested in ten ranches and ranges, placing 2,000 head on each range, by selling the beeves as fast as they mature, and all the cows as soon as they were too old to breed well, and investing the receipts in young cattle, at the end of five years there would be at least 45,000 head on the ten ranges, worth at least $18.00 per head, or $810,000. Assuming the capital was borrowed at 10 per cent interest, in five years the interest would amount to $125,000, which must be deducted; $250,000 principal, and interest for five years, compounded at 25 per cent per annum, would only be $762,938, or less than the value of the cattle exclusive of the ranches and fixtures. I have often thought if some enterprising persons would form a joint-stock company for the purpose of breeding, buying, and selling horses, cattle, and sheep, it would prove enormously profitable. I have no doubt but a company properly managed would declare an annual dividend of at least 25 per cent.

Bingo! — the beef rush was on. Entrepreneurs rushed to the plains and established a wave of new ranches, quickly striking gold in the new treasure chest. Just like Brisbin had promised, cattle that were worth $11 each in Texas could be sold in Kansas for $22 a head, and then at the slaughterhouses in Chicago for $44 each. With so much money to be made, the frenzy to fence off the range reached a new pitch. It was clear that the cattle boom would soon be over, and everyone wanted a piece of it before it ended. Old rivalries became more pronounced, and new ones erupted. Cattlemen were pitted against sheep men, whose nomadic ways required open territory. In one case, to discourage Wyoming senator Warren from running sheep, cattle ranchers crippled and killed hundreds of his range horses by trapping them while they drank from troughs and then stampeding them into a barbed-wire fence. "Wagons groaning with wire came rumbling out to the cattle ranches," reported the *Cattleman* magazine. "Posts every thirty feet and four strands of wire spider-webbed the West. In some sections, fencing bees were held. In western Kansas and the Indian territory, small cattle companies combined into huge pools and fenced off thousands of acres." On the Frying Pan Ranch in the Texas Panhandle, cattlemen enclosed 250,000 acres at a cost of $30,000. In Nebraska, a rancher claimed one million acres with the devil's rope, and in New Mexico, Charles Goodnight fenced off three times that amount. Production of barbed wire went from five tons in 1874 to two hundred thousand tons by the end of the nineteenth century, and during that time, people began cutting the fences down.

The fence wars began in 1882. Gangs of fence cutters with names like the Owls, the Blue Devils, and the Javelinas headed out on midnight rides, laying waste to the barbed wire that locked up the land. The *Wyoming Sentinel* seemed to approve of their tactics and summed up the situation this way: "Some morning we will wake up to find that a corporation has run a wire fence about the boundary lines of Wyoming, and all within the same have been notified to move." But in the Lone Star State, the Texas Rangers were called in to patrol areas where fence-cutting was rampant, and it soon became a felony.

Battles continued to rage across the West, and nature finally intervened, rendering General Brisbin's happy beef bonanza a scene of carnage and despair. The grasslands were overgrazed and barren. A long drought beginning in 1883 aggravated the situation, producing cattle that were thin and weak. Beef prices fell. Then, on November 13, 1886, it started to snow and did not stop for an entire month. In mid-December, there was a thaw, and the snow turned to slush. In late December, the temperature dropped again, to 30 degrees below zero, and the slush turned to a vast and solid sheet of ice. January of 1887 was the coldest month in memory, bringing with it one blizzard that raged for seventy-two hours. "It was all so slow," wrote Teddy Abbott, "plunging after [the cows] through the deep snow ... The horses' feet were cut and bleeding from the heavy crust, and the cattle had the hair and hide wore off their legs to the knees and the hocks. It was surely hell to see big four-year-old steers just able to stagger along. It was the same all over Wyoming, Montana, and Colorado, western Nebraska, and western Kansas."

Much of the cattle had wandered as far as drift fences, built to keep them from running off. Now, the cows died there, huddling together for shelter, falling over, impaled on the wires, freezing to death, cracking into pieces, piling up high enough for men to walk over. In March, Teddy Roosevelt rode the stretches of his Dakota ranch. "The land was a mere barren waste," he wrote, "not a green thing could be seen; the dead grass eaten off till the country looked as if it had been shaved with a razor. Occasionally among the desolate hills a rider would come across a band of gaunt, hollow-flanked cattle feebly cropping the sparse, dry pasturage, too listless to move out of the way; and the blackened carcasses lay in the sheltered spots, some stretched out, others in as natural a position as if the animals had merely lain down to rest."

The winter of 1886 to 1887 came to be known as the Great Die-Up, and it is regarded as the marker for the closing of the range. It was also the same year that Geronimo and his band of Apache, the last Native American holdouts, were captured and shipped by boxcar to Florida to perform hard labor. "All in all," Goodnight said when it was over, referring to the infancy of the era, "my years on the trail were the happiest I ever lived. Most of the time we were solitary adventurers in a great land as fresh and new as a spring morning. And we were free, and full of the zest of darers."

But there was another side to the story and it came out as the snows blanketed the range. It was about the brute force used against the mustang on the trail and it was part of a book called *A Texas Cowboy, or, Fifteen Years on the Hurricane Deck of a Spanish Pony*

— *Taken from Real Life.* The memoir was penned by Lone Star native Charles A. Siringo. Despite its disturbing account, the book would go on to sell hundreds of thousands of copies, drawing many to the cowboy life in the West even as it was fully enclosed by the devil's rope and controlled by large syndicates based elsewhere.

Siringo was born in Matagorda, Texas, on February 7, 1856. Wild steers roamed the Matagorda peninsula, and for fun, cowboys would come from the mainland to polish up their roping skills. Young Charles would copy them, taking his stick horse out on the beach, making a lariat out of fishing line, and trying to lasso the crabs that traveled in droves. Soon he moved on to riding real horses and roping real cows, and when he was a teenager, he joined a cattle outfit and hit the Chisholm Trail. Along the way, he was drawn to writing and soon felt compelled to speak for the beast of burden.

"Dear reader," he asked in *Texas Cowboy,* "may I use you for a few moments? Lean back, close your eyes, and pretend that you're an old knee-sprung, poor, sore-backed pony whose hips and shoulders are scarred up with Spanish brands and spur gashes." Now, it's early spring, he continued, the grass is showing, and you're feeling happy after being turned out since the fall—there are lots of tender shoots for the taking, and you don't have to paw through the snow and ice for a few sprigs of dry tasteless herbs. But the old hands on their fat corn-fed ponies have come to get you, for spring work is about to begin.

"You break and run," he said, "to try and get away, but you are too weak; they soon overtake you, and start you toward the 'home-ranch.' They drive you into a corral, along with the rest of your skinny companions. Last year's sore on your back has healed up and a new coat of hair is just starting to grow over it," Siringo observed. Now, here comes the boss with the new summer hires. "You are leaning against the fence scratching yourself when a rope is pitched over your head. 'Here, Curly! You can take this fellow for one of yours,' yells the boss as he drags you towards the gate." Curly throws an old saddle on your back and you snort and start pitching, which angers Curly. So when you stop bucking, he ties you up and starts beating you over the head and back with a doubled rope.

Finally, he gets you saddled, but when he mounts, you start bucking again. Somehow he stays on. The boss tells the hands to drive down San Pedro Canyon to Buzzard Flat for the roundup. Along the way, you step into a badger hole and fall, throwing Curly hard against the ground. "You jump up and stand trembling from the shock you received," Siringo wrote, "while your mad master takes hold of the bridle-reins and goes to abusing you for falling—not only with his tongue, but by jerking the reins, which are attached to the severe Spanish bit, causing your mouth to bleed, and kicking you in the stomach with the toe of his boot."

Finally you reach San Pedro Canyon, and the hands dismount to move their saddles back in place and tighten the girths. "The ponies are white with sweat," Siringo continued, "and panting like lizards." After surveying the country, the boss orders Curly to head west about five miles and run the cattle down the canyon. Curly buries his spurs deep into your bloody sides. As you close in on the cows, they take off at full speed, in the wrong direction . . . At nightfall, you return to camp. Curly can't wait to get to the grub, so he jerks your saddle off and turns you loose without washing your back, kicking you with his boot. "You are by this time a pitiful looking sight as you trot off . . . But the worst part of it is your back," Siringo said. "The day has been very hot, causing the old last year's sore to become scalded. When the saddle was jerked off, the old scab with its new growth of hair, also went, having adhered to the blanket."

Now it's morning; the sun peeps over the trees, where little birds greet daybreak with joy. "But there is no joy nor happiness for you," Siringo said. You are roped and dragged to the hitching post. You're bridled "and then your lazy master picks up the dirty, hard, saddle blankets—which have not been washed for a month—and throws them over your raw and swollen back."

Finally comes the saddle, which makes you squirm and twist, and then once again comes Curly himself. "You can now wake up, dear reader," Siringo concluded, "for we know you are disgusted playing the role of a sore-backed Spanish cow-pony."

And how fared Siringo's own horses? In 1922, as Siringo faltered with pleurisy, he raffled off his beloved Sailor Gray, a horse who had served him for years, for a hundred dollars in cash. That left eighteen-year-old Patsy, his one-and-only. "He was hog-fat," he wrote, "and I had been offered $150 for him. But I wouldn't risk selling him, for fear that he might, in time, fall into cruel hands." Deciding that Patsy would be better off in horse heaven with his father, Rowdy, Siringo took him into the woods and put a .45 in his brain.

In his later years, Siringo became a celebrity, penning other tales about his life and moving to Los Angeles, where he became part of a salon of cowboy writers that included Will James and Zane Grey. At the end of his last book, *Riata and Spurs,* he requested that his tombstone bear the following inscription, written by the legendary cowboy poet Badger Clark Jr.:

> *'Twas good to live when all the range*
> *Without no fence or fuss,*
> *Belonged in partnership with God,*
> *The Government and us.*
>
> *With skyline bounds from east to west,*
> *With room to go and come,*
> *I liked my fellow man the best*
> *When he was scattered some.*
>
> *When my old soul hunts range and rest*
> *Beyond the last divide,*
> *Just plant me on some strip of west*
> *That's sunny, lone and wide.*
>
> *Let cattle rub my headstone round,*
> *And coyotes wail their kin,*
> *Let hosses come and paw the mound,*
> *But don't you fence it in.*

Along with the Buffalo Bill shows of the late nineteenth century, there was another horse spectacle growing in popularity. This was the rodeo, from the Spanish for "to surround." With roots in Extremadura and other regions of Spain, rodeos had been popping up all over the West since the 1700s, starting with the Days of the Bulls at the Spanish missions in Texas and California. In a ritualized display of the vaquero's work, a man on horseback would run down a group of longhorns, cut one from the herd, grab it by the tail, and hurl it to the

ground. The practice was called bull-tailing. Later, after cowboys finished long drives, they would gather in stockyards and hold competi-
tions to see who was best at cutting, roping, and branding. The men
would also display their equestrian skills, demonstrating how well
they worked with the horses in their remudas.

But there was another aspect of the early rodeos that had nothing
to do with the tasks of a cattle drive. This was a display of how long a
cowboy could remain aboard a bucking bronco. The harder and longer it bucked, the more it seemed to dare the rider to stay on, endure,
tough it out through every contortion and leap. Of course, those who
lasted the longest before getting thrown off became heroes, men who
could wear down "the outlaw hoss," "the vicious son-of-a-gun," and
"the devil hisself" and walk away unscathed. The first references
to mustangs as being outside the law surfaced at rodeos, and, as we
shall see, the terminology — even more insidious — continues to be
used on the modern range (today some wild horses are subject to a
"three-strikes" law that condemns them to the slaughterhouse). This
language — all variations on the theme of *wild* — was also used to describe the land; with the closing of the range, it was as if the mustang
itself had become the West and the cowboy were reenacting its conquest.

There is much debate in certain quarters about exactly where the
first official rodeo was held. Three places claim to be that historic location, but they all agree on one thing — it happened on July 4. The
earliest of the first rodeos occurred in 1883 in Pecos, Texas. Up and
down the Chisholm, two trail veterans were regarded as the best rop-
ers in the business. Someone suggested holding a contest to settle the
score, and as word of the event spread, other cowboys signed on, eager to display their skills. Since the rodeo was scheduled for a holiday, people traveled for miles on horseback and by wagon to watch
their favorite riders in action. The event was a hit and has since been
held every year in the same location.

In 1884, the town of Payson, Arizona, held its own rodeo, although
some contest the use of the term *rodeo* in this case, pointing out that
the event was just some cowboys roping cows. Today, the town bills
the show as the "oldest continuous rodeo." In 1888, the nearby town
of Prescott, Arizona, held a "cowboy tournament," which was added

to the July 4 celebration program like a Wild West show to increase attendance. A century later, the town applied to the U.S. Patent Office for appropriate billing of its signature event; it was granted in 1985, and since then the contest has been called the World's Oldest Rodeo.

By the early 1900s, the rodeo circuit had spawned celebrities with their own followings, including such infamous characters as the black cowboy Bill Pickett, who pioneered the strange practice known as bull-dogging. In this event, a steer was released, Pickett galloped to its side, leaped toward the animal, grabbed its horns, twisted the steer over onto its back, sank his teeth into its lip, then released the horns and jerked himself backward. A mustang finally put Pickett out of business, kicking him in the skull.

Equine superstars also traveled the circuit; in the West, they were as legendary as Seabiscuit later became. You can see their photographs in old rodeo programs and hear their names in today's rodeo fanfare, but generally their stories have been lost to the ages. The famous Frontier Days rodeo in Cheyenne, Wyoming, featured these horses every July in a program that included wild horse racing, bucking contests (with a prize of twenty-five dollars going to the worst horse), exhibits of hitching wild horses to wagons and driving them, barking dogs, wolf roping, trick roping, floats that portrayed frontier hangings, and horse and steer stampedes.

One of the mustangs on the circuit was Gin Fiz, described in a 1908 program as "an exceptionally bad actor, and one of the best performers. He is known as a high bucker from start to finish, usually landing his rider before exhausting his different stunts." One of the most famous of all bucking broncs was Midnight, who was on the circuit from 1923 to 1933. He was born in 1916 on the Cottonwood Ranch in Alberta, out of a Thoroughbred mare and a Percheron-Morgan cross. For the first few years of his life, he was a cow horse. According to legend, his bucking career began at a roundup on the Blood Indian reservation, when he ejected an Indian cowboy who was trying to ride him into the chuck wagon for dinner. The bucking was so impressive that his owner put him on the rodeo circuit, and Midnight went on to appear at the Calgary Stampede and Wild West shows in Canada and the United States.

"One by one," said a reporter at the time, "the best riders came to grief by the chain lightning actions of the 1300-pound Canadian champion." In 1926, the famous bucking-horse rider Bobby Askins traveled from Montana to Toronto to show Midnight his stuff. For four days in a row, he studied the horse in the preliminaries. "I think I can ride him if the judges will let me spur him once in the shoulders," he said, "and then high behind for the remainder of the ride." On the day of the event, twenty thousand people gathered at the Toronto exhibition grounds to watch the heavily hyped ride. When the chute gates opened, Askins raised both of his feet and "clawed Midnight high behind the ears," said one account. "The big black was so astonished that he stood stock-still. The crowded grandstand roared with laughter as the horse walked out of the chute with short, mincing steps."

Expecting all hell to break loose, a spectator grabbed a friend's arm in excitement. "Midnight went into action," the report continued. "Down went his head and then one terrific leap almost shot the Montana cowboy out of the saddle. Bobby clawed his way back desperately," spurring the horse again. Midnight jumped eight times, throwing Askins aloft, then pitching high and fast for another four jumps, throwing the rider from his back and sending him to the first-aid tent. "He's even better than they said he was," Askins said.

They say that Midnight bucked off countless riders and once jumped a stunning twenty-seven feet from the chute before he hit the ground. Outside the arena, he was a gentle horse, and he never argued when he was saddled. He would even stand quietly when the bucking rig was cinched to his back, according to a tribute in the *Western Horseman.* He just did not like to be ridden; he always stopped bucking as soon as the rider was thrown. In fact, he was known as a gentleman. "Once at a rodeo in Nebraska," reported the *Denver Post,* "Midnight's rider was thrown and knocked unconscious. Midnight turned and trotted toward the man. The crowd screamed in horror, thinking the famed bronc intended to jump on the cowboy. But Midnight merely sniffed at the rider, then gently nuzzled him and tried to turn him over, as though to say, 'C'mon, cowboy, get up.'"

But all the years of bucking took a toll on his feet. He was always shod in front with flat shoes because his feet were tender, and he later developed ringbone. In 1936, he died at the Denver Rodeo, of "infir-mities" (that's as far as the record goes). He was given a full funeral and buried at his owners' ranch in Colorado, then exhumed and re-buried in 1966 at the National Cowboy Hall of Fame in Oklahoma City, next to another famous bucking horse, Five Minutes to Mid-night, in an elaborate service attended by the country's foremost ro-deo riders and marked by wreaths and prayer and media fanfare.

In the annals of rodeo lore, there is no more legendary steed than Steamboat. Steamboat was named for the sound he made while buck-ing, a loud hissing of sorts that became his calling card. It was the re-sult of his being thrown to the ground when he was castrated and hit-ting his head so hard that he broke a bone in his nose. The big black horse — part Percheron and part Mexican hotblood — was born on a Wyoming ranch in 1896. "I bitted him several times in the corral," recalled the hand who named him when asked about his first ride. "And I rode him about four times in the corral. He was kind of stub-born and I would get right on to him and he would just stand there and when you screwed him a little bit with spurs he would go to. He would buck and when he bucked, he bucked hard. And so I decided I would take him out there one day. When he came out of the corral he looked that way and this way. He blowed up at me and we had one of the damnedest saddle fights you ever saw ... I guess he thought bucking was his business."

By 1901, Steamboat began his career, quickly becoming known as "the horse who couldn't be rode," ejecting thousands from the hur-ricane deck. Until 1908, that is, at Frontier Days in Wyoming, when a notorious cowboy named Dick Stanley was not thrown off. Steam-boat was by then past his prime. In fact, he was not able to get a foot-hold in the heavy turf, and so he could not perform his astonishing leaps and arcs. But the bighearted horse kept trying, his bones weary from absorbing countless impacts, reminiscent of an old song-and-dance man crooning and shuffling to give people a smile.

In 1914, he was taken to Salt Lake City to perform with the Irwin brothers' Wild West show. While penned up with other horses during a storm, he was frightened by thunder and lightning, and he cut him-self on the very thing that cowboys had feared years earlier — barbed wire. They took him back to Wyoming, but blood poisoning had set

Guy Edward Holt on Steamboat, "the horse who couldn't be rode,"
Cheyenne, Wyoming, 1903.

in. Veterinarians couldn't save him, and he was shot in the skull with
a gun that had belonged to the famous outlaw Tom Horn. Conventional wisdom has it that he was buried in Frontier Park in Cheyenne,
where he had thrilled audiences for so many years.

But Paul Hansen, the man who rode Steamboat more than anyone, claimed otherwise. Years after the acclaimed bronco had passed
away, Hansen told the *Cheyenne Tribune* that Steamboat on the night
of his injury was loaded onto a truck and returned to Cheyenne. "He
was terribly swollen and dying," he remembered. "The only humane
thing to do was to destroy him." It was at the city dump that he took
his last breath; there, said Hansen, they shot and left him.

If you played the game of license plate as a child, you may have noticed the bucking horse and rider insignia on the Wyoming tag. Or you may have noticed it more recently, on a road trip, for it is still used on Wyoming plates today. No one knows for sure, but most likely, the horse is Steamboat. The famous logo was first used by Wyoming troops in World War I, then emblazoned on the license plate in 1936 (and trademarked as the Bucking Horse and Rider). Since then, Steamboat and his mysterious cowboy, one hand on the reins and the other brandishing his hat, have accompanied Wyoming National Guard units to Korea, Vietnam, and Iraq.

But what this logo does not convey, and what all the rodeo lore leaves out, is what Will James wrote about in *Smoky,* in a chapter called "When the Good Leaves." Smoky has become separated from Clint after the cowboy put him out to graze in the fall. He wanders off during a blizzard, and just as the cowboy Siringo had feared for his own horse, Smoky comes into the hands of a cruel man who beats him until he becomes mean, then puts him on the rodeo circuit as a vicious killer called the Cougar. As James wrote:

> The first two years he put in as The Cougar and bad horse was the most ferocious two years any horse went thru. It was wicked times, not only for the horse, but for all who handled and tried to ride him. There was so much poison in that pony's heart that the only way he could live was by hating and being hated; he fed on it, and the bars or poles that was between him and whoever he wanted to get at in his fits of wickedness showed signs a-plenty of his hankering to murder — the destroying ability of that pony's teeth and hoofs sure was visible, and convincing.

Over time, the Cougar gave out, becoming the broken-down rodeo horse known as the Old Cougar. He was sold and resold and finally, a bag of bones, he was reduced to hauling a vegetable cart.

One day, as the horse is about to endure another beating, Clint happens by; he's in town because of rumors about "the wickedest bucking horse the country had ever layed eyes on," now on his last legs and heading for the slaughterhouse. In his heart of hearts, Clint knows it's Smoky, his one true love; a conversation with the sheriff leads to the arrest of the vegetable man and Smoky's rescue. For a while, it seems Clint may have gotten there too late. He takes the weary mustang home, where he rests in a stall, starts to eat, and begins to fill out. But it appears he does not recognize Clint.

One day, as Smoky starts to enjoy the company of some colts in the corral, the cowboy realizes it's time for him to go. He opens the gates of his ranch, and Smoky hesitates, then joins some young horses who are heading for the winter range. For months, Clint doesn't see the horse and is occupied with running the ranch. Then one morning, stepping out for a bucket of water, he hears a nicker in the distance. "Standing out a ways," James wrote, "slick and shiny, was the old mouse-colored horse. The good care the cowboy had handed him, and afterwards the ramblings over the old home range, had done its work. The heart of Smoky had come to life again, and full size."

As for Will James, he became a prisoner of his own persona, and he could not do for himself what his alter ego Clint had done for Smoky. With the success of the novel, James was summoned to Hollywood and was supposed to appear in the 1933 version of the film that starred Victor Jory as Clint and the famous horse Rex, "King of the Wild Stallions," as Smoky. But James had begun drinking heavily and slurred the words on his cue cards, and he was dropped from the film.

Yet he kept writing and drawing, producing a book a year, to the delight of his legions of fans. In Tinseltown, everyone wanted a piece of the famous and talented cowboy, and he was commissioned by a producer to write the Great American Novel. It told the story of three generations of cowboys, each named Bill, each unable to accept the changing West. It spanned the early days on the trail to the advent of fencing to the modern era, when cows began to grow fat in feedlots instead of on the range. As James worked on this epic book, his drinking got worse; he was often arrested for drunk driving, was in and out of the hospital, and became overwhelmed with debt. On September 3, 1942, he died.

At his Hollywood funeral, to the surprise of everyone, his brother showed up, explaining to the mourners that James was, in fact, not really named James. He was not a cowpuncher from Montana. In fact, he was not American at all. His real name was Joseph Ernest Nephtali Dufault, and he was from a small town in Quebec. Being asked to write the big novel about the thing he was supposed to have been but really wasn't may have destroyed him — in effect, breaking his wild spirit. Today, many of his drawings and original manuscripts are in the Yellowstone Museum in Billings, Montana, where he lived and worked on ranches and gave due credit to the cow horse.

I went to the museum on a recent trip to Billings but it was closed. Instead I found myself outside the Chamber of Commerce office, to take a look at a famous statue of a cowboy astride a horse, driving a herd of longhorns. The whole bronze parade was splayed out across the sidewalk. The statue is called *The Great Montana Centennial Cattle Drive Monument* and commemorates a two-years-in-the-making, five-day cattle drive, with 3,000 cows, 3,500 horses, and a human cast of thousands that took place in 1989 to mark the state's one hundredth birthday. The plaque says, in part: "Dedicated to every child who dreamed of being a cowboy ... every cowboy who dreamed of clear water and rolling prairies." Under the dedication there's a long list of those who were involved in the drive, including the board of directors, the Latigo Drovers, horse wranglers, members of law enforcement, media wranglers, the medical team, the press, veterinarians, the lead herd, riders, sponsors, swampers, wagon cooks, wagoneers, teamsters, outriders, and walkers. Was the animal that the cowboy sang of, wrote poems to, and could not live without really not cited in this monument to the country's most glorified era? I wondered as I studied the plaque. Later, I placed a call to the Chamber of Commerce. Had I read the inscription correctly? I asked. Yes, came the answer, you have.

And across the West, our cattle cult continues to reign supreme. General Brisbin's promise of a never-ending beef bonanza in the land of plenty endures: four million cows now graze on depleted public lands that are leased from the government, mostly by large ranching corporations for a little over a dollar on the head. As Will James wrote, "The cowboy will never die." It was the last sentence of his final novel, the one that would never be published, and he wrote the sentence in uppercase letters. As for his four-legged, hard-working, and fleet-footed partner, that, as we shall see, is another story.

7

The Wonder Horses
That Built Hollywood

AFTER PLAYING THEMSELVES in Wild West shows, driving cattle up the trail, and starring in rodeos, horses proceeded to become America's first movie icons, serving as the backbone of Hollywood in the burgeoning new genre of Westerns. While dime novels, Buffalo Bill spectacles, cowboy poetry, and frontier art and literature had already launched our dream of self, it would take the big screen to inscribe it for all time. In fact, it was as if the land itself had mandated the Western: not only was no other art form up to the task, but the one element necessary to make film, silver, came from Nevada. Soon after miners converged on the Comstock Lode in 1857, new coins were minted, mirrors were manufactured, and the practice of still photography exploded. Within two decades, the captured image would move — and it hasn't stopped.

The first recorded moving image could have been anything — a herd of antelope, a dancer, crashing surf — but as it happens, it was a horse, suggesting that just as the land brought forth the Western, so too did the animal that helped us conquer the land. After completing the transcontinental railroad in 1869, financier Leland Stanford sought medical advice about a serious problem that today would be described as career burnout. His doctor advised him to spend time in the outdoors, especially with horses. "He became passionately fond of the animals," a biographer wrote, "and would drop business at any time to talk about them." He began acquiring racehorses, and he soon wanted to improve training techniques so his horses would run faster. By 1872, as various new theories of science and animal breeding began to emerge, he was ready to weigh in on a popular question of the time: when a horse galloped, was there a point at which all four of its legs were off the ground? "The possibility that horses briefly flew had seized the attention of scientists, artists and 'turfmen' alike," Mitchell Leslie later wrote in *Stanford* magazine. "Stanford sided with the advocates of 'unsupported transit,' who swore they could discern all four hooves in the air. Their opponents denied the possibility with equal certainty, arguing that the horse would collapse without the support of at least one leg."

To prove his belief, Stanford enlisted the aid of acclaimed landscape photographer Eadweard Muybridge. A classic British eccentric, Muybridge was a flamboyant and tortured soul, described by a contemporary as resembling "Walt Whitman ready to play King Lear." According to legend, Stanford was so convinced of his view that he had twenty-five thousand dollars riding on the outcome. At first, Muybridge turned down Stanford's initial offer of two thousand dollars to produce the evidence — it was impossible, he said; camera shutters were simply too slow to record an animal that moved at forty feet per second. But the pair soon developed a friendship, and Stanford convinced Muybridge to take the photographs, a long-term production that ultimately cost fifty thousand dollars.

On a June morning in 1878, racing fans and reporters assembled at Stanford's estate to watch the experiment unfold. Muybridge had constructed an elaborate rig — a forerunner of movie cameras. From a shed on one side of the track, a dozen large cameras bulged through an opening, "lined up like cannons in a galleon," wrote Leslie. On the other side, a white backdrop had been raised to enhance contrast. The trotting horse Abe Edgington took the track, pulling a two-wheeled sulky driven by one of Stanford's trainers. There were twelve wires underneath the track at twenty-one-inch intervals, each connected to a different camera. As the sulky wheels ran across the wires, the shutters were tripped, "firing in quick succession," Leslie recounted, "sounding like a drumroll." It took half a second to take all twelve photographs, and twenty minutes later, Muybridge emerged from his darkroom with the plates. Indeed, the horse was briefly airborne—all four legs had left the ground. Stanford won his bet, and within a few years, the motion pictures were upon us. Once again, the country embarked on a great transformation, all because of the horse—which in this case had taken its own picture.

Four days after Abe Edgington made history, Muybridge repeated the experiment, photographing Stanford's horse Occident carrying a jockey at the gallop. The same results were recorded, and Muybridge went on to take pictures of other horses as they walked, trotted, and ran. He soon patented the first moving-picture projector, the zoopraxiscope, and in 1881, his pictures were published in the famous work *Attitudes of Animals in Motion*. In 1893, three years after Wounded Knee, Muybridge gave a series of lectures at the Columbian World Expo in Chicago as Plains Indians danced in the Bazaar of Nations exhibit on the midway. Inside Zoopraxigraphical Hall, Muybridge regaled audiences with moving pictures of galloping horses. Soon movies would be the best place to see horses; America's loyal partner, no longer needed, was about to follow the path of the Indian and make its long and bloody fade from the American West to the silver screen.

"The frontier is closed," announced Frederick Jackson Turner at the World Expo in the speech that has influenced our view of the West to this day. Across Chicago, depending on which way the winds were blowing, a person could actually smell the end, the very reason the range was cleared: every day, great swarms of livestock—now including mustangs—were harried across the Bridge of Sighs to the slaughterhouse floor at the Union Stock Yards. The odor that emanated was "elemental," Upton Sinclair wrote in *The Jungle*, "raw and crude; it was rich, almost rancid, sensual and strong." But historian Turner pegged his case to something else—the 1890 census report: "Up to and including 1880 the country had a frontier of settlement," it said, "but at present the unsettled area has been so broken into by isolated bodies of settlement that there can hardly be said to be a frontier line." The report's summary was even more dire, forbidding further mention of "the frontier" in official population reports. Its disappearance, Turner observed, marked the end of the first period of American history. By that, he meant the era that had begun with Christopher Columbus.

In fact, the fair — named after the conquistador — was a celebration of the four hundredth anniversary of the European conquest of the New World. A mind-bending spectacle that ran for six months and culminated in the introduction of Columbus Day, it presented the past, present, and future in thousands of stunning, historical, and goofy exhibits of nearly every accomplishment known to man, appropriating the animal, plant, fish, and mineral kingdoms along the way, and wrapping it all up under the glittering bow called progress. In effect, the burgeoning new land of America was consuming the world and rolling out the things that would assert dominion for decades: technology and pop culture. Later, observers would mark the fair as the beginning of the twentieth century.

"Let us hold fast to the meaning which underlies this ceremony," President Grover Cleveland said at the fair's opening ceremony on May 1, 1893, "and let us not lose the impressiveness of this moment. As by a touch the machinery that gives life to this vast Exposition is now set in motion, so at the same instant let our hopes and aspirations awaken forces which in all time to come shall influence the welfare, the dignity, and the freedom of mankind." Then he flicked a switch that turned on the lights, the rides, and everything else; for the first time, alternating current was introduced to the public. Now, in addition to watching the flashing images on Muybridge's zoopraxiscope, viewers could also stop at various points around the fair and watch the first moving picture to be shown through a kinetoscope, the movie projector invented by Thomas Edison. It was another first that had to do with the horse. Called *The Blacksmith Scene*, the movie lasted less than a minute and portrayed two men at an anvil hammering a horseshoe as a third looked on.

Among all the exhibits at the fair named after Columbus, there was nary a tribute to the horse that had helped tame the frontier. Some horses did appear: Comanche, who was making his first postmortem appearance at the expo but as a novelty, not as a representative of his kind; and the horses at a midway display of a Bedouin encampment called "The Wild East Show," featuring fine Arabian horses from "the Syrian desert" (although at the time, their connection with America's wild horses was not well known). Fair-goers seeking mustangs of the Wild West had to take the elevated railway to the Buffalo Bill show that was playing nearby. Oddly, the spectacle was deemed "too Western" for the expo itself. Perhaps frontier reenactments were not in keeping with the fair's theme of looking to the future. Perhaps the conquest of the West was still too raw, even when reflected in Buffalo Bill's fun-house mirror. Or perhaps fair organizers feared that the staged shoot-'em-ups would compete with other exhibits. In any case, the fair's closing was marked by the real thing — two days before the final ceremonies, the mayor of Chicago was felled by an assassin's bullet. Was the frontier really finished? The census report may have banned the term, but with every constriction upon the land, the frontier lived on, an imaginary space that spilled over into reality in many ways. And it was forever preserved on film.

In 1894, a few months after the fair closed, Edison launched the Black Maria studios in New Jersey, where he produced a wave of documentary-style Westerns, sometimes using cast members from *Buffalo Bill's Wild West* show as his subjects. In the fall of that year, Edison filmed several Lakota players in his twenty-one-second movie *Sioux Ghost Dance.* "One of the most peculiar customs of the Sioux tribe is here shown," said the studio catalog, "the dancers being genuine Sioux Indians, in full war paint and costumes." A month later, he shot *Bucking Broncho,* which featured a mustang named Sunfish and "a genuine cowboy" named Lee Martin. "This particular broncho is an unusually wicked one," the catalog said.

In 1897, Edison went to the Northwest and filmed a deployment of horses to Alaska ten minutes before the ship sailed. He called it *Horses Loading for the Klondike.* "The wharf is crowded with livestock," stated the catalog, "and the huge derrick slowly drops the large box or sling into the bunch. Into this cradle a horse is led, and is slowly hoisted and swung over to the deck of the steamer." Most of the horses shipped to Alaska for the Gold Rush were culled from the range and perished in the nether reaches of the icy wilderness. A year later, the inventor produced *Trained Cavalry Horses,* which featured the army steeds of Troop F, Sixth Cavalry, that had served in the Spanish-American War. "At a command," the catalog said, "they lie down promptly, and at another order, scramble to their feet."

What Edison was not filming — and what Westerns have yet to portray — is the actual life of the warhorse. At the time he made his short about the steeds of the Spanish-American War, and while Buffalo Bill was portraying Teddy Roosevelt's famous Rough Riders of the same war in his shows, Frederic Remington was covering it for the *New York Journal*, with drawings and text. On January 24, 1897, the paper published this dispatch:

> The appearance of the Spanish cavalry in the field is really pathetic. Fresh supplies of ponies, which are arriving daily from Texas, may occasionally lessen the extent of the misery somewhat, but for only a short time, for the hard usage which the poor brutes receive soon renders them pitiable objects.
>
> These little ponies are in the last stages of exhaustion and disease, due to the hard work they are subjected to and the poor fodder they receive. The saddles used on these equine martyrs are of two kinds, and both are bad and cruel and torturing beyond description . . .

While mustangs were being taken from the range and shipped to war or to the slaughterhouse, Edison again made cinematic history with production of the first feature-length Western, *The Great Train Robbery,* which presented people and horses in twelve thrilling minutes and nine action-packed scenes and played to packed nickelodeons around the country. Released in 1903, it was ripped from reality, like dime novels and Wild West shows, based on a turn-of-the-century holdup by Butch Cassidy and his gang. They had stopped a train in Wyoming, blown up the mail safe, and made off with five thousand dollars. The film introduced cinematic techniques such as camera movement, location shooting, and jump cuts, as well as elements of Westerns that quickly became standard, including gunshots that made someone dance, throwing a person from a train, and bad guys being chased by good guys on horseback.

It also featured the first cowboy star, Bronco Billy Anderson, formerly a janitor named Gilbert Max Aronson who had worked at Edison's East Coast studios. In *The Great Train Robbery*, Bronco Billy played three parts, then went on to launch his own movie studio and star in five hundred Westerns. His movies were wildly popular, and people flocked to theaters for thrills and spills in our cactus-studded Garden of Eden. Of course, his fans didn't know that he was an inferior rider and used stunt doubles for hard falls. And they didn't seem to mind that he lacked an equine partner. But that all changed in the next wave of films—not only were cowboys the real thing, but they acquired four-legged costars.

These horses quickly became Hollywood's biggest draw. Some are memorialized in the cement plains of the Walk of Fame, where their hoof prints are preserved forever, as if they had galloped straight from the Miocene walls of Death Valley to the corner of Hollywood and Vine. Others have nearly faded from the record, including the first equine celebrity. He's buried on a hilltop in the town of Newhall on the outskirts of Los Angeles. On a fine spring day a couple of years ago, I paid him a visit. A train in the near distance wailed the sad/hopeful note that we all know, the note of progress, new beginnings, of things left behind. The plot was marked by a white picket fence, and it was sparely and tastefully landscaped. A few bunches of wild rosemary were growing at its edges and some patches of daisies flourished here and there. A vine of bougainvillea climbed up the stone shrine at the head of the grave and at the top of the rise there was a stand of prickly pears. A metal plaque embedded in the shrine hinted at our story:

> *BILL HART'S*
> *PINTO PONY*
> *"FRITZ"*
> *AGED 31 YEARS*
> *LOYAL COMRADE*

Before Trigger and Silver and Mr. Ed, after Bucephalus and Incitatus, there was Fritz. Fritz is an important character in American history. Without Fritz, Hollywood would have stalled at Bronco Billy, the cowboy who couldn't ride and didn't even have his own horse. "Fritz is the greatest all around horse that ever lived," said his celebrated cowboy partner, William S. Hart. Hart coined the "strong, silent" movie character—silent not just because cowboys didn't say much, but also because talkies hadn't been invented yet. And he appeared to dominate the landscape, seemingly touched by it. At six feet two inches and 180 pounds, he was lanky and had a long face —horselike, almost—with a brooding, mournful look that audiences loved. And he was utterly devoted to Fritz, in the movies and in life, marrying once and only briefly, ultimately retiring to his ranch with the little pinto, his devoted sister, and other animals he had acquired along the way.

Originally from upstate New York, Hart grew up on the Great Plains where his father found work as an itinerant mill hand. According to legend, he spent his boyhood with Lakota children, learning their ways, living with them for a time, and cultivating a love for wide-open spaces. A penchant for acting led him to New York and London, where he performed on stage in the works of Shakespeare and inaugurated the role of the Roman emperor Messala in *Ben-Hur*. He also appeared in *The Squaw Man* and *The Virginian,* which drew on

William S. Hart and his celebrated pony Fritz during the filming of *Testing Block* in Felton, California, 1920.

his love of the West and helped him refine his cowboy persona. In 1914, already forty-eight years old, he signed with producer Thomas Ince and moved to Hollywood to make Westerns, determined to end what he called "libels" on the frontier. "It was awful!" he later wrote, recalling an early popular silent in which "the sheriff was dressed as a cross between a Wisconsin woodchopper and Gloucester fisherman." With the offer from Ince, he said, "The opportunity I had been waiting for years to come was knocking at my door."

At the time Hart came to California, World War I had erupted, and the country was locked in a debate about whether to enter it. Yet our involvement had already begun — in a further depletion of the range, we were shipping mustangs to French and British armies on the front. Three years later, when America joined the war, horses from the range would be mustered out for our own troops. By the time the war ended, in 1919, about two hundred thousand mustangs had perished in Europe, many of them killed and eaten by starving soldiers in bloody, icebound bunkers.

On the home front, the country was experiencing a frenzy of change, with the various themes of progress introduced at the 1893 fair now in full play. Houses were lit by electricity, new ad campaigns were proffering booze, and the assembly line was cranking out new products such as canned soup. Yet behind the sparkling lights and whirring conveyor belts, there was another story. The shrinking frontier sent many people from rural areas to cities for jobs in the many new factories. Wages were low, hours were long, and the workplace was dangerous. Labor strikes erupted outside sweatshops, and they were often deadly. Soon, their effects were felt in Hollywood, involving actors and animals alike.

But there were those who had no desire for employment at a steel mill or a shirt factory or any other place where they were fenced in; hundreds of rangeland exiles converged on Tinseltown, where they got paid to preserve the disappearing past in a country that was quickly moving on. In today's parlance, they had been downsized, wiped out by syndicate takeovers of cattle empires and the blizzard of 1887 from which many operations never recovered. In her book *The Hollywood Posse,* Diana Serra Cary, the daughter of early stuntman Jack Montgomery, described the scene:

Dispossessed and disillusioned, the old hands moved on, as ranch after ranch went under or was broken up for farms. For older men, rendered obsolete by change, only the hope of a miracle remained. Younger punchers trailed rodeos working as trick riders, or took part in the ever-stiffening competition for bronc-riding and bull-dogging prize money. Not a few hired on with one or another of the still-solvent Wild West shows—whose tents were likewise tattered—hungry for the hazardous work they savvied and which in turn salvaged their self-respect and pride.

In Los Angeles, the cowboys hung out at a ramshackle bar called the Waterhole, on the corner of Hollywood and Cahuenga. Those who had their own horses could tether them outside. The area soon developed a reputation that earned it the nickname that still exists today, Gower Gulch, derived from a nearby street and a deadly shoot-out over a cowboy's girlfriend. But more than that, the bar became the heart of a lost culture where men swapped tales of stampedes, ran into war buddies from Cuba, and found out where wild horses were still running and who might be interested in buying them. The bar also functioned as a way station for work, not unlike twenty-first-century storefronts where day laborers wait to be offered jobs. At any time of day or night, producers could find a cowpuncher with a craggy face or a crew of Indians who would paint themselves for a war party. Sometimes, Thomas Ince sent over his own car to pick up an instant cast of rough-and-tumble extras and take them back to his movie ranch in Santa Monica.

The ranch was called Inceville, which was where Hart met Fritz, his equine life partner. Inceville was a Wild West town with all the trappings, sprawling across eighteen thousand acres of canyons and chaparral, and home to the horses, buffalo, mules, burros, and cows that Ince had purchased for his films. Many of the horses came from the range, passing through the hands of Fat Jones, a famous broker who supplied animals for the big Hollywood herds that lived on studio lots or in company bergs on the outskirts of Los Angeles. The best horsemen could often be found at Fat's stable, working with animals and preparing them for careers in the movies; one of those horsemen was former rodeo cowboy Jack "Swede" Lindell, the "granddaddy of all horse trainers." Lindell developed new techniques for teaching animals not to fear cumbersome motion-picture equipment, methods still in use today.

One of his star students was Rex the Wonder Horse, a beautiful black stallion who became one of the biggest wage earners of the silent era. In 1923, while scouting the West for the lead in *King of the Wild Horses*, Lindell heard about a "killer stallion" who was living at a detention home in Golden, Colorado. After dragging a rider to death, the horse had been condemned to solitary confinement for two years, to be used only for breeding. Lindell went to the prison and was impressed by the horse's look and spirit. He convinced the warden to let him work with the inmate. One week later, Rex displayed his new skills for prison officials, and he was on his way to Hollywood to star in his first film. *King of the Wild Horses* was a huge hit, and Rex's career was launched. In a career that spanned fifteen years, he made nineteen movies, often costarring with a pinto stallion named Marky, and even participating in stunt billing with Rin Tin Tin Jr. in a twelve-part serial called *The Adventures of Rex and Rinty*.

Yet Rex remained essentially wild. His eagle's stare was so intense that Navajo extras often wore special amulets for protection. And it was clear that he did not like being held captive. There was the time on a set in Nevada when he simply took off, running for seventeen miles in response to a particular command. While filming *Smoky*, he charged an actor and knocked him down. That should have been the end of the stunt, but he kept on going, ripping into the actor's clothes with his teeth. Audiences never saw the stallion's flight from the set or the attack on his rider, but they loved Smoky, who, after traveling from the wild to the trail to the rodeo and almost to the slaughterhouse, finally got to run free. Rex finally returned to the desert too, retiring to a ranch in Flagstaff, Arizona, where he again became king, living with a band of mares and siring a parade of foals. He died sometime in the early 1940s.

Unlike Rex, there is no record of where Fritz was found or how he made his way to the mythmaking corrals. But it would seem that he was one of the wild ones. His size is the first clue: at a thousand pounds and just over fourteen hands, he was small, a classic mustang. Then there is his "autobiography," a bestseller William Hart later penned for the animal's many fans. In it, Fritz said he was from Nevada. He also said he had descended from a horse named Red Top. Red Top, he wrote, was a gift from an Arab to Ulysses S. Grant, who then gave him to a man in Nevada, who in turn set Red Top free. "And in a few years," Fritz recounted, "there was lots of little Red Tops running across the mesa and playing in the rivers. And one of them was my great-grandfather." This may have been true. According to legend, a prominent Turkish breeder did indeed give Grant a horse, although it had a different name. When Grant died, the horse was sold and then re-sold until it landed in Nevada and joined up with a band on the open range. One day, unto Hollywood came the little pinto with the red forelock that recalled his possible forebears. Someone called him Fritz. On the day he met Hart, he was practicing a stunt, rearing up with actress Anne Little in the saddle. He almost landed on Hart, and from then on man and horse were a pair. "Better a painted pony than a painted woman," proclaimed an ad for one of their movies.

From 1914 to the time of his retirement in 1927, Hart and Fritz made over a dozen films. Hart played complicated characters, bad guys who were forced to do good, and they had names like Jack O'Diamonds, Frosty Blake, and Shark Monroe. Hart directed and wrote most of the movies himself, and, true to his word, delivered a gritty, authentic portrayal of the West. He wore real cowboy hats, hired real Indians, and avoided the practice of spraying down dirt with water so camera shots wouldn't be obscured by grit—when horses were running, he wanted real dust. Man and horse quickly developed a large following, and soon the pinto's popularity eclipsed Hart's. Fritz was all the rage in the United States and Europe, receiving truckloads of mail and causing massive traffic jams when he stopped to greet fans in parades.

One of the pair's first movies was *The Taking of Luke McVane*, made in 1915. Luke McVane, Hart's character, kills a man who cheated him at cards. Fleeing a posse into the desert, he is carried to safety in a cloud of dust by Fritz. Although Fritz was small, "his power and endurance were remarkable," Hart said in his popular autobiography *My Life—East and West*. In one scene, he and the sheriff are attacked by Indians. When the sheriff's horse is killed, he mounts Fritz, behind McVane, and they are chased until Fritz is shot while running at a full gallop. The men go down with Fritz, then fight to the end behind his body. The combined weight of the actors, their guns, and a heavy stock saddle was nearly 450 pounds. "Yet that little horse carried us for hours," Hart wrote, "until all our scenes were taken. But when I was lying across his neck shooting Injuns, he rolled eyes at me that plainly said: 'Say, Mister, I sure was glad when you give me that fall.'"

Because of his distinct look, Fritz did not have a stunt double like other horses. He went on to fall hundreds of times in the pair's parade of films, which included *The Man from Nowhere, The Darkening Trail, A Knight of the Trail, The Return of Draw Egan, The Gun Fighter, Wolves of the Rail, Selfish Yates, Breed of Men, Sand, O'Malley of the Mounted, Wild Bill Hickok,* and *The Narrow Trail*—a rugged chase movie that Hart dreamed up especially for Fritz. The pony barely survived its making, nearly drowning in a sequence shot in a cave with swiftly running water and no footing. Hart attributed Fritz's stamina and endurance to his pedigree as a wild horse, repeatedly putting the horse through his paces. In one film, Fritz jumped through a window and cut his nose. In another, he slid off a fallen tree that bridged two sides of a canyon, slicing his side open on some rocks. Fritz himself explained the accident:

> They wanted a close-up of me in the middle of the log, pausing like, and Bill petting me and talking nice, and it couldn't be got in the long shot without me standing there for a week for Joe to switch his camera, SO WE HAD TO DO IT AGAIN! ... Well, we started, and when we got to the center (the highest place, of course), Bill stopped me and started to his acting and what makes him a hero — and me a-doing it all, trying to stand there like I was a wire-walker in a circus ... My hind end went first, and quicker'n lightning, Bill cued for my front end too (you got to hand it to him he thinks kind of quick in a pinch), so I throw'd my front end with my hind end, and we went down sideways instead of me trying to hold on in front and going over backwards ... I was a mess and Bill said, "Pardner, whether you like it or not, you're going to eat grass for the rest of your days. No more pictures or work for you."

As it happened, Fritz was sidelined, but not out of concern for his health; Hart was involved in a prolonged studio dispute, and Ince

locked Fritz in a dark box stall for weeks until the dispute was resolved. Fans were outraged, clamoring for the mustang's comeback,
and two years later, in 1919, Fritz returned in *Sand*. Like any star, Fritz
had his requirements. He issued unspoken but well-understood demands that Hart happily met: for Fritz's performances to go well, he
had to be accompanied on the set by his two longtime stable mates, a
bucking mare named Cactus Kate and a big pack mule named Lizabeth. *Sand* was a huge success; President Woodrow Wilson, a Western fan, proclaimed it his favorite Hart film. Yet even the on-set presence of Kate and Lizabeth was not enough for Fritz while making
Singer Jim McKee in 1924, a railroad story that involved breakneck
galloping and a leap from a cliff. He simply would not perform unless
both animals, or at least one of them, were standing close enough so
he could see them. So his companions looked on, and as he galloped
to the cliff, Fritz caught their gaze. When the movie was released, fans
were outraged that Fritz had been made to perform such a treacherous stunt. But it wasn't really Fritz in that particular scene. Hart had
ridden him to the edge of the cliff, then for the jump switched to a
dummy that was animated by piano wires.

In 1925, Hart made *Tumbleweeds,* a classic Western epic. Too old
to perform, Fritz had retired a year earlier. The movie tells the story
of the great Oklahoma land rush on the Cherokee Strip, a fifty-thou-
sand-square-mile parcel of land that the government had bought
from the Cherokee and leased to ranchers, who fenced it off for cattle; the government then decided to purge the ranchers and open up
the land for pioneers. The call went out in May of 1893 as the world's
fair came alive with lights and rides: "Uncle Sam is desirous of homesteaders," the Department of the Interior announced, "and all who
would stake a claim are invited to enter a horse race in which the
winners will come into possession of their own piece of land." Great
swarms of people flocked to the edge of the strip, with only a few dollars in their pockets and a dream of making a home on the prairie.

On September 16, guns sounded and the rush began — a hundred
thousand people took off across the dry and dusty plain on horseback, in wagons, on bicycles, and on foot, with people and animals
trampled along the way as they raced for the forty-two thousand
claims. In the movie, Hart played a ranch hand who has lost his job,
falls in love, and decides to stake a claim. The complicated stampede

sequences were painstakingly shot, and Hart himself did the riding at full speed, using three different horses to film his scenes. (They are still regarded by movie buffs as among the best Western action sequences ever filmed.) As the range is taken by farmers and the last cattle are rounded up, Hart sounds the note of loss: "Boys," he says, "it's the last of the West."

Critics loved the movie but it did not do well at the box office. Yet Hart was still popular enough to win an invitation to the Little Bighorn battlefield for the fiftieth-anniversary commemorations in 1926. For a famous movie cowboy to speak at the memorial was no small thing; three movies about Custer had already been made, and a "renegade" Indian named Willie Boy had recently been gunned down by a white posse in the Mojave Desert and was billed as the last "wild Indian." At the commemorations, Hart spoke of old warriors in full regalia, "the volleys fired over the graves of the dead, the soft sound of 'Taps' echoed back by the hills like a benediction, the low, weird death song of the Indian women." When he returned to Hollywood, a lifelong fascination with Indians became a defense of Crazy Horse. "Crazy Horse was a very plain man," Hart said, "simple in all his habits, and a great statesman, and always looking out for the Indians."

A year later, Hart donated a statue of himself atop Fritz to the city of Billings, where it was erected on a rise above the Yellowstone Valley, and still stands, rarely visited, on a remaining parcel of open space — a highway median near the airport. In 1926, Hart retired. "My friends," he said in his farewell statement, "I loved the art of making motion pictures. It is as the breath of life to me ... The rush of the wind that cuts your face. The pounding hooves of the pursuing posse. Out there in front, a fallen tree trunk that spans a yawning chasm, and an old animal under you that takes it in the same low, ground-eating gallop. The harmless shots of the battled ones that remained behind. And then, the cloud of dust ... Oh, the thrill of it all!"

Hart passed away in 1946, still pining for his equine partner, who had died in 1938. He became the prototype for a long line of cinema cowboys who are caught out of time and place. Fritz too blazed the trail for a parade of superstar horses of the West. When he died, there was a modest service for the pinto pony, attended by ranch hands, a few friends, and some local children. A string band from the local town of San Fernando played while Fritz was placed in the ground. On the metal plaque above the grave, there is a portrait of America's first equine movie star. He is wearing his bridle and chain bit, immortalized in service. Other than the modest fanfare arranged by Hart, Fritz received little public attention when he died. Yet in a way, he had already died, and the country had already mourned his passing. It happened in one of the pair's most popular movies, *Pinto Ben*, which was based on a famous poem of Hart's that was published in the *New York Morning Telegraph*. The poem, about a martyred cow pony, is a tribute to both Fritz and the character that he played:

> . . . *When that sea o' cattle stopped comin',*
> *They wus piled up a mountain high;*
> *I sat in their blood, Ben's head in my lap,*
> *A-listenin' to his last sigh.*
> *Then the greatest light I ever see'd,*
> *Come into that Pinto's eyes;*
> *He pulled up them poor broken laigs,*
> *An tried to stand, — an' died.*
> *Reckon some o' that blood come out o' my heart,*
> *This heart that Ben had won,*
> *So long, Ben — all in a day's work!*

In 1927, as Hart's star was waning, talkies arrived. The silver in Nevada was nearly depleted, but it seems that the West never runs out of mines. Now, Hollywood found a new one: the silent movies. Many of the old silents were destroyed in order to retrieve the element and use it for the next wave of films, and countless other reels simply rotted away on the shelves. Most celebrities of the silent era were left behind as well, but one who managed to make the transition was Tom Mix, Hart's longtime rival. In every way, Mix was Hart's opposite. He did not brood but smiled. He preferred glitter to grit, wore fancy cowboy clothes instead of authentic garb, and drove a white Rolls-Royce with his initials in 14-karat gold on every door.

Born in 1880 in Mix Run, Pennsylvania, Mix learned how to ride from his father, a stable master. As the story goes, he fought in the Spanish-American War, the Boer War, and with the Texas Rangers against Pancho Villa. In the early 1900s, he joined up with the *Miller Brothers 101 Ranch Real Wild West* show and became a top performer. He was soon discovered by the Selig Polyscope Company, and after he had made just a few movies, it was clear to cowboy stuntmen and fans alike that Mix was the best horseman of them all. By the 1920s, he was producing his own films on his LA lot, Mixville, where a crew of rangeland exiles lived in a bunkhouse. "Roll out, you sons o' bitches!" came the call every morning, just like on the old cattle drives, and the cowboys would have breakfast in the cookhouse, saddle up, and ride to the day's location — the Mojave, which was a stand-in for Arizona, Vasquez Rocks for the Khyber Pass, or the old mission of San Fernando Rey, which was used for the Alamo.

Mix had a series of equine partners, but the most famous was Tony, another officially labeled Wonder Horse. At the height of his career, Tony was so well known that he received mail addressed to "Just Tony, Somewhere in the USA," visited the White House, and appeared on Broadway, posing for his debut as he got a manicure and pedicure while photographers snapped away. Like Mix himself, there are various stories about his origin. Most agree that Tony was discovered in 1914 by Mix's wife, Olivia, when she spotted him following a chicken cart that Tony's mother was pulling on Glendale Boulevard near downtown Los Angeles. He was about two years old. Olivia contacted Mix's trainer, Pat Chrisman, who lived nearby. He liked the look of the sorrel with the long white blaze and white stockings on his hind legs and bought him for fourteen dollars. Over the next couple of years, Chrisman taught Tony the tricks that would make him one of the country's most beloved stars. Among other things, he prefigured Mr. Ed by decades, learning to respond to lines of dialogue that were more than just simple commands like "whoa," and appearing to engage in conversation with Mix. These conversations made the pair wildly popular and launched the trend in which actors talked to their animal partners.

He also became the first horse to receive equal billing with his rider, and was even included in a few movie titles — *Just Tony, "Oh! You Tony,* and *Tony Runs Wild.* Together, Mix and Tony made dozens of hits, with Tony often bailing Mix out of trouble, rescuing damsels in distress, and performing breathtaking stunts — although sometimes a double named Black Bess was used for long shots. But like

Fritz, Tony's life was periodically endangered. In one film, because of an error made by the special-effects man, Mix and Tony got too close to a dynamite blast and were thrown fifty feet. Mix was knocked unconscious and Tony suffered a serious cut. The accident did not impede the pair's career and probably added to the lore that presented them as equals. "Tony was very much like his owner," one director said. "Pat Chrisman would rehearse him in some tricks and he would perform beautifully, but when it came time to shoot—nothing! He could be whipped, pulled, jerked, have bits changed, but still no performance. Come out the next morning and he would run through the whole scene with barely a rehearsal. Then he'd look at you as much as to say, 'How do you like that? Yesterday, I didn't feel like working.'" But on he toiled, until 1932, when he was retired and replaced by Tony Jr.

In 1933, the first concrete was poured at the site of Hoover Dam, on the border of Arizona and Nevada. The unfettered Colorado River that conquistadors had followed into the red-rock heart of the West was about to be walled up forever. Within two years, the biggest reclamation project in American history diverted billions of gallons of water to quench the growing cities of the Southwest. The taming of the river provided jobs for the many unemployed of the Depression era, and propelled the country into an almost desperate embrace of the great wide open.

Dude ranches proliferated everywhere, especially in the East, offering work to the ongoing parade of dispossessed cowhands and a taste of freedom to beleaguered and wealthy city slickers. "If we can't go west, we can nevertheless go western," proclaimed a *New York Times* ad for a popular ranch in the Adirondacks, in answer to railroad come-ons for trips to the glittering new national parks. Of course, another way to go western was the movies, which now offered a new kind of horse-cowboy partnership, thanks to the technology of recorded sound. This was the singing cowboy, who traversed a sage-studded set on board a beautiful horse with a fancy saddle, crooning of trail drives and lost love. Together, horse and rider brought a giddy version of the West to movie fans, who flocked to theaters for relief from hard times and who otherwise might never have listened to country music.

The first of the singing cowboys was Gene Autry, the so-called

World's Greatest Cowboy, whose partner was Champion, the World's Wonder Horse. Autry was born in 1907 in the small town of Tioga, Texas. He grew up around horses, but his passion was music. He was steeped in the songs of his church choir, and as a young boy he learned to strum a mail-order guitar. In 1924, he met Will Rogers while working in a telegraph office. That famous cowboy had come in to send a telegram and heard Autry singing and playing the guitar. Rogers encouraged Autry to pursue a career as a musician, and soon Autry got a job at a Tulsa radio station. He quickly became known as Oklahoma's Yodeling Cowboy. The job launched his career in radio, and he soon made his way to Hollywood. A producer paired him up with Champion, who was owned by Tom Mix and had been used as a double for Tony Jr. Champion was a beautiful chestnut with four white stockings, a Tennessee walking horse about fifteen hands high. Trainer Tracy Layne taught him to play dead, outrun cars and trucks, kneel in prayer, nod his head yes, shake his head no, answer to Autry's famous whistle, and do the hula.

Unlike the movies of Tom Mix and William Hart, the pair's early films, such as *Tumbling Tumbleweeds,* highlighted Champion's tricks rather than action. This was because Autry could barely stay on a horse even when it was standing still. "If horses was dollars," went the stuntman's joke, "Autry could ride." Later, his horsemanship improved; when he sang "Back in the Saddle Again" for the umpteenth time, he was finally making an authentic claim — or at least one that insiders no longer scoffed at. Champion died in 1947, at the age of seventeen; he was replaced by a series of Champions.

By then, the pair's legacy was already quite apparent — a galloping choir of singing cowboys and their loyal partners had overtaken the screen. There was Tex Ritter and White Flash; black cowboy Herbert Jeffrey and Stardusk, who appeared in *Harlem Rides the Range* with an "all-colored cast"; Rex Allen and Koko; and, of course, Roy Rogers and Trigger, the Smartest Horse in the Movies. Together Roy and Trigger made eighty-seven films and crisscrossed the country multiple times. The celebrated golden palomino entertained fans by dancing, rearing and pawing the air, playing dead on ballroom floors — he had fifty-two tricks in all. He passed away at the age of thirty-three and was stuffed and mounted and put on display at the Roy Rogers Museum in Victorville, California. In 2003, he was moved to the more heavily trafficked country-themed town of Branson, Missouri, along with Buttermilk, who belonged to Roy's wife, Dale Evans, Trigger Jr., and their German shepherd, Bullet.

Of course, the singing cowboy and his four-legged partner alone could not carry the country's dream of self. The fantasy is rooted in blood and born of action, and, sooner or later, that part of it returns. As Autry and the others crooned their way across the frontier, countless lesser-known actors and anonymous horses appeared in hundreds of B movies about the West. Many celebrity horses were palomino or white so the audiences could spot them in the distance and know that rescue was at hand, but the working-class steeds were usually darker (like the movies themselves) — bays, blacks, and chestnuts, with few distinctive markings. Another reason for this preference was that producers did not want fans paying more attention to the horse than the actor. Also, horses of solid color could be used in multiple scenes and play various parts — herding cattle, pulling a plow, hauling the stagecoach, and carrying an outlaw away from a high-plains theft.

Another thing that differentiated these unsung horses from their famous counterparts was that they were the ones who died in service to Hollywood. While Fritz, Tony, and other famous steeds were sometimes overworked, harshly treated, and at times forced to risk their lives, once back in the barn, they were pampered and well fed. Lesser-known horses often received little medical care — some had ancient and festering saddle sores, bad legs, dispositions in need of nurture rather than fear. But beyond that, they frequently participated in treacherous stunts. While many horses performed these stunts without incident, falling as they were trained and getting up to do it again if the shot didn't work out, countless others were killed — and sometimes together, in large numbers.

"With rare exceptions, most early equine actors were tricked into the stunts," write Petrine Day Mitchum and Audrey Pavia in *Hollywood Hoofbeats*. "Pits were dug and disguised so that galloping horses would simply tumble into them." For jump or dive sequences, a horse was blinkered or blindfolded and then urged through a curtain into a greased chute, which was then tilted to send the horse flying into a lake or river. There was also a particularly cruel stunt called the Running W. It was named for an old range method of breaking wild horses in which they were tied to a moving wagon with a long rope. If they fought the line or tried to run in a different direction, the moving wagon simply pulled them down.

In the movies, the practice was modified and became deadlier. Piano wire was attached to a horse's front legs with a leather strap and then run up through a ring on the saddle horn, where it was secured; the other end of the wire was connected to a buried stake. On cue, the horse would begin to run, and the rider would jump just before the wire ran out, and the horse took a hard and often fatal fall. In 1936, 125 horses were rigged with Running Ws for the big scene in *The Charge of the Light Brigade,* which was shot in the Mojave Desert and starred Errol Flynn. At the call of "Action!" the cavalry took off across a dry lakebed, but when the wires were triggered, the stunt quickly turned into a bloody pileup, each horse tripping and falling headfirst into the horses ahead of it. By the time it was over, many animals and riders were seriously injured, and twenty-five horses had died — either killed in action or destroyed later because of broken legs. "I never saw so many good men and horses smashed up in one day in all my years in the picture business," stuntman Jack Montgomery told his family that night over dinner. "I've always thought those Humane Society people with their 'reps' snooping around on every set or location were a bunch of busybodies. But by God, today every cowboy on the set stood behind the rep when he set up a howl."

Such a collective action startled producers; it violated the code of the West, in which everyone and every critter took care of himself. And it was the first time that stuntmen — unsung cast members like the horses who routinely got killed during performances — had joined together in protest about conditions on a movie set, a concern that fueled the growing call for an actors' union. Meanwhile, Errol Flynn had gone public with the story of what had happened in the making of *The Charge of the Light Brigade.* In spite of the ensuing outcry for reform, many more horses would die before new guidelines moved through the approval process and Hollywood began following a stricter code for treatment of equine actors.

By 1939, the country had embarked on a new era, kicked off by a world's fair that built on the legacy of the previous expo. But this one did not display the few remaining and aging survivors of the Little Bighorn, and Comanche was a long-lost curio consigned to a glass case at the Kansas museum where he had been stuffed. In fact, the past was barely acknowledged at the latest exposition, which was dubbed the World of Tomorrow. Its theme was the future, and it was located on the marshlands just outside New York, the new cosmopolis. It was an unfettered paean to science and technology, referring to the future everywhere ("I Have Seen the Future," proclaimed a souvenir button), and popularizing the wacky word-ending "o-rama." Playing on the suffix, it even offered a Futurama exhibit—a model of the American landscape as the 1939 expo producers imagined it would look in 1960, with futuristic homes and a complex highway system that permitted Wild West speeds of a hundred miles an hour.

The fair also unveiled the first television broadcasts; TV sets were placed around the grounds and featured broadcasts of smiling consumers who happily discussed the various new products that were being launched at the extravaganza. But for those who had a hankering for yesteryear, there was the remotely situated Cavalcade of Centaurs exhibit, featuring cowboys and Indians on horseback; it was located across the way from the exhibit sponsored by the Doughnut Corporation of America, which offered the baked good along with Maxwell House coffee.

Elsewhere in New York, a more sophisticated reworking of emerging cultural themes was under way: the big musical was in full flower, and throughout the 1930s, America's song of self was shouted and tap-danced to the world. Some of the musicals were odes to the high life in Manhattan, such as Cole Porter's *Anything Goes,* and others took on the urban condition, such as George and Ira Gershwin's all-black opera *Porgy and Bess,* about a man who tries to rescue a prostitute from her pimp—using today's jargon, hip-hop in reverse. Regardless of theme, many of the stage spectacles of those years reflected a burgeoning East Coast provincialism in which the West was merely a place or an idea to be referenced in a bill of clever and ironic songs. For instance, the hit production *Babes in Arms* featured a song called "Way Out West," about the Upper West Side, with the lyric "Git along, little taxi." The Rodgers and Hart musical *Too Many*

Girls included the catchy tune "Give It Back to the Indians," which suggested that Manhattan had become so inconvenient that the Indians must have put one over on the Dutch. A few years later, Irving Berlin created his most famous rendition of the West, *Annie Get Your Gun,* the musical in which Sitting Bull actually issues dating advice, telling Annie Oakley to lose a shooting match to the man she loves in order to win him over. Considering that in 1869 the Wyoming Territory became the first place in the United States to grant women's suffrage, this was an idea that was beyond glib — it obliterated the frontier. But of course, Annie follows the elder's advice and a wedding ensues, with Ethel Merman as Annie belting out the show-tune classic "There's No Business Like Show Business" while Sitting Bull and the rest of the cast — including actors dressed as wild horses — join her in the finale.

But no matter how hard the country tried to put a smiling face on the past, it always came back with a vengeance. When World War II threatened, Broadway turned to patriotic extravaganzas, but in Hollywood, the big action-packed Western that has since come to define us exploded onto the screen with *Stagecoach,* the epic that made John Wayne a national stand-in. Shot by John Ford in Monument Valley, it was the first movie to make use of the stunning scenery that did not yet have a paved road, elevating it to the iconic status that the Navajo had long assigned it. The film told the story of a party of disparate characters crossing the desert on a stage pulled by six big bay steeds during a time of Apache uprisings led by Geronimo. Local Navajo played the Apache, and John Wayne played the Ringo Kid, a prisoner on the stagecoach who helps the cavalry fend off an Indian attack. The movie was accompanied by a new kind of soundtrack — traditional American folk songs coupled with orchestration, a stirring background that became a character; it sent the singing cowboy down the road and launched many years of memorable Western soundtracks.

In the spectacle's most elaborate scene, the Indians chase the stage, their ponies churning up the red-rock dust. When they attack, the Ringo Kid (actually, John Wayne's stand-in) jumps from horse to horse in front of the stage, a radical new stunt devised by legendary stuntman Yakima Canutt. Alas, the Running W was also used in *Stagecoach*. "I have done some 300 Running Ws and never crippled a horse," Canutt said in his autobiography. There are no reports of animal accidents on the set of *Stagecoach,* but the same cannot be said of *Jesse James,* starring Tyrone Power as James and released later that same year. In this popular film, a horse was blinkered and forced to gallop into a tripwire stretched across the edge of a cliff. The wire flipped the animal over the edge, and it plummeted upside down into the rapids below, smashing its back on the rocks. "The result," reports *Hollywood Hoofbeats,* "was a few shocking seconds of film, clearly depicting a hideously contorted horse tumbling through the air." The stuntman was paid a record fee of $2,350 for the jump. Word of the incident quickly spread, and in response to the public outrage, the industry-run Hays Office on censorship consulted with the American Humane Association and within a year issued a new code for the treatment of animals in the movies. The Running W and the tripwire were finally banned, although, since then, the horse that took its own picture and went on to issue many calls for help has continued to perish in the making of movies.

The popularity of the epic Westerns launched by *Stagecoach* began to fade after World War II, an authentic saga of good versus evil in which America rode off into the sunset — and returned at dawn in a Cadillac. This was the America with the smiling face, a happy, victorious country whose future had arrived: families flocked to the suburbs for a guaranteed comfortable life in convenient tract housing, sampling the first TV dinners (which came in a box that resembled a television) as they sat in front of their sets and watched the entertainment of the 1950s. The singing cowboy and his trusted horse had found a new home in TV land, along with other cowboys who didn't sing but had equine partners with names. There was Hopalong Cassidy and Topper, Gene Autry and another Champion, the boys from *Bonanza,* including Hoss, and their horses Sport, Ginger, and Cochise, and, of course, the Lone Ranger and Silver. According to the show's legend, "the fiery horse with the speed of light" had been found near a silver mine in Nevada. By the end of the decade, the West had been completely consigned to the small screen in the form of two dozen Westerns. The widely watched shows were running in prime time as the ever-vanishing frontier was festooned with shopping malls, trussed with freeways, and blown up with atomic bombs that were being tested in case of a nuclear attack. The tests rendered the land poison for decades, destroying wildlife in the process and triggering deadly cancer clusters in people who lived downwind from the blasts.

Notes of dismay and alienation were sounded in various quarters in many ways, from street protests to jazz clubs to poets. In 1957, *On the Road* was published, Jack Kerouac's beautiful unfettered love song to the America that was not on television but in dive bars and crumbling motels, all the human shipwrecks, never to enter the glittering kitchens of suburbia, finding solace in the promise of starting over in the next town, down the road. "I'd often dreamed of going West to see the country," Kerouac wrote, "always vaguely planning and never taking off."

Kerouac exalted the road, but it took a true desert rat to see it as the thing that was killing the West. In 1956, *The Brave Cowboy* by Edward Abbey was published. It tells the story of a latter-day cowboy who still lives by the old code, under the stars with his chestnut mare named Whisky, in what's left of the wilderness outside Albuquerque. In 1962 it was made into a movie with Kirk Douglas called *Lonely Are the Brave*. It's a classic among the new breed of Westerns produced during this era of social upheaval and reappraisal of the past, and perhaps the greatest equine/cowboy love story ever told on screen. In the movie, Douglas has a run-in with the law, breaks out of jail, then flees on his horse. The pair is pursued across the desert by a reluctant Walter Matthau, who secretly hopes that they'll get away. They almost make it to Mexico, but of course there's one more obstacle — the interstate. It's nighttime, and there's a rainstorm. Douglas urges his faltering horse across the wet asphalt, but Whisky is frightened by the lights and sounds of onrushing traffic. She wheels in confusion as Douglas flails at her with his hat. A cranked-up trucker spots them in his headlights but it's too late — he hits Whisky, knocking the pair to the side of the road. Douglas survives but his horse cannot go on. The sheriff arrives and puts her down as the old cowboy watches. "From the black arroyo came the scream of the horse," Abbey wrote, "then the sound of the first shot and another scream; — while over the great four-lane highway beside them the traffic roared and whistled and thundered by, steel, rubber, and flesh, dim faces behind glass, beating hearts, cold hands — the fury of men and women immured in engines."

In 1970, *Monte Walsh* was released. Based on a novel of the same name by Jack Schaefer, who wrote the screenplay for *Shane,* it too is a dark story about a lost cowboy. Set in the late nineteenth century, it starred Lee Marvin as a jobless ranch hand who is too proud to take a job at a two-bit rodeo. When a city slicker comes to town and takes credit for western progress, Walsh explodes. "You damned accountants!" he says. "We did it!" He finally proposes to his longtime love, a prostitute played by Jeanne Moreau, but she rejects him; unknown to Marvin, she is dying of syphilis. Pressed to his limits, he approaches a corralled mustang and says, "You know what I'm gonna do? I'm gonna teach you some manners before you leave." Then he mounts him and rides the bucking horse as it rampages through town, demolishing buildings and starting a cattle stampede, until the pair keels over in exhaustion. The horse gets up, and Walsh remounts; with head bowed the horse carries the aging cowboy into town. "Yeah, well, thanks," Walsh, the obsolete cowboy, his spirit broken, says to the spent mustang. Meanwhile, Mama Cass croons the movie's theme song, "The Good Times Are Coming."

The most harrowing Western to come out of the postwar era was *The Misfits,* about mustangers in Reno, with Clark Gable and Marilyn Monroe and directed by John Huston. Released in 1961, it was based on a short story of the same name written by Arthur Miller (who also wrote the screenplay) and published in *Esquire* in 1957. Years earlier, Will James had lamented the plight of the mustang in *Smoky.* Now, Miller conveyed the same story to a different audience, by way of the twentieth-century cowboy whose desperation Abbey had also expressed. Shortly after Arthur Miller met and fell in love with Marilyn, he went to Nevada to get a divorce. He took a cottage at Pyramid Lake outside Reno, next to the novelist Saul Bellow, who had also come to the quickie-divorce haven to legally split with his wife. Every day, they wrote. Miller had met some down-and-out cowboys who eked out a living by rounding up wild horses and selling them to the slaughterhouse for dog food, and he decided to write their story.

"The Misfits" opens at a makeshift camp east of Reno. Three men have gone into the outback to hunt mustangs and sell them to a cannery. "Wind blew down from the mountains all night," the story begins. "A wild river of air swept and swirled across the dark sky and struck down against the blue desert and hissed back into the hills. The three cowboys slept under their blankets, their backs against the first upward curve of the circling mountains, their faces toward the desert of sage. The wind and its tidal washing seethed through their dreams, and when it stopped there was a lunar silence that caused Gay Langland to open his eyes." Gay Langland (played by Clark Gable in the movie) is a forty-five-year-old jack-of-all-trades with a wife and two kids. She betrayed him and he left, though he still longs for his family. When the wind stops, Gay Langland knows it's a good day to catch wild horses. He wakes his partner, the pilot Guido Racanelli (played by Eli Wallach); his battered old fixed-wing plane with the rattling valves and weak shock absorbers is tethered nearby. Then the third man wakes up, a drifter named Perce (Montgomery Clift). "Better'n wages, huh, Perce?" Gay says. "Damn right," Perce responds, relieved at the chance to augment his meager income as a bucking-bronc rider in local rodeos.

Gay and Perce had met five weeks earlier in a bar, striking up the kind of friendship born of immediate need and a lifetime of defying the conventional world. Three days before the mustang hunt, Gay had introduced the drifter to his girlfriend, Roslyn (Marilyn Monroe), an eastern-educated woman who was "a good sport" with a soft heart. Now Perce had joined him in wild horse country, and the three broke Romeos were hoping to return to civilization with a few bucks. "Well, let's get gassed up," Guido says to his compadre as the sun begins to warm the desert, then climbs into the cockpit and cranks the ignition while Gay turns the propeller. Guido taxis across the white desert gravel and takes off. Gay, Perce, and Gay's dog climb into Gay's pickup and head to a sprawling playa — later it became a Nevada landmark named Misfits Flat. In the movie, Roslyn joins them.

After a couple of hours, Gay and Perce stop, get out, and scan the ridges for Guido's plane. "I sure hope they's five up in there," Perce says. "Guido saw five," Gay replies. "He said he wasn't sure if one wasn't only a colt," Perce says. After a while, Perce says that he's getting tired of this life. Gay reminds him that "it's better than wages" and Perce agrees. "You're a real misfit, boy," Gay says. "That suits me fine," Perce says. "I don't want nothin' and I don't want to want nothin'." "That's the way, boy," Gay replies.

Presently the pair spot Guido driving the mustangs — four and a colt — out of the mountains and toward the salt flats. Gay slides off the truck bed and opens the cab door, snapping his fingers for his dog, who jumps out and quivers like she always does when wild horses are coming. Perce is watching the plane through binoculars as it dives toward the mustangs. "God, they sure can run!" he says. They had been running for over an hour and would slow down when the plane climbed after a dive, and then speed up when it came back in for another clip. The heat waves swirl across the desert and the horses are alarmed at the sight of the barren terrain that gives off no scent of water. Guido tries a few times to get them onto the flats, and before long, Miller writes, "they closed ranks and slowly galloped shoulder to shoulder out onto the borderless lakebed. The colt galloped a length behind with its nose nearly touching the mare's long tail."

Exhausted, the herd slows to a halt in the middle of the bed, and Gay and Perce drive out to meet them. "As they roared closer and closer they saw that this herd was beautiful," the story goes. "There had been much rain this spring, and this herd must have found good pasture. They were well-rounded and shining. The mare was almost black, and the stallion and the two others were deep brown. The colt was curly-coated and had a gray sheen. The stallion dipped his head suddenly and turned his back on the truck and galloped." The others turned and followed, with the colt running next to the mare. Now Guido was back in the truck and surged after the band. "They were slim-legged and wet after running almost two hours in this alarm," Miller writes. But again they wheel away — "like circus horses" — when the truck approaches.

Guido maneuvers the truck between the stallion and the two browns, cutting off the mare and the colt at the left. From the truck bed, Gay throws a lasso over the stallion, "whose lungs were hoarsely screaming with exhaustion." The rope falls around his neck and the stallion swerves off, pulling a giant truck tire that the rope is attached to off the truck bed and dragging it along the hard clay for a few yards. "The three men watch as the stallion, with startled eyes . . .

Marilyn Monroe, Clark Gable, Montgomery Clift, and Eli Wallach
on the set of *The Misfits*, 1960.

leaped up with his forelegs in the air and came down facing the tire
and trying to back away from it. Then he stood still, heaving," Miller
writes, "his hind legs dancing in an arc from right to left and back
again as he shook his head in the remorseless noose." The cowboys
repeat the process with the other horses. The mare had never seen a
man, and her eyes were wide with fear. Blood trickled out of her nostrils and she was breathing hard. The colt tried to keep the mare between itself and the men, and the mare kept shifting to shield the colt.

Finally all the horses were roped and tethered to tires. The men gather around the stallion. "They're just old misfit horses," says Gay as he flings a rope around the horse's forelegs and pulls it tight, hoping to make him fall. But he would not. Gay hands the rope to Perce, gets another one, and ropes the stallion's hind legs. Still he would not fall. Guido tries to push him over but the horse swings his head and bares his teeth. The men pull harder on the ropes. "The stallion's forefeet slipped back, and he came down on his knees," Miller writes, "and his nose struck the clay ground and he snorted as he struck, but he would not topple over and stayed there on his knees as though he were bowing to something." Perce lays his hands on the horse's neck, pushes, and the horse falls over.

After a while, the men open the ropes around his hooves, and when the stallion felt free, he "clattered up and stood there looking at them, from one to the other, blood dripping from his nostrils and a stain of deep red on both dusty knees." With the band of mustangs tied to the tires, except for the colt, the men leave. "That mare might be six hundred pounds," Gay says. "About four hundred apiece for the browns and a little more for the stallion." Then they quiet down and figure their take. With a total of two thousand pounds at six cents per pound, all together they would make $120. The colt would bring in a few more dollars. Factoring in gas for the plane and truck and twelve dollars for groceries, the take boils down to a hundred dollars. Guido would get forty-five dollars, since he had used his plane; Gay would get thirty-five dollars because they had used his truck, and Perce would get the remaining twenty dollars. "We should have watered them," Gay says. "They can pick up a lot of weight if you let them water."

They stop at their camp to retrieve their supplies and then continue back to town. Perce looks at the mare in the distance. Her colt is lying next to her on the clay bed. "Ever hear of a colt leave a mare?" he says to Gay. "Not that young a colt," Gay says. "He ain't goin' nowhere." As the desert fades, the men approach town, driving in silence. After a while, Perce says, "I'm never goin' to amount to a damn thing." As for the wild horses, here's how they endured their last day before the men returned:

> The sun shone hot on the beige plain all day. Neither fly nor bug nor snake ventured out on the waste to molest the four horses tethered there, or the colt ... Toward evening the wind came up, and they backed into it and faced the mountains from which they had come. From time to time the stallion caught the smell of the pastures up there, and he started to walk toward the vaulted fields in which he had grazed; but the tire bent his neck around ... The cold of night raised the colt onto its legs, and it stood next to the mare for warmth [and then the five horses] closed their eyes and slept. The colt settled again on the hard ground and lay under the mare ... When the first pink glow of another morning lit the sky the colt stood up, and as it had always done at dawn it walked waywardly for water. The mare shifted and her bone hoofs ticked the clay. The colt turned its head and returned to her and stood at her side with vacant eye, its nostrils sniffing the warming air.

Of course, the Hollywood ending was different; instead of selling the horses to the cannery, the cowboys are convinced by Roslyn to set them free. But the true West trumps the movies every time. In Nevada, as we shall see, such roundups had been going on for decades; wild horses had become the new silver mine, and no one was letting them go. "We stand today on the edge of a New Frontier," John Fitzgerald Kennedy said on July 15, 1960, when he accepted the presidential nomination of the Democratic National Convention. His words launched the space age, and the frontier that he charted would ultimately include the moon.

Four years later, there was a new world's fair, located on the same site in Queens as the 1939 fair. It sounded the popular theme of space travel in many exhibits and was a valentine to corporate culture, several companies once again showcasing new products. On April 17, crowds gathered at the fair for an important event. Ford unveiled the Mustang—a name chosen from a list of six thousand possibilities because, as a company executive said, "It was American as hell." Its logo—the galloping horse on the grille—was adapted from Remington's portraits of the Old West. Two days after its unveiling, the car was advertised on all three television networks, and the campaign was widely hailed as "one of the greatest product launches in history." Millions of people placed orders for what soon became the ultimate road-trip car, but on the old frontier, a battle to save the real mustangs was under way as desperate misfits continued to prey on our greatest partner.

PART III

LAST STAND

8

The Mustang Besieged

THE FIRST TIME I saw mustangs in the wild, it was as if I had come home. There they were on a hillside near Reno, grazing, making their way down. They were a small band of mares and foals that had not yet shed their winter coats, and in every way they were perfect. A stallion stood nearby and watched. I walked through some brush to greet them. Surely they would be excited to see me, I thought; after all, I'm here to tell their story, and can't they tell that I like them? I flattened my hand and extended it, palm up — a gesture that domestic horses take as a sign of friendship, especially when the hand has an apple or a carrot. But the mustangs ran away and I was crushed.

The feeling only added to my sadness. It was just a few months after members of their herd had been gunned down in the massacre that I had read about in a desert bar. From the moment I saw the story, I started to make inquiries. Soon, I began traveling to Nevada to find out what happened. Over time, I got to know a wide range of people. I talked to the first people to arrive on the scene and the detectives who were horrified as, day after day, the body count got higher. I talked to people who were dismayed that mustangs were under siege and to those who wanted them gone. But most important, I began visiting the Virginia Range, where the mustangs are living and dying.

I grew up around racehorses and show horses, and later, when I moved to the West, logged a lot of time exploring the desert on horseback. But the only place I had seen mustangs was on television and in the movies. "That's not how you approach them," my guide said when the mustangs ran away. I was accustomed to being around domestic horses and it was difficult to realize these horses were actually wild. A few days later I returned and tried it again. This time, the horses were crossing a gulley deep in the range. My guide stopped the truck and we got out. She demonstrated a kind of sideways walk in which you move toward the horses on a diagonal, so they can see you fully and not feel threatened. "Don't stare at them," she said. I followed the instruction and tried to erase myself, edging quietly into their territory. For a while they didn't move. I could see their ears twitch and hear them breathe, and in the sky, a hawk rode a thermal. The moment was primal and basic, and since then I have visited them many times.

I have thought about the mustang massacre for years. To this day, I try to understand why someone would kill them. I have read thousands of pages of trial testimony and forensic reports and lists of what shells were found where and who said what to whom in the days before and after the crime. I have even met men who carry automatic weapons and go into the desert to kill things. Once, one of them asked me for a date. I declined, explaining that I wouldn't be able to listen to his stories. "That's okay," he said. "I won't tell you." In one of his novels, Tim O'Brien wrote that people go to war out of love, not patriotism. As they go about the business of destruction, they acquire nicknames that they savor, and are later ashamed of, and they become intimate in the performance of certain acts and the knowledge that they did it and in the silence or acclaim that follows. They are the only ones who know how and why an incident occurred, and then, sometimes, they don't; their pathologies sync up with greater forces, and in the wide-open space, things happen.

When the men approached, the black foal might have been nursing. Or she might have been on her side, giving her wobbly legs a rest, leaning into her mother under the starry desert sky. At the sound of the vehicle, the band prepared to move and did move at once; their withers twitched, their ears stiffened, their perfect, unshod hooves dug into the scrub for traction, and then they began to run. The black foal might have taken a second or two longer than the others to rise. Perhaps the mare, already upright, bolted instantly, turning her head to see if the foal had followed. The headlights appeared on a rise. The men were shouting and then there was another bright light—it trained from the roof of the vehicle across the sunken *ba-jada*. It swept the sands, illuminating the wild and running four-legged spirits as their legs stretched in full perfect extension, flashing across their hides, which were dun and sorrel and bay, making a living mural in three dimensions, in which the American story—all of it—was frozen in the desert forever as bullets hissed through the patches of juniper and into the wild horses of the old frontier. It was Christmas, 1998, and in the distance, the lights of Reno glittered and the casinos presented their holiday shows.

At about one in the afternoon on December 28, the phone rang at Wild Horse Spirit. Washoe County Animal Control officer DeDe Monroe was calling Betty Lee Kelly and Bobbi Royle at their sanctuary for injured and abused mustangs. The sanctuary is about half-way between Reno and Carson City, past the fast-food joints with the keno machines, past the various strip malls, in the rural zone on the eastern side of the Sierra Nevada where civilization trails off into high desert.

"Hey, Bobbi," Betty called. "A horse has been shot and wounded." Bobbi was in the corral with Art Majeski, an ex-Marine who fought on Guam in World War II, later worked as a ranch hand around Nevada, and had seen how some cattlemen treated mustangs on the range and didn't like it. Bobbi and Art immediately grabbed lead ropes and halters while Betty ran to their big Dodge pickup with her camera and video camcorder. Art remained at the sanctuary with the twenty-two resident mustangs, and the women drove quickly from Washoe Valley across the icy roads toward Reno and the Virginia Range to the east.

At Mira Loma Park, the women met up with two vehicles—Washoe County Animal Control and the Washoe County Sheriff's Department—and followed them toward the mountains. After a while, Betty and Bobbi stopped to pick up Craig Kelly (no relation to Betty), a hiker who had spotted an injured mustang in the gravel earlier that day and made the initial call to authorities. Kelly led the way to the scene, heading south up Mira Loma Road, past the old wagon-wheel tracks of the Donner Party and past the Sage Hill Gun Club until the road faded from relatively smooth and well-traveled dirt into an old and rugged path. Then the caravan turned left onto another desert road and headed east past a power station, slipping the tentacles of civilization as it inched its way toward the remote shooting gallery in Lagomarsino Canyon.

Because of recent snows, the road was slippery and washed out. The Washoe County vehicles fell behind, but Bobbi and Betty continued to follow Kelly, onto the upper power-line road, deeper into the piñon and juniper mountain terrain, past a dry lakebed way down below on the right. The two women knew this terrain well. They had begun exploring it years earlier, when they were learning about wild horses. Often they would go up into the Virginia Range and spend time with the local herds, photographing them, observing them, and and studying their behavior.

Now, as they headed into the range, they were about to come face to face with the dark heart of the thing they had been fighting for years, a crime so horrific that it would cause hundreds of thousands of people all over the world to pose some disturbing questions: Exactly what is America doing to its wild horses? And what is going on in Nevada? Bobbi's cell phone was ringing but the connection kept cutting out. In a few minutes, Kelly stopped at two large electrical towers. Bobbi and Betty got out, and Bobbi followed Kelly to the wounded filly he had seen earlier. Betty began to tape the scene, now spotting a dead stallion.

The filly was light bay, lying on the left side of the dirt road if you were heading to the nearby small town of Lockwood. Her head was facing the west, toward the land of thunder in Black Elk's vision, the place where horses are from. Her back legs were paralyzed. She was covered with dried body fluids. There was a hole near her front legs, where she had been thrashing and trying to get up. At her tail, there was a large pile of manure. Her eyes were open and she was clinging to life. Betty, a doctor, estimated that she had been there for a day or a day and a half, unable to move. She looked to be about six or seven months old.

While waiting for officials to arrive, Betty came across two more dead horses under a juniper tree—a nursing brown mare and her bay filly, also about six or seven months old. Both horses would soon be referred to in the record as #9 and #10. The women quickly realized that there was nothing to be done for the wounded filly. Knowing that it's difficult to kill a horse, even with a shot to the head in what passes for the right spot, they considered picking her up and taking her to the vet's to be euthanized with an injection. Since her back legs were paralyzed and she was small, she could have been carried by the group to their truck. But the risk of transporting her across the ice-covered slope was too great. If someone fell, the horse would have been hurt again.

"Would a handgun be appropriate?" asked Washoe County sheriff's deputy Daryl Spratley, who had just arrived. Betty said yes. Unlike some residents of Reno, Spratley liked seeing wild horses come down from the mountains as he headed to work in the morning. To him, they were not nuisance animals that tied up traffic but thrilling reminders of our past. He radioed for permission to put the filly down, then shot her in the head. Betty noticed a slight tremor in the horse, and he shot her again. Then, he turned away in tears. She was later identified in the record as horse #7. But Betty and Bobbi were keeping a different kind of record, and they called her Hope.

From that point on, things only got worse. On the right side of the road, once again heading toward Lockwood, Betty spotted a dead stallion with an exit wound in his chest. "There's another horse over here," Craig Kelly said, pointing to the left of the dirt road, just off a jeep trail. Bobbi got there first in the truck. "Jesus," Bobbi said, and then Betty arrived and started taping. There was a dark bay colt, about four to six months old, lying on his right side, facing south toward Hidden Valley. He had been sprayed around the mouth, nostrils, genitals, and rectum with a strange white substance. But there was an additional mutilation—a crude white circle had been painted across and around his left eye, as if someone could not take his gaze.

Throughout the day, a stallion had been standing at the edge of the kill zone, watching Betty, Bobbi, and the investigators as they found each dead horse. As the last rays of the winter sun faded, they headed to their cars. For a while, the horse remained at the perimeter, then he trotted on down the road. "His family had been wiped out," Betty recalled later, "but we still didn't know how bad it was."

In the American West, a bizarre war is underfoot. It is a variation of the old range wars of the nineteenth century, and it is waged by stockmen and sagebrush rebels with copies of the Second Amendment tucked into their back pockets, and it is backed by Republicans and Democrats and a federal agency that circumvents the Wild Free-Roaming Horses and Burros Act of 1971, along with small-town officials who march to the great American battle cry "Don't tread on me." Their target is the wild horse, and the war rages most intensely in Nevada, where more than 50 percent of the country's remaining mustangs still roam.

Nevada is the country's most extreme state, a stunning geographical wonderland that is a proving ground for mustang and man alike. It's the seventh-biggest state, and most of it — a full 67 percent — is made up of public, or federally owned, lands. It's also the most parched state in the Union, with the least amount of rainfall. The moisture that travels into the state from the Pacific generally doesn't make it past the tallest peaks of the Sierra Nevadas, where in the winter it becomes snow. In addition to the Sierra Nevadas, there are more than three hundred separate mountain ranges in the state, described by writer William L. Fox as "a geological maze no one has yet fully deciphered."

Many of Nevada's rivers drain down from the various ranges and have no place to go, so the water pools and evaporates in vast sinks, leaving alkali mud flats and dry lakes where pioneers and oxen and mules became mired and then baked to death, and once in a while, you can still see the old rut of a wagon wheel, crusted over and petrified until the next geologic age.

With so much wide-open space, there is plenty of room for extreme behavior; the West is a personal-rights fest, and Nevada is ground zero. Part of the state was blown to smithereens during the age of atomic testing while spectators in Cadillac-fin sunglasses gathered to watch the distant show. Rivers are bled dry so faux dolphins can spout perpetual streams of H_2O in the hotel fountains, and some say that an alien was once captured and filleted on the military base that the military says isn't really a military base, the one that's known as Area 51. Today the Nevada state tourism commission sells the extreme image, running a full-page ad in various adventure magazines that shows a photo of a dusty woman—a modern pioneer—at the foreground of desert scenery, having just climbed Bloody Shins Trail, "challenge #6" on the state's list of notorious mountain-biking paths. "Rage before beauty," the caption says. "This is a 91,000-square-mile provocation to seize life by the throat and throttle it like a rag doll." Or, as Bernard DeVoto put it in 1955, "The West is systematically looted."

At the end of the nineteenth century, there were two million wild horses ranging across seventeen states, from California to Missouri, Texas to Montana. While official counts were not taken at the time, then, as now, most of them had retreated to Nevada, staking out territory in the remote mountains and deserts, steering clear of those who would round them up and ship them off to wars or the slaughterhouse, or simply shoot them for sport. The great cattle drives had come to an end, but that did not mean that there were no more cows. The ranching industry had retrenched and was well on its way to becoming the powerful lobby that it is today. Across western rangelands thousands of cows and sheep were competing for grasslands that had already been badly depleted.

Nevada had not been as severely affected by the catastrophic blizzards of the 1880s as the other western states, and a parade of ranchers converged on the Silver State to start anew. Some of them brought their own horses, but others needed to purchase fresh stock. Suddenly, the value of mustangs increased and Nevada was no longer a safe haven. In addition to being taken for urban populations that needed transportation or foreign consumers of horsemeat, they were now rounded up to supply the state's many newcomers in their ranch work.

In 1897, Nevada passed a law authorizing the killing of wild horses —another way to make a profit. Within a year five thousand had been shot and sent to a rendering plant in Elko, where they became fertilizer, glue, or hog food. In 1899, the Boer War broke out in South Africa, and their value increased again. Over the next three years, nearly 230,000 wild horses were sent to the front. Many came from Texas and Canada, but some came from the other western states, including

Nevada, where the price quickly jumped from three dollars a head to ten. Some cowboys rounded up so many wild horses during the war years that they made a small fortune.

Meanwhile, across the West, the rangelands were nearly bereft of forage, particularly Nevada because it had been so badly overgrazed. The winter of 1889 was the worst ever for the state, with harsh weather and deep snows killing off about 75 percent of its cattle and sheep. Wild horses suffered as well, but they endured—to the dismay of ranchers. Many stockmen considered them mostly expendable animals that shouldn't have been on the range in the first place, recent arrivals to the ecosystem who were stealing food from cows. This view created a new alliance among old enemies, cattlemen and sheep men, who found a common foe in the mustang even as they continued their own war. A couple of decades later, *Cattleman* magazine summed up the ongoing complaint:

> They eat too much grass, these horses drink too much from streams which else would sustain peaceful and profitable herds and flocks of cattle and sheep. There have grown to be too many of them; 70,000 it is said in Montana alone; 40,000 in Eastern Oregon and so on.

But as ranchers well knew, horses were not the problem on the range. Cattle had been grazing for 350 years without regulations. In 1898, a group of cattlemen asked the government for limits on grazing, fearing that the land was becoming depleted. Their plea went unheeded. In 1901, conservationist Teddy Roosevelt was elected president. After the cattle die-off in the 1880s, he had visited the western rangelands and was heartbroken. The land, he said, was "a mere barren waste; not a green thing could be seen; the dead grass eaten off till the country looked as if it had been shaved by a razor." One of his first acts as president was assembling a group of experts to make recommendations for rangeland reform. A year later, the agriculture department issued a warning: "The public ranges are in many places badly depleted. This is directly traceable to overstocking." In 1906, after rounding up support from 78 percent of the ranchers in the West, Roosevelt's Public Land Commission presented its report to Congress. Its major finding was this:

The general lack of control in the use of public grazing lands has resulted, naturally and inevitably, in overgrazing and the ruin of millions of acres of otherwise valuable grazing territory. Lands useful for grazing are losing their only capacity for productiveness, as, of course, they must when no legal control is exercised.

The report was ignored, and the range got worse. By 1920, the age-old tension between cattlemen and sheep men had escalated, with the groups battling over the remaining forage. In Colorado, 350 sheep were clubbed to death by masked men. Various grazing bills were introduced, but, like Roosevelt's report, they were derailed by political infighting, an uninterested public, and the cry for states' rights — some of the issues that continue to interfere with rangeland protection today, and contribute to the mustang's demise.

But the greater threat to the wild horse was greed, the thing that had propelled Nevada for decades.

In 1857, the Comstock Lode was discovered at Virginia City, Nevada. It was the biggest silver strike in American history. The town quickly became a geologic slot machine, with swarms of miners crawling through its veins and removing the precious metal. "I have just heard five pistol shots down the street," Mark Twain wrote to his mother while living in the violent town in 1860. "The pistol did its work well ... two of my friends [were shot]. Both died within three minutes." After three years, Virginia City went bust, and the parade moved on to other caches. But its silver linked it forever to the fate of the nation: the town had helped the Union finance the Civil War, and later, when the silver was plundered to make movies, America looked at the screen and saw its reflection — a cowboy on a horse.

As the nineteenth century came to a close, the silver mines were stripped bare, and Nevada turned its attention to wild horses, a readily accessible treasure in seemingly endless supply. With fortunes to be made, a Hydra-headed horseflesh industry arose and flourished in one way or another for the next seventy years, until federal protection for mustangs was finally enacted after a hard-fought battle.

In its early stages, the wild-horse industry involved the collusion of mustangers and transportation networks that supplied slaughterhouses with a steady stream of horses that could be rendered into products such as pet food, glue, clothing, and meat. "The wild horse returns to Europe in a tin can," proclaimed an early twentieth-century headline in the *Cattleman,* and soon it also returned on four legs, to serve in the American, British, and French cavalries of World War I.

So many mustangs were taken from 1920 to 1935 that the era is known in certain circles as "the great removal." Wild horses had gone from "cow pony to cauldron," writes Walker D. Wyman in his important book *The Wild Horse of the West,* published in 1945, the first work to fully document the demise of the mustang. In fact, the icon of freedom had become chicken feed. Offering a special "chicken feed rate" on horse shipments, railroad companies provided a system whereby thousands of horses were bought for one cent a pound or less on ranges as far east as the Dakotas and then transported to the California towns of Vernon, Petaluma, and Hayward — the primary centers of chicken breeding.

"By designating a carload of horses as 'chicken feed,'" Wyman writes, "the railroad was under no legal obligations to give humane treatment to the cargo ... This was almost the only market for scrub horses caught by cooperating cattlemen, mustangers, and one or two government bureaus in the 1920s." Around 1923, another market for wild horses emerged — canned dog and cat food. "When the country was agricultural," Wyman writes, "food for the dog was not a problem — scraps, left-overs, and rodents constituted the diet. But as the urban population increased, the delicatessen came into its own ... The dog then entered the discussion."

To supply these burgeoning markets, men hunted mustangs in droves, and some became famous. The most celebrated mustanger was Charles "Pete" Barnum, who came from South Dakota to Nevada around the end of the 1890s, drawn by the thing called mustang fever. Within six years, he had revolutionized the practice of hunting wild horses, devising a method that is still used today, in which the animals are run through a jute-lined chute into a portable trap. During his career, he shipped about seven thousand horses to stockyards in the Midwest. Considering that about 25 percent were killed in the process before they even got to the stockyards, that means that he had actually rounded up about nine thousand horses.

When he arrived in Nevada, he was around twenty-five years old. He had the innocent, boyish look of Billy the Kid, which masked a particularly American trait that is nasty and accountable to no one. Like countless other characters who came before and would come after, Barnum took the great American promise of life in a free country as more than a right; to him, it was a commandment, and it led him into the heart of the high Nevada desert, on the eastern side of the Sierra Nevadas. This was a harsh region that sprawled across six counties where the only railroad that crossed the state was a hundred miles away, and it was a three-day ride from one ranch to another.

In 1929, the Western writer Rufus Steele wrote a glowing profile of Barnum in *McClure's Magazine,* titled "Trapping Wild Horses." "I have ridden neck and neck with these game old stallions," Barnum said. "I have beaten them across the nose with my quirt until their faces were drenched with blood, only to have them slacken sufficiently to dodge behind my horse and thence to continue on their contrary way." But embedded in the article was Steele's own tribute to wild horses:

> Their endurance is phenomenal, and as for agility, the marks of their unshod hoofs are found at the summits of monumental boulder-piles which even a mountain goat might reasonably be expected to cut out of his itinerary ... The water-holes are from twenty to fifty miles apart, but when the taint of man is upon a drinking place, they will turn aside from it, even in midsummer ... In winter the water-holes may be solid ice, but the horses are not inconvenienced — they eat the snow ... In extremity they gnaw at scrub pines and cedars, the sparse chaparral, greasewood, and rabbitbrush, and with starvation ahead, they eat the bitter brush of the black sage.

Curiously, such odes to the mustang seemed only to hasten its demise. At the time Steele's article appeared, the war against wild horses was raging on two fronts, as stockmen and mustangers ripped into the herds, often in tandem (with a slight difference in tactics: whereas ranchers frequently killed horses on the spot, horse drovers had to bring them in alive — as required by contract). Countless equine death runs were carried out across the high desert, in which the animals were harried with little food or water across hundreds of miles to railheads, then shipped to the slaughterhouse. Many mustangs ended up at the country's first major processing plant in Rockford, Illinois, an operation that figured prominently in the plundering of the West. It was started in 1923 by the notoriously dapper Englishman P. M. Chappel and his brother Earl. Officially called the Chappel Brothers Corporation, or CBC, it was known among cowboys as "the Corned Beef and Cabbage." In its first year, Wyman reports, "about half the 1446 horses processed under federal jurisdiction were canned, and it is certain most of them were wild." The result was 149,906 pounds of meat from the Chappel plant alone; the total yield from the nearly two hundred plants that were operating across the country that year was 22,932,265 pounds.

In 1925, Montana entered the market, signing a death warrant for "abandoned horses running at large upon the open range." Over the next four years, about four hundred thousand mustangs were removed from the state. On June 5, 1929, a *New York Times* reporter filed a heated account of the roundups, as if he too had been struck by mustang fever. "The first chapter has been written in the greatest wild horse roundup ever held in the West," he said, "and today hundreds of horses — large and small, vicious and indifferent, mustangs, 'fuzz-tails' and bronchos — are in pastures ready for the first sale and elimination check. The roundup will continue through most of the summer, with the hardest work still ahead, for the horses are retreating."

It seemed there was no end to the demand for mustangs: Scandinavians were eating tons of horseflesh, and glue and mattress factories were buying up all the spare parts. Adolph C. Kreuter, a cowboy who worked mustangs at the Chappel corrals, recalled the era in an article called "I Herded the Wild Ones" for *Frontier Times:*

> Ladies were demanding pony coats, in the manufacture of which the hair side was used much as the hide of unborn calf is used in some western apparel. Frequently as many as five to seven hundred horses daily were being sashayed up the ramp to the killing floor. I heard that this was very often done with great difficulty, due to the spooky natures of the condemned.

Despite protests from the Humane Society, the killing continued. Finally, the supply of wild horses in America had so dwindled that even Chappel's ranch in Montana, populated with his own mares and stallions, failed to keep him in style. So he moved his business to Argentina, where he died in a freak accident—like others who have trafficked in the misery of horses. "I like to think that his spirit will always be among us," Kreuter wrote. "I've also wondered what P. M. Chappel might have accomplished if he had the benefits of automation in his day."

Buried in Kreuter's article is the story of an unnamed cowboy who worked for a time at the Chappel plant and did not like what he saw. One day he tried to burn the plant down. Then he tried again and again, pouring a flammable liquid on burlap sacks and placing them in the shallow, narrow gutters that ran from room to room. Some of his fires did a great deal of damage, but he could not shut the slaughterhouse down. His methods became more extreme. Once, he climbed a telegraph pole and cut the wires, sending off huge flares of flashing light—an SOS seen for miles. Finally, when that did not end the slaughter of his beloved mustangs, he packed a suitcase with dynamite, wrapped it with baling wire, and attached a fuse.

On a dark night, he carried it to a smokestack at the main power plant. "What are you doing?" asked a guard. He would not say and started to light the fuse. "Put that down!" the guard called. The cowboy dropped the match and the dynamite, backed away, and took off. Scrambling up a railroad trestle, the guard spotted the cowboy, took aim, and fired. His gun was loaded with birdshot. The next day, children were playing in some tall grass near the slaughterhouse. They found the wounded cowboy. He was arrested and charged with attempting to blow up a horse-meat canning plant. "I plead guilty," he said. "I couldn't help it. I am a cowboy and I love horses. I can't bear to think of people eating them." Later, he went insane, at which point he disappeared from the record.

By the 1930s, the Great Depression had gripped the country, with thirteen million people out of work. In the west, vast hurricanes of dust swept the land, the result of a drought, overgrazing, and high winds. By the middle of August 1934 "a good third of our part of the continent was one wide crisp," said *Fortune* magazine. The government's relief office listed 1,100 counties among the 1,400 in twenty-two western states as "harmed beyond all help." As historian T. H.

Watkins observed, "Economic desolation combined with a largely human-caused environmental disaster to inspire the cattle industry to give up its fondly held delusions of rugged individualism — just long enough to plead with the New Deal government for help."

Later that year, Congress finally responded to pressure from the livestock industry and passed the Taylor Grazing Act, named for prominent ranching representative Edward Taylor. For the first time in American history, livestock grazing would be managed by a federal oversight agency. The act's mandate was "to stop injury to the public grazing lands by preventing overgrazing and soil deterioration." To carry out the new law, a new division of grazing was created within the Department of the Interior. Wild horse advocates mark passage of the act as the beginning of the end for the mustang (although even at the time of its passage — and to this day — there were ranchers who didn't like the act, regarding it as a federal intrusion into paradise on the range).

The Taylor Grazing Act was an invisible fence that constrained the West in a new way, dividing millions of acres of public lands in the eleven western states into allotments. These were lands where wild horses roamed, about seventy thousand of them at the time of its enactment, and where ranchers had been running livestock for generations. Each allotment was allowed a certain number of cows or sheep, based on how many the range could carry in a particular region. To determine how many the range could carry, the grazing service — which soon merged with the newly formed Bureau of Land Management within the Department of the Interior — was later tasked with carrying out annual studies of rainfall, soil conditions, wildlife populations, flowers, trees, and so on.

To graze on an allotment, ranchers were required to have a permit. The fees for the permits — pennies on the head in 1934, and today about $1.39 per cow — has led to what many rangeland observers call "welfare ranching," a subsidized industry in which stockmen receive a government handout in the form of cheap land in exchange for relaxed grazing regulations. One would think that such easy access to public lands involved a practice that was crucial to the nation. But in an explosive series of articles called "Cash Cows," published in 1999, the *San Jose Mercury News* presented a finding that rocked certain quarters in the West: the large livestock operations of the eleven western states supply the country with just 3 percent of our beef. In recent years, these operations have become more entrenched; as two BLM scientists revealed in 2005, their grazing studies were altered by agency officials who wanted the latest rules to favor ranchers.

Five years after passage of the Taylor Grazing Act, the government declared its view of the mustang. It was a view shared by many stock-men — the one that they had been promoting for years to reporters who were entranced by mustang roundups and to a public that was accustomed to seeing horses on the racetrack or the show circuit and did not realize that many were still wild. "A wild horse consumes forage needed by domestic livestock, brings in no return, and serves no useful purpose," said a grazing service spokesman in August 1939. "[The agency is] interested in the removal of wild horses from the public ranges but the population of these animals in grazing districts is localized and for this reason the Division has not attempted removal on a general scale but has relied on efforts made by individuals who have worked in cooperation with the Division." In other words, the only thing standing between mustangs and oblivion was time.

Mustang roundups continued unchecked until one day in 1950 when an intrepid Nevada character who would come to be known as Wild Horse Annie saw blood spilling out of a truck and followed it to a slaughterhouse outside Reno. From then on, she gave her life over to the horses, winning passage of the first legal protections for mustangs — four times, in county, state, and national battles that endangered her life and raged for two decades. Finally, in 1971, Richard Nixon signed the landmark Wild Free-Roaming Horses and Burros Act into law — a gesture that harked back to Ulysses S. Grant, and one that would be undone years later by George W. Bush, a president whose home state presided over two of the country's three remaining horse slaughterhouses.

Although generally overlooked in discussions of the era's great environmental advocates (like her animal constituents themselves), Annie was as influential and courageous as Rachel Carson in her fight to save songbirds or Dave Brower in his fight for the wilderness: with nothing but a typewriter and a telephone in a Reno office, she launched a discussion of the meaning and purpose of public lands that continues to this day. And she still stands as an example of how one person can change the course of events — something that seems almost quaint in today's cynical times.

Velma Johnston — aka Wild Horse Annie — was born in Reno on March 5, 1912, the first of Joseph and Gertrude Clay Bronn's four children. A pioneer family, the Bronns were intimately connected to the land and wild horses. In fact, wild horses had once saved Joseph Bronn's life. The story of how that happened contains the DNA of Annie's difficult and ultimately victorious journey to protect mustangs. In the 1870s, Annie's paternal grandfather was the foreman of a silver mine in Ione, Nevada, another boom-and-bust town that now feeds on its ghosts, a shadow of an outpost where tourists pose for pictures in front of boarded-up miners' shacks and stop for a drink at the local watering hole where a famous bartender spins tales of a violent and voracious yesteryear.

When the silver veins were tapped out in 1884, Annie's grandfather took what was left of his meager earnings, paid his men, and then left for California. "There would have been an early-morning chill in the air that is always a part of the desert climate," Annie wrote in an unpublished memoir, "and the horses would be frisky, the colt playful." She was referring to the team of four mustangs that her grandfather had caught in the wild and tamed, the ones he was now feeding, harnessing, and watering, and the foal, still nursing, recently born to one of the team's mares. "The children, Ben and Ella, would be lifted into the box-bed of the spring wagon, sleepy-eyed and querulous, as children are when they are faced with the unknown. Grandma and Grandpa would climb to the high seat, Grandma with the infant in her arms."

As they trekked across the desert, they refreshed whenever there was a spring and some sparse grass for the horses. After a journey of several days, they camped at Sand Mountain, a giant dune that is now a haven for off-roaders and others who come for its marvels. "The land is cumbered here and there with drifted ridges of the finest sand, sometimes 200 feet high and shifting before every gale," Sir Richard Burton wrote in his diary in 1860 while traveling with Pony Express riders. At night when the winds dance, the mountain sends forth a soft whistle — said to carry the stories of all who have passed by — and perhaps when the Bronns rested here, they were comforted by the strains of the tuneful sand before they moved on through the lower elevations.

Their trip was more difficult now, as the terrain became more desolate; in the noonday heat, they were crossing a desert plateau through valleys pocked with gravel and sage. "The dust would form a mask of discomfort," Annie recounted. "The sun reflected on the sand and alkali would be blinding; and the cloth cover of the wagon that protected the children and the meager store of possessions would attract the heat and multiply it into a furnace."

Soon the Bronns ran out of food and could not afford to purchase a cow from passing wayfarers. This particular leg of the trip — thirty-five miles from Sand Springs to Ragtown — was a classic desert joke; there was a shimmer of hope in the distance, and the alkali flats continued to throw off a glare that seared the eye as the team plodded along the perimeter of the Carson Sink, a deadly scape littered with the dregs of earlier pioneer crossings. Gertrude's breast milk had dried up, and the baby was shriveling in the desert wastes. But the horses had found succor in the rabbit brush and sparse grasses along the road, and the nursing mare was feeding her foal. So Joseph milked the mare and nourished the child, knowing that she would not have enough milk for her colt and his boy for much longer.

The painful decision was made: the next morning, Joseph would sacrifice the colt by slicing its throat. But when the sun rose, the horses were gone. Later that day, a band of Paiute Indians returned, offering to trade back the horses for food. In exchange for the mare, Joseph gave them sacks of sugar and flour. But the Indians would not part with the foal — and they left with the ransom tied to his back. For the rest of the trip, Joseph's son, Wild Horse Annie's father, was fed mare's milk. When the family arrived in the promised land and introduced their newborn son to his grandparents, they told the story that would be passed down through the generations: how a little boy in the desert was saved by a wild horse.

A few years later, the Bronns returned to Nevada and purchased a small ranch near Reno. Annie's father was running the Mustang Express, a desert freighting service, using wild horses he had found on the range to haul goods through the Great Basin. Sometimes Annie would pass time with the itinerant desert workers who helped out on the ranch. Some of these men were well known in the region, such as Sanitary Bill, a pole cutter whose name derived from his never having taken a bath. Annie got to know them well, and years later, when she learned that some of them eked out a living by destroying wild horses, her knowledge of their ways helped her navigate through a dangerous maze of threats and social castigation.

In 1923, when she turned eleven, she was struck by polio—a scourge of the era that attacked the nervous system and wreaked havoc on the limbs, affecting millions. Its debilitated victims were often kept behind doors or sent away to places known only to a few family members. Annie wore leg braces and was ridiculed at school. Her parents sent her away for a special treatment—months of confinement inside an upper-body cast at a sanatorium in California. When doctors took the cast off, the polio was arrested but Annie's face had stuck to the plaster, and she was permanently disfigured. No one told her what had happened, and she found out on her own when she went home. Her parents had removed all the mirrors, but she finally found one, took a look—and was stunned. Afraid to show her face, she retreated into a world of learning and began to write and paint. But mostly, she was healed by the desert.

Meanwhile, a newfangled style of mustang roundup was being carried out all over the West by a pilot named Chance Parry. Like Annie, he was from a pioneer family. He grew up in southern Utah and started hunting wild horses when he was ten. He was a World War I vet and a trophy hunter, with a penchant for bagging cougars in the Grand Canyon. But it was mustang fever that really had him in its grip. "Hunting wild horses is the greatest sport in the world," he said. "The wild horse is not only the swiftest, but the cleverest of animals." Parry paved the way for the characters Arthur Miller wrote about in his story "The Misfits" and for other hunters who now penetrated the nooks and crannies of the wilderness.

Their tales were often recounted in breathless prose published in high- and lowbrow journals, from the *New York Times Magazine* to brochures produced by wilderness outfitters. In November 1925, *Popular Science Monthly* published an article about Parry under the headline "How a Cowboy-Aviator Hunts: The World's Most Thrilling Sport Found in Ridding Western Grazing Land of a Million Outlaw Animals — Adventures of a Famous Buckaroo." It was a typical adventure piece of the time, using language not so different from that used by those involved in wild horse roundups of today, framing the mustang as criminal, unwanted, or fugitive.

Other cultures used the same language long ago. In the Middle Ages, wolves were tried as killers, said to have stolen babies, and pigs and even monkeys were placed in the docket and cross-examined, then convicted of being demons, and hanged. The *Popular Science Monthly* article relished the idea of chasing down the outlaw horses. Beneath the lurid headline was an illustration of two rugged cowboys roping a wild stallion on its hind legs. "Breaking a Wild Captive — Desperate Struggle," screamed the caption, and the article went on:

> The great white stallion snorted, wild-eyed, muscles tensed, his gorgeous mane tossing in the breeze that swept across the vast desert of the Colorado Plateau. Behind their leader a shaggy band of mustangs trembled in terror.
>
> Out of the mighty depths of the Grand Canyon rose a humming roar that thundered through the spacious silence of the plateau as a great winged creature shot from the chasm at the North Rim and swooped downward, like a giant bird of prey.
>
> With a scream of warning the big stallion lunged forward, a flashing streak of white, while the pack of wild mustangs pounded the desert at his heels. Madly they tore across the waste of sagebrush and cactus in a terrified pace to shake off the strange menace from the skies.
>
> The pursuer swung lower. Closer and closer it flew, until its great wings cast a shadow over the tossing, straining herd, and its roar drowned out the beat of flying hoofs. Mile after mile the relentless pursuit continued. Now a raw-boned mare at the rear of the band faltered, stumbled, and fell. Now a spotted colt wavered and lagged behind, all atremble. The terrific pace was beginning to tell . . .

When Annie graduated from high school, she got a job at the First Mutual Bank of Reno as an executive secretary, where she worked for the next forty years. On her first day at work, she was introduced to the instrument that would help her wage the coming battle — the typewriter, which she had never used before. "I made so many mistakes that day," she said, "I was afraid to throw all the ruined letterheads and second sheets into the wastebasket to give proof of my inefficiency, so I tucked them all up my bloomer leg and fairly rustled home that night."

Soon Annie met the love of her life — a tall handsome half Native American named Charlie Johnston who had come to Reno for a divorce. They dated over five-cent beers, talked about their love of poetry and the West, went square-dancing and for long rides through the desert canyons. They soon married and bought sixteen acres in Wadsworth; they called it the Double Lazy Heart Ranch and proceeded to build a ranch with horses and cows. They even registered their brand, but they never used it because Annie thought branding was cruel. Not able to have children, the Johnstons turned their spread into a retreat for young boys and girls, paving the way for the hippotherapy used in many programs today.

The morning in 1950 that changed Annie's life had started out like all the rest. She put on her customary suit, pumps, and hat, and got in her car and headed for work. Somewhere along the old Kit Carson Trail, she saw a truck carrying live animals, to market, she thought, but then something disturbed her — she noticed the blood. Annie followed the truck to a rendering plant, and when it stopped, she was sickened at the sight. The animals were tightly packed horses, suffering from buckshot wounds. There was a stallion whose eyes had been shot out and a badly trampled colt. Some of the horses were bleeding from their hooves, which were worn down from being chased across hard rocks.

Annie asked the driver where the horses had come from and why they were in such terrible condition. He told her they had been run in by plane. "For many years I had heard about the capturing of wild horses by airplane," she would later say. "I pretended it didn't exist. After that day in 1950, it touched my life directly and I could no longer pretend. In the decades to come it would reach and change the lives of many others as well."

Annie was up against a very powerful force, an entrenched illness, the old affliction called mustang fever. *Fever* was the appropriate term; what ailed many men of the West was very similar to the gold fever that had driven the conquistadors, the sickness in their hearts that led them to great heights of violence. Yet it differed in one respect. Because wild horses were alive and could run and hide in the vast reaches of the Great Basin, they had to be chased down. With gold, all one had to do was find it. Pure and simple, mustang fever was bloodlust that became its own culture—it made money, it had

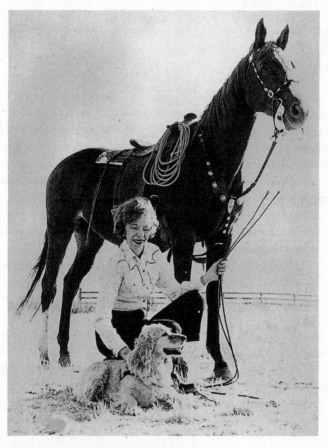

An iconic image of Wild Horse Annie with her dog
Daiquiri and her horse Hobo.

its own gear, and it provided people with identities. Often, it drove them mad. As Nevada writer Anthony Amaral described in his book *Mustang:*

> One summer there was a wild horse spree that ended with nine of the saddle horses crippled and their value hardly compensated by the sale of the few captured mustangs ... A seasoned mustanger who wouldn't think of running his top saddle horse in a demanding stakes race would force his horse after mustangs until the saddle horse collapsed in a convulsive shudder. One rider chased a wild horse until his horse dropped. In a rage the rider jerked out his Winchester from the saddle scabbard and fired recklessly into the herd. Then he threw his arms around his dying horse and cried like a baby.

Although Annie's life had changed the moment she saw the trail of blood, she didn't know how to proceed. In some ways, she was like the hardscrabble ranch hands she had met long ago. She too had come from a pioneer family that eked out a living in the West, proud of making something from nothing on their own. She could handle a rifle and six-shooter and had an iron will. And she did not need outsiders — government — to understand right from wrong.

But for her, Nevada was not a place to plunder. Wild horses — which *were* Nevada — should be left alone. Without them, she said, we have no heritage. So where to start? First, she needed to do some research. Why were the roundups legal? Poring over documents in the Reno library, she found out about the Taylor Grazing Act — which answered her question. She also learned that permits to hunt horses were required, but they were also easy to get. In Nevada, the only thing needed was a petition seeking permission and a two-thousand-dollar bond. Yet the hunts were only whispered about, sometimes boasted about in certain bars — people didn't want to draw attention to what they knew was a disturbing practice.

As Annie discovered, during the eight years after World War II, a hundred thousand wild horses were seized in Nevada alone — for use as pet food. She started writing letters to local papers; best to start slowly and see who else out there was in her corner. Very quickly Annie began to receive mail in response — a lot of it, often with no full

mailing address, just her original name, Velma Johnston. Tex Gladding, the Virginia City postmaster, knew exactly where to take it.
Cautious coverage of her campaign began to surface in local papers,
articles that were in favor of what she was doing but were worded
so as not to offend the old-timers who had been making a living as
mustangers.

Soon people came to Annie with terrible stories — roundups they
had seen over the years, unreported atrocities involving the deaths of
who knew how many mustangs. One night, Annie and her husband,
Charlie, followed up on a tip. There had been another aerial hunt.
They tracked the horse thieves to a makeshift corral in a desert canyon seven miles from their ranch. They found four hundred horses.
The next morning, the horses would be heading for the slaughterhouse. With Charlie behind the wheel of their truck, Annie stood on
the hood so she could see over the bars of the corral and snapped
pictures. "The mustangs were milling around in the dry dust, hyster-
ical with fear," Annie told *Desert* magazine. "Their hoofs and mouths
were bleeding ... They emitted strange tortured cries." The only
thing that mattered to their captors was that they were breathing — as
required in the contract issued by the pet food company.

As Annie clicked the camera, its flash alerted the men. "A set of
headlights careened toward the station wagon," Annie later told Alan
Kania, who drove from Boston to Colorado after graduating from
college to work with Annie, inspired by an article about her battle.
"I jumped off the hood and into the passenger side just as the truck
swerved off. The men in the truck were yelling things, obscenities,
then they turned around and headed right for Charlie. He pulled out
his .38 and took aim. The men left." Back home, Annie and Charlie
developed the film. Early the next morning, Annie waited outside the
county commissioner's office until the first official arrived. "Look,"
she said, handing him the photos.

He followed her back to the corral where he confronted the men,
accused them of cruelty to animals, and ordered them to release
the mustangs. As word of the horses' release spread across Storey
County, the range war against the horse exploded, and it now had
a human target. Annie received death threats and began responding
to knocks on her door with a rifle in her left hand. But she didn't

hide — in fact, she and Charlie and Tex Gladding often met in the neighborhood tavern, along with other locals, to talk about the situation. And then Annie got another tip: the Reno BLM office had given two pilots from Idaho permission to round up wild horses in Storey County, and the county commissioners were about to meet to consider the pilots' application for a bond.

"You have to testify," Tex told her. Others agreed. "I don't know," she said. "I know I can make a good argument but . . ." And then her voice trailed off because she was reluctant to show her disfigured face in public. Charlie always told her not to worry, she was beautiful to him and that was all that mattered. Soon she was aided by local papers; in June of 1952, the *Territorial Enterprise* in Virginia City, the paper that Mark Twain had written for, enraged half the town when it announced support for Annie in the following editorial:

> Every so often there is put in motion agitation for the destruction by one means or another of the bands of wild horses which still roam the Washoe Hills. The current pressure is being applied solely for the gratification of two sheep ranchers who claim their grazing lands are impaired by the horses. In view of the practically unlimited grazing lands available in Western Nevada and the absurdly small number of the horses, such claims are purely fictional. The wild horses, harmless and picturesque as they are, are a pleasant reminder of a time when all the West was wilder and more free, and any suggestion of their elimination or the abatement of the protection they now enjoy deserves a flat and instant rejection from the authorities within whose province the matter lies.

A few days later, Annie traveled to the Storey County courthouse, once the battleground for miners' claims. The famous nineteenth-century statue of Lady Justice without a blindfold still guarded the front door. Annie was accompanied by Charlie and a band of supporters; they sat on one side of the courtroom, across the aisle from the stockmen who had vowed to shut Annie down. A Western showdown was under way, and the overflow crowd gathered next door in the Bucket O' Blood Saloon; the same place where, years later, local wags would await the verdict in the 1998 horse massacre trial that would unfold in the same hallowed hall.

"Gentlemen," Annie said now, rising to speak, and immediately, the cattlemen and the owners of sheep and the defenders of animals stopped shouting and jockeying and eyeing each other and got very quiet, for Annie had a way. "I'm fighting to save a memory." She recited a litany of abuses against the mustang, and her gaze did not waver — not because she wanted it that way but because her childhood polio treatment prevented her from moving her neck. When she was finished, others added their voices, including Ted, who testified that he had recently seen pilots driving mustangs down a canyon, shooting them from the air. "Resolved!" said the commissioners; for the first time in local history, "the use of any airborne equipment, including airplanes, helicopters, etc. as a means of chasing, rounding up or spotting during a roundup of wild horses or burros in Storey County" was outlawed.

It was an important victory, but "infinitesimal," Annie said; the war against the mustang was far from over. Since the resolution applied only to Storey County, meat dealers could run the horses over the county line the old-fashioned way, then pick up the airborne chase. But public support for wild horses and burros was gathering steam, and Annie set her sights on the Nevada state legislature. She received more death threats as the mail poured in, and the roundups outside Storey County continued. Bills were introduced, killed, then reintroduced. Unwavering, Annie sent letters to every newspaper in the state, and some of them ran shocking editorials in favor of mustang protection. As she stood to address one local meeting, a cattleman derided her as Wild Horse Annie. The joke quickly backfired, and the nickname became her calling card.

Paradoxically, Annie was anything but wild. She never shouted. She never swore. She never broke rules. She always dressed like a lady. She always said please and thank you and, if the occasion warranted, made a point of letting people know — including stockmen who had little regard for wild horses — that they had been helpful in situations when other activists might not even have said hello. "A woman can go far with a girdle and a can of hair spray," she once told an admiring crowd, puffing on a trademark Chesterfield. In 1955, after she had blazed through miles of typewriter ribbon in letter-writing campaigns, the State of Nevada followed Storey County's lead and banned the use of airborne and mechanized vehicles to capture wild horses and burros. It even outlawed another common practice — the poisoning of water sources where the animals gathered. But in another way, the bill was simply a piece of paper; most lands in Nevada were public, and stockmen made sure that public lands were omitted from the new law. That meant the animals could still be run down by air or any other vehicle in the state's vast backcountry.

Once again, it was time to take the fight to the next level. The country was beginning to examine its natural heritage, and a wave of environmental activism was building. In 1951, Rachel Carson had published *The Sea Around Us,* the groundbreaking book that portrayed the ocean as part of an ecology to which we were all linked. It blazed the trail for her seminal work *Silent Spring,* which warned of the impact of pesticides on birds. Meanwhile, Dave Brower was becoming a voice for the wilderness through the burgeoning Sierra Club. Others were speaking on behalf of various beleaguered wild animals. Over the next few years, the dirty secret of the range began to leak out — a semi-stealth government program called predator control carried out at the behest of ranchers.

For decades, tax-funded hunters had been laying waste to coyotes and wolves in the most vicious of ways, setting coyote dens on fire and trapping wolves in agonizing steel traps. Often they killed wild horses for bait, lacing them with strychnine and placing them at stations where the animals would gather and feed on the tainted meat. As word of these practices began to spread, people complained to their representatives, and the media picked up the stories of wildlife carnage. In December of 1957, shortly after *Esquire* had published "The Misfits," *Reader's Digest* published an article about Annie and her battle. In May of the following year, *True* magazine followed the trend, reversing an old policy in men's adventure magazines by celebrating Annie, a person who was trying to save mustangs, instead of someone who was hunting them down.

Meanwhile, the country was awash in TV Westerns. The show featuring Roy Rogers and his beloved Trigger, which first aired in 1950, had given way to more sophisticated series such as *Maverick, Have Gun — Will Travel, Rawhide,* and *Bonanza,* which took place in Virginia City, Nevada, and, in addition to the famous fictional

Cartwright family, featured the popular horses Big Buck, Beauty, Ginger, Paiute, Chubb, Paint, and Cochise. Out of the frontier came Wild Horse Annie, putting city slickers and politicos off their guard because she dressed like a schoolmarm and did not talk tough like Miss Kitty on *Gunsmoke.*

With a groundswell of support sweeping the country, Annie had a series of meetings with Congressman Walter S. Baring of Nevada, and in 1959, he introduced a bill banning use of aircraft and motor vehicles to hunt wild horses and burros on all public lands in the country. In the Silver State, opposition to the bill was fierce. It was one thing to enact protection of wild horses on the local and even the state level; with the old attaboy networks in place for nearly a century, it was fairly easy to circumvent laws that the ranching establishment didn't like. But federal protection was another matter. It would bring greater scrutiny from outsiders who had nothing to lose and possibly everything to gain.

"We have all been exposed to, and are afflicted with a severe case of mustang fever," Annie told members of the House of Representatives when she testified for the bill, turning the old concept on its head. She now had a far-flung network of supporters — nuns in Wisconsin, a Lakota chief, a blind man in New Jersey, a missionary in the Congo, secretaries everywhere — and some of them had traveled to Washington, D.C., to sit in the gallery as Annie spoke. "This fever is raging at high temperatures throughout the nation, is highly communicable, not only by exposure to a person already having it, but also through the written word," she continued. "Once having contracted it, there is no known cure. But our reputation as a great humanitarian nation becomes a bit less enviable as people of other countries read about the mustang hunters, and they write and express their surprise and disgust."

Then, taking a breath, for what was coming always disturbed her, she displayed a series of horrifying photographs that had been published in *Life* magazine and have since become iconic. In the middle of an empty alkaline flat, a rearing horse bleeds through his nostrils after being chased by a plane and then captured by men throwing rope from a moving truck; in the middle of the same flat, with a mountain range on the horizon, an exhausted horse stands tethered to a huge tire — exactly the scene that Arthur Miller had written about in his short story.

"The continued ruthless harassment of the mustangs has kept them constantly fleeing for their lives," she concluded, "into higher, more barren places where their chances for survival are slim. It is incredible that one should have to furnish any argument to bring about laws to save the mustang. But if there must be an argument, let it be this: That of all living things that have played their part in the development of this country, except man, the horse has played the most prominent and beneficial role ... he portrays the West as all people like to think of it; he is a symbol of wild freedom to us all."

The Department of the Interior tried to gut the bill, but it cleared the House and Senate by wide margins. On September 9, 1959, President Dwight D. Eisenhower signed it into law, and thus it became illegal to hunt mustangs and burros on all public lands with airplanes or motorized vehicles. The bill became known as the Wild Horse Annie Act. But such is rangeland politics and so extreme is the rights fest in some parts of the West — in fact, so impossible is it to legislate behavior — that stronger protection for the mustang and burro did not deter airborne roundups and killings. While the law was better than no law, Annie returned to Nevada to fight another day — or, more precisely, for the next eleven years.

Annie got the first tip that ranchers were ignoring the law just a few months after Eisenhower had signed the bill. On a hot July day in 1960, the phone rang at her office. Someone had spotted a silver plane at the head of Lagomarsino Canyon (later the site of the 1998 wild horse massacre). The tipster had heard gunshots, then saw the co-pilot harrying mustangs into the canyon with his rifle. Annie relayed the information to the Washoe County sheriff, who immediately dispatched four deputies to the area. They blocked the road leading out of the canyon and then combed the rough terrain for trapped horses. But the only tracks they found were a week old.

The next day, Annie got another tip. This time, someone had spotted a truck in the canyon. Meanwhile, the plane had been identified as belonging to veteran mustanger Chug Utter. Annie figured there was some kind of grudge match going on, to see who could round up the most horses and not get caught while at the same time blaming a rival. The next day, twenty horses were found shot to death in the hills. And the rest of that particular herd of three to four hundred horses had vanished — most likely into a caravan of trucks sometime in the night.

A little while later, the phone rang with more disturbing news. Some Indians in Fallon were rounding up mustangs, the caller said. They weren't using planes, so the roundup was legal. But it was terribly cruel. They had dug a hole in a horse trail, then covered it with a piece of slashed tin. The whole piece of tin was rigged with cable, and the entire trap had been camouflaged with a scattering of dirt. When the horses were run down the trail, their legs went through the tin, the cable was tightened, and their tendons were shredded. Other horses were simply run to death by relay teams of riders. Later that year, this same group of mustangers was hired by the feds to round up wild horses on Nellis Air Force Base. Many wild horses reportedly died as they were being run across the harsh desert wastes.

In 1962, public sentiment in favor of wild horses led to the creation of the Nevada Wild Horse Range on the base at Nellis, the first such federally protected mustang domain. A harsh terrain, it consists of thousands of acres of broad alkali flats that sweep down from rocky desert mountains. Water is scarce, and sometimes horses travel as much as fifteen miles per day to get to a source. In recent years, there have been two instances of horses dying at poisoned water holes, filled with toxins from base operations under mysterious circumstances.

"For God's sake, Mrs. Johnston," said Stanley Rouston in a surprise visit to Annie at her Reno home in 1967. "I was just called to inspect 38 horses that had been shipped out of Nevada to California. They were taken in an aerial roundup. Their eyes were shot out and I had to put them down." Rouston was the supervisor of livestock identification for the Nevada Department of Agriculture, an agency that represented the interests of stockmen. He knew he had witnessed a violation of the Wild Horse Annie Act, and, to the dismay of many of his colleagues, it had so disturbed him that he joined Annie's campaign. "If something isn't done," he told Annie, "the wild horses of Nevada have no future." A few days later, he made an astounding offer: he invited Annie to review his department's records, which, she suspected, would reveal information about how mustangers were literally getting away with murder. She found that pilots were inventing ruses to hunt down horses. They would mix their own private stock, which was branded, with wild horses, which were unbranded. When they went to cull their own herds, wild horses would be killed in the process — a mistake, they said.

With more allies flocking to the cause, Annie's fight was gaining momentum. Many people were joining her newly formed group, the International Society for the Protection of Mustangs and Burros, one of the first such organizations in the country. Along with the Humane Society and a Montana rancher named Lloyd Tillett, it lobbied the Department of the Interior to create the next federally protected mustang refuge; this was the Pryor Mountain Wild Horse Range on the Montana-Wyoming border. These horses were a distinctive herd whose members each had a dorsal stripe down the back; there was speculation that the markings linked them directly to the horses of the conquest, but it was not until years later that the connection was proven through DNA analysis. "This is only one instance involving 200 animals," Annie said when the range was created, "while the rest of the colorful heritage known as 'the wild ones' continues to be the object of exploitation, starvation, slaughter . . . Time is running out."

In 1968, the law was violated again, and in the process a father-son aerial hunting team collided over the Red Desert in Wyoming. In one plane, Barlow H. Call had been chasing mustangs toward a trap, and at the same time, from a second plane, his son had been shooting coyotes. They flew into each other and died. The incident did not deter hunting expeditions, and as killings mounted across the West, Annie's health deteriorated. Her husband had passed away a few years earlier, and she knew that their lifelong battle to save wild horses and burros — all the roundups they had documented, the death threats, the heartbreak — had taken its toll. She never spoke of it, but her childhood polio had weakened her immune system. She was in constant pain, a chain smoker, and on a diet of what she called "slow and go" pills.

But the wave of passion for the environment that had begun in the 1950s was reaching a peak, and it was now carrying Annie. Many of the country's landmark protections for the air, sea, and endangered species were about to be passed with great fanfare — partly because of the activism of children. In May of 1970, Boy Scouts discovered a number of dead eagles while hiking in the Wyoming backcountry. An investigation by the Audubon Society revealed that they had been poisoned by eating sheep carcasses laced with deadly thallium salts; the carcasses had been meant for coyotes. Finally, the full story of the government's predator control program emerged. Congressional hearings were called, and the public outcry was so great that even *Sports Illustrated* ran a three-part series called "The Poisoning of the West." Bills were introduced, and the program was overhauled.

A few months after the incident in Wyoming, Annie's campaign was joined by the famous pencil brigade, a far-flung grassroots action waged by schoolchildren. It was so engaging that even today, many of those who participated have great nostalgia for the moment when they pasted stamps on envelopes and addressed them to their representatives. The brigade started with the Christmas of 1969, when Gregory Gude, the eleven-year-old son of Maryland congressman Gilbert Gude, got a present that changed his life, and the law. It was a copy of *Mustang: Wild Spirit of the West,* a children's book about Wild Horse Annie by the popular writer Marguerite Henry, who was adored for her *Misty of Chincoteague* series about the wild ponies of the islands off the Virginia coast.

After reading the book, Gregory wrote a letter to his father's colleagues. "I think we need a law to protect our wild mustangs before they are all killed," he said. Today, such a letter would be lost in the 24/7 noise machine, but back then, it's safe to say, things were different. Among those who responded to Gregory's call was Joan Bolsinger, a fourth-grade teacher at Eastwood Elementary School in Rosebud, Oregon, who told her students about the vanishing wild horses of the West and suggested that they could help. They wrote letter after letter in support of a bill cosponsored by Oregon senator Mark Hatfield and Washington senator Henry Jackson, who had spearheaded some of the great wilderness legislation of the era. Soon, they were joined by thousands of children at schools in every state. Meanwhile, Annie received an anonymous tip. Mustangers in the mountains outside Virginia City had built a hidden corral and were preparing to run horses in via airplane, in violation of the original law. Hoping to catch them in the act, a team of locals began a five-month-long period of surveillance as the bill moved through the Senate.

With deep wells of public support, the bill still faced the traditional network of opposition. Since the Northwest Ordinance of 1787, Congress had passed thousands of laws regarding public lands. On June 23, 1970, House representative Wayne Aspinall made one more recommendation. Once called the "scourge of the environmental movement" by Dave Brower, conservative Democrat Aspinall had tried to defeat nearly every piece of land and animal protection that was moving through legislatures at the time. His political mentor was Ed Taylor, the father of the Taylor Grazing Act. Now, in a Rose Garden ceremony at the White House, he presented Richard Nixon with a hefty months-in-the-making report. Called "One-Third of a Nation: A Report to the President and the Congress," it suggested that all public land issues should be administered by a new department of natural resources. "Public land forage policies should be designed to attain maximum economic efficiency," the committee report said, "and to support regional economic growth." In other words, animals that depended on public lands for sustenance but did not yield income, such as wild horses and burros, did not have a chance of survival.

The Aspinall report was denounced in many newspapers, but it laid the foundation for a rebellion that would erupt across the West in a few years. It also began a polarizing debate about public lands that now rages out of control. In the heated political climate following the Nixon meeting, the Virginia City sheriff who had permitted locals to monitor the mustang trap told them to tear it down, then he joined a crew of high school students who picked up the wire and posts and hauled them away. The men who had built the corral came forward and sued for damages. As the case headed to court, the *Elko Daily Free Press* in Nevada accused Annie of running a mustang cult.

In a way, the paper was right: like the ancient goddess Epona, Annie had stepped out of a distant place and called many to a new path. Anticipating that the new bill would pass, the cattle lobby launched a public relations campaign of its own, asserting that wild horses weren't really wild but feral newcomers to this country ("varmints"), and therefore, protecting them would be the same as protecting alley cats or invasive weeds. Moreover, as a non-native "foreigner," the mustang was a threat to the limited food and water supply on the range. The view of the wild horse as feral was shared by hunters, who were concerned that public lands would not have enough forage for trophy animals; the various extraction lobbies, which wanted the land for gas and oil drilling without having to follow new regulations for wild horse protection; and certain environmental groups, which tended to defend sexy predators such as wolves and raptors. To them, the West was supposed to look as it did when the conquistadors came, a Paradise Lost that did not have the horse, considered at that time to be a non-native species.

Given that the science of the era had not linked mustangs on the range to the horses of the Ice Age (or, at least, the fossil record was not as definitive as the genetic record that would come later), the stockmen's analysis was accurate: many wild horse populations were indeed a mixed American breed of cavalry horses, horses that had fled wagon trains, the horses of the conquest, and so on. But calling them varmints was disingenuous; ranchers assigned the term to any animal they didn't like, including those that were indisputably native, such as coyotes. The other indigenous animals that they regarded as threats, such as wolves and bobcats, were dubbed outlaws—a term they also used for mustangs.

Of course, such hypocrisies were not enough for a legal argument. Annie well knew how difficult it was to claim that a non-native species deserved protection. There were too many indigenous birds, fish, and mammals that were under siege, and the battles to save them were also on center stage, soon to culminate in the Endangered Species Act. "Wild horses exist in a limbo," she said. "Being a domestic animal gone wild, they can't qualify as an endangered species. They're not considered wildlife in the sense that deer, elk and antelope are. Yet obviously they are not domestic animals." After giving it much thought, she realized that the only way to save them was to give them a new and distinct designation—a national heritage species.

On April 20, 1971, Annie again traveled from Reno to Capitol Hill to make her case. By then, she was so famous that she had even appeared on the popular game show *To Tell the Truth,* in which celebrities posed a series of questions to a panel of guests until they figured out who was authentic. "Do you save wild horses?" Kitty Carlisle finally asked, to much applause. Yet Annie was not affected by fame, and on her trip to Washington, she traveled with little fanfare and only two people—publicity-shy scientists from the University of Nevada who were studying wild horses. One of them was Steve Pellegrini, who had grown up in mustang country and had written the first academic paper on mustang behavior.

"Annie told me not to dress like a cowboy," he remembered years later. They were joined on the Senate floor by James Feist, a Montana biologist who was dressed like Buffalo Bill. Pellegrini spoke of the tightly knit wild horse herd of the Wassuk Range, of their intricate family connections and what happened when those bonds were broken. Feist had been studying the Pryor Mountain horses and made a persuasive case for their Spanish heritage, which implied that perhaps other herds had the same bloodlines (later, it turned out that they did). Then the reporter Hope Ryden testified. In 1968, after learning that wild horses were under siege, she had quit her job as a television news producer to write a book about them. The influential book was published shortly before the hearings and mailed to every congressperson. "I am not normally a crusader," she said; as she testified, wheelbarrows overflowing with mail were rolled down the aisles. They contained the thousands of letters sent by the pencil brigade—more mail than Congress had ever received about anything except the war in Vietnam.

But the opposition was not going down without one last hurrah. A spokesman for the Nevada Cattlemen's Association rose to make a statement. "Who can manage the range better than the people who have lived there for generations?" he said to the appreciation of stockmen in the gallery. "If this bill passes, it will be one more encroachment on a way of life that is fast disappearing."

Then it was Annie's turn. "Today," she began, "I am here to save a memory." It was a stirring echo of the very first speech she had given in Virginia City so long ago. A few days later, Congress unanimously passed Public Law 92-195, the federal Wild Free-Roaming Horses and Burros Act. For the first time since Annie had seen blood spilling out of a truck on a Nevada highway, it was illegal to capture, brand, harass, or kill the wild horses that roamed public lands.

And finally, the term *wild* as it applied to horses was legally defined. "Wild free-roaming horses and burros" referred to "all unbranded and unclaimed horses and burros on public lands." They would "be managed in a manner that is designed to achieve and maintain a thriving natural ecological balance" and "considered in areas where presently found, as an integral part of the system of public lands." Those areas were called ranges, referring to the amount of land that was needed "to sustain an existing herd or herds." The ranges were to be devoted "principally but not necessarily exclusively" to the welfare of mustangs and burros, and within a few years, the government would designate three hundred of them for wild horses.

Shortly before Christmas, Richard Nixon, the president who has since gone down in history for spying on Americans, who has been perpetually mocked for his social awkwardness, for sweating during the debates with JFK, for not being *cool,* not being a *cowboy,* after all, signed the bill. "We need the tonic of wildness," he said at a crowded ceremony, quoting Thoreau — a moment that has been overlooked in the annals of his presidency. "In the past seventy years, civilization and economics have brought the wild horse to 99 percent extinction. They are a living link with the conquistadors, through the heroic times of the western Indians and pioneers to our own day ... More than that, they merit protection as a matter of ecological right — as anyone knows who has stood awed at the indomitable spirit and sheer energy of a mustang running free."

Under the new law, management of wild horses fell to the Forest Service and the Bureau of Land Management, agencies inside the Department of the Interior. Soon the bureau opened the first new wild horse range under its oversight — the Little Book Cliffs, near Grand Junction, Colorado. Here the bays, blacks, and sorrels, the pintos, roans, and palominos could roam forever in rugged canyons and sandstone plateaus, where mountain lions, bobcats, bald eagles, hawks, and elk also made their livings. The thirty-thousand-acre preserve was dedicated to Annie, and on opening day, a plaque with Annie's portrait was unveiled. Too exhausted to attend, Annie celebrated at her ranch with some kids from the pencil brigade.

Three years after the act was passed, she received yet another disturbing tip. Stockmen in Howe, Idaho, had hunted down some of the last mustangs in the state — a herd of thirty-two horses — chasing them for forty-five days, driving them into a narrow canyon and trapping them on a shelf in the dead of winter. Some jumped off the cliff to their deaths. Others panicked and jammed their hoofs into rocks. To make the horses more manageable, ranchers sewed hog rings into their noses. The fear escalated, and some horses broke their legs as they scrambled on the rocks. With dead mustangs piling up, ranchers tried to hide the evidence by sawing off the horses' legs.

When it was over, the six surviving horses were shipped to a packing house in Nebraska. A few days later, the dead and mutilated horses were found at the foot of the cliff. Annie arrived at the scene, and reporters from New York rushed west to report the carnage. Locals hunkered down, claiming that city slickers just didn't understand how hard it was for ranchers to get by. Like the ranchers, Annie viewed the incident as a test case under the new law. But the case fell apart and there were no convictions, setting the stage for an endless wave of similar incidents.

Soon after the infamous Howe massacre, Annie's health began to deteriorate. "I'm just a lowly housewife who has lived and loved in Nevada," she said to a friend. In 1977, at the age of sixty-five, she died. Doctors said that her system had failed. Fearing that she had made so many enemies in Nevada that her archives would be destroyed, Annie left her vast acreage of papers, documents, photographs, and letters to the extensive western collections at the Denver Public Library. Her suspicion may have been right—there is little mention of her in the Nevada state collections, and few officials know where she is buried. It happens to be on a bluff outside Reno, near her father, the man who was saved by mare's milk.

Alas, Annie had another fear that came to fruition. Enforcement of the act to which she had dedicated her life depended solely on the desire of those sworn to carry it out. Knowing that the Bureau of Land Management was the domain of stockmen, she had worried that, in addition to the illegal killings, the war against the wild horse would continue on another front—under cover of law, by way of the mustang's legal guardians. And paradoxically, it rages most fiercely in the Virginia Range, where descendants of the very horses that Annie first tried to save are without federal protection because they live on state lands. They are now surrounded by freeways, making their last stand.

9

The Mustang Endures

N THE SUMMER OF 2004, I traveled to the Diamond Mountains of eastern Nevada to watch a series of wild horse roundups. Such roundups, or gathers, as the government calls them, are generally done under the auspices of the Bureau of Land Management, but sometimes involve other agencies as well, depending on which herd is being culled. To get to the roundup site, a companion and I headed from Reno across Highway 50, the officially proclaimed "Loneliest Highway in America," past Misfits Flat, where the Marilyn Monroe movie was filmed, stopping at the Pony Expresso café (near an actual stop on the old Pony Express trail), and then arriving in Ely the night before the roundup and staying at the Best Western along with the roundup crew. The next morning, we got up early and drove to the site of the gather in the mountains to the north.

A few weeks before the roundup, the crew had carried out reconnaissance, determining where in the mountains the horses usually congregated, what was the best place for the trap, and from what points the helicopter should take off and refuel. Then they returned with their considerable team, their ventilated big rigs, their water trucks, their chopper and portable corral and chute, and they set the trap. When I arrived, they had just erected the metal fencing that would form the small pen into which thousands of mustangs had been chased before and thousands were going to follow.

The chopper took off and swept across the boulders and sage and gravel and up into the juniper and pine and then higher where the horses were grazing. Spotting them, the pilot radioed back and dropped altitude, slowing as he approached the band. At five hundred feet, the horses started to move and were harried out of their home, down ancient paths used by Indians, Spanish explorers, cattlemen, coyotes, hikers, and drivers of jeeps and ATVs. As the horses neared the trap, the chopper peeled off, and out raced the lead cowboy on his Judas horse. They galloped in front of the onrushing band, leading it toward the trap, peeling off as the chopper had just before the mustangs ran into the dead-end corral.

Panicked, the horses shifted and banged against the fence. Some of the stallions tried to break out, leaping over the pack and battering smaller horses in the frenzy. After a while, the mustangs tired and lowered their heads. Then they were funneled into trucks and hauled to a nearby gravel pit where they were sorted by gender and numbered with chalk.

In 1830, French scientist Jean Louis Berlandier had come to Texas to observe flora and fauna. Among the things he wrote about was a wild horse roundup. The vaqueros had certain words for what happened to mustangs once they were penned in. *Sentimiento* meant that a horse had died of heartbreak. *Despecho* meant that a horse had died of nervous rage. *Hediondo* referred to a corral that reeked of frightened and dying horses. In the holding pen at the gravel pit a few miles from the roundup site, I saw many horses that appeared to be on the verge of the first two conditions. I saw a foal trampled by frightened mares and another horse whose leg was bleeding, perhaps injured while being run into the trap. A veterinarian was called, and a few hours later he arrived to treat the horse. On the ground near one of the pens was a cattle prod. When I asked some crew members why it was there, they said they didn't know.

As the sun went down, the horses raced nervously to one end of the pen and back, arching their necks, straining to look beyond the fence, some climbing on the backs of others, looking for an escape. Dusk faded to black and floodlights powered by a generator lit up the

corral. It was then that I heard a disturbing sound. In other circumstances, it would have symbolized all that's right with the world. It
was the shrieking and laughing of two children—the grandson and
granddaughter of the crew chiefs—running just outside the fence
that circled the horses, spooking the wild animals that only hours ago
had known no such sounds, peering through the sheets of jute and
calling loudly into the pen as the rest of the crew prepared dinner.
The mustangs were scared and had nowhere to run except into one
another. After a while the children moved on, and the horses grew
less restive. Soon, their heads dropped, lower this time—the spark
was fading.

The following morning, they were loaded onto two big rigs and
hauled away, to the government's Pyramid Lake holding facility, 240
miles to the east. My companion and I left a little while later, and
when we arrived at the corrals, the horses had already been offloaded
and were fenced in with a desert view that ran all the way to the sky.
Perhaps some of the scents that drifted in were familiar to them, but
others—traffic from the highway nearby, diesel exhaust from the trac-
tors that carried their hay—were not. Soon, they would be given vac-
cinations and freeze brands indicating government registration, year
of birth, state of origin, and their own identification numbers—not
unlike the information that the warhorse Comanche carried on his
shoulder.

Within a few months, they would meet varying fates. Many would
be marketed as "living legends" through the government's adopt-a-
horse program. Some would go to good homes. Others would end
up with cruel owners. A few would be returned to the land after being injected with birth control. Over time, hundreds would make
their way to the various sanctuaries and conservancies around the
country. A small number would become famous, like Nevada Joe, a
wild horse used for children's hippotherapy; J. B. Andrew, the dressage star; Eeyore, the mascot at the Great Smoky Mountains National
Park; and Montezuma Willy, Peking Luke, and the mustang palominos of the U.S. Marines' Mounted Color Guard, the last of its kind
in the country. Still others would fall victim to a new piece of legislation that has unraveled the 1971 law. Passed during the George Bush
administration, it sent the mustangs straight back to the slaughter-

house; out of the three then operating, two were in Texas, which had purged wild horses from its lands long ago.

Shortly after the mustangs from the Diamond Mountains had been rounded up, the crew headed to the next site for another cull. They would add several hundred more horses to those they had just removed, as well as the 150,000 that they had taken off the range since 1974, when they had begun working under contract for the government. "Wild horses really fascinate me," Dave Cattoor once told an interviewer. He's the cowboy with the craggy face who was in charge of the operation. "They've dominated my whole life. I think I must have been reincarnated from one of those old-time mustangers."

In 1973, the government began implementing the new law. But it wasn't long before ranchers launched a prolonged assault, trying to take the law down through four presidential administrations until they finally found their best friend. They pressed the old claims that the mustang degrades the range and is not wild, and added some new ones along the way: it's not worth the taxpayer expense to manage, and the mustang is deformed. Surely, they said, if outsiders visited the range and saw for themselves what problems inbreeding had wreaked on wild horses, they would change their minds about saving them. Behind the scenes, they tried to take the horse out in other ways, such as surrounding water sources with fences that only cows could walk under, or, more secretively, looking the other way when mustangs were shot, figuring that local authorities would do the same.

In November of 1974, the BLM issued a notice to ranchers across the West: they had two months to brand wild horses that were living on their allotments and claim them as their own. After that, any unclaimed mustangs would belong to the federal government and fall under its policies. The locations where the horses were found would become herd areas, or HAs, inside of which were herd management areas, or HMAs — artificial zones that created a situation in which a mustang with two hooves outside the zone could be considered out of bounds and eligible for capture by the government, and those inside the zone would be periodically culled for population control. As ranchers quickly moved to claim the mustangs on their turf, the BLM began advertising for contract cowboys to round up any that were not branded. "Man, oh man, I was right there!" Dave Cattoor said to a reporter a few years ago. "My first contract was to move horses onto a preserve in Colorado, and I gave the lowest bid. That's what put me in business." Today, Cattoor earns $3.46 per horse.

Once the first roundups were completed, management of wild horse ranges was taken to the next level. In most HMAs, the mustang's natural predators had been nearly wiped out by man. Now, the government had to assume the role of mountain lion or wolf—although in a less obvious way. Depending on where the wild horses lived, culling of what the bill called "excess horses" fell either to the BLM or to other agencies. The new law said that herds should be maintained at the numbers found when it was passed, and anything more than that would place too much stress on the range. In 1974, the BLM published its first count. On the public lands in the eleven western states, it said there were seventeen thousand wild horses and burros. Most of this population were mustangs.

From then on, this figure—called the appropriate management level, or AML—has been hotly debated, because maintaining AML has involved the rounding-up of over two hundred thousand horses since the act went into effect. Wild horse advocates say that it has not been necessary to remove so many and that the original figure was too low. They point out that just two years later, the agency said there were fifty-four thousand wild horses and burros, a number that would have been impossible for such a small population of mustangs to have reached so quickly, considering natural attrition and that not all of them were mares. Wild horse advocates also argue that shortly before the act was passed, the agency had released a series of conflicting counts, perhaps anticipating that it would soon have to announce an official baseline census. Further complicating the issue is the fact that over the years, the BLM itself has changed the appropriate management levels, to thirty-six thousand in the 1980s and to twenty-three thousand just a few years ago.

It's difficult to count wild horses. In the beginning, the BLM relied on ranchers for its figures. Then it made aerial counts, which posed their own problems. Hiding in remote canyons or simply blending into the brush, horses are not always easy to spot. Even the National Research Council, an organization that operates under a federal mandate and advises the National Academy of Sciences, found that mustang census figures are frequently lower than actual levels. According to a 1982 report, at least 7 percent of the horses in open areas and as much as 60 percent of those on tree-covered valleys and hills can be overlooked. In the past few years, the goal of returning to the original figure of seventeen thousand has been vigorously pursued and, some say, met and surpassed — although the government claims otherwise. Yet the fact remains that when it comes to counting mustangs, the 1971 act has been repeatedly violated since its inception.

"Wild horse censusing is not carried out scientifically by the BLM," says Dr. Patricia Fazio, environmental historian and longtime student of the mustang. "Range monitoring, to determine range condition, utilization, and trend, is often outdated, due to lack of funds and personnel. Appropriate management levels are frequently inaccurate, outdated, and not determined in accordance with the law. Where oh where has scientific management and substantive public input for federal lands gone?"

Compounding the problem of outdated studies that result in unnecessary roundups based on erroneous counts is a host of troublesome issues. For instance, herd management areas are vanishing. When the law went into effect, the wild horse and burro protection act mandated that mustangs be maintained where they were found. To that end, 303 herd areas were designated on forty-seven million acres of public lands, inside of which there was the further designation of herd management areas. Now, according to the American Wild Horse Preservation Campaign, there are 192 HAs, which means that mustangs and burros have been completely removed from about one-third of their natural habitat. With fewer herds, the survival of the rest of the populations becomes more urgent.

In many of the remaining areas, the AMLs are now set too low for genetic viability. "For a herd to be genetically diverse over the long term, it must have at least 150 horses," according to Dr. Gus Cothran, director of the Equine Blood Typing Research Laboratory at the University of Kentucky. Some herds are currently at target figures of one hundred. If their habitat is further reduced, suggests Andrea Lococo of the Animal Welfare Institute, they cannot be expected to survive. "I have always believed that we made a huge mistake in 1971, when the act was passed," says Dr. Jay Kirkpatrick, a noted endocrinologist who has studied mustangs for decades and advises various groups about equine birth control. "We should have identified a single range as the best of its kind in each of the eleven states with horses and put them there and restricted grazing by domestic livestock. That way we would have only had eleven HMAs to manage and every state would have had its own wild horse population. We didn't, and now, we have a nightmare on our hands."

In 1976, federal protection for mustangs was hit with its first challenge. On behalf of stockmen, New Mexico sued the Department of the Interior, claiming that mustangs were a natural resource that belonged to the state, not the federal government, and therefore, the new law was unconstitutional. New Mexico won the case. It was immediately appealed; a few months later, all nine justices of the Supreme Court reaffirmed the wild horse and burro protection act, stating that mustangs were indeed wildlife and they belonged to the public. Later that year, official erosion of the bill began.

Congress passed the Federal Land Policy and Management Act, or, in the acronym mania that characterizes government policy, FLPMA. The new law introduced the term *multiple use management,* and assigned to the BLM the oversight of the country's 261 million acres of public lands for a wide range of uses. In addition to the job of overseeing grazing and mineral extraction, the BLM mandate now included timber production, wildlife habitat, hunting, preservation of archaeological sites, off-road vehicle travel, and other areas. Many of these uses were in competition, and once again, wild horses and burros felt that competition keenly. Under FLPMA, the 1971 act was amended to permit mechanized roundups, this time by helicopter, considered more humane than the old fixed-wing method. From then on, mustangs began coming off the range in large numbers.

But what would replace their home? To solve the problem, the BLM launched the Adopt-a-Horse or Burro Program. A well-meaning plan with a cute name, it soon became a deathtrap for countless animals. "Anyone with a large backyard and a hankering for a four-footed part of our national heritage could get a mustang by filling out a form and paying a small fee of twenty-five dollars," wrote Richard Symanski in *Wild Horses and Sacred Cows.* "If one is to judge only by numbers, the first decade of the adoption program was a conspicuous success. By 1984, more than thirty-five thousand wild horses had found foster homes in forty-nine states." But the many animals who were not adopted fell into an Orwellian maze of government housing, and some began to disappear from the record.

There were early signs that mustangs in the BLM pipeline were at risk. Over a ten-month period in 1977 and '78, two thousand wild horses were rounded up and taken to corrals at Palomino Valley near Reno. Once a vast feedlot, the corrals were filled with manure. "The animals were haunch to haunch in the pens," Symanski reports. The caretakers threw their hay on the ground, and it mixed with the sand and detritus. Then the rains came and the pens flooded and people stopped showing up for scheduled adoptions. The muck froze and the animals couldn't move. Within days, 146 mustangs died and another 98 had to be destroyed. They were buried in mass graves — or "death ditches," as *Bonanza* star and horse advocate Lorne Greene said when photographs surfaced in newspapers. "Here in Nevada," he said, "we have our own holocaust."

People clamored for an investigation, and Senate hearings were held. A wide range of citizens testified, including BLM employees, happy foster parents who loved the adoption program, and those who decried it. As a result, conditions at the corrals improved, and the rate of wild horse losses dropped from about 10 percent since the program's inception to 2 percent, according to a BLM spokesman at the time. But the reprieve was temporary; across the West, citizens were joining forces in the sagebrush rebellion — a campaign fueled by classic American distrust of big government and hefty donations from wealthy conservatives. Sagebrush rebels wanted to take down the Endangered Species Act, dismantle national parks, and unravel restrictions on grazing. They managed to move ahead on two fronts, forcing confrontations with park rangers in remote areas and lobbying for local management of natural resources through sympathetic members of Congress. Later, some became elected representatives themselves. Colorful characters who attracted the media, they snagged the cover of *Time* magazine at their peak, and nowhere were they more vocal than in Nevada. "Why can't I cut Christmas trees where I want to?" a Tonopah resident said to the *Time* reporter. He was voicing a minor complaint but one that underscored the broader themes of the sagebrush activists.

In 1977, a Nevada rancher who was part of this group put together a slide show and took it to Washington. Called "The Trouble with Mustangs," it featured a series of images of range degradation that was attributed to wild horses. "The trouble began with passage of the 1971 Wild Horse Act," the narrator said to a group of western congressmen who assembled in a hall for the presentation. His first slide depicted wild horses on a parched hill. "The act was literally shoved down the throats of Congress because of the tremendous letter writing of the school children," he continued. At the conclusion of the show, the rancher dropped a bombshell: the BLM should have "sale authority" — rangeland code language for permission to sell mustangs to the slaughterhouse. The profits from such sales should be used to pay for wild horse management — more code language, in this case meaning "why should taxpayers foot the bill for animals that are pests?" If the BLM could profit from wild horses as ranchers did in the old days, went the argument, then it would want to remove more and more mustangs from the range, until they were all gone. The rancher's suggestion was ignored, but two years later the sagebrush rebels tried again.

This time, the state of Nevada tried a fresh take on New Mexico's earlier attempt to derail mustang protection. It filed suit against the BLM itself for mismanagement of the wild horse program. Mustangs, it claimed, were taking food from wildlife, destroying cover for small game around water holes, and trampling riparian habitats, which made it impossible for fish to spawn. The only answer to the problem was local control. On paper, the lawsuit was a defense of the environment. But really, it was a move against the wild horse on the part of the hunting and fishing communities, which produced revenue for the state by way of licensing fees. The suit failed, but the sagebrush rebels planned and waited.

In 1981, they found their first friend in the White House — Ronald Reagan. "I am a sagebrush rebel," proclaimed the horseman, and he appointed James Watt as director of the Department of the Interior. Notorious for his anti-environment views, Watt ran a legal foundation that was trying to gut wilderness protection and viewed public lands as a treasure chest that belonged to the private sector. "We will mine more, drill more, and cut more timber," he announced. Years later, one of his key protégés would emerge in the George W. Bush administration, profoundly influencing the fate of wild horses.

Midway through the Reagan era, there were ten thousand wild horses in government corrals. It was a record high, and the BLM had another problem — too many horses and not enough adopters. Some were moved to federally funded sanctuaries in Oklahoma and Kansas, where they would live out their lives. But there was not enough room for all of them, and rather than pay for more sanctuaries, the BLM decided to get the remaining animals adopted quickly. So it launched a disastrous fee-waiver program in which almost anyone who agreed to take at least a hundred mustangs could have them for free. Three years later, the program was stopped, when it turned out that thousands of mustangs had been sold to slaughterhouses. Meanwhile, Congress appropriated fifty-one million dollars for roundups, the most ever allotted to the task. From 1984 to 1987, forty thousand horses were taken from the range, even though the government had no intention of paying for additional sanctuaries and there were still too few adopters.

In 1990, the government's accounting office issued its own take on the situation. According to the law, mustangs were removed because there was not enough forage to support them. But the report said that the takings had not improved range conditions. "Wild horses are vastly outnumbered on rangelands by livestock," the GAO stated. "Wild horse behavior patterns make them somewhat less damaging than cattle to especially vulnerable range areas. Wild horse removals have taken place in some areas not being damaged by widespread overgrazing." But the BLM ignored the report, and mustang roundups escalated.

Meanwhile, mustangs fell prey to people who worked inside the pipeline. In 1992, Shoshone Indians in Nevada hired Dave Cattoor and his crew to remove horses that were dying from thirst on their reservation and load them onto trucks bound for a rendering plant in Texas. (Drought is a frequent excuse for roundups. Sometimes the horses are actually thirsty, but many other times, they are not. After being given a drink, they are rarely returned to the range, and they are the only wild animals to be consistently captured because of perceived thirst.) Tipped off about the illegal Nevada capture, government agents arrived just after the mustangs had been herded onto the trucks. They told the drivers to stop. But the trucks left anyway, filled with 130 horses. Cattoor testified at a trial that some of the ani-

mals were actually "in fairly good shape." He pleaded guilty to a misdemeanor charge of using an aircraft to capture wild horses without
federal protection. "I've been out here a long time," Cattoor told me
as I watched the roundups in the Diamond Mountains. "I like wild
horses but they make a lot of problems."

Concerned with the government removal program, screenwriter
Michael Blake decided to mount his own investigation. With an
Academy Award for *Dances with Wolves*, the veteran animal advocate hired a team of wild horse experts to fly across Nevada and carry
out their own census. In 1993, they found that in certain parts of the
range, there were far fewer horses than the BLM had said there were.
Blake paid for the construction of two giant billboards, one in Reno,
and the other on Sunset Boulevard in Los Angeles. Each featured a
photograph of a downed wild horse being restrained by four cowboys. CALL BRUCE BABBITT, the signs said. At the time, Babbitt was
the Clinton-appointed secretary of the Department of the Interior,
and his phone number was emblazoned on the ads.

This billboard outside Reno, Nevada, was subsidized by Michael Blake,
who wrote the screenplay for *Dances with Wolves*, and John Densmore,
the drummer of the Doors, whose song "Horse Latitudes" lamented the
conquistadors' practice of throwing horses overboard.

The ill-fated June 2006 roundup at the Sheldon Wildlife Refuge, on the border of Oregon and Nevada.

Several horses died or were injured during the roundup, including the foal shown here. The casualties prompted Representative Nick Rahall of West Virginia to call for a moratorium on roundups at Sheldon until environmental impact reports were brought up to date.

Under Clinton and the Republican-controlled Congress, the branches of government were at war. A crew of sagebrush rebels was now in Washington, elected to the House and Senate. Babbitt took them on and tried to raise grazing fees. Meanwhile, mustangs were being triaged by the thousands, and the BLM was rocked by the worst wild horse scandal in its history. After a grand jury looked into it for four years and as indictments were about to be handed down, the investigation was suddenly scuttled — by Bruce Babbitt, or so it seemed to many involved in the case. Since 1992, agency employees had allegedly been siphoning mustangs out of government pipelines, fattening them up in corrals, and then selling them to killer buyers — that is, brokers from the rendering plants who purchased horses by the pound. The brokers covered up the sales with bogus documents and computer records. Investigators estimated that as many as thirty thou-

Inmates on mustangs in a wild horse gentling program at the Warm Springs Correctional Facility in Carson City, Nevada, July 2007. After 120 days of training, the horses are offered for adoption.

sand mustangs had disappeared from the pipeline. As the grand jury hearings were wrapping up, key witnesses were apparently tipped off, and they disappeared. In 1996, the case was dropped, and the BLM director resigned in protest. "I was told not to make waves," he said to AP reporter Martha Mendoza, who broke the story in a series of explosive articles. "Someone actually said to me, why the hell are you raising problems about horses?"

Across the West, the reports were so alarming that people began making radical changes in their lives, quitting jobs and leaving the familiar so they could devote themselves to saving mustangs. Their actions were the flip side of the sagebrush rebellion — a citizens' response to government failure, but in this case, the people wanted a federal law upheld. In California, Neda DeMayo walked away from a well-paying position in Hollywood and began learning about wild horses. She visited them in the range and buried herself in obscure records. She read the 1971 act and studied its modifications and moved on to the numbers and statistics of lengthy government reports. Some of the herds, she found out, were about to be greatly reduced or "zeroed out" — agency parlance for complete removal from their homes. She knew that this was illegal but couldn't stop it. So she raised money and started a sanctuary near Santa Barbara. Soon she found herself in the role of conservator, taking in large portions of historic, genetically distinct herds — descendants of cavalry horses who were living at the Sheldon National Wildlife Refuge on the border of Oregon and Nevada, conquistador horses from the Cerbat range in Arizona, and the Sulphur Springs mustangs in Utah whose ancestors escaped from Wakara's drives across the Mojave.

In suburban Phoenix, equestrienne Karen Sussman was also joining the fray. While married and raising a family, she had heard about the frequent mustang and burro roundups across the West and did not like the stories. She contacted protégés of Wild Horse Annie, and soon she was running the organization that Annie had started. In 1996, she found out that the BLM was planning to remove wild horses in the Gila Bend area of her home state. "At that time, I didn't even know there were wild horses in central Arizona," Karen told me during my extended stay at her conservation center in South Dakota, where the band now lives. She and an assistant began traveling to Gila

Bend every Friday to observe the horses as they roamed through the salt cedars planted during the Teddy Roosevelt era. During their visits, they interviewed the local old-timers — ranchers and mustangers — and learned that one of them had captured twenty thousand wild horses, chasing and shooting them from his motorcycle, until one day, in 1936, he was just too tired and he quit.

The surviving Gila Bend horses were mostly dun with the telltale dorsal stripes on their backs — a sign of Spanish heritage. Putting together rancher stories with historical information gleaned from other sources, Karen surmised that they were descendants of the mustangs that had flourished in the 1700s at Father Kino's mission a hundred miles away. By the time she wrapped up her studies, the BLM was closing down their range. There were seventy-five horses left, of which the BLM had removed about half. Another four died during the roundup. Someone adopted a stallion. Before the rest could be captured, Karen offered to take them, and Secretary of the Interior Babbitt intervened on her behalf.

When her marriage dissolved, she began looking for land on which to provide a home for more of the country's disappearing wild horses and burros. A vision led her to the Cheyenne River Lakota of South Dakota, from whom she purchased her land and where she established headquarters for the International Society for the Protection of Mustangs and Burros. Soon she left the sprawl of suburban Phoenix and moved into a modest ranch home on the property in Lantry, in the heart of the prairie, surrounded by trails once followed by Sitting Bull and Crazy Horse and thousands of Indian ponies. When she arrived at Lantry, she had the Gila Bend band with her.

She immediately took in part of the Sheldon herd, as well as a third herd that was designated for zeroing out. These were the wild horses of the White Sands Missile Range in New Mexico, descendants of the steeds that had carried Billy the Kid and Pat Garrett and countless lesser-known cowboys and outlaws. Named for the pure white gypsum flats that make up most of its two million acres, the range is one of the most severe terrains in the country, marked by occasional outbursts of yucca and sage and intersected by the Malpais, a miles-long strip of obsidian that winds through the sands. At one time thousands of mustangs lived on the two million acres of this top-secret army test site, where in 1945 the first atomic bomb had been detonated.

Over time, the herd survived and took on mythical status as outlaw mustangs that were tough enough to live in a strange moonscape of shattered missiles and leaked toxins and hidden water springs and stunning cactus flowers during a good year, roaming free while somewhere on the range, a stealth bomber cruised in for a starlit landing. In the mid-1990s, Karen received the kind of phone call that has become all too common for wild horse groups: a person who was afraid to identify herself stated that eighty-nine wild horses on the White Sands range had died after their water source had somehow dried up—whether through drought or chemicals that had leached from an experiment or perhaps because the water source had suddenly been obstructed was never determined to anyone's but the army's satisfaction.

Karen contacted the army. They agreed to take her into the range. She and her guide and a few others soon encountered a phalanx of people in goggles and protective gear. Realizing that they had accidentally headed for the site of the day's missile launch, Karen's group quickly reversed course, and hours later they found the wild horses drinking at the site of the source where a few weeks prior so many had perished. Apparently, once word had gotten out that observers were on the way, the army had modified or cleaned up the water supply, and while the group watched, a beautiful bay stallion came in to join his band at the spring.

Over the next four years, hundreds of horses were removed from the range by a team of cowboys and soldiers led by a local veterinarian, while Karen tried to save them as well. Some were adopted, but many others met a harsher fate. By 1998, with just seventy horses left, the military finally agreed to let Karen take the horses to South Dakota. There they joined the mustangs of Father Kino and cavalry mounts and the ghosts of Indian ponies who thundered past as the northern lights sparkled on certain evenings when it was very clear and the prairie winds whispered of other times.

To many ranchers across the West, it was apparent that their time had come: Bill Clinton was about to be impeached, and they escalated efforts to take back the range. Utah representative James Hansen, a sagebrush rebel and chairman of the House subcommittee on national parks and public lands, called a meeting to discuss how to end the "Horse Act." "Wild horses are like feral alley cats," he said at the hearing in Reno. The only reason mustangs were protected, he explained, was that "some pretty good PR people" had somehow convinced citizens to mobilize on their behalf. "The intentions behind the act were quite laudable," he said. "Unfortunately, things have not worked out. Adoptions are lagging. The health of the animals on the range is deteriorating and disease is becoming a problem."

Then he played the conservatives' favorite card. "It costs $18 million a year to administer the wild horse and burro program," he said. "Last year, 8,692 animals were adopted. This works out to over $2,000 per animal, and yet, these horses sell for $200 per animal. Two thousand to sell a $200 horse. As our friend Pat Shea, director of BLM, has noted, these animals are livestock, and we need to give the BLM the authority to start managing them as livestock." The meeting ended with renewed calls for "sale authority," and his colleagues picked up the cry. It was an important moment for sagebrush rebels. Their message was now being delivered from the halls of Congress, and it was not lost on those who understood the code: except for a paltry adoption fee, the wild horse was officially worthless.

Mustang murders are hard to crack. There are few arrests and even fewer convictions. In 1989, the carcasses of at least five hundred wild horses were found in the rough terrain outside Lovelock, Nevada. The horses had been gunned down over a period of months, and some were used as bait for coyotes. "Whoever is killing these horses should get a medal," one local told a reporter at the time. But the incident was so extreme that even those who were no great friends of the wild horse were appalled. "The horses built this country," said Jimmy Williams, who had made his living as a mustanger until the passage of the 1971 law. "They deserve better than this. It just ain't right. It's my way of life they're killing out there." After multiple trips to the burgeoning crime scene, BLM criminal investigator Len Sims was heartbroken. "We'll make an arrest," he said. "Count on it." Following a two-year investigation, authorities zeroed in on several suspects, including a popular local named Dave Thacker. Thacker had a history that ran deep; he belonged to an old cattle-running family, and his great-great-grandfather was a lawman who had busted Black Bart. When a posse of BLM cops and local sheriffs converged at Thacker's remote ranch in the dark, they narrowly avoided a shootout. As the trial date approached, there were high hopes for a guilty verdict. But one complication led to another, and in the end, Thacker had an alibi for the narrow time frame of the charges — he was at a rodeo in Idaho. The case was finally dropped.

In 1998, it was time for a reckoning. Within days of the Reno massacre, cop shops were besieged with tips — names of possible suspects who were heavily armed, addresses of strange characters who hated animals, information about shifty-eyed drifters with Alabama plates, meth freaks who drove monster trucks with lightning bolts and all manner of Mad Max vehicles, drunks who went out into the desert and came back with dead wildlife — the sad roll call of the modern West, where ex-felons were dumped after stints in the slammer and a lot of other citizens were on their way.

One RP, or reporting person, said that during the time frame in question, he had heard rifle shots in the Lagomarsino Canyon area and then talked to a man in a Ford pickup who said he was hunting coyotes; another led investigators to pelts on the front seat of a truck that was owned by a man who had boasted of killing wild horses; another said there was a man with a ponytail wearing a camo jacket who was walking toward a beat-up Chevy station wagon, carrying a rifle with a scope; a fourth told cops that there was a man who once killed a horse with a bow and arrow; a fifth said he saw two neighbors in camo gear and carrying weapons take off in a four-by-four and return later that same night; a sixth fingered an unstable employee of the local humane society who may have been using the job as a cover; a seventh mentioned a Marine who frequented gun shows accompanied by his mother; and an eighth named a drunk and his girlfriend who lived in Sparks and liked to drive into the desert to kill horses. As it turned out, even the hiker who had initially called Animal Control after spotting the dying filly briefly came under suspicion when it was found that he had a machete and guns in his apartment.

Soon, a witness came forward and said some men had been talking at a Christmas party about killing horses. Two of those men were

Marines who were home on leave. After making inquiries, detectives were led to Lance Corporal Scott Brendle. Armed with a warrant, they searched his truck. In the back, they found the front page of the *Reno Gazette-Journal* that had a banner headline about the crime. That in itself might have proved nothing, but they also found a stack of photographs. One of them was very strange — a picture of the other Marine, Lance Corporal Darien Brock, standing on a dead horse. The photo had been taken the day before the carcasses were found.

As it turned out, detectives were already questioning Brock, along with a third suspect, Reno construction worker Anthony Merlino. Merlino and Brock had been friends since elementary school in the mid-1980s. At Earl Wooster High, Brendle had made it a threesome. Brock was a brilliant student, detectives learned, and had been placed in honors English. His dark essays had drawn the attention of school officials, and when military investigators searched his barracks, they found some troublesome drawings. Merlino was of a different stripe; blustery and loud, he played malicious pranks on classmates, such as yanking chairs from students just as they sat down. Brendle, investigators theorized, was the go-along, get-along type; rather than make waves, he would generally consent to whatever program the others had cooked up.

Among some cliques at Earl Wooster, it was known that the three would go into the mountains and shoot horses. But the information was never passed on; or if it was, authorities ignored it. Yet, like many establishments in Nevada, the school derives its identity from wild horses. The newspaper is called *Hoofprints.* The yearbook is named *Pegasus.* The newsletter is called *Pony Tales,* and the school's website features a beautiful painting of multicolored mustangs running across the desert. WELCOME TO EARL WOOSTER HIGH SCHOOL! proclaims a banner beneath the painting. HOME OF THE UNSTOPPABLE COLTS!

When detectives announced that three suspects were under arrest, a Virginia City deejay played "Chestnut Mare" by the Byrds. Their names were broadcast around the world as the melancholy tune wafted across the sagebrush sea. Later, the incident would be included in a popular timeline of Nevada history that covered events from the Ice Age through the present. But *Hoofprints* did not mention the high-profile arrest of the three alumni, and to this day it has not covered the mustang massacre.

After hours of questioning by a military investigator, Brendle cracked and told a disturbing tale. Two nights after Christmas, he said, he and his friends hopped in his '92 Ford Ranger, drove to a local Wal-Mart, bought a hand-held spotlight and some ammunition, and headed to the Virginia Range. "When we left the road," he said, "Anthony and Darien got into the bed of the truck so driving would be easier. The spotlight was plugged into the cigarette lighter and passed out the rear window. As I drove, both of them pounded on the truck. I stopped and got out to see what they were looking at. They said, 'Hey, look, there is a horse.'" Brendle grabbed the bolt-action .270 in the cab of the truck, trained the scope, and squeezed the trigger. The hind legs of the horse dropped, and then it buckled to the ground. Brendle fired again, but the horse was still on its front legs. Merlino finished the job. Brendle grabbed a Bud and changed the CD, and then the three friends picked up the shells and moved on.

Meanwhile, Brock was offering his own version of the evening and explaining what had happened when the men were finished. Somewhere in the mountains, he said, the three friends stopped to build a campfire. They exchanged stories around the hearth, possibly engaging in end-of-the-year reminiscing about past exploits, and perhaps toasting Brendle, who was about to turn twenty-one. They took a few photos and talked about the evening's events. Then, they had a few more beers, shot up the cans and a tree, and went home. Two days later, a detective announced on television what kind of gun had probably been used to kill the horses. That night, the three friends drove to the far side of the range so no one would see them, separated, and crawled up the mountains. It was a Marine-style assault, Brock said, and it worked; they picked up some shells, fled down the hillside, and dumped the evidence in a garbage can.

While the trio remained in custody, detectives questioned their friends and associates. One of them emerged as a ringleader — Anthony Merlino. Shortly before the mustangs were killed, Merlino's hunting and trapping licenses had been suspended because wildlife officials had discovered in his refrigerator a kit fox that he had shot and killed. "It was kind of a tradition," he told detectives when they asked why the friends brought guns into the Virginia Range. "You know, we used to go out and shoot rabbits or do whatever and it was, just catching up on old times basically."

While Merlino's female friends described him as "sweet" and a "teddy bear," his male friends saw another side. Some regretted that they hadn't contacted law enforcement long ago. There were dead ducks all over his apartment, a neighbor said. Once, he had gutted a deer on the living room floor. While growing up in Hidden Valley, a community of tract homes next to the Virginia Range, he had complained to neighbors about a wild horse that had come down from the mountains and kicked his truck. "One day we went into the hills to hunt chukker," a friend told investigators. When it got dark, they headed back down the mountains. On the way, they saw some horses in the distance. Merlino stopped the truck and retrieved a .270 from behind the seat. "He jacked a round into the gun," the friend said, "and started shooting horses." After a few shots, he hit one. "I saw its leg flopping in the wind," he continued. "I told him to get out of there before we'd get in trouble." As the pair left the Virginia Range, the friend turned around. The injured horse was on the ground. "I saw two or three other horses jumping on its head and back," he recalled. They were trying to put it out of its misery because they could see that he was wounded.

How do you feel about horses? a detective asked Merlino. "Personally I think they are a beautiful animal," he said. "I mean that might sound kind of hard to believe from everybody judging by what's going on here, but ... uh ... I mean I have nothing against them. They're not, you know, they don't hurt anyone. You know, they take a dump here and there, but who doesn't do that? Um ... I ... uh ... I don't have anything against them. Uh ... and that [the killings] shouldn't have happened."

A few days later, the men were arraigned in Storey County, at the same courthouse where Wild Horse Annie had waged her first battle, next to the old miners' pub called the Bucket O' Blood Saloon. Death threats were pouring in, and sharpshooters patrolled the roof. Spectators were searched and then packed the courtroom, which was guarded by four deputies and a bailiff named Bearclaw. The infamous lawman from Tombstone, Arizona, was over six feet and weighed about 330 pounds. He had a handlebar mustache and wore his customary necklace of twenty black bear claws. He was dressed in black and sported a badge. At his waist was a pair of crossed and holstered .44 magnums.

The men were charged with several felonies — grand theft, grand larceny and poisoning, and killing or maiming another person's animal — and they faced up to fifteen years in jail. In the gallery, spectators placed bets on the outcome of the trial; after all, Nevada was a gambling state, and when it came to mustangs, anything could happen.

Among the spectators were Bobbi Royle and Betty Kelly, the women who had gotten the call from Animal Control on the day the murders were discovered. As Bobbi studied Merlino, she was reminded of something. Years earlier, the women had lived in Hidden Valley, near Anthony Merlino — although they didn't know that at the time. It was there that they had their first contact with wild horses. The animals would come down from the mountains and wander the yards of residents, occasionally even foaling in a carefully landscaped garden. Some were thrilled at the sight. Others did not want the animals trampling their flowers or dropping manure on their lawns, and blamed the horses themselves for causing accidents when they happened to cross local streets and highways. The women knew that the local wild horse population was being picked off by people with guns.

You can't live in Nevada and not hear the stories. Perhaps you're in a bar in Elko and someone makes a reference to some mustangs he had just run down, or maybe you're on one of the university campuses and a biologist just in from the range reports that he saw a couple of wild horse carcasses with their ears cut off, or maybe you're a teenager at a local school and you hear some kids talking about going out into the desert to waste critters. It's not news, and yet to those who aren't comfortable with such things, it's disturbing, and so one day when Bobbi saw a boy on his bike with a rifle across the handlebars, she stopped her truck and asked what he was doing. "Going out to shoot," he said. "You're not planning to shoot wild horses, are you?" she asked. He shrugged and then pedaled away. Bobbi floored her truck and sent a swath of dirt across the boy's path. In her rear-view mirror, she watched as he continued up into the hills where the mustangs made their home. Now, as Bobbi watched the men in the courtroom, she was convinced that one of them, Anthony Merlino, was the boy she had confronted so long ago.

A month after the arraignment, another man was hiking in the mountains near the kill site at Lagomarsino Canyon. It was a cold and sunny afternoon. Something made him look to his left, up a hill. He saw a dark foal lying down in the sagebrush, not able to get up. A bachelor stallion—one without mares and offspring—had been watching from a distance and came over and nibbled at the foal's neck. She tried to get up but couldn't, and the stallion rejoined his little band. The hiker called for help. A vet arrived and could find no injuries. Once again, the Animal Control agent called Bobbi and Betty and asked for a rescue.

They immediately hitched one of their two horse trailers to one of their two Dodge pickups with the big diesel engines and four-wheel drive, and again, they headed north through the ice and snow toward Reno, then retraced the long and winding dirt road into the mountains in the Virginia Range, as far as the truck could go until the road was blocked by snowbanks. It was getting dark, and it was freezing. In their layers of flannel and down, Bobbi and Betty knew how to dress for such weather, but sometimes nothing protects you from the dry winter chill of the Great Basin, a desert tomb unless you're an animal with a thick coat or hide.

As they trudged through the snow in their lug boots to unhitch the trailer, the hiker, the vet, and the Animal Control officer came to help them, and they hauled the trailer across the frozen washes and gullies until they approached the filly, about a hundred yards away and downhill. The stars were particularly bright that night and helped the rescue party, who were equipped only with flashlights, as they lumbered across the sands and then up the rocky rise where the filly was lying on her side with her head down. The men lifted her onto a platform and carried her down the hill and into the trailer. "She was a carcass with a winter coat," Betty later told me. She was covered with ticks and parasites, weak and anemic. She was six months old. Two days later, at their sanctuary, Betty and Bobbi helped her stand. But she kept falling. Over the weeks, they nourished her, and she grew strong and regained muscle and she began to walk without falling down.

But she was nervous, not skittish as a lot of horses are, especially wild ones, but distracted, preoccupied, perhaps even haunted. Because of her location when rescued, and because she was starving, her rescuers reasoned that she had been a nursing foal who had recently lost her mother. Without mother's milk, a foal can last for a while in the wilderness, sometimes as long as a couple of months. And because a band of bachelor stallions had been nearby when she was found, her rescuers figured that they had taken her in, looking after her until it was time to go, standing guard as she lay down in the brush to die. "Something made me stop," the hiker who found the filly later said.

Betty and Bobbi named her Bugz, because she was permanently spooked, not unlike another twitchy Nevada character, Bugsy Siegel, said to have been demon-possessed and therefore buggy, and no doubt he was, having witnessed — and been the progenitor of — great rivers of desert carnage. Although she could not be returned to the wild, Bugz was the luckiest horse in Reno.

Shortly after the three men went on trial for the horse killings but before a verdict had been rendered, rumors swept through certain circles that a senator rose to make a speech on the Nevada House floor. "If a wild horse comes to your property," he said, "shoot him." There is no record of such a statement on the official record of legislative sessions during the time period in question. But in Nevada, information has a way of disappearing, or of simply not being recorded, and according to the rumors, some in the gallery applauded, which only added to the feeling among those who had wagered on the trial outcome that things weren't looking good for a guilty verdict. Yet because of the trophy photo, others felt that for the first time in Nevada history, there would be a conviction in a horse killing.

State veterinarian David Thain had presented the evidence at pretrial hearings. From the beginning of the investigation, autopsies had been run on each horse, and there were extensive forensic tests, with close scrutiny of bullet fragments and casings, entry and exit wounds, shattered bones, ruptured organs, collapsed lungs, and shredded hearts. Horse #1, for instance, was a male, from three to four years old, brown, 850 pounds, with a chest wound made by a projectile that went through his neck and into his heart. No bullets were recovered, although nearby there were seventeen .223 casings. Horse #2, a female, was two and a half years old, 900 pounds, with neck wounds. No bullets were found. Horse #4, the one who had been sprayed by the fire extinguisher, was between one and two, brown, 400 pounds, and had wounds in his left hip. A few casings were found nearby, but no bullets. Horse #5 was a pregnant mare, black, six years old, 850 pounds. She had wounds in her sinus and gluteals. A .30 caliber bullet was retrieved and there was a black powder slug nearby. On the list went, and by the time Dr. Thain had gotten to horse #7, his years of dealing with downer cattle and other rangeland horrors could not steel him, and he broke down and cried.

Investigators and numbered mustang carcasses at the scene of the 1998 massacre in the Virginia Range, Nevada.

Defense attorneys countered with a battery of issues, including the thorny question of which county the horses had been found in. Some said Washoe, others said Storey. The two counties met somewhere in Lagomarsino Canyon, though there was some dispute as to exactly where that merger was, even after close scrutiny of satellite maps. What if a horse had fallen with two hooves in Storey and two in Washoe — who should have investigated? Were any of the horses under the jurisdiction of the BLM? If so, which ones? Had some been privately owned horses that had escaped and joined the Virginia Range mustangs? What if someone came forward and claimed one of them? Shouldn't the killing of that horse be tried separately?

Meanwhile, the first batches of what would be at least fifty thousand pieces of mail had made their way to Storey County. The tables had turned — the outside world had become the frontier, and all the letter writers were demanding revenge. Indeed, the case was so horrific that, from the start, the DA had decided to try a novel approach. How much is a wild horse worth? she asked as she formulated the case. It was the one question that went right to the heart of the matter.

At the time of the murders, killing a mustang in the state of Nevada was a gross misdemeanor. In fact, the law didn't even refer to them as wild horses; they were legally deemed "estrays." The fine for such an act was a thousand dollars. Prosecutors did not think it feasible to pursue thirty-four separate misdemeanor charges. Moreover, that idea seemed to trivialize the case. To qualify as a felony, lost property belonging to the state — the horses — had to be worth more than five thousand dollars. So the prosecution decided to add up the value of each horse so that the crime carried a more serious penalty. Chris Collis of the Nevada Bureau of Livestock Administration took the stand to explain how he had come up with the aggregate worth of the mustangs, which was based on the per-pound value of the animals at the time of their deaths.

"I got a list of the horses that were destroyed," he testified, "and asked buyers to list a value according to age and weight . . . [generally] they give you a range of ten to fifty cents a pound . . . Smaller horses are not worth as much as larger horses. So you ask them, you know, 'What's an 850-pound horse worth,' or what a 500-pound horse is worth and they will break it down, narrow the category to, you know, eight weights are worth such and such. Six weights are worth what-ever, and so on."

On cross-examination, it was pointed out that one buyer would not provide a value because the horses were dead. Two others gave widely varying estimates, due to the fluctuating market and individ-ual ways of doing business. When Collis was finished testifying, ex-hibit B was entered in the record. It was a list of each equine victim, with gender, age, color (most were bay or brown, with a few blacks and sorrels), weight, cause of death (gunshot for each one), evidence retrieved (if there was any), and value as provided by a buyer from Fallon, Nevada. It was not unlike the list of pony claims that the Sioux had presented to the government a hundred years earlier. In this case, the total value of the thirty-four horses was $6,656.50.

Like so many cases involving alleged horse killers, this one fell apart. There were two trials, a change of venue, and the state su-preme court even stepped in. But the high-profile defense attorneys had made their case: by the time the bullets had moved through the flesh and bone of the horses, they were too shattered to match the one gun that was linked to the accused. The case was knocked back down to various misdemeanor counts, and Merlino pleaded guilty to disturbing the peace — killing horse #12, to put him out of his misery after Brendle had shot him, while Brock was holding the light. It was the story they had first told detectives. Brock and Brendle, kicked out of the Marines before the trial, pleaded no contest to charges of kill-ing or maiming an animal. All three received light sentences. Many cried foul, and others collected on their bets. But a few months later, there came a vindication — a sad one, but perhaps the Virginia Range mustangs had not died in vain: for the first time in Nevada history, it became a felony to kill a wild horse.

When he came to the White House in 2000, George W. Bush wore a cowboy hat. Like Ronald Reagan, he was from a ranch. They both liked to clear brush. And they kept Western art in the Oval Office. For Bush, it was the inspirational painting *A Charge to Keep,* in which a frontier circuit rider is charging up a rocky trail on a mustang. Al-though Reagan had invited sagebrush rebels to Washington, it took the false cowboy Bush to launch the mustang's final takedown.

Shortly after Bush was elected president, wild horse roundups escalated ferociously. At the time of the election, there were about 25,000 wild horses and burros in Nevada. By 2003, there were 17,900. As the situation worsened, wild horse advocates began weekly protests in front of the Nevada state capitol building in Carson City, yards away from a statue of Kit Carson on his horse. They waved American flags and carried placards that said PUBLIC LANDS IN PUBLIC HANDS and GOODBYE, SPIRIT OF THE WEST. "Remember Wild Horse Annie," someone called out from a car on the day I visited, and inside other cars on the stretch of old Highway 395, people honked their horns in response. "Keep up the heat," a woman identifying herself as a BLM employee said as she walked quickly past protesters during a spring rain. She was on the verge of tears. "Things are going to happen fast in the next few years. The wild horse is in big trouble. But you didn't hear that from me."

When I watched the roundups in the Diamond Mountains in 2004, I asked Dave Cattoor about his work. Cattoor is one of the two primary contractors for wild horse and burro removals around the country. Based in Nephi, Utah, he and his wife, Sue, and their sizable crew are on the road much of the year and have been since the inception of the removals. He grew up with wild horses in Colorado, and from the time he was six years old, horses have been all he thinks about. As a kid, he would follow them on horseback through their range, living with them for weeks at a time with only his bedroll, a can of beans, and some jerky. "I'd stay within two hundred yards of those horses all day long," he said in *Honest Horses,* a collection of interviews about wild horse management. "If they moved, I'd move. If they'd run, I'd keep with them. I'd get up on a rock and sit there for hours and watch them. Then I'd ride around and move them, one way and then another."

Sometimes Cattoor sees a harsh truth on the range — starving mustangs, or foals that have been orphaned. He has been known to rescue some of these youngsters, and long ago, even Wild Horse Annie herself sent him a characteristic thank-you note, expressing gratitude for his expertise. But he has also been criticized for rough handling of animals during roundups, such as at the one I witnessed. While the government allows for a 1 or 2 percent loss of animals during the captures, sometimes more die. It is often not possible to find out exactly how many, as the reports that the contractors file after each roundup are trademarked and not available outside the BLM. Often the roundups happen at remote locations on short notice, which gives independent observers little time to prepare visits. Then the horses are rushed into the overwhelmed adoption program. "Look at all the horses that no one wants!" Cattoor told me. "It would be more humane to send them to the slaughterhouse." A few months after I spoke with Cattoor, a BLM employee forgot to turn on a spigot in a corral in eastern Nevada, and five mustangs died of thirst after languishing in the hot sun for several days. Supposedly, they had been rounded up because of a drought.

Ill-intentioned government plans are often hatched in nondescript places at meetings that go unnoticed. That year, 2004, the Wild Horse and Burro Advisory Board held its annual meeting at the Marriott Hotel in Phoenix. The board advises the BLM about mustang and burro management and is mostly made up of political appointees who are pro-ranching range experts. Every year, it comes together to formulate plans for the following fiscal year and to hear public testimony about the state of mustangs and burros.

By 2004 there were dozens of wild horse advocates across the country, taxpaying citizens who were trying to head off a disaster created by mismanagement of a tax-funded program. Many of them had arrived in Phoenix to testify. There was Ginger Kathrens for the Pryor Mountain horses in Montana; Toni Moore and Val Stanley for the dwindling Douglas herd in Colorado; the crucial "Tahoe" Barry Breslow for the burros in the Mojave National Preserve and Death Valley National Park; Craig Downer for the mustangs of Nevada; and Kathleen Hayden for the recently captured Coyote Canyon herd in the Anza-Borrego Desert of Southern California — the last wild horses in the region.

The advocates made brief statements on behalf of the herds that they had been monitoring as longtime unofficial guardians. Attorney Val Stanley asked for range studies to be brought up to date — something that the 1971 law requires but that was not always done. Tahoe Barry asked that the last burros of the Mojave be permitted to stay in the land where their families had lived for over four hundred years. Ginger Kathrens wondered why, with only a hundred wild horses in Montana, more roundups were being discussed. Craig Downer pointed out that study after government study had shown that cattle did more damage to the range than any other animal and that wild horses benefited the land by spreading seeds through their manure. Kat Hayden argued for a new kind of protection for wild horses, with the places they roamed designated as historic districts under the National Register of Historic Places.

"Any more comments?" a board member asked in the final moments of the meeting. A tall guy with a square jaw stood up. He was wearing boots, jeans, and a cowboy hat, a rancher from central casting. This was Montana cattleman Merle Edsall. In wild horse circles, there had been a great deal of talk about a peculiar plan of his that he had floated long before this meeting. He and some investors had acquired a large parcel of land in Mexico, just south of the Arizona border. They planned to use it as a sanctuary for wild horses from America, the thousands that had been rounded up but were still living in government sanctuaries because they had not been adopted.

His plan was gaining traction, and wild horse advocates rightly protested, pointing out that in Mexico people were still eating horses, and when it came to the treatment of animals they did not have a particularly good record. Moreover, if American mustangs were going to be "repatriated," as the plan suggested, why not repatriate them by returning them to their actual home on the range, from where they shouldn't have been removed in the first place? Under Bush's Department of the Interior, which was looking to appease certain lobbies and reduce what it termed unnecessary spending, and all while being largely unwatched by the media, there was now an atmosphere in which Edsall could make his move.

"Right now there are fourteen thousand horses that you can't adopt out," Edsall said to the board. "It's costing you money to feed them, to give them their shots, vet care is expensive." It was the standard Republican argument about a useless government program, but the kind of thing that could easily gather momentum in the media as a scare story. The wild horse advocates did not like where this was going and exchanged glances. "You've all seen the proposal for my sanctuary," Edsall continued, referring to a glossy, full-color kit that he had sent to various key people in the months prior to this meeting. "Well, I can take care of your problem easily. Why doesn't the BLM offer horses that are over ten years old or haven't been adopted on the third try for a buck a head?"

If the government decided to go for his program, he said, he could immediately buy eight thousand of its rounded-up mustangs and take them to Mexico. The others could go to churches, kids' groups, "someone might want a pony to pull a cart—it's a way that these horses can pay for themselves. Think of all the money you can save!" And he continued, "Title for the horses should pass immediately." Wild horse advocates knew right away what horses "for a buck a head" meant—easy purchase and a trip to the slaughterhouse, earning buyers a fast grand, more or less, depending on the day's price for horseflesh. Although Edsall's suggestion made people nervous, when the meeting broke up, most everyone brushed it off, whistling past what would turn out to be literally a graveyard.

Eight months later, Montana senator Conrad Burns attached a stealth rider to the 2005 federal appropriations bill just as senators were going home for Thanksgiving. They hurriedly voted to pass it, and left. When they returned after the Christmas holiday, they—and the rest of the country—were in for a terrible surprise. The very language that Edsall had floated at the Phoenix meeting—"three strikes and you're out"—had become the law, and in a throwback to the nineteenth century, it made horses sound like felons. Known as the Burns rider, it unraveled the 1971 act and granted the BLM sale authority—the thing that stockmen had sought for decades. Now, for the first time in twenty-five years, mustangs could be taken from the range and sent to the slaughterhouse.

Wild horse advocates predicted that within a matter of days, the animals would be purchased by killer buyers at BLM corrals and quickly hauled to the three foreign-owned slaughter plants in the country, two in Texas and one in Illinois. Government officials discounted the idea, claiming that they were watching matters closely. An emergency meeting of wild horse defenders was quickly organized. Although frequently at odds over how to save horses, hundreds of mustang fans from across the land trekked through a nationwide cold snap and converged for the historic session on January 2 and 3 at the Casino Fandango in Carson City, Nevada. The group was a wide-ranging constituency of Republicans, Democrats, sagebrush rebels who didn't like the government taking away "their" mustangs, government employees, rednecks who used to round up mustangs for profit, cowboys, cowgirls, and kids. "Every morning when I get up, I see mustangs on the hillside," said casino owner George Carriou, who had donated the meeting room, as the conference began. "Don't let them take our horses."

The meeting was presided over by Karen Sussman, who had flown in from her 680-acre spread in Lantry, South Dakota, where she lives with her adopted wild horses, several burros, nine cats, and two dogs. She held a microphone before the concerned citizens in the room, and on a large screen behind her a phalanx of wild horses stood on the plains like ancient guardians. "Take a look at these horses," she said, "and feel their power. That's what we have on our side, and as we go through the next few hours together and try to formulate a plan to save their lives, don't stop thinking about that power. In fact, now, as we begin, I'd like everyone to inhale with the wind-drinkers and imagine yourselves running with them."

For the next few hours, people strategized, swapped stories of mustangs they had known, mourned the state of the world, and vowed to do something about it. When the conference ended, local singer Lacy Dalton belted out her famous song "Let 'Em Run" as an American flag waved behind her. Alas, a few days after the meeting, the fears of wild horse advocates were realized. The first mustangs to fall victim to the Burns rider were sold for a dollar a head to a rodeo clown, who promptly turned them over to a slaughterhouse in Texas. It is not widely known what goes on at slaughterhouses. Some time ago, an ex-worker was interviewed by investigators at a secret location about one such place. The account was entered into the record of a meeting held by the Assembly Committee on Natural Resources, Agriculture, and Mining of the Nevada state legislature on March 29, 1999. Here it is:

> I saw a lot of terrible things. When the colts come in, they're not worth anything because they're so small. So they hit them in the head and throw them in the gut pile.
>
> I used to go into the corrals at night to be with the mares. They were still trying to take care of their young, like in the wild. Some of them got tangled up in the fences.
>
> The most difficult thing for me to talk about was the time I heard a big ruckus and I looked down and there was this black wild stallion that they were trying to get up the chute. But he knew what was coming. He reared. He turned around and tried to crawl over the

top of the other horses to get back down the chute. And, of course, man is always stronger and he is always going to figure out a way to get the job done because we're talking about a dollar bill here. So they got all the crew out there. And they used the electric prods to prod him up. They used ropes around his neck to jerk him up. And they did everything they could. They finally got him into the chute where they could use a stun gun. Supposed to kill them instantly. And this horse took six shots and still didn't go down.

And finally the guy on the kill floor came up, running upstairs, laughing. And he says, "You know that son of a bitch just didn't want to die. But we got him. He got loose on the kill floor and they had to get a rifle before they could finally take him down."

Soon after the Burns rider triggered the first sale, some members of the Rosebud Sioux tribe bought forty-one wild horses and turned them over to a plant in Illinois, just down the road from the one where D. M. Chappel had made his fortune. After getting word of the impending slaughter, the Ford Motor Company — maker of the Mustang — stopped the clock as the horses were heading to the killing floor, buying and transporting them to a safe haven. A few days later, they issued a press release and started a Save the Mustangs fund to aid rescue groups, but they did not want to make too big a deal, lest they offend some of their most loyal buyers — drivers of pickup trucks, many of whom are ranchers.

Since the Burns rider was passed, the country's three equine slaughterhouses have been shut down, as a result of the historic Carson City gathering of wild horse advocates and the nationwide campaign that followed. But the BLM still has sale authority and has continued to market three-strikers and horses over ten years old to the lowest bidder, who can sell them to rendering plants in Canada and Mexico. Sagebrush rebels and cattlemen are pressing for more removals. In August of 2007, President Bush signed an executive order that sped up grazing permits. As of this writing, in some herd management areas, the mandated annual studies have not been carried out for many years. There are four million cows on the range, and more horses in government corrals and long-term pastures (thirty thousand) than on public lands (now about twenty-five thousand), although that figure, as always, is hotly disputed.

At some corrals, the BLM is offering mustang closeout sales —

mare-and-foal pairs in two-for-one deals. At another, there has been a disaster: 178 horses — already weakened by poor range conditions and a recent roundup — contracted salmonella and died or had to be put down. The corral was briefly shuttered, pending an investigation. On the range, some herds are at dangerously low numbers. If the roundups don't stop, the horses may vanish from the range. And still, there are those who take matters into their own hands. In February 2006, a mare and a stallion were shot to death in Gerlach, Nevada. The mare had aborted her foal during the incident, and it too perished. In fall of that year, seven horses were shot and killed near Pinedale, Arizona. Among them were a pregnant mare and a yearling. The BLM has offered rewards, but no one has come forward.

America is bleeding and a dedicated crew around the country keeps trying to stanch the wounds. In her small apartment in Cody, Wyoming, Pat Fazio sits at her computer late at night, every night, organizing thirty years of painstaking research, filing statistics and obscure documents from ancient BLM files, transferring her vast archives from boxes to cyberarchives, posting important findings online, convinced that if people were aware of the science, all the studies, the range conditions, then surely they would insist that the government stop spending tax dollars on unnecessary roundups that the public doesn't even know it's paying for.

While Fazio amasses her considerable library, there are now sanctuaries in every time zone and climate, in every size, from five-acre pastures to seven-hundred-acre wilderness spreads, and concerned citizens across the land respond to the perpetual mustang emergency. At any given time, a call goes out, and hundreds of people across the country spread the word. Can anyone take in a wild mare that the adopters can no longer afford to take care of? What about a little brown mustang that just won't let anyone put a saddle on its back? He's a pistol, the owner says. I know he'll make someone very happy. I hope I can find someone. If I don't, I'll have to put him down. Can you send out the information and cross-post? In the past, individuals who had only single empty stalls stepped up, but nowadays many of these people are simply too cash-strapped to take in even one more horse. And some of the Virginia Range mustangs who had found safe haven on the Cheyenne River Sioux reservation in South Dakota were recently sold because the Iraq War forced cutbacks in government aid, and the tribe leased the horses' land to a cattle company.

Carrying on the heritage of that herd now falls to Bugz and the dwindling numbers of horses who still eke out a living in the mountains near Reno. I met Bugz eight months after her family was killed. Since then, I have gone to see her many times. Once when I visited, she was on her way to the hospital for surgery on her right front leg, which she had been having trouble with since her arrival at Wild Horse Spirit due to lack of nourishment as a foal. Now she had a check, or crooked, ligament, which needed to be repaired lest she develop further and perhaps life-threatening problems.

While doctors operated on Bugz, Betty, Bobbi, and an associate, Mandy, paced the waiting room for hours, and even after word came that the operation was over and Bugz was coming out of anesthesia, they continued to pace, for the hours after surgery are touch-and-go for a horse — if it falls while getting up after an operation, the horse could re-injure a leg or hurt another one, and then it might have to be destroyed. But late in the day, Bugz shook off the narcotic and stood

Mustangs at Lifesavers Wild Horse Rescue in Lancaster, California.

up just fine. A few days later, she went home. As soon as she came out of the trailer, she was greeted by her buddy Mona, a sweet little brown mustang with a BLM freeze brand. Mona trotted to the rail of a corral and called out a welcoming sound. Bugz whinnied back and then went to her stall for dinner.

Bobbi and Betty, now in their sixties, live in a house adjacent to the corrals and stalls, along with several rescued dogs and cats. Their house is big and comfortable but can barely accommodate all the horse stuff—art, books, files, and so on—that the women have acquired over the years. From early in the morning until late in the evening, Bobbi takes care of the horses along with twenty-four-year-old Mandy McNitt, a neighbor who found refuge from her strict family at Wild Horse Spirit. Art Majeski doesn't come by much anymore, although he did recently hire a pilot to fly over the Virginia Range to see how many horses there were. He counted sixty-eight, a number that is far below the state's estimated five hundred and that, if accurate means the days of the horses that Wild Horse Annie first tried to protect are not just numbered but close to gone. (Officer Spratley, the sheriff's deputy who was called to the Virginia Range when the wounded filly was discovered, tells me that as of this writing, he does not see wild horses on his way to work anymore.)

At Wild Horse Spirit, Bobbi and Mandy carry on, feeding and watering the horses twice a day, and spending the rest of their time mucking out stalls, grooming the horses, checking them for ailments, taking them to the vet, making repairs around the stalls and corrals, and finding additional time to hold garage sales so they can raise money for feed and equipment. When their work outside is finished, they sit down with Betty and watch the horses on monitors from the living room because some of them are recovering from injuries or wounds. Late at night, Betty is often online, informing a circuit of people of the latest news in the ongoing battle to save wild horses, and Bobbi is organizing the next day's work. "Can I call you back?" Bobbi says one recent evening when someone calls to chat. "I got two colicky horses I'm trying to get into a trailer."

A few days later Betty and I drove out to Lagomarsino Canyon to pay our respects, see how it's changed since the massacre. As we climbed up the rutted road leading into the Virginia Range, past sites where men used to trap wild horses and haul them away, I thought about the old mustanger accounts that I had read over the years. Toward the end of their lives, some of the hunters expressed regret for the loss of wild horses and their part in it. I had heard the same thing from people I talked with — old-timers who used to hunt horses and were not happy about seeing strip malls and minimarts in their place. What will today's government contractors think in two or three decades, I wondered, when they may have worked themselves out of a job because there are too few horses to take, or the only mustang left in Nevada is on a sign in front of a brothel, or their grandchildren ask them where all the wild ones have gone? Will they leave in sadness someday, like Pete Barnum, their progenitor, the "king of mustangers," the very man who invented the portable canvas corral, when the fate of the animals becomes too much to bear? Will they become like the cowboy who sent so many horses to the slaughterhouse that one day he tried to blow one up and then went mad? "I've lived my whole life in the West," Dave Cattoor once said, "away from towns and out on the range with these horses. Maybe you could call it an obsession, but I've just had to do something with them, to be working with them, to be following them around. My life belongs with them, these wild horses."

As we came closer to the graveyard, I thought of others who ran with the wild ones, Buffalo Bill and Custer and Crazy Horse. A couple of years earlier, on the mustang trail, I had visited the Crazy Horse Memorial in South Dakota. Work began on the memorial in 1948. It's a massive stone carving of the legendary Indian on his steed — or will be someday, when it's finished. A group of Native Americans hired the Polish American sculptor Korczak Ziolkowski to carve the tribute in response to Mount Rushmore; he had been one of the sculptors of the four presidents, and the Indians wanted him to do the same for Crazy Horse in the mountains nearby, overlooking their tribal home.

Ziolkowski raised his family at the site of the memorial, and they all worked on the sculpture until he died in 1982. Since then, his children and grandchildren have continued the mission, and so too will their children and their children's children until the memorial is completed, perhaps in another fifty years. When I was there, I hiked up a trail to the work-in-progress, stood near the ten-story-tall rendition of warrior and horse, and watched the blasting of rock as the pair continued to take shape. I learned from a guide that the face of Crazy Horse was completed in 1998 — coincidentally, at the time of the Reno horse killings. Soon afterward, the crew began to carve the horse's head. By the time of my visit, the rippling mane had emerged, and out of the granite of the Black Hills had also come the big, sad, wise horse eye.

Now, Betty and I were just a few hundred yards from the kill site. I thought of a conversation I had once overheard in the Reno airport — a big guy on a cell phone complaining that the ammo in the steel toe of his boot had been confiscated — and I thought of the mustang whose eye had been mutilated and then of something that was on my mind throughout the writing of this book — the astonishing play *Equus*. Written by Peter Shaffer in 1973, it tells the story of a young man who is drawn to the mysterious power of horses. As he comes of age, he is gripped by an ecstatic frenzy and blinds six of them with a spike. The play is based on a real incident that occurred in the English countryside, and examines the underlying reasons for such attacks. The horses have roiled the young man, stirred his juices, mirrored his wild side and even stoked it. But they have also seen his shame and must be destroyed. While the Virginia Range massacre had an especially American bent, filled with rage but not passion, in the end it was the same: the horse is our great silent witness, as Elizabeth Atwood Lawrence described Comanche long ago; he knows too much and we can't take it. "Is it possible," a character asks in *Equus*, "for a horse at a certain moment to add its sufferings together, and turn them into grief?" Today, I thought, almost five hundred years after Cortés traveled to the New World, we are still throwing them overboard, into the horse latitudes, trying to lighten our load. And there they swim with Moby Dick, whose big eye watched as Ahab hunted him down.

We had arrived, and we parked near the site and walked up a rise. It was springtime and the stands of sage were puffy with rain and fragrant. Except for our footsteps, it was quiet. The horse skulls and cages of ribs and shins and intact hooves and manes and tails were still there, forever preserved in the dry Mojave air. There was a pair of leg bones and they were crossed, as if running in repose. They were as pure a white as you will ever see, polished and caressed and battered by the winds of the Great Basin, radiating almost, a reverse silhouette of wildness paralyzed in movement and time. Betty knew exactly which horse this was, and had told me about her on our first visit to the site. She was horse #1 in the court record, or Hope, as she and Bobbi had named her — the one who had prompted the phone call from Animal Control.

"She had probably been here for a day or two," Betty recalled, and as she continued, it was like a prayer. "She was lying in the sand. She had dug a small hole with her front legs, intermittently trying to get up." I knew the story well, and in bearing witness there was comfort and then Betty's voice trailed off and we walked on. After a while, we came across the horse known in the Nevada court system as #4. Like the others, Bobbi and Betty gave him a name. It was Alvin. He was the one who was shot in the chest and whose eye was mutilated with a fire extinguisher. His carcass — the barrel of his chest — was picked and blown clean by time, wind, and critters, rooted always in the great wide open. His spine was vanishing but still flush against the sand, and his ribs curved toward the sky. "There was a stallion watching us that day," Betty had told me long ago, now reciting the rest of the prayer. "Just standing at the perimeter as we found each dead horse. When the sun went down and we got in our cars, he trotted on down the road. His family had been wiped out, but we still didn't know how bad it was."

As I walked the site this time, I saw that someone or something, maybe a coyote or perhaps the weather, had moved a few of the large stones in the cross under a juniper tree that Betty had made on the one-year anniversary. But it was still very much a cross, and I decided that a natural force had disturbed the stones — a person who wanted to vandalize the scene would have done more damage. And then I discovered something new: an empty box of Winchester cartridges, lodged between the branches of another juniper tree.

Winchester — the gun that won the West, the ammo that brought it to its knees — now back as a reminder, probably placed intentionally and maybe by the people who killed the horses. Did someone have us in his sights? I wondered as I sat on a rock and looked out across the range. The latest NOTHING DOWN subdivisions of Reno were just beyond the peaks on the horizon, but no one would know if someone decided to take us out that day; maybe someone would hear the gunfire — others who came out here to shoot, perhaps — but gunshots in the desert outside Reno, in the desert outside any American town or city, would not be a surprise and no one would rush to our aid.

"I think it's time to go," I said, but as we walked back to the pickup there came a wonderful sight — a few horses, down from a rise. Since the massacre, Betty rarely saw them in the canyon, and she had visited it several times a year, as a kind of a groundskeeper for the kill site. On my visits, I had not seen any horses either, nor had I seen any hoofprints, which made me think that they had been avoiding the area, because in the desert, tracks last for a very long time. The horses that approached were brown with black manes — the scruffy and beautiful Nevada horses that nobody asks for at the adoption centers. We stopped in our tracks and watched them, and they watched us back. After a while, we bid them farewell. As we headed down the mountain, I turned for one more look. They were walking across the boneyard toward the stone cross, reclaiming their home.

And in the higher elevations of the Nevada desert, and in certain pockets across the West, mustangs still roam, unfettered, in pretty herds, each herd with its own story — the Cerbat in Arizona, the Little Bookcliffs in Colorado, in Idaho the Challis, the Kiger in Oregon, the Chemehuevi in California, the South Shoshone, the West Douglas, the Sinbad, the Cibola, the herd at Wheeler Pass, the mustangs at Havasu, the Whistler Mountain horses, the four-leggeds of Jakes Wash, Chokecherry, Clover Creek, Reveille, and Alamo — galloping, walking, grazing, trying to make more of their own, pawing through the ice in winter to scrounge for forage, appearing in the back yards of the new Levittowns that are replicating across the desert, straddling land where they are federally protected and land where they are not, spreading seeds so new grasses can grow, stopping for a drink, trying to cross highways, fleeing trappers, running from bullets, on they go, but for how much longer, we cannot say. "They really belong not to man," Will James wrote, "but to that country of junipers and sage, of deep arroyos, mesas — and freedom."

They Also Served

THERE'S A STATUE of Brighty the burro in the Grand Canyon Lodge. Brighty lived at the Grand Canyon from 1892 to 1922, along with countless other burros whose ancestors had come with the Spanish and had carried the ensuing parade up mountains, across deserts, and into mines and history. Named after the Bright Angel Creek in the canyon, Brighty originally belonged to a gold prospector. When the prospector was killed, Brighty was adopted by the park service. He helped build the canyon's first suspension bridge across the Colorado River and carried Teddy Roosevelt's packs on a hunt for mountain lions. He was an icon of the West when he died, and Wild Horse Annie made sure that his kind was included in the 1971 act, which placed most burros under the mandate of the Bureau of Land Management because they lived on public lands.

Those that found themselves managed by other agencies, such as the National Park Service, had no protection — as a non-native species, they had to go. In 1979, the extirpation began — with Brighty's descendants. Because getting them out of the Grand Canyon would be difficult, all 577 of them were to be shot. The late writer and animal defender Cleveland Amory intervened, along with his organization, the Fund for Animals, putting together a daring and complicated rescue in which the burros were airlifted from the canyon and taken to his Black Beauty Ranch in Texas, which he had founded for this occasion.

But that was the beginning of the end for the burro in national parks and preserves. Since then, NPS has continued its policy of "direct reduction," and thousands of burros have been shot by contract hunters, harried to their doom, and packed into overcrowded government adoption pipelines in airborne roundups. From 1987 to 1994, the park service shot four hundred burros in Death Valley alone — just one of various burro sites all over the desert West. When Death Valley went from monument to park status in '94, the park service escalated its plans to remove burros — and Death Valley's remaining wild horses.

Nineteenth-century burro train hauling gold from a mine near Ouray, Colorado.

In Wild Horse Annie's footsteps came another friend of the burro. This was Diana Chontos. In 1990, the longtime rescuer of burros had taken six of them and made a two-year cross-country wilderness trek through California to draw attention to their plight. When she heard about the plan for the Death Valley burros, she approached the agency with an idea. After lengthy and difficult talks, it was agreed that the agency would not shoot burros if her organization, Wild Burro Rescue in Olancha, California, would organize the burro removal, pay for it, and remove them on its own.

And that's what she's been doing since then, along with her late partner, Tom Allewelt, who trimmed the hooves of rescued burros and horses and helped to gentle them at their sanctuary in the Owens Valley. There are still a few burros in Death Valley, and it is a matter of conjecture as to who will get to them first, contract hunters or those who want to provide them with a new home.

In 2007, the last burros of the Mojave Desert were rounded up. These belonged to the Clark Mountain herd, whose home turf was the highest peak in the Mojave Desert, at 7,929 feet. This is on the north side of the Mojave National Preserve, and until the final roundup, you could have seen them hanging out at Excelsior Mine Road, if you were driving east on I-15 toward Las Vegas and you were lucky. A couple of years earlier, another herd had been taken off the preserve. According to the desert grapevine, two may have been shot in the process. There are photos of one burro with a bullet to the head circulating the ether — the rumor is that he died a slow and painful death as the contractors stood by.

Like wild horses, burros are part of the government's adoption program. Not as glamorous as the mustang, they receive less attention from the press. And so their obliteration is carried out in total darkness, and burro sanctuaries across the West are counting on new arrivals as the government gets ready to zero out Brighty's descendants.

Like wild horses, burros have much to tell us. In 2000, Diana Chontos rescued a burro from Death Valley and called him Yaqui. "He was respected by all of the younger jacks," she wrote, "and they didn't chase him from food or water. He loved to be brushed and hugged. But one day he began to grow weak and could no longer get up from his naps without our help and towards the end we rigged a blanket for shade and called a vet to ease his passing. One by one all 32 jacks came by and touched him some place on his body, then went back to their hay. Shortly after the last jack paid his respects, Yaqui took a deep breath and died." He was fifty years old, the vet said, the oldest equine he had ever seen. Had he helped a miner named Peg-leg Pete find water? Maybe he had once led a lost pilgrim back to the trail. Or maybe he just lived in the Mojave Desert—for a long time, until he had to go.

Acknowledgments

THIS PROJECT WAS a large undertaking, and many people have helped me bring it to fruition. First, I want to thank my publisher, Janet Silver, for acquiring it and understanding its potential. I also want to thank my editor, Anton Mueller, for his great insight into my story and helping me shape it. His assistant, Nicole Angeloro, has been generous with her time and suggestions. I extend appreciation to manuscript editors Laurence Cooper and Tracy Roe for their thoughtful work. Thanks also to Lindsey Smith for looking after the softcover edition. A tip of the hat to Kathy Anderson as well, for early help with my proposal and selling the book, and to my agent Liz Darhansoff for guidance as I moved through the editorial process. I am also grateful to her associate Michele Mortimer and her partner Chuck Verrill. In addition, I would like to thank Mark Lamonica, student of things ancient and modern, who gave me an early key to my story, and it helped me follow the horses through time.

The following people have offered aid, comfort, insight, and knowledge (and apologies to those whose names I may have omitted — please know that it's an oversight):

Shirley Allen, Detective Allan Artz, Pamela Berkeley, Sonja Bolle, Walter Brasch, John Brian, Dave and Sue Cattoor, Troy Cattoor, Leslie Caveny, Harry Charger, Diana Chontos, Jim Clapp, Eileen Cohen, Lacy Dalton, Joey Deeg, Neda DeMayo, Steve and Jeri de Souza,

Craig Downer, Meredith Dunham, Samantha Dunn, Ed Dwyer, Merle Edsall, Elaine and Frida Etchell, Judi Farkas, Terri Farley, Dr. Patricia Fazio, Marva Felchlin and the staff of the Autry National Center, Olivia Fiamingo, Jennifer and Ken Foster, Judith Freeman, Louie Freiberg, Grandpa Yahoo, C. J. Hadley, Holland Haig, Amy Handelsman, Kathleen and Robert Hayden, Kim Henrick, Diana Mara Henry, John Holland, Laurie Howard, Valerie James-Patton, Alan J. Kania, Ginger Kathrens, Dylan Kato, Michael and Lenora Kelley, Betty Lee Kelly, Nancy Kerson, Dr. Jay Kirkpatrick, Sharon Klassen, Elissa Kline, George Knapp, Willis and Sharon Lamm, Andrea Lankford, Cindy Lawrence, Jay Levin, Julie Littman, Andrea Lococo, Cindy McDonald, Art Majeski, Bobbi McCollum, Irv McMillan, Mandy McNitt, Toni Moore, Laila Nabulsi, Joanne O'Hare, Sherry O'Mahoney, Lynne Oyama, Virginie Parant, Bobby Parker, Judy Belushi Pisano, Victor Pisano, Rob Pliskin, Tom Pogacnik, Susie Pohlman, Dr. Paula Powers, Betty and Bob Retzer, Andrea Riggs, Patricia Roth, Bobbi Royle, Nylene Schoellhorn, Sheila Schwadel, Maxine Shane, Rosie Shuster, Paul and Sabine Skelton, Pam Slipyan, Deputy Daryl Spratley, Valerie Stanley, Jill Starr, Paul Steblein, the late Peter and Susan Stern, Cindy Stevens, Jon, Denise, and Ariana Stillman, Ron Stillman, Susie Stokke, Nicoline, Richard, and Sabrina Storey, Sally Summers, Karen Sussman, Tom Teicholz, Pamela Turner, Barbara Warner, Jean Blackmon Waszak, Terry Watt, Rex Weiner, Connie White, John Winniepenix, Billie Young, and many people at the Huntington Library, including Chris Adde, Jill Cogen, Susi Krasnoo, and finally, Peter J. Blodgett, who told me about Charles Siringo and his groundbreaking account of the cowboy's horse.

Of course, when everyone gathers round the chuck wagon at the end of the day, there's always someone out on the range, looking after things. In the case of *Mustang,* that would be Patrice Taddonio, publicist extraordinaire; her endeavors on behalf of my book and the wild ones have been mighty and enduring.

Notes on the Writing of This Book

TO WRITE THIS BOOK, I traveled to Montana, Wyoming, Texas, and parts of California north and south of my home in Los Angeles. Often, I was in Nevada, where most of the country's wild horses still roam. I went to their ranges in the northeastern part of the state, the southwest near Las Vegas, and outside Reno in the Virginia Range. I also visited government corrals where mustangs and burros are taken after roundups, adoption centers where they await new homes, and sanctuaries and conservancies in Nevada, South Dakota, and California. Along the way, I spent time at a burro range in the Mojave National Preserve, one of the last in the West. My travels also took me to powwows, rodeos, parades, and events such as the Wild Horse and Burro Exposition, an annual gathering where gentled mustangs trained by prison inmates show their stuff as ceremonial cavalry mounts and partners on the range.

In 2006, when the expo was in Reno, I watched BLM employees ride wild horses that had just graduated from the mustang program at Carson City's Warm Springs Correctional Facility. Here comes Johnny Ringo, the announcer called, and then Starbuck and Buddy, followed by Mikey the Comstock horse from the Virginia Range. Here's Tough with three strikes against him, a four-year-old from the White River Herd, Mojave from the Calico Mountains, a six-year-old with "trust issues," Will, at just two years old, another three-striker (perhaps like some of the inmates who trained him), and then Charlie, Lookin Good, Dutch, Gravy, Goldrush, Cletus, Sundown, Gauge, Shaggy, Brownie, and Harriet the burro, who, the announcer explained, had been trained by all the inmates at the prison, was one year old, and "would make a great yard ornament or a pet." Beautiful animals all, and later in the day, when a stunning black mustang had been auctioned off to a prominent Nevada rancher for the reported sum of $20,000, some in the crowd took heart, thinking that if this particular rancher would pay that much for a wild one, perhaps other ranchers would follow his lead and reconsider the notion that mustangs were worth only their weight at the meat market. But of course there were other magnificent horses that would not go adopted that day, particularly the little brown ones that people often passed over for more glamorous paints and palominos.

There's a big market for the classically western mustangs — people want them for shows and parades. In fact, some palominos are surviving thanks to the Marine Corps Mounted Color Guard, which uses only palomino mustangs from the Nevada range for its breathtaking spectacles that recall the days of the horses' participation in war. The horses are named after battles, and since we are a nation that likes visuals, it is often through such spectacles — with riders in full dress blue, festooned with ribbons and badges, and horses outfitted with fine English saddles and handmade bridles and breast collars with Marine emblems and blankets with the corps colors of red and gold — that the full meaning of equine service is passed on. Fortunately for me, the color guard is part of the annual Rose Bowl Equestfest in Pasadena, and I make a point of seeing them every year.

Of course, traveling was only one aspect of what went into the writing of this book. My work generally draws from many sources, and *Mustang* was no exception, although in this case, there were more than usual. I consulted scientists, range experts, politicians, cowboys and Indians, horse killers and horse saviors, the diaries of long-gone historical figures, tepee skins, petroglyphs, books, articles, poems, artwork, the Old and New Testaments, government documents, trial transcripts, songs, movies, television shows, and plays. Several books were key to the writing of this one, including *The Horse of the*

Americas by Robert Moorman Denhardt, *The Mustangs* by J. Frank Dobie, and *The Wild Horse of the West* by Walker D. Wyman. These sources are cited in my text, so I am not including them in the following chapter-by-chapter list of references, presented in alphabetical order by author's last name. Other sources are cited in the text as well, and may not be listed here. To keep this section at fighting weight, a few additional sources have been omitted; they are all listed in my extensive bibliography.

For chapter 1, "The Horses Return," I relied on Eliyahu Ashtor's *The Jews of Moslem Spain,* volume I; Paul Brown and Fairfax Downey's *Horses of Destiny; Don Quixote* by Miguel de Cervantes; *Cholent & Chorizo* by Abraham S. Chanin; Martin A. Cohen's *The Martyr: Luis de Carvajal, a Secret Jew in Sixteenth-Century Mexico; The Inca's Florida* by Garcilaso de la Vega; David Ewing Duncan's *Hernando de Soto: A Savage Quest in the Americas; The Horses of the Conquest* by R. B. Cunninghame Graham; Seymour Leibman's *The Jews in New Spain* and his translation of *The Enlightened: The Writings of Luis de Carvajal, El Mozo; Pioneer Jews: A New Life in the Far West* by Harriet and Fred Rochlin; *Dark and Dashing Horsemen* by Stan Steiner and his article "Jewish Conquistadors: America's First Cowboys," which appeared in *American West;* Arthur Strawn's *Sails and Swords; Who's Who of the Conquistadors* and *Rivers of Gold: The Rise of the Spanish Empire from Columbus to Magellan* by Hugh Thomas; *The Spanish Riding School: Its Traditions and Development from the Sixteenth Century until Today* by Mathilde Windisch-Graetz; and *Conquistadors* by Michael Wood.

For chapter 2, "Dawn of the Mustang," I drew from *Unbroken Spirit: The Wild Horse in the American Landscape,* a special publication done under the auspices of the Buffalo Bill Historical Center and edited and written by various contributors; the documentary *El Caballo;* Mark Cohen's *Equus Evolves: The Story of the Hagerman Horse;* "Wild Horses As Native North American Wildlife" statement for the 109th Congress, 2005, by Dr. Patricia Fazio and Dr. Jay Kirkpatrick; Dr. Ann Forsten's 1992 paper "Mitochondrial-DNA Time-Table and the Evolution of *Equus*" from *Annales Zoologici Fennici; The Western Pony* by William R. Leigh; *Horse Watching* by Desmond Morris; *The Centaur Legacy* by Bjarke Rink; "Vertebrate Tracks,

Death Valley" by Vincent L. Santucci and Torrey G. Nyborg for the *San Bernardino County Museum Association Quarterly;* "Camel and Horse Footprints from the Miocene of California" by William A. S. Sargeant and Robert E. Reynolds for the *San Bernardino County Museum Association Quarterly;* and *The First Horsemen* from the Emergence of Man Series by Frank Trippett and the editors of Time-Life Books.

The opening story of chapter 3, "Hoofbeats on the Prairie," is from Victor Mandan for the Turtle Island Storytellers Network. The myth about the Horse Nations comes from *Black Elk Speaks* by John G. Neihardt. The rest of the chapter is derived from interviews with various Native Americans, including Cheyenne River Lakota elder Harry Charger and Little Bighorn National Monument park personnel, and from a wide range of other works, including George Douglas Brewerton's *Overland with Kit Carson: A Narrative of the Old Spanish Trail in '48;* George Catlin's *Letters and Notes on the Manners, Customs, and Conditions of the North American Indians,* volumes 1 and 2; LaVerne Harrell Clark's *They Sang for Horses;* Joseph Medicine Crow's *From the Heart of the Crow Country: The Crow Indians' Own Stories;* Ann W. and LeRoy R. Hafen's *Old Spanish Trail: Santa Fé to Los Angeles; Appaloosa: The Spotted Horse in Art and History* by Francis Haines; "Slavers in the Mojave" in *The Westerners Brand Book,* volume 11, edited by Russ Leadabrand; *Death Valley and the Amargosa: A Land of Illusion* by Richard E. Lingenfelter; Dr. Michel Pijoan's article "The Herds of Onate" for *El Palacio* magazine; Frank Gilbert Roe's *The Indian and the Horse;* Conway B. Sonne's *World of Wakara;* and Clark Wissler's *Indians of the United States: Four Centuries of Their History and Culture.*

To write chapter 4, "Comanche," I spent several days exploring the battlefield and talking to a range of authorities on the subject. The chapter is derived in part from that trip, but from much else as well, including accounts of Native American and U.S. cavalry history before the battle; government documents and treaties of the era; Native American and army reconstructions of the battle as told in period art, oral histories, and written accounts; transcripts of the investigation that followed the battle; and accounts and histories of the era that immediately followed and what happened to various battle participants, including Comanche. These are most of the works I used: *Crazy Horse and Custer* by Stephen Ambrose; *Comanche* by David Appel; Michael Blake's *Marching to Valhalla: A Novel of Custer's Last Days; The Horses of Gettysburg* (DVD), produced and directed by Mark Bussler; Walter Camp's *Custer in '76;* Evan S. Connell's *Son of the Morning Star: Custer and the Little Bighorn;* Forrest W. Daniel's "Dismounting the Sioux" for *North Dakota History;* "The Cavalry and the Horse," Ph.D. dissertation by Emmett Essin III; *Great Plains* by Ian Frazier; Richard G. Hardorff's *Indian Views of the Custer Fight; The Battle of the Washita* by Stan Hoig; Edward and Mabel Kadlecek's *To Kill an Eagle: Indian Views on the Last Days of Crazy Horse;* Elizabeth Atwood Lawrence's *His Very Silence Speaks — Comanche, the Horse Who Survived Custer's Last Stand; Keogh, Comanche, and Custer* by Captain Edward S. Luce; *Wooden Leg: A Warrior Who Fought Custer* by Thomas B. Marquis; *The Journey of Crazy Horse* by Joseph M. Marshall III; Don Rickey Jr.'s *Forty Miles a Day on Beans and Hay;* George F. Shrady's *General Grant's Last Days;* Robert M. Utley's *Little Bighorn Battlefield: A History and Guide to the Battle of the Little Bighorn;* and "The Battle of the Washita, Revisited" by Howard F. Van Zandt for *The Chronicles of Oklahoma.* The story about Chief Joseph and his request for a horse comes from the writer N. Scott Momaday, in the PBS documentary *The West.* Its website, www.pbs.org/weta/thewest/program/, was immensely helpful in many other ways.

For chapter 5, "All Roads Lead to Buffalo Bill," I drew from a range of material on Buffalo Bill, the era, and on the ensuing events in the lives of the Plains Indians. First, there was *Buffalo Bill's Life Story,* an autobiography. There was also *The Diamond's Ace: Scotland and the Native Americans* by Tom F. Cunningham; *Last of the Great Scouts (Buffalo Bill)* by Zane Grey and Helen Cody Wetmore; *The Colonel and Little Missie* by Larry McMurtry; *Buffalo Bill in Bologna: The Americanization of the World, 1869–1922* by Robert W. Rydell and Rob Kroes; *Buffalo Bill and His Horses* by Agnes Wright Spring; *Buffalo Bill's America: William Cody and the Wild West Show* by Louis Warren; and also the very useful website www.wyoming talesandtrails.com. For material regarding the death of Long Wolf and the return of his remains to Pine Ridge, South Dakota, I relied on

Thirteen Stories by Robert Cunninghame Graham, the man who first told the story long ago, and the article "Brompton Cemetery" at this link: www.bbc.co.uk/london/content/articles/2005/05/10/brompton_cemetery_feature.shtml.

For chapter 6, "Rawhide," I traveled to Fort Worth, Texas, where the old Chisholm Trail started and where every day there are cattle-drive reenactments at the historic stockyards, featuring a veteran longhorn named Jake who has been given a permanent reprieve. I visited the grave of Midnight, the famous bucking horse, located outside the Will Rogers Coliseum, and I toured the Cowgirl Hall of Fame as well as the Amon Carter Museum, which has extensive holdings of works by Frederic Remington and Charles M. Russell. My extensive readings on the cattle-drive era included Anthony Amaral's *Will James: The Gilt-Edged Cowboy;* William Gardner Bell's *Will James: The Life and Works of a Lone Cowboy; AG Man: The Comic Book* by Baxter Black; *Cowboy Love Poetry: Verse from the Heart of the West,* edited by Paddy Calistro, Jack Lamb, and Jean Penn; "Midnight: Story of a Champion Bucker" by Susan Childs; *Tales of the Wild Horse Desert* by Betty Bailey Colley and Jane Clements Monday; *California Cowboys* by Dane Coolidge; *In the Days of the Vaqueros: America's First True Cowboys* by Russell Freedman; *My Reminiscences As a Cowboy* by Frank Harris; *Steamboat, Legendary Bucking Horse: His Life and Times, and the Cowboys Who Tried to Tame Him* by Candy Vyvey Moulton and Flossie Moulton; Candy Moulton's "Kings of the Hurricane Deck"; and Martin W. Sandler's *Vaqueros: America's First Cowmen.* I also reread Owen Wister's *The Virginian,* the classic work regarded by many as the first Western novel. Of note is the fact that Wister includes a harrowing passage about a cowboy who beats his horse. According to Bernard DeVoto in *The Western Paradox,* the account had originally appeared in *Harper's Magazine* and was so brutal that Teddy Roosevelt wrote a letter to the editor to complain. In *The Virginian,* Wister toned it down.

For chapter 7, "The Wonder Horses That Built Hollywood," I drew from my own knowledge of Westerns (a favorite genre) as well as *The Hollywood Posse* by Diana Serra Cary; *The Encyclopedia of Westerns* by Herb Fagen; and the works of William S. Hart. There were several websites that I referred to for the history of the first

movies, including http://xroads.virginia.edu/~ma96/WCE/title.html
(1893 World's Fair); http://memory.loc.gov/ammem/edhtml/edfict.
html; http://memory.loc.gov/ammem/edhtml/edmvhm.html; http://
www.nps.gov/edis/; http://www.filmsite.org/milestonespre1900s_2.
html; and http://www.wildwestweb.net/flicks.html. I also found various movie facts on the Internet Movie Database website, www.imdb.
com.

The final chapters, about the modern range wars, are based on
interviews and discussions, in person, through e-mail, and on the
phone, with a wide range of people. They include Maxine Shane,
Susie Stokke, John Winniepenix, and other BLM personnel; David
Cattoor; Alan J. Kania, Betty Lee Kelly, Bobbi Royle, Mandy Mc-
Nitt, Karen Sussman, Neda DeMayo, Virginie Parant, Joey Deeg,
Rob Pliskin, Grandpa Yahoo, Craig Downer, Harry Charger, Nylene
Schoellhorn, Dr. Patricia Fazio, Dr. Jay Kirkpatrick, Toni Moore, Val-
erie Stanley, Andrea Lococo, Willis and Sharon Lamm, Lacy Dalton,
Olivia Fiamingo, Terry Farley, Kathleen Hayden, Jennifer Foster, Jill
Starr, Ginger Kathrens, Terry Watt, C.J. Hadley, and others.

This part of my narrative is also based on various books, articles,
and documents, including Anthony Amaral's *Mustang: Life and Leg-
ends of Nevada's Wild Horses; Orphans Preferred* by Christopher
Corbett; *The Wild Horse in Nevada: I Thought I Heard a Discour-
aging Word* by Amy Dansie, Don Tuohy, Ann Pinzl, and Cheryl A.
Young; C.J. Hadley's "Wild Horses: No Home on the Range?" in
Range magazine; the documentary *Last of the Spanish Mustangs* by
Len Johnson; *Welfare Ranching: The Subsidized Destruction of the
American West,* edited by Mollie Matteson and George Wuerth-
ner; *Honest Horses* by Paula Morin; Frank Mullen's series of articles
about the Reno horse massacre for the *Reno Gazette-Journal;* Paul
Rogers's article "Cash Cows" in the *San Jose Mercury News*; Scott
Sonner's article "$25,000 Reward Sought in Shooting Death of 33
Wild Horses," *Las Vegas Sun; The Pony Express in Nevada,* compiled by the U.S. Department of the Interior, Bureau of Land Management; and *Coyotes and Town Dogs: Earth First! And the Environmental Movement* by Susan Zakin.

I've also referred to various websites, including http://www.fort.
usgs.gov/WildHorsePopulations/default.asp regarding government

counts of wild horses and burros; http://www.blm.gov/nv/st/en.html regarding wild horses and burros in Nevada; and http://www.wild horseandburro.blm.gov/index.php regarding wild horses and bur- ros across the West.

Information about the 1998 horse massacre comes from the exten- sive official record, including arraignment, pretrial hearing and trial transcripts, arrest and police reports, witness statements, newspa- per accounts, a video of the crime scene, and my own interviews with various people who are cited in the text, including detectives, other members of law enforcement, and rescuers called to the scene.

Finally, I'd like to make a point about 1998 itself. In the annals of the modern West, that year was a particularly strange and violent one, as I learned while looking into the events surrounding the mas- sacre. The Clinton impeachment proceedings were under way, and the country was in a sort of free fall. In May, Kip Kinkel killed his par- ents, then gunned down two students at his Oregon high school and wounded twenty-five others. The incident kicked off a wave of school shootings that has yet to subside. In October, in Laramie, Wyoming, Matthew Shepard was brutally beaten and tied to a fence, where he later died. Then came the horse killings as the year closed out. Now, on the ten-year anniversary of these events, I leave it to others to fully explore the forces that converged in 1998, a moment in time that may have been a turning point for the country — for our culture as well as our spirit.

Bibliography

BOOKS

Abbey, Edward. *The Brave Cowboy*. New York: Avon Books, 1956.

Amaral, Anthony. *Will James: The Gilt-Edged Cowboy*. Los Angeles: Westernlore Press, 1967.

———. *Mustang: Life and Legends of Nevada's Wild Horses*. Reno: University of Nevada Press, 1977.

Ambrose, Stephen E. *Crazy Horse and Custer*. New York: Doubleday, 1975.

Appel, David. *Comanche*. Cleveland: World Publishing Company, 1951.

Ashtor, Eliyahu. *The Jews of Moslem Spain*. 3 vols. Philadelphia: The Jewish Publication Society of America, 1973.

Bama, Lynne, et al. *Unbroken Spirit: The Wild Horse in the American Landscape*. Cody, WY: Buffalo Bill Historical Center, 1999.

Bancroft, Hubert H. *The Works of Hubert Howe Bancroft*. Vol. 25. San Francisco: The History Company, Publishers, 1890.

Barnard, Edward S. *Story of the Great American West*. Pleasantville, NY: Reader's Digest Association, Inc., 1977.

Bell, William Gardner. *Will James: The Life and Works of a Lone Cowboy*. Flagstaff, AZ: Northland Press, 1987.

Berger, Joel. *Wild Horses of the Great Basin: Social Competition and Population Size (Wildlife Behavior and Ecology)*. Chicago: University of Chicago Press, 1986.

Black, Baxter. *AG Man: The Comic Book*. Benson, AZ: Coyote Cowboy Company, 2003.

Blake, Forrester. *Riding the Mustang Trail*. New York: Charles Scribner's Sons, 1935.

Blake, Michael. *Marching to Valhalla: A Novel of Custer's Last Days*. Tucson, AZ: Hrymfaxe, 2002.

Bowman, John S., ed. *The World Almanac of the American West*. New York: World Almanac, 1986.

Brewerton, George Douglas. *Overland with Kit Carson: A Narrative of the Old Spanish Trail in '48*. Lincoln: University of Nebraska Press, 1993.

Brown, Paul, and Fairfax Downey. *Horses of Destiny*. New York: Charles Scribner's Sons, 1949.

Budiansky, Stephen. *The Nature of Horses: Exploring Equine Evolution, Intelligence and Behavior*. New York: Free Press, 1997.

Calistro, Paddy, Jack Lamb, and Jean Penn, editors. *Cowboy Love Poetry: Verse from the Heart of the West*. Santa Monica, CA: Angel City Press, 2005.

Camp, Walter. *Custer in '76*. Provo, UT: Brigham Young University Press, 1976.

Cary, Diana Serra. *The Hollywood Posse*. Boston: Houghton Mifflin, 2003.

Catlin, George. *Letters and Notes on the Manners, Customs, and Conditions of the North American Indians*. 2 vols. Minneapolis: Ross and Haines, Inc., 1965.

Caughey, John Walton. *California*. New York: Prentice-Hall, Inc., 1940.

Cervantes, Miguel de. *Don Quixote*. Translated by Edith Grossman. New York: HarperCollins Books, 2003.

Chalfant, William Y. *Cheyennes and Horse Soldiers: The 1857 Expedition and the Battle of Solomon's Fork*. Norman: Oklahoma Press, 1989.

Chanin, Abraham S. *Cholent & Chorizo*. Tucson: Midbar Press, 1995.

Clark, LaVerne Harrell. *They Sang for Horses*. Tucson: University of Arizona Press, 1983.

Cody, William. *Buffalo Bill's Life Story*. New York: Turtle Point Press, 2002.

Cohen, Mark. *Equus Evolves: The Story of the Hagerman Horse*. Boise, ID: Black Canyon Communications, 2002.

Cohen, Martin A. *The Martyr: Luis de Carvajal, a Secret Jew in Sixteenth-Century Mexico*. Albuquerque: University of New Mexico Press, 2001.

Cohen, Paula Marantz. *Silent Film and the Triumph of the American Myth*. New York: Oxford University Press, 2001.

Colley, Betty Bailey, and Jane Clements Monday. *Tales of the Wild Horse Desert*. Austin: University of Texas Press, 2001.

Connell, Evan S. *Son of the Morning Star: Custer and the Little Bighorn*. New York: North Point Press, 1997.

Convis, Charles L. *Horses and Riders: True Tales of the Old West*. Carson City, NV: Pioneer Press, 1998.

Cook, James H., and Howard R. Driggs. *Longhorn Cowboy*. Yonkers-on-Hudson, NY: World Book Company, 1942.

Coolidge, Dane. *California Cowboys*. 2nd ed. Tucson: University of Arizona Press, 1967.

Corbett, Christopher. *Orphans Preferred*. New York: Broadway Books, 2003.

Cortés, Hernando. *Five Letters of Cortés to the Emperor*. Translated by F. Bayard Morris. New York: W. W. Norton and Company, 1969.

Crow, Joseph Medicine. *From the Heart of the Crow Country: The Crow Indians' Own Stories*. New York: Orion Books, 1992.

Crowell, Ann. *Dawn Horse to Derby Winner*. New York: Praeger Publishers, 1973.

Cunningham, Tom F. *The Diamond's Ace: Scotland and the Native Americans*. Edinburgh, Scotland: Mainstream Publishing, 2001.

Custer, Elizabeth R. *Boots and Saddles, or, Life in Dakota with General Custer*. New York: Harper and Brothers Publishers, 1885.

Custer, George Armstrong. *My Life on the Plains, or, Personal Experiences with Indians*. Norman: University of Oklahoma Press, 1962.

Dagget, Dan. *Beyond the Rangeland Conflict: Toward a West That Works*. Flagstaff, AZ: Good Stewards Project, 1998.

Dansie, Amy, Don Tuohy, Ann Pinzl, and Cheryl A. Young. *The Wild Horse in Nevada: I Thought I Heard a Discouraging Word*. Carson City: Nevada State Museum, 1985.

Dary, David. *Comanche*. Lawrence: University of Kansas Publications, 1976.

Davis, Ronald S. *William S. Hart: Projecting the American West*. Norman: University of Oklahoma Press, 2003.

de la Vega, Garcilaso. *The Inca's Florida*. Austin: University of Texas Press, 1951.

Denhardt, Robert Moorman. *The Horse of the Americas*. Norman: University of Oklahoma Press, 1949.

DeVoto, Bernard. *The Western Paradox*. New Haven: Yale University Press, 2001.

DeWall, Robb. *The Saga of Sitting Bull's Bones*. Crazy Horse, SD: Korczak's Heritage, Inc., 1984.

Díaz del Castillo, Bernal. *The Conquest of New Spain*. Translated by J. M. Cohen. London: The Folio Society, 1963.

Dines, Lisa. *The American Mustang Guidebook: History, Behavior, and State-by-State Directions on Where to Best View America's Wild Horses*. Minocqua, WI: Willow Creek Press, 2001.

Dobie, J. Frank. *The Mustangs*. Boston: Little, Brown and Company, 1936.

———. *The Voice of the Coyote*. Lincoln: University of Nebraska Press, 1949.

———, and John D. Young. *A Vaquero of the Brush Country: The Life and Times of John D. Young*. Austin: University of Texas Press, 1998.

Dodge, Richard Irving. *Our Wild Indians*. New York: Archer House, Inc., 1959.

Donahue, Debra L. *The Western Range Revisited: Removing Livestock from Public Lands to Conserve Native Biodiversity*. Norman: University of Oklahoma Press, 1999.

Duncan, David Ewing. *Hernando de Soto: A Savage Quest in the Americas.* New York: Crown Publishing, 1995.

Erbsen, Wayne. *Cowboy Songs, Jokes, Lingo 'n Lore.* Asheville, NC: Native Ground Music, Inc., 1995.

Essin, Emmett M. *Shavetails and Bell Sharps: The History of the U.S. Army Mule.* Lincoln: University of Nebraska Press, 1997.

Evans, E. P. *The Criminal Prosecution and Capital Punishment of Animals.* London: William Heinemann, 1906.

Fagen, Herb. *The Encyclopedia of Westerns.* New York: Facts on File, 2003.

Fergus, Jim. *One Thousand White Women: The Journals of May Dodd.* New York: St. Martin's Griffin, 1998.

Fischer, David Hackett. *Paul Revere's Ride.* New York: Oxford University Press, 1995.

Franklin, George Cory. *Wild Horses of the Rio Grande.* Boston: Houghton Mifflin, 1951.

Frazier, Ian. *Great Plains.* New York: Penguin Books, 1989.

Freedman, Russell. *In the Days of the Vaqueros: America's First True Cowboys.* New York: Clarion Books, 2001.

Fremont, John Charles. *Narratives of Exploration and Adventure.* New York: Longmans, Green and Co., 1956.

Gallagher, Carole. *American Ground Zero: The Secret Nuclear War.* New York: Random House, 1993.

Garland, Hamlin. *The Captain of the Gray-Horse Troop.* New York: Harper and Brothers, 1901.

Garrard, Kenner. *Nolan's System for Training Cavalry Horses.* New York: D. Van Nostrant, 1862.

Goodwin, Grenville. *Western Apache Raiding & Warfare.* Edited by Keith H. Basso. Tucson: University of Arizona Press, 1971.

Graham, R. B. Cunninghame. *The Horses of the Conquest.* Edited by Robert Moorman Denhardt. Norman: University of Oklahoma Press, 1930.

——. *Thirteen Stories.* Freeport, NY: Books for Libraries Press, 1969.

Graham, W. A. *The Reno Court of Inquiry: Abstract of the Official Record of Proceedings.* Mechanicsburg, PA: Stackpole Books, 1995.

Grant, Richard. *American Nomads: Travels with Conquistadors, Mountain Men, Cowboys, Indians, Hoboes, Truckers and Bull Riders.* New York: Grove Press, 2003.

Gray, Charles Wright. *Horses: An Anthology of Short Stories.* Garden City, NY: Garden City Publishing Co., Inc., 1927.

Grey, Zane, and Helen Cody Wetmore. *Last of the Great Scouts (Buffalo Bill).* New York: Grosset and Dunlap Publishers, 1918.

Hafen, Ann W., and LeRoy R. Hafen. *Old Spanish Trail: Santa Fé to Los Angeles.* Lincoln: University of Nebraska Press, 1993.

——, editors. *The Diaries of William Henry Jackson, Frontier Photographer.* Glendale, CA: Arthur H. Clark Company, 1959.

Haines, Francis. *Appaloosa: The Spotted Horse in Art and History.* Austin: University of Texas Press, 1963.

Hampton, Bruce. *The Great American Wolf.* New York: Owl Books, 1997. Hanson, Victor Davis. *Carnage and Culture: Landmark Battles in the Rise of Western Power.* New York: Doubleday, 2001.

Hardorff, Richard G. *Indian Views of the Custer Fight.* Norman: University of Oklahoma Press, 2005.

Harris, Frank. *My Reminiscences As a Cowboy.* New York: Charles Boni Paper Books, 1930.

Hart, Mary, and William S. Hart. *Pinto Ben — and Other Stories.* New York: Brilton Publishing Company, 1919.

Hart, William S. *My Life — East and West.* North Stratford, NH: Ayer Company Publishers, Inc., 2000.

——, ed. *Told Under a White Oak Tree.* Boston: Houghton Mifflin, 1922.

Henry, Marguerite. *Mustang: Wild Spirit of the West.* Chicago: Rand McNally and Company, 1966.

——. *A Pictorial Life Story of Misty.* Chicago: Rand McNally and Company, 1976.

——. *Sea Star: Orphan of Chincoteague.* Chicago: Rand McNally and Company, 1949.

Hernández, Marie Theresa. *Delirio: The Fantastic, the Demonic, and the Réel.* Austin: University of Texas Press, 2000.

Herr, Major General John K., and Edward D. Wallace. *The Story of the U.S. Cavalry.* Boston: Little, Brown and Company, 1953.

Hintz, H. F. *Horses in the Movies.* New York: A. S. Barnes and Company, 1979.

Hoig, Stan. *The Battle of the Washita.* Lincoln, NE: Bison Books, 1976.

Horse Capture, George P., and Emil Her Many Horses, editors. *A Song for the Horse Nation.* Golden, CO: Fulcrum Publishing for the National Museum of the American Indian, 2006.

Howey, M. Oldfield. *The Horse in Magic and Myth.* Mineola, NY: Dover Publications, Inc., 2000.

Hunt, Frazier, and Robert Hunt. *Horses and Heroes: The Story of the Horse in America for 450 Years.* New York: Charles Scribner's Sons, 1949.

Hutchins, James S. *Boots & Saddles at Little Bighorn: Weapons, Dress, Equipment, Horses and Flags of General Custer's Seventh U.S. Cavalry in 1876.* Harden, MT: Custer Battlefield Historical and Museum Association, Inc., 1976.

——. *Horse Equipment and Cavalry Accoutrements.* Tucson: Westernlore Press, 1984.

Jaffe, Mark. *The Gilded Dinosaur: The Fossil War Between E. D. Cope and O. C.*

Marsh and the Rise of American Science. New York: Crown Publishers, 2000.

James, Will. *Cowboys North and South.* New York: Charles Scribner's Sons, 1942.

———. *Lone Cowboy: My Life Story.* New York: Charles Scribner's Sons, 1930.

———. *Smoky the Cowhorse.* New York: Grosset and Dunlap, 1926.

Johnson, James Ralph, and Bill Milhollen. *Horsemen Blue and Gray.* New York: Oxford University Press, 1960.

Kadlecek, Edward, and Mabel Kadlecek. *To Kill an Eagle: Indian Views on the Last Days of Crazy Horse.* Boulder, CO: Johnson Books, 1981.

Kathrens, Ginger. *Cloud's Legacy: The Wild Stallion Returns.* Irvine, CA: Bow-tie Press, 2003.

Korda, Michael. *Ulysses S. Grant.* New York: HarperCollins, 2004.

Koszarski, Diane Kaiser. *The Complete Films of William S. Hart: A Pictorial Record.* New York: Dover Publications, Inc., 1980.

Langellier, John Phillip. *Custer: The Man, the Myth, the Movies.* Mechanicsburg, PA: Stackpole Books, 2000.

Larson, Eric. *Devil in the White City.* New York: Crown Publishers, 2003.

Lawrence, Elizabeth Atwood. *His Very Silence Speaks — Comanche, the Horse Who Survived Custer's Last Stand.* Detroit: Wayne State University Press, 1989.

Lawrence, Robert Means. *The Magic of the Horse-Shoe; with other Folk-Lore Notes.* Boston: Houghton Mifflin, 1891.

Leadabrand, Russ, editor. *The Westerners Brand Book, Los Angeles Corral.* Number 11. Los Angeles: The Ward Ritchie Press, 1964.

Leigh, William R. *The Western Pony.* New York: Huntington Press, 1933.

Leighton, Margaret. *Comanche of the Seventh.* New York: Berkeley Publishing Corporation, 1957.

Liebman, Seymour B. *The Jews in New Spain.* Coral Gables, FL: University of Miami Press, 1970.

———, editor and translator. *The Enlightened: The Writings of Luis de Carvajal, El Mozo.* Coral Gables, FL: University of Miami Press, 1967.

Lingenfelter, Richard E. *Death Valley and the Amargosa: A Land of Illusion.* Berkeley: University of California Press, 1986.

Lopez, Barry. *Of Wolves and Men.* New York: Scribner, 1979.

Luce, Captain Edward S. *Keogh, Comanche and Custer.* Ashland, OR: Lewis Osborne, 1974.

Lucey, Donna M. *Photographing Montana, 1894–1928: The Life and Work of Evelyn Cameron.* New York: Alfred A. Knopf, 1990.

Lyons, Dorothy. *Midnight Moon.* New York: Harcourt, Brace and Company, 1941.

Mails, Thomas E. *The Mystic Warriors of the Plains.* Tulsa, OK: Council Oak Books, 1972.

Marquis, Thomas B. *Wooden Leg: A Warrior Who Fought Custer.* Lincoln: University of Nebraska Press, 1931.

Marshall, Joseph M., III. *The Day the World Ended at the Little Bighorn.* New York: Viking, 2006.

———. *The Journey of Crazy Horse.* New York: Penguin Books, 2004.

Martin, Russell. *Cowboy: The Enduring Myth of the Wild West.* New York: Stewart, Tabori and Chang Publishers, 1983.

Mason, Theodore K. *The South Pole Ponies.* New York: Dodd, Mead and Company, 1979.

Matteson, Mollie, and George Wuerthner, editors. *Welfare Ranching: The Subsidized Destruction of the American West.* Washington, DC: Island Press, 2002.

Matthiessen, Peter, and Bob Hines. *Wildlife in America.* New York: Penguin, 1978.

McDermott, John D. *A Guide to the Indian Wars of the West.* Lincoln: University of Nebraska Press, 1998.

McMurtry, Larry. *The Colonel and Little Missie.* New York: Simon and Schuster, 2005.

Miller, Arthur, and Serge Toubiana. *The Misfits.* New York: Phaedon Press, Inc., 1995.

Miller, Clyde A., II, Carol A. O'Connor, and Martha A. Sandweiss, editors. *The Oxford History of the American West.* New York: Oxford University Press, 1994.

Miller, David Humphreys. *Custer's Fall: The Native American Side of the Story.* New York: Meridian Printing, 1992.

Mitchum, Petrine Day, with Audrey Pavia. *Hollywood Hoofbeats.* Irvine, CA: Bowtie Press, 2005.

Morin, Paula. *Honest Horses.* Reno: University of Nevada Press, 2006.

Morris, Desmond. *Horse Watching.* New York: Crown Publishers, Inc., 1988.

Moulton, Candy Vyvey, and Flossie Moulton. *Steamboat, Legendary Bucking Horse: His Life and Times, and the Cowboys Who Tried to Tame Him.* Glendo, WY: High Plains Press, 1992.

National Live Stock Association. *Prose and Poetry of the Live Stock Industry of the United States.* Denver: National Live Stock Historical Association, 1904.

Neihardt, John G. *Black Elk Speaks: Being the Life Story of a Holy Man of the Oglala Sioux.* Lincoln: University of Nebraska Press, 1988.

Neil, J. M., editor. *Will James: The Spirit of the Cowboy.* Lincoln: University of Nebraska Press, 1985.

Otis, George A. *A Report to the Surgeon General on the Transport of Sick and Wounded by Pack Animals.* Edited by John M. Carroll. Washington, DC: Government Printing Office, 1877.

Overfield, Loyd J., II. *The Little Big Horn, 1876: The Official Communications, Documents and Reports.* Glendale, CA: Arthur H. Clark Company, 1971.

328   BIBLIOGRAPHY

Paskett, Parley J. *Wild Mustangs.* Logan: Utah State University, 1986.

Plummer, Alexander, and Richard H. Power. *The Army Horse in Accident and Disease.* Washington, DC: Government Printing Office, 1903.

Pomeranz, Lynne. *Among Wild Horses.* North Adams, MA.: Storey Publishing, 2006.

Rickey, Don, Jr. *Forty Miles a Day on Beans and Hay.* Norman: University of Oklahoma Press, 1963.

Rivas, Mim Eichler. *Beautiful Jim Key: The Lost History of a Horse and a Man Who Changed History.* New York: William Morrow, 2005.

Rochlin, Harriet, and Fred Rochlin. *Pioneer Jews: A New Life in the Far West.* Boston: Houghton Mifflin, 2000.

Roe, Frank Gilbert. *The Indian and the Horse.* 5th ed. Norman: University of Oklahoma Press, 1979.

Rojas, Arnold R. *California Vaquero.* Fresno, CA: Academy Library Guild, 1953.

Roosevelt, Theodore. *Wilderness Writings.* Salt Lake City: Gibbs M. Smith, Inc./Peregrine Smith Books, 1986.

Rosenblum, Robert. *Remembering the Future: The New York World's Fair from 1939 to 1964.* New York: Rizzoli International Publications, 1989.

Russell, Sharman Apt. *Kill the Cowboy: A Battle of Mythology in the New West.* Lincoln: University of Nebraska Press, 2001.

Rydell, Robert W., and Rob Kroes. *Buffalo Bill in Bologna: The Americanization of the World, 1869–1922.* Chicago: University of Chicago Press, 2005.

Ryden, Hope. *America's Last Wild Horses.* Guilford, CT: Lyons Press. 1970.

———. *Wild Horses I Have Known.* New York: Clarion Books, 1999.

Sandler, Martin W. *Vaqueros: America's First Cowmen.* New York: Henry Holt and Company, 2001.

Sandoz, Mari. *The Cattlemen: From the Rio Grande Across the Far Marias.* New York: Hastings House, Publishers, 1958.

Scanlan, Lawrence. *Wild About Horses: Our Timeless Passion for the Horse.* New York: Perennial, 1998.

Settle, Mary Lund, and Raymond W. Settle. *Saddles and Spurs: The Pony Express Saga.* Lincoln: University of Nebraska Press, 1955.

Shrady, George F. *General Grant's Last Days.* New York: privately printed, 1908.

Sides, Hampton. *Blood and Thunder.* New York: Doubleday, 2006.

Siringo, Charles A. *Cowboy Detective.* Lincoln: University of Nebraska Press, 1979.

———. *Riata and Spurs.* Cambridge, MA: Riverside Press, 1912.

———. *A Texas Cowboy.* Lincoln: University of Nebraska Press, 1979.

Sloan, Jim. *Nevada: True Tales from the Neon Wilderness.* Salt Lake City: University of Utah Press, 1993.

Smythe, R. H. *The Mind of the Horse.* Brattleboro, VT: Stephen Greene Press, 1965.

Snyder, Swan, editor. *The California Grizzly Bear in Mind.* Berkeley, CA: Heyday Books, 2003.

Sonne, Conway B. *World of Wakara.* San Antonio, TX: Naylor Company, 1962.

Spring, Agnes Wright. *Buffalo Bill and His Horses.* Fort Collins, CO: B&M Print Co., 1953.

Steiner, Stan. *Dark and Dashing Horsemen.* New York: Harper and Row, 1981.

Stewart, Edgar I. *Custer's Luck.* Norman: University of Oklahoma Press, 1955.

Strawn, Arthur. *Sails and Swords.* New York: Brentano's Publishers, 1928.

Symanski, Richard. *Wild Horses and Sacred Cows.* Flagstaff, AZ: Northland Press, 1985.

Thomas, Heather Smith. *The Wild Horse Controversy.* New York: A. S. Barnes, 1979.

Thomas, Hugh. *Rivers of Gold: The Rise of the Spanish Empire, from Columbus to Magellan.* London: Weidenfeld and Nicolson, 2003.

———. *Who's Who of the Conquistadors.* London: Cassel and Co., 2000.

Trippett, Frank, and the editors of Time-Life Books. *The First Horsemen.* The Emergence of Man Series. New York: Time-Life Books, 1974.

Tuska, Jon. *The American West in Film: Critical Approaches to the Western.* Lincoln: University of Nebraska Press, 1988.

Twain, Mark. *Roughing It.* New York: New American Library, 1962.

Urwin, Gregory J. W. *The United States Cavalry: An Illustrated History 1776–1944.* Norman: University of Oklahoma Press, 2003.

Utley, Robert M. *Little Bighorn Battlefield: A History and Guide to the Battle of the Little Bighorn.* Washington, DC: Division of Publications, National Park Service, 1994.

———, general editor. *The Story of the West: A History of the American West and Its People.* London: Dorling Kindersley, 2003.

Wagner, Glendolin Damon. *Old Neutriment.* Lincoln: University of Nebraska Press, 1989.

Wallace, Lew. *The Fair God, or, the Last of the 'Tzins: A Tale of the Conquest of Mexico.* Boston: Houghton Mifflin, 1901.

Warren, Louis. *Buffalo Bill's America: William Cody and the Wild West Show.* New York: Knopf, 2005.

Windisch-Graetz, Mathilde. *The Spanish Riding School: Its Traditions and Development from the Sixteenth Century until Today.* New York: A. S. Barnes and Company, 1958.

Wissler, Clark. *Indians of the United States: Four Centuries of Their History and Culture.* Garden City, NY: Doubleday and Company, Inc., 1946.

Wister, Owen. *The Virginian.* New York: Forge Books, 1998.

Wood, Michael. *Conquistadors.* Berkeley: University of California Press, 2000.

Worcester, Don, editor. *Western Horse Tales.* Plano, TX: Wordware Publishing, Inc., 1994.

Wormser, Richard. *The Yellowlegs: The Story of the United States Cavalry.* Garden City, NY: Doubleday and Company, 1966.

Wyman, Walker D. *The Wild Horse of the West.* Lincoln: University of Nebraska Press, 1945.

Zakin, Susan. *Coyotes and Town Dogs: Earth First! And the Environmental Movement.* New York: Viking, 1993.

ARTICLES AND OTHER SOURCES

Aikens, C. Melvin, John L. Fagan, and Judith A. Willig, editors. "Early Human Occupation in Far Western North America: The Clovis-Archaic Interface." In *Nevada State Museum Anthropological Papers* 21. Carson City: Nevada State Museum, 1988.

Amaral, Anthony. "How Will James Got His Start." *Frontier Times,* June/July 1966.

Anderson, Tim. "More Horse Slaying Suspects Arraigned." *Reno Gazette-Journal,* February 2, 1999.

Arambulo, Adrian. "Feds Answer to Wild Horse Neglect Charges." KLAS-TV.com, January 13, 2006.

Associated Press. "180 More Wild Horses Found Dead in Nevada." *New York Times,* October 12, 1988.

———. "Two Navy Airmen Held on Charges of Killing Seven Cows." *Las Vegas Review-Journal,* September 24, 1999.

Barnes, Will G. "The Passing of the Wild Horse." *American Forests,* November 1924.

Blunt, Judy. "Live Free and Die." *New York Times,* January 4, 2005.

Brenner, Anita. "Cavaliers and Martyrs." *The Menorah Journal,* n.d.

Brininstool, E. A. "Unwritten Seventh Cavalry History." *Middle Border Bulletin* (Spring 1945): 1–2.

Brower, Monty, and Bill Shaw. "Lawman Len Sims, Alone on the Range, Hunts the Killers of Nevada's Wild Mustangs." *People,* November 21, 1988

Burkhardt, J. Wayne. "Steppes in Time." *Range* magazine (Fall/Winter 1992).

Chapman, Arthur. "How a Cowboy-Aviator Hunts Wild Horses." *Popular Science Monthly,* November 1925.

Childs, Susan. "Midnight: Story of a Champion Bucker." *Johnstown Breeze,* April 2, 1981.

Cline, Don. "Battle Over Billy the Kid's Horse." *Quarterly of the National Association and Center for Outlaw and Lawman History* (Winter 1988): 12.

Coates-Markle, Linda, with Emily Kilby. "Choosing to Survive." *Equus,* January 1997.

Conway, C.R.G. "Hernando Alonso, a Jewish Conquistador with Cortés in Mexico." *Publications of the American Jewish Historical Society* 31: 9–31.

Daniel, Forrest W. "Dismounting the Sioux." *North Dakota History* (Summer 1974): 9–13.

Devereaux, Linda Ericson. "Philip Nolan and His 'Wild Horses.'" *Texana* 12 (1974): 89–100.

Downer, Craig C. "Wild and Free-Roaming Horses and Burros of North America: Factual and Sensitive Statement—How They Help the Ecosystem." *Natural Horse* magazine 7, no. 3 (2005).

Eigell, Robert W. "Rounding Up 'Canners' for the 'Corned Beef and Cabbage.'" Montana 36, no. 4 (1986): 64–68.

Essin, Emmett M, III. "The Cavalry and the Horse." PhD diss., Texas Christian University, May 1968.

Fazio, Patricia M. "The Fight to Save a Memory: Creation of the Pryor Mountain Wild Horse Range." *Wyoming* (Spring 1997).

———. "Wild Horses As Native North American Wildlife." Written for the International Society for the Protection of Mustangs and Burros, 2003.

———, and Jay Kirkpatrick. "Wild Horses As Native North American Wildlife." Statement prepared for 109th Congress, 2005.

Fenwick, Robert W. "Horse Heaven Hour Strikes for Great Bronc, Midnight." *Denver Post,* March 31, 1966.

Fialka, John J. "Wild No More: The Odyssey Begins for Horse 96563288." *Wall Street Journal,* August 25, 1998.

Flores, Dan. "Where All the Pretty Horses Have Gone." *Horizontal Yellow: Nature and History in the Near Southwest.* Albuquerque: University of New Mexico Press, 1999.

Gerleman, David J. "Unchronicled Heroes: A Study of Union Cavalry Horses in the Eastern Theater; Care, Treatment, and Use, 1861–1865." PhD diss., Southern Illinois University at Carbondale, June 1999.

Hadley, C. J. "Wild Horses: No Home on the Range?" *Range* magazine (Fall/Winter 1992).

Haederle, Michael. "The Hidden Jews of the Southwest." *El Palacio* 2 (Spring 1993): 38–57.

Haines, Francis. "Horses and the American Frontier." *American West* (March 1971): 10–14.

Hildebrand, Kurt. "Not Everyone in Love with Horses." *Nevada Appeal,* December 16, 2001.

Knapp, George. "Wild Horses: Nowhere to Run." KLAS-TV.com, February 5, 2004.

Kreuter, Adolph C. "I Herded the Wild Ones." *Frontier Times,* June/July, 1966.

Lawrence, Elizabeth A. "'That By Means of Which People Live': Indians and their Horses' Health." *Journal of the West* (January 1988): 7–15.

Liebman, Seymour B. "The Mestizo Jews of Mexico." *American Jewish Archives* (November 1967): 144–74.

Lord, Russell. "The Mustang Returns to Europe in Tin Cans." *The Cattleman,*
October 1928.

Lowe, Percival G. "Five Years a Dragoon ('49 to '54) and Other Adventures on
the Great Plains." *Journal of the United States Cavalry Association* (October 1905): 251–52.

McInnis, Doug. "Report Acknowledges Wild Horses Are Being Sold for Slaughter." *New York Times,* January 29, 1997.

Mendoza, Martha. "Feds Slaughtered Wild Horses: Probe, Documents Show."
AP, March 23, 1997.

Miller, Arthur. "The Misfits." *Esquire,* October 1957.

Montini, E. J. "Seven Wild Horses Shot in Arizona." *Arizona Republic,* January
11, 2007.

Moulton, Candy. "Kings of the Hurricane Deck." *Ketch Pen* (Spring 1998).

Mullen, Frank. "Suspect in Horse Massacre Had Hunting License Lifted." *Reno
Gazette-Journal,* January 14, 1999.

———. "Friends Describe Shooting Suspects as Kind, Thoughtful." *Reno Gazette-Journal,* January 15, 1999.

———. "Vet Testifies Horses Died Agonizing Deaths." *Reno Gazette-Journal,*
September 9, 1999.

Nack, William. "They Have to Be Free." ESPN.com, May 20, 2005.

O'Toole, Sharon Salisbury. "Managing a Western Icon." *Range* magazine (Fall
2005).

Pellegrini, Steven W. "Wild Horses and Other Phantoms." *Nevada Historical Society Quarterly* (Summer 1997): 207–14.

Peterson, Martin E. "On the Nature of the Horse of the American West in Nineteenth Century American Art." *Great Plains Quarterly* (Winter 1986):
34–43.

Pijoan, Michel. "The Herds of Onate." *El Palacio* 81, no. 3 (1955): 8–17.

Radke, Jace. "State Mourns Loss of Wild Horses." *Las Vegas Sun,* December 31,
1998.

———. "Reward for Slain Horses, Burros Grows." *Las Vegas Sun,* January 11,
2000.

———. "Wild Horse Slaughter Continues." *Las Vegas Sun,* January 19, 2000.

Robinson, Sherry. "Finding Common Ground." *Albuquerque Tribune,* January
28, 2002.

Rogers, Keith. "71 Horses Die at Tonopah Test Range." *Las Vegas Review Journal,* August 22, 2007.

Rogers, Paul. "Cash Cows." *San Jose Mercury News,* November 7, 1999.

Santucci, Vincent L., and Torrey G. Nyborg. "Vertebrate Tracks, Death Valley."
San Bernardino County Museum Association Quarterly 46 (1999): 21–26.

Sargeant, William A. S., and Robert E. Reynolds. "Camel and Horse Footprints
from the Miocene of California." *San Bernardino County Museum Association Quarterly* 46 (1999): 3–19.

Schneider, Wolf. "The Horses Called Spanish Barbs." *El Palacio* (Spring 1993): 34–39.

Shetterly, Caryn. "Company Fined for Poisoning Horses." *Las Vegas Review Journal,* January 25, 1989.

Shurtleff, Marianne G. "My Husband Is a Mustanger." *Desert* magazine (February 1962).

Sink, Mindy. "National Briefing/West: Colorado: Killing Wild Horses." *New York Times,* December 21, 2001.

Smith, Cornelius C. "The Iron Men." *Montana, the Magazine of Western History* (January 1959): 47–56.

Sonner, Scott. "$25,000 Reward Sought in Shooting Death of 33 Wild Horses." *Las Vegas Sun,* December 30, 1998.

Steele, Rufus. "Trapping Wild Horses in Nevada." *McClure's Magazine* (December, 1909).

Steiner, Stan. "Jewish Conquistadors: America's First Cowboys?" *American West* (September/October 1983): 31–37.

U.S. Department of the Interior. Bureau of Land Management. *The Pony Express in Nevada.* BLMNVGI890048200.

——. Wild Horse and Burro Program. *Legends* (booklet), 2005.

——. *Annual Report on Performance and Accountability,* fiscal year 2005.

Van Zandt, Howard F. "The Battle of the Washita, Revisited." *The Chronicles of Oklahoma* (Spring 1984): 57–69.

Vasquez, Susie. "Wild Horses of Storey Caught in Political Trap." *Nevada Appeal,* December 16, 2001.

Welling, Angie. "Two Utahns Admit to Killing Nine Wild Horses." *Deseret Morning News,* February 23, 2005.

Whitaker, Nancy. "Wild Horses: The Feral Animal Label." *The Southeast Horse Report* (November 1999).

White, Captain Herbert A. "The Yellowstone Expedition of 1873." *Journal of the United States Cavalry Association* (October 1905): 218–21.

Woodmansee, Karen. "Wild Horses Die in Highway 50 Crashes." *Nevada Appeal,* October 19, 2005.

DVDs

El Caballo. Produced by Doug Hawes-Davis and Drury Gunn Carr. Directed by Doug Hawes-Davis. The Fund for Animals and High Plains Films for Bullfrog Films, 2001.

The Desert Speaks. Produced by KUAT-TV, Tucson, in cooperation with the Arizona-Sonora Desert Museum and the Nature Conservancy of Arizona, 2001.

The Great Train Robbery with Tumbleweeds, the Heart of Texas Ryan and the

Battle of Elderbush Gulch. 100th Anniversary Special Edition. VCI Entertainment, 2003.

The Horses of Gettysburg. Produced and directed by Mark Bussler. An Inecom Entertainment Company Production, 2006.

Last of the Spanish Mustangs. Produced and directed by Len Johnson. Len Johnson Productions, 2005.

Lessons from the Wild . . . Wild Horse Wisdom. With Mary Ann Simonds. Mystic Horse Productions, n.d.

Return to Freedom. Directed by Allison Argo. An Argo Films Production, 2004.

CDs AND TAPES

Autry, Gene. *25 Cowboy Classics*. Autry Qualified Interest Trust, the Autry Foundation and Flying A Pictures, Inc., 2001.

Don't Fence Me In: Western Music's Early Golden Era. Rounder Records Corp., 1996.

Great Songs about Horses. CMH Records, 2002.

The Horses: Pow-Wow Songs of the Northern Plains. John and Katherine Windy Boy, Rocky Boy, Montana; Thomas Oldman Sr., Wind River, Wyoming. Cool Runnings Music, 2004.

Laine, Frankie. *On the Trail*. Bear Family, 1990.

Songs of the Seventh Cavalry. Funded by *Bismarck Tribune*, 1989.

WEBSITES

www.blm.gov/nv/st/en.html
    Bureau of Land Management site for Nevada.
www.filmsite.org
    for history of first Westerns.
www.fort.usgs.gov/WildHorsePopulations/default.asp
    government's wild horse counting methods.
www.imdb.net
    for facts related to individual films.
www.pbs.org/weta/thewest/program/
    accompanied PBS documentary *The West*.
http://net.unl.edu/artsFeat/wildhorses/
    accompanied PBS documentary *Wild Horses: An American Romance*.
www.ndow.org/
    Nevada Department of Wildlife, regarding information about other wild animals in Nevada.
www.wildwestweb.net
    on history of Westerns.

http://wyomingtalesandtrails.com/
> wide-ranging and comprehensive site that includes western history and photographs.

www.wildhorseandburro.blm.gov/index.php
> BLM website for wild horse and burro program; links to facts and statistics.

www.wildhorse.nv.gov/
> Nevada state commission for the preservation of wild horses; links to facts and statistics.

http://xroads.virginia.edu/~ma96/WCE/title.html
> information about the 1893 World's Columbian Exposition.

ARCHIVES AND COLLECTIONS

Autry National Center / Southwest Museum of the American Indian, Los Angeles, California. Programs from Buffalo Bill's and other Wild West shows, frontier memorabilia and art; Captain Myles Keogh family scrapbook with extensive information about Keogh's service in the cavalry and his horse Comanche.

Buffalo Bill Historical Center, Cody, Wyoming. Records and news accounts of Buffalo Bill, his travels, and his horses.

Buffalo Bill Museum and Grave, Golden, Colorado. Records and news accounts of Buffalo Bill, his travels, and his horses.

Cowgirl Hall of Fame, Ft. Worth, Texas. Exhibits, records, diaries, and news accounts of ranching and rodeo women.

Crazy Horse Memorial, Crazy Horse, South Dakota. Exhibits, books, and film relating to Plains Indian life, especially during the nineteenth century.

Custer Battlefield Museum, Garryowen, Montana. David F. Barry photograph collection; Plains Indian and cavalry memorabilia and art.

Huntington Library, San Marino, California. Extensive holdings in American history, especially the West, including rare books and early cavalry manuals; accounts of the Indian wars, settlement of the frontier, and era of cattle drives in newspapers, magazines, academic journals, and periodicals published by historical associations; explorer, settler, and war veteran diaries and memoirs; nineteenth-century documents and records.

The Jacob Rader Center of the American Jewish Archives, Cincinnati, Ohio. Material relating to Jewish conquistadors and Jewish settlement of the West.

Library of Congress — American Memory digital archives for a range of material, including clips of Thomas Edison's first films and nineteenth-century treaties, documents, and memorabilia.

Little Bighorn Battlefield National Monument, Crow Agency, Montana. Exhibits, books, periodical accounts of battle, cavalry history, and history of Plains Indians.

Ralph Case Papers, Box Six. Richardson Collection, I. D. Weeks Library at the University of South Dakota, Vermillion, South Dakota. Newspaper clippings and legal filings regarding the Sioux pony claims.

Rodeo archives at the National Cowboy and Western Heritage Museum, Oklahoma City, Oklahoma. Transcript of memorial service for re-interment of Midnight and Five Minutes to Midnight, various undated newspaper clippings, reminiscences of early rodeo riders.

Extensive wild horse and burro records and histories in the private collection of Betty Lee Kelly and Bobbi Royle at Wild Horse Spirit, Carson City, Nevada, including records of Nevada horse herds, with focus on the Virginia Range horses; the 1998 Reno horse massacre and others; range history in Nevada; public lands ranching in Nevada.

Extensive wild horse and burro records and histories in the private collection of Karen Sussman at the International Society for the Protection of Mustangs and Burros in Lantry, South Dakota, including Velma C. Johnston / Wild Horse Annie archives; history of various wild horse herds, including the White Sands Missile herd, the Gila Bend herd, and the Sheldon herd; history of burro herds; roundups, adoption program, public lands, and grazing-permit regulations and statistics; history of investigations and legal actions against the BLM and other government agencies regarding mismanagement of wild horses and burros.

Private archives of Alan J. Kania, associate of Velma C. Johnston / Wild Horse Annie, Denver, Colorado, including Wild Horse Annie's testimony at congressional hearings, newspaper and magazine clippings, and letters.

Private archives of Dr. Patricia Fazio, Cody, Wyoming, including BLM wild horse and burro management history, legislative history regarding wild horses and burros, and public testimony.

A band of mustangs with foal heading toward an
unpaved jeep road and Misfits Flat.

Index

Numbers in italics refer to illustrations.